Rev. 3 April 2013

CELESTIAL NAVIGATION CALCULATIONS
(UPON OCEANS ENDORSEMENT)
WORKED-OUT FOR

MASTER 500 GT THROUGH 2ND MATE UNLIMITED

VOLUME 3

Alexander F. Hickethier MBA
and
Dr. Hu Jia-Shen

Rev. 3 April 2013

Every effort has been made to assure that this book is accurate, current, and complete as of date of publication. However, as in the case of all human endeavors, there can be no guarantee that this work does not contain errors or omissions. Therefore, the prudent mariner will not rely only on this or any other single source when guiding his vessel.

Please report any errors or omissions to the publisher. Last correction 04-01-2013

Printed in the United States
First Edition
ISBN **978-1480175341**

Published by:
Alexander F. Hickethier MBA
20555 Bee Valley Road;
Jamul, CA 91935

Forward

We have developed this series of training manuals to assist the Merchant Mariner in passing the U.S. Coast Guard Licensing Examinations, from Master 500 GT to 2nd Mate Unlimited upon Oceans.

These manuals have been developed to augment our current textbooks for Mariners and are modular in design incorporating practical exercises and actual U.S. Coast Guard examination questions with all questions worked-out.

A description of each manual follows:

Volume I: Deck Calculations worked-out for Master 500 GT through 2nd Mate Unlimited Upon Oceans.

Volume I provides an in-depth understanding of Basic Deck and Stability Calculation found US coast Guard Merchant Mariner Examinations through 2nd Mate Unlimited,

Chapter 1	including Stowage Calculations, Lumber and Dunnage Stowage, Stowage Factors, Size of lines and Block and Tackle, lifting stress, Anchoring calculations, Humidity and Dew Point Calculations and Rules for bearings.
Chapter 2	includes Stability Terminology, Calculating Period of Roll and Estimating GM, Freesurface, Floodable Length Curves, Loll, Final Draft, TPI, Trim< LCG, Final KG, Freeboard Draft, LCG and Double Bottom Tankage.

Volume II: Terrestrial Navigation Calculations worked-out for Master 500 GT through 2nd Mate Unlimited Upon Oceans.

Volume II provides an in-depth understanding of Terrestrial Calculation found US Coast Guard Merchant Mariner Examinations through 2nd Mate Unlimited.

Chapter 1	Tides and Currents.
Chapter 2	Speed by RPM, SOA, Slip and Fuel Consumption Calculations
Chapter 3	Compass Deviation Table Construction, Deviation by Celestial Observation (Amplitude and Azimuth), and Deviation by Terrestrial Observation.
Chapter 4	Time Zone Calculations, (Sunrise and Sunset, Time Tick, and Estimated Time of Arrival).

Volume III: Celestial Navigation Calculations worked-out for Master 500 GT through 2nd Mate Unlimited Upon Oceans Endorsement.

Volume I provides an in-depth understanding of Celestial Calculation found on the US Coast Guard Merchant Mariner Examinations through 2nd Mate Unlimited.

ACKNOWLEDGMENTS

There are numerous people who made this book possible. In particular I profusely thank my co-author, Master mariner and educator Dr. Hu Jia-Shen.

ALEXANDER F. HICKETHIER MBA

ABOUT THE AUTHORS

Alexander F. is the Vice-President Maritime Institute Inc. for Curriculum Development and International and Academic Affairs. He is a visiting navigation department professor at Shanghai Marine University, Shanghai, China and National Kaohsiung Marine University, Kaohsiung, Taiwan. He is an approved instructor of 23 Marine/STCW US Coast Guard (USCG) approved courses. He has designed and implemented 25 USCG approved Maritime courses of which 7 are approved e-Learning courses, Authored or co-authored 7 maritime textbooks, 3 navigation workbooks and 3 Engineering workbooks. He holds a BBS and MBA from National University.

Hu Jia-Shen is the associate professor of the Shipping Technology Department, National Kaohsiung Marine University, Kaohsiung, Taiwan. He is an approved Maritime Education and Training instructor who hold the certificates of Marine Navigation Instructor, GMDSS Instructor, ARPA Radar Instructor, Full Mission Shiphandling Instructor, Cargo Handling Instructor (Tanker, LNG, LPG and Chemical Carrier; the Diplomas of ISO 9000 Internal Audit, STCW In-service Assessment, STCW Course Design Workshop, etc. He holds a PhD. Degree from Australian Maritime College.

TABLE OF CONTENT

x

NAUTICAL PUBLICATIONS
and
EQUIPMENT

Chapter 1

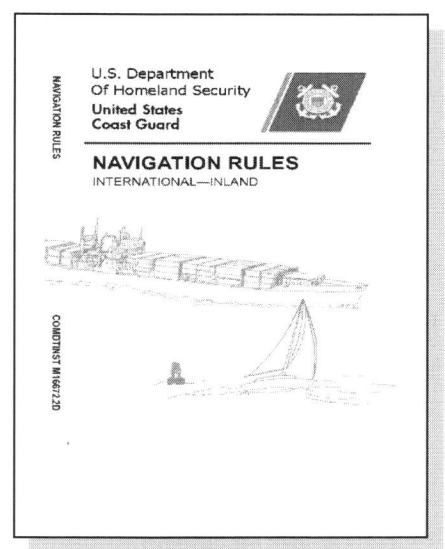

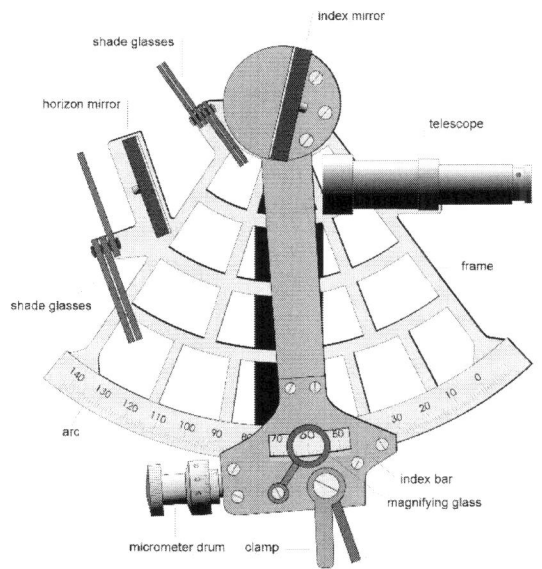

NAUTICAL PUBLICATIONS

Every vessel should carry the charts and publications required for its safe operation. These include the Navigation Rules - International-Inland, all charts applicable for the vessel's navigational area of operation, and appropriate publications pertinent to navigation.

Included here is a listing of the some of the more commonly used publications, and the agencies responsible for publishing them. Naturally, not all of them will be applicable to all vessels.

Rules of the Rules of the Road

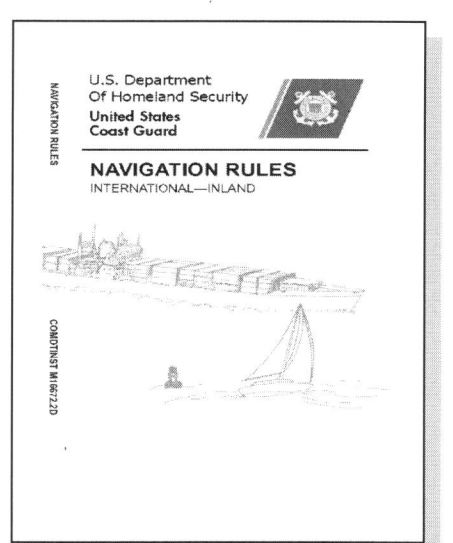

The U.S. Coast Guard publishes *Navigation Rules* **for international and inland waters**. This publication, officially known as Commandant Instruction M16672.2d, contains the Inland Navigation Rules enacted in December 1980 and effective on all inland waters of the United States including the Great Lakes, as well as the *International Regulations for the Prevention of Collisions at Sea*, enacted in 1972 (1972 COLREGS). Mariners should ensure that they have the updated issue.

Sailing Directions (Enroute and Planning Guides)

National Imagery and Mapping Agency *Sailing Directions* consist of **37 Enroutes** and **5 Planning Guides**. *Planning Guides* describe general features of ocean basins; *Enroutes* describe features of coastlines, ports, and harbors.

Sailing Directions are updated when new data requires extensive revision of an existing volume. These data are obtained from several sources, including pilots and foreign Sailing Directions.

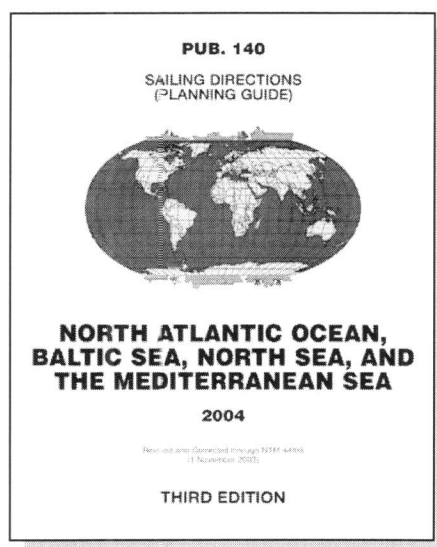

One book comprises the *Planning Guide* and *Enroute* for Antarctica. This consolidation allows for a more effective presentation of material on this unique area.

The *Planning Guides* are relatively permanent; by contrast, *Sailing Directions (Enroute)* are frequently updated. Between updates, both are corrected by the *Notice to Mariners*.

Sailing Directions (Planning Guide)

Planning Guides assist the navigator in planning an extensive oceanic voyage. Each of the Guides provides useful information about all the countries adjacent to a particular ocean basin.

The limits of the *Sailing Directions* in relation to the major ocean basins are shown in the below:

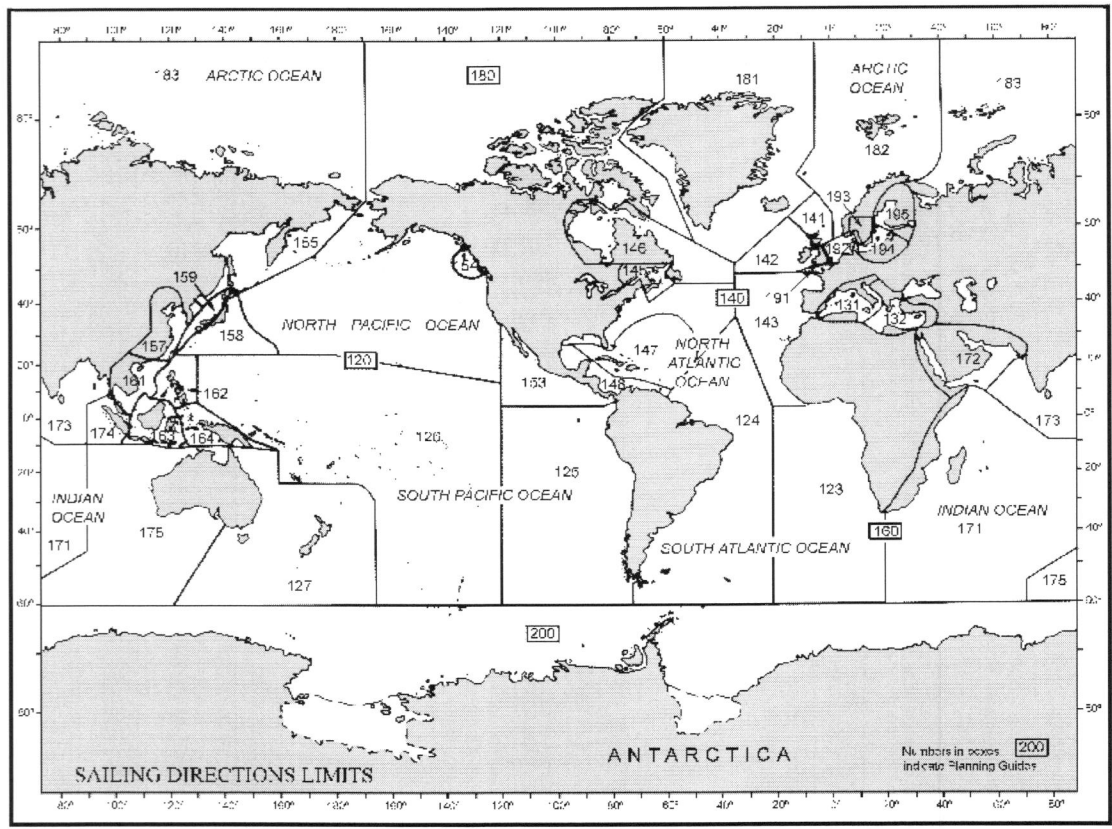

Alexander F. Hickethier MBA © 2011-2113

Planning Guides are structured in the alphabetical order of countries contained within the region. Information pertaining to each country includes Buoyage Systems, Currency, Government, Industries, Holidays, Languages, Regulations, Firing Danger Areas, Mined Areas, Pilotage, Search and Rescue, Reporting Systems, Submarine Operating Areas, Time Zone, and the location of the U.S. Embassy.

Sailing Directions (Enroute)

Each volume of the *Sailing Directions (Enroute)* contains numbered sections along a coast or through a strait. Figure 403a illustrates this division. Each sector is sub-divided into paragraphs and discussed in turn. A preface with information about authorities, references, and conventions used in each book precedes the sector discussions. Each book also provides conversions between feet, fathoms, and meters, and an Information and Suggestion Sheet.

A foreign terms glossary and a comprehensive Index- Gazetteer follow the sector discussions. The Index-Gazetteer is an alphabetical listing of described and charted features. The Index lists each feature by geographic coordinates and sector paragraph number.

U.S. military vessels have access to special files of data reported via official messages known as Port Visit After Action Reports. These reports, written in text form according to a standardized reporting format, give complete details of recent visits by U.S. military vessels to all foreign ports visited. Virtually every detail regarding navigation, services, supplies, official and unofficial contacts, and other matters is discussed in detail, making these reports an extremely useful adjunct to the *Sailing Directions*. These files are available to ".mil" users only, and may be accessed on the Web at: http://cnsl.spear.navy.mil, under the "Force Navigator" link. They are also available via DoD's classified Web.

Coast Pilots

The National Ocean Service publishes nine *United States Coast Pilots* to supplement nautical charts of U.S. waters. Information comes from field inspections, survey vessels, and various harbor authorities. Maritime officials and pilotage associations provide additional information.

Coast Pilots provide more detailed information than *Sailing Directions* because *Sailing Directions* are intended exclusively for the oceangoing mariner. The *Notice to Mariners* updates *Coast Pilots*.

Each volume contains comprehensive sections on local operational considerations and navigation regulations.

Following chapters contain detailed discussions of coastal navigation. An appendix provides information on obtaining additional weather information, communications services, and other data. An index and additional tables complete the volume.

Light Lists

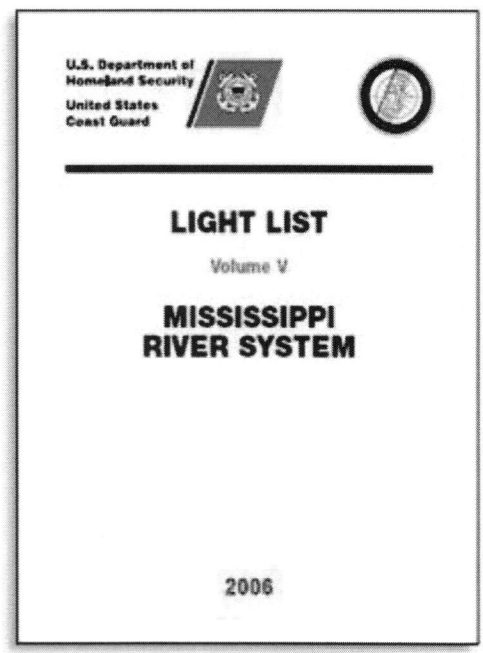

The United States publishes two different light lists. The U.S. Coast Guard publishes the *Light List* for lights in U.S. territorial waters; NIMA publishes the *List of Lights* for lights in foreign waters.

Light lists furnish detailed information about navigation lights and other navigation aids, supplementing the charts, *Coast Pilots*, and *Sailing Directions*. Consult the chart for the location and light characteristics of all navigation aids; consult the light lists to determine their detailed description.

The *Notice to Mariners* corrects both lists. Corrections which have accumulated since the print date are included in the *Notice to Mariners* as a *Summary of Corrections*. All of these summary corrections, and any corrections published subsequently, should be noted in the "Record of Corrections."

A navigator needs to know both the identity of a light and when he can expect to see it; he often plans the ship's track to pass within a light's range. If lights are not sighted when predicted, the vessel may be significantly off course and standing into danger.

A circle with a radius equal to the visible range of the light usually defines the area in which a light can be seen.

On some bearings, however, obstructions may reduce the range. In this case, the obstructed arc might differ with height of eye and distance. Also, lights of different colors may be seen at different distances. Consider these facts both when identifying a light and predicting the range at which it can be seen.

Atmospheric conditions have a major effect on a light's range. Fog, haze, dust, smoke, or precipitation can obscure a light. Additionally, a light can be extinguished.

Always report an extinguished light so maritime authorities can issue a warning and make repairs.

On a dark, clear night, the visual range is limited by either: (1) luminous intensity, or (2) curvature of the Earth.

Regardless of the height of eye, one cannot see a weak light beyond a certain luminous range. Assuming light travels linearly, an observer located below the light's visible horizon cannot see it. The Distance to the Horizon table gives the distance to the horizon for various heights of eye.

The light lists contain a condensed version of this table.

Abnormal refraction patterns might change this range; therefore, one cannot exactly predict the range at which a light will be seen.

The American Practical Navigator (Pub 9)

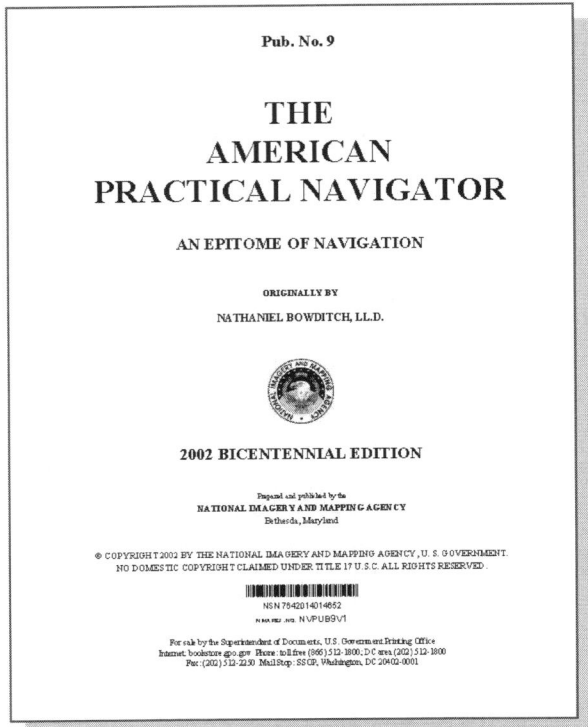

The American Practical Navigator (Pub 9) is a publication, which describes the modern principles of marine navigation and includes the formulas, tables, data and instructions required by navigators to perform the computations associated with dead reckoning, piloting, and celestial navigation. The publication also contains sections addressing the Practice of Navigation, Navigational Safety, Oceanography, Weather, and Electronic Navigation.

Notice to Mariners

The ***Notice to Mariners*** is published weekly by the National Imagery and Mapping Agency (NIMA), prepared jointly with the National Ocean Service (NOS) and the U.S. Coast Guard. It advises mariners of important matters affecting navigational safety, including new hydrographic information, changes in channels and aids to navigation, and other important data. The information in the *Notice to Mariners* is formatted to simplify the correction of paper charts, sailing directions, light lists, and other publications produced by NIMA, NOS, and the U.S. Coast Guard.

It is the responsibility of users to decide which of their charts and publications require correction.

Suitable records of *Notice to Mariners* should be maintained to facilitate the updating of charts and publications prior to use.

Notice to Mariners No. 1 of each year contains important information on a variety of subjects which supplements information not usually found on charts and in navigational publications. This information is published as ***Special Notice to Mariners Paragraphs***. Additional items considered of interest to the mariner are also included in this *Notice*.

Summary of Corrections

A close companion to the *Notice to Mariners* is the ***Summary of Corrections***. The *Summary* is published in five volumes. Each volume covers a major portion of the Earth including several chart regions and their sub-regions. Volume 5 also includes special charts and publications corrected by the *Notice to Mariners*. Since the *Summaries* contain cumulative corrections, any chart, regardless of its print date, can be corrected with the proper volume of the *Summary* and all subsequent *Notice to Mariners*.

Local Notice to Mariners

The *Local Notice to Mariners* is issued by each U.S. Coast Guard District to disseminate important information affecting navigational safety within that District. This Notice reports changes and deficiencies in aids to navigation maintained by the Coast Guard. Other marine information such as new charts, channel depths, naval operations, and regattas is included. Since temporary information of short duration is not included in the NIMA *Notice to Mariners*, the *Local Notice to Mariners* may be the only source for it. Since correcting information for U.S. charts in the NIMA *Notice* is obtained from the Coast Guard local notices, there is a lag of 1 or 2 weeks for NIMA *Notice* to publish a correction from this source. The *Local Notice to Mariners* may be obtained free of charge by contacting the appropriate Coast Guard District Commander. Vessels operating in ports and waterways in several districts must obtain the *Local Notice to Mariners* from each district. See below for a complete list of U.S. Coast Guard Districts.

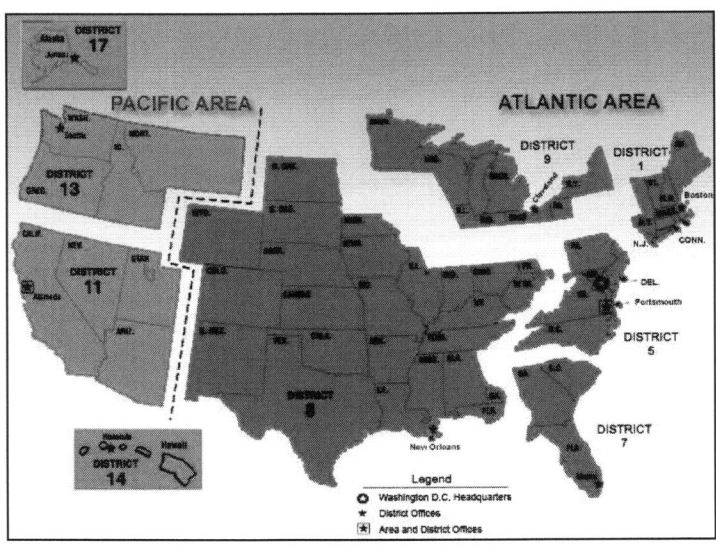

Electronic Notice to Mariners

One major impediment to full implementation of electronic chart systems has been the issue of how to keep them up to date. The IMO, after reviewing the range standards which might be employed in the provision of updates to ECDIS charts, decided that the correction system must be "hands off" from the mariner's point of view. That is, the correction system could not rely on the ability of the mariner to enter individual correction data himself, as he would do on a paper chart. The process must be automated to maintain the integrity of the data and prevent errors in data entry by navigators.

Chart No. 1 Chart Symbols and Abbreviations

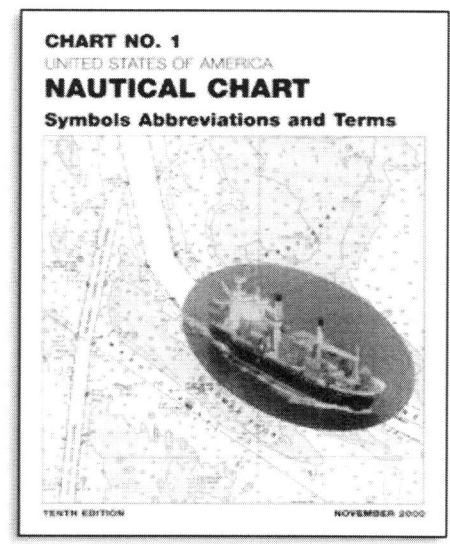

Chart No. 1 is not actually a chart but a book containing a key to chart symbols. Most countries which produce charts also produce such a list. The U.S. *Chart No. 1* contains a listing of chart symbols in four categories:

1.   Chart symbols used by the National Ocean Service
2.   Chart symbols used by NIMA
3.   Chart symbols recommended by the International Hydrographic Organization
4.   Chart symbols used on foreign charts reproduced by NIMA

Subjects covered include general features of charts, topography, hydrography, and aids to navigation. There is also a complete index of abbreviations and an explanation of the IALA buoyage system.

NIMA *International Code of Signals (Pub. 102)*

This book lists the signals to be employed by vessels at sea to communicate a variety of information relating to safety, distress, medical, and operational information. This publication became effective in 1969.

According to this code, each signal has a unique and complete meaning. The signals can be transmitted via Morse code light and sound, flag, radio telegraph and telephone, and semaphore. Since these methods of signaling are internationally recognized, differences in language between sender and receiver are immaterial; the message will be understood when decoded in the language of the receiver, regardless of the language of the sender.

The *Notice to Mariners* corrects *Pub. 102*.

Sight Reduction Tables Pub. 229

Without a calculator or computer programmed for sight reduction, the navigator needs *sight reduction tables* to solve the celestial triangle. Two different sets of tables are commonly used at sea.

NIMA *Pub. 229, Sight Reduction Tables for Marine Navigation*, consists of six volumes of tables designed for use with the *Nautical Almanac* for solution of the celestial triangle by the **Marcq Saint Hilaire** or **intercept** method. The tabular data are the solutions of the navigational triangle of which two sides and the included angle are known and it is necessary to find the third side and adjacent angle.

Each volume of *Pub. 229* includes two 8 degree zones, comprising 15 degree bands from 0 to 90 degrees, with a 1 degree overlap between volumes. *Pub. 229* is a joint publication produced by the National Imagery and Mapping Agency, the U.S. Naval Observatory, and the Royal Greenwich Observatory.

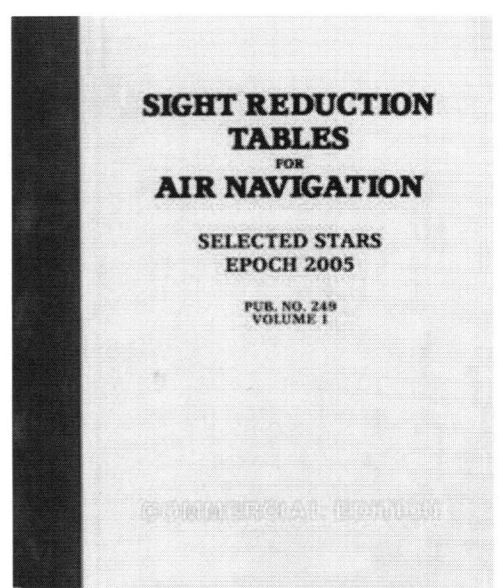

Sight Reduction Tables for Air Navigation, Pub. 249, is also a joint production of the three organizations above. It is issued in three volumes. Volume 1 contains the values of the altitude and true azimuth of seven selected stars chosen to provide, for any given position and time, the best celestial observations. A new edition is issued every 5 years for the upcoming astronomical epoch. Volumes 2 (0 to 40) and 3 (39 to 89) provide for sights of the Sun, Moon, and planets.

Radio Navigational Aids PUB. 117

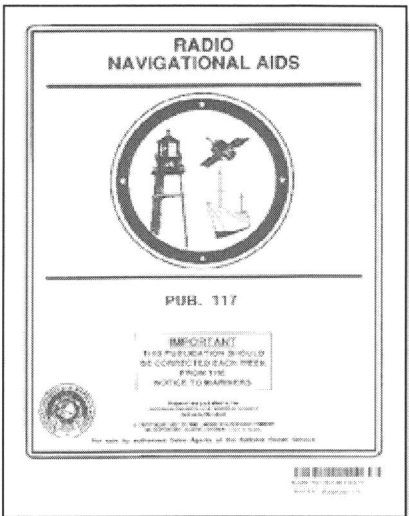

The Radio Navigational Aids (Pub 117) publication contains a detailed list of selected worldwide radio stations that provide services to the mariner. The publication is divided into chapters according to the nature of the service provided by the radio stations. The services include RDF and Radar Stations; stations broadcasting navigational warnings, time signals or medical advice; communication traffic for distress, emergency and safety including GMDSS; and long range navigational aids. It also contains chapters describing procedures of the AMVER System, and the interim emergency procedures and communication instructions to be followed by U.S merchant vessels in times of crisis

The Nautical Almanac

For celestial sight reduction, the navigator needs an **almanac** for ephemeris data. **The *Nautical Almanac,*** produced jointly by H.M. Nautical Almanac Office and the U.S. Naval Observatory, is the most common almanac used for celestial navigation. It also contains information on sunrise, sunset, moonrise, and moonset, as well as compact sight reduction tables. The *Nautical Almanac* is published annually.

Current Tables

2007 Atlantic Coast Tidal Current Tables informs the reader on the expected behaviors of the oceans along the eastern coasts of North and South America, as well as the western coasts of Europe and Africa, and its waves through charts, graphs, and informative writing.

Topics include daily predicted times of slack water and predicted times and velocities of maximum current (flood and ebb), the speed of a current at times between slack water and maximum current, and the duration of weak current near the time of slack water. This book is published as one part in a set of four volumes listed below:

Tidal Current Tables: Atlantic Coast of North America
Tidal Current Tables: Pacific Coast of North America
Tide & Tidal Current Tables: New York Harbor to Chesapeake Bay
Tide Tables: Central & Western Pacific Ocean

Tide Tables

2007 Central and Western Pacific and Indian Ocean Tide Tables contains full daily predictions for

76 reference ports and differences and other constants for about 2,600 stations in North America, South America, and Greenland.

It also contains a table for obtaining the approximate height of the tide at any time, a table of local mean time of sunrise and sunset for every 5th day of the year for different latitudes, a table for the reduction of local mean time to standard time, a table of moonrise and moonset for 8 places, a table of the Greenwich mean time of the Moons phases, apogee, perigee, greatest north and south and zero declination, and the time of the solar equinoxes and solstices, and a glossary of terms.

This book is published as one part in a set of four volumes as listed below

Tide Tables: East Coast of North and South America, 2007
Tide Tables: Europe and West Coasts of Africa, 2007
Tide Tables: West Coast of North and South America, 2007

Chemical Data Guide for Bulk Shipment by Water

Chemical Data Guide for Bulk Shipment by Water: Marine Technical and Hazardous Materials Division.

The data in this guide was compiled from a number of sources in the interest of safe water movement of bulk chemicals. Hopefully, by providing key chemical information in an easy to use form, this guide can help prevent or at least minimize the harmful effects of chemical accidents on the waterways.

CELESTIAL NAVIGATION EQUIPMENT

Chapter 1

TELESCOPIC ALIDADE

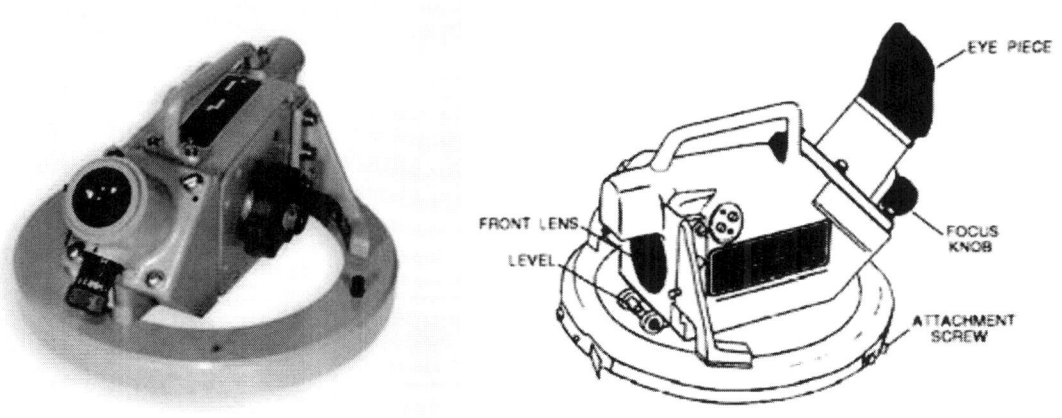

 A **telescopic alidade** is a telescope equipped with crosshair, level vial, polarizing light filter, and internal focusing. The telescope is mounted on a ring that fits on a gyro repeater or magnetic compass. The optical system simultaneously projects an image of approximately 25 degrees of the compass card, together with a view of the level vial onto the optical axis of the telescope. By this means, both the object and its bearing can be viewed at the same time through the alidade eyepiece. Older models of the telescopic alidade have a straight-through eyepiece telescope, whereas the model shown in the figure has the eyepiece inclined at an angle for ease in viewing.

AZIMUTH CIRCLE

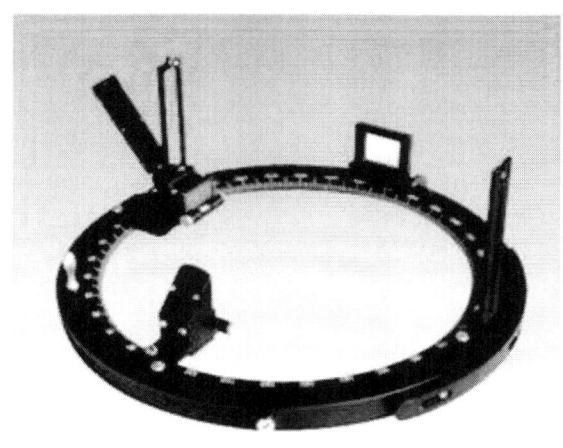

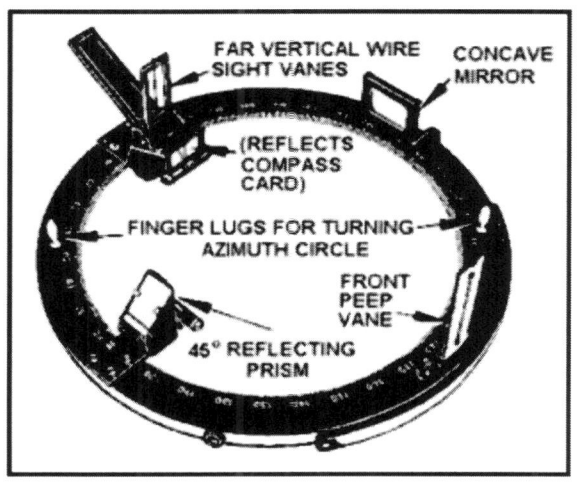

To take an azimuth of a celestial body, you must use the **azimuth circle.** An azimuth circle is a nonmagnetic metal ring sized to fit upon a 7 1/2 inch compass bowl or upon a gyro repeater. The inner lip is graduated in degrees from 0° to 360° in a counterclockwise direction for taking relative bearings. Two sighting vanes (the forward or far vane containing a vertical wire and the after or near vane containing a **peep sight**) facilitate the observation of bearings and azimuths. **Two finger lugs** are used to position the instruments exactly while the vanes are being aligned. A hinged **reflector vane**, mounted at the base and beyond the forward vane, is used for reflecting stars and planets when you are observing azimuths. Beneath the forward vane a **reflecting mirror** and the extended **vertical wire** are mounted, enabling the navigator to read the bearing, or azimuth, from the reflected portion of the compass card. For observing azimuths of the Sun, an additional **reflecting mirror and housing** are mounted on the ring, each midway between the forward and after vanes. The Sun's rays are reflected by the mirror to the housing where a vertical slit admits a line of light. This admitted light passes through a **45 degree reflecting prism** and is projected on the compass card from which its azimuth is directly read. When both bearing and azimuths are observed, two spirit levels, which are attached, must be used to level the instrument.

SEXTANT

glass filter — index mirror
— telescope
horizon mirror — telescope clamp
glass filter — eyepiece
screw to regulate small mirror — telescope printing
index arm — frame
— graduated arc
drum — locking device

One of the better known navigational instruments is the **sextant.** It is used to measure angles that ultimately result in determining the ship's position at sea. The sextant is capable only of measuring the angle between two objects. Its principal function in navigation is measuring the angle between a heavenly body and the visible horizon.

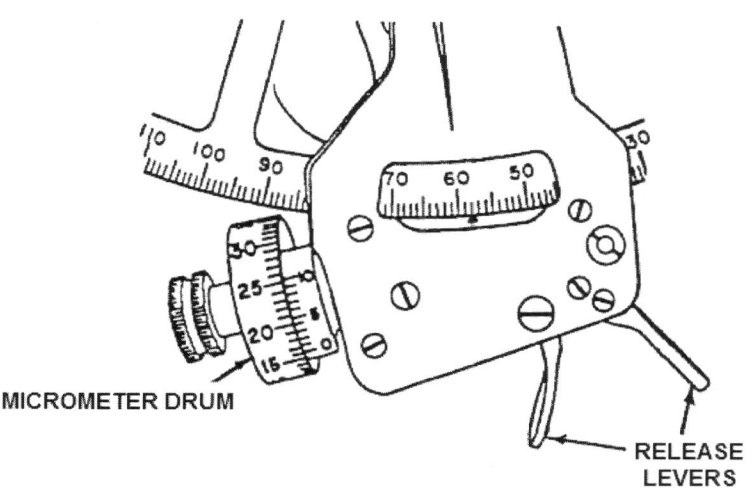

MICROMETER DRUM

RELEASE LEVERS

The figure above shows the parts of a marine sextant. The **frame** on which the other parts are mounted. The **graduated arc or limb**, graduated in degrees. (The word sextant is derived from the Latin word sex; meaning six. In old-fashioned sextants the limb was one-sixth of the arc of a circle. The **limb** on a modern sextant, however contains more than one-sixth of the arc of a circle.) The **index arm**, which pivots about the exact center of curvature of the limb. The lower end of the arm is provided with an index mark (to indicate the reading) and with a **micrometer drum.** The **index mirror** is mounted perpendicular to the plane of the **limb** at the upper end of the **index arm.** Half of the horizon glass is silvered over like a mirror; the other half is clear. At zero reading, the **horizon glass** is supposed to be exactly parallel to the index mirror. The **telescope** is supported in a collar attached to the **frame**. It directs the observer's line of sight to the **horizon glass**, a line parallel to the plane of the **frame,** and also magnifies the horizon. **Glass Filters** reduce the glare of light reaching the eye.

MICROMETER

The figure below shows the micrometer arrangement on a sextant. The limb on this sextant has teeth that mesh with teeth on the **micrometer drum**. One complete rotation of the drum moves the index arm 1 degree along the limb. The limb and micrometer drum can be separated by disengaging the tangent screw. This process is accomplished by squeezing the two small **levers** that project below the arm.

Looking at the figure to the right, see if you can figure out how to read the altitude. On this type of sextant, altitude can be read to the nearest tenth of a minute. It's easy to see that the altitude is somewhere between **57 degrees and 58 degrees** -the indicator on the arm shows you that on the main scale. Inboard of the tangent screw is the micrometer drum, graduated from 0 to 60. Each graduation represents 1 minute (1'). A smaller cylinder, inboard of the drum, is graduated from 0 to 10. It is the vernier of this type of sextant. Each graduation on it represents one-tenth of a minute (0.1') The index mark for the drum is the 0 on the vernier, **which is between 16 and 17**. Thus, the altitude is a little more than 58 degrees 16 minutes. To find, to the nearest tenth of a minute, how much more the altitude is, start along the vernier scale from 0 and locate the **first graduation that lines up with a graduation on the drum**. Here, it is readily apparent that the first graduation that so lines up is 3. Therefore, the sextant shows an altitude of **58 degrees 16.3 minutes**.

Index Correction

Practically every sextant has a small error, called the **index error,** which is allowed for by applying the index correction (IC) to every sextant reading. To find the IC, place the index mark at 0 degrees on the limb scale, and level the sextant toward the horizon. If there is no IC, setting for zero altitude will bring the direct and reflected images of the horizon exactly into line. If the two images are not exactly in line when the instrument is set at zero, the IC is the amount shown to the right or left of zero after they are brought into line. A few graduations have been inserted to the right of the 0 degree mark to allow for an IC that might occur on that side.

After the images are lined up, if the index lies to the **right** of 0 degrees, then the IC is plus and must be **added** to all sextant readings. If the index lies to the **left**, the IC is minus and must be **subtracted**.

This little jingle will help you remember how to apply the IC to the sextant reading: **When it's on, it's off, when it's off, it's on.** In other words when the reading is on the drum scale, the correction is subtractive; when the reading is off the drum scale, the correction is additive.

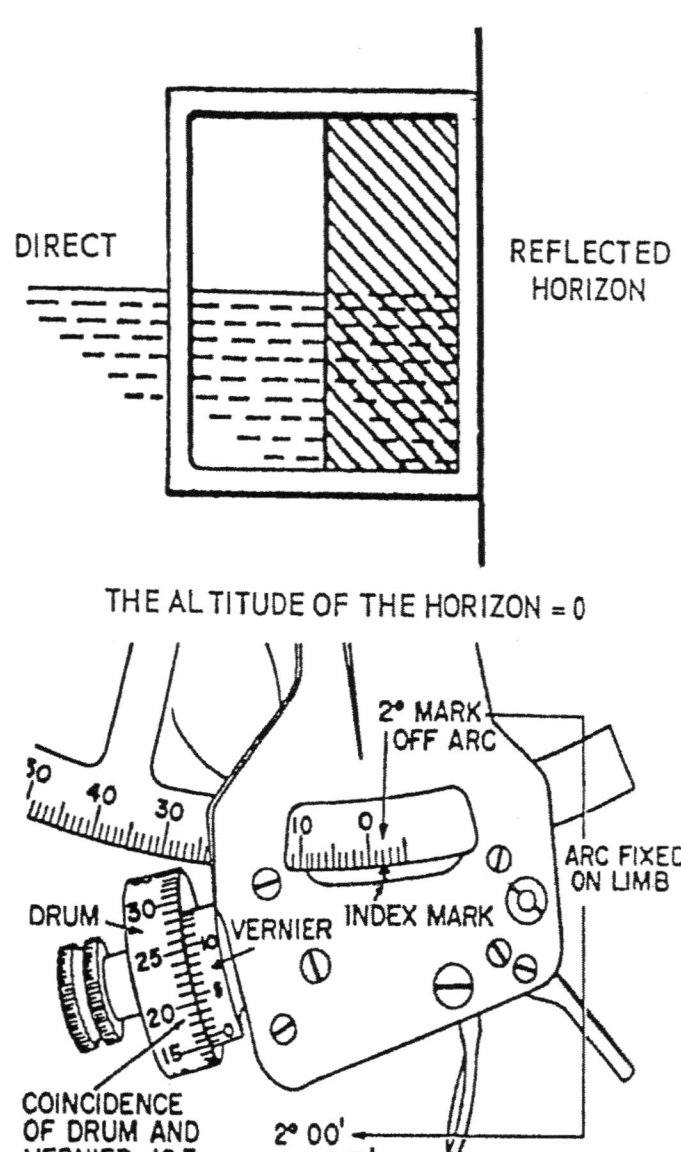

Care of Sextant

Accuracy of the sextant depends on exact adjustment and alignment of its various parts. A slight shock, for instance, can disturb the adjustment and alignment enough to produce a material error. **In handling the sextant, exercise great care** to avoid striking it accidentally against any object. Accidental dropping will, of course, either temporarily or permanently destroy its value as a navigational instrument. **Protect it** against exposure to **salt spray** while you are waiting to get a sight. If no shelter is available, use a towel to protect the sextant.

Moisture must not be permitted to accumulate on the mirror or glass surfaces. These surfaces should

1- 20

be dried with a good grade of lens paper or a piece of clean, soft linen. Si k or chamois may scratch the mirrors, and cotton cloth or waste may leave particles of lint adhering to the glass. **Alcohol** is an **excellent glass cleaner** and is safe to use on a sextant.

Never use brass polish on the arc or vernier because it eventually abrades the graduations on the scale. When **cleaning** becomes necessary, use **ammonia**. Subsequent rubbing with thin oil and lampblack will restore the distinctness of faded markings. A drop or two of light oil should be applied occasionally to the **sextant's working parts**.

Adjusting screws on the sextant should never be manipulated unless absolutely necessary and then only by authorized persons who must exercise the greatest possible caution. Minor adjustments are described below. All other adjustments should be made by trained personnel or at an authorized optical shop.

Sextant adjustment

The navigator should measure and remove the following adjustable sextant errors in the order listed:

1. **Perpendicularity Error:** Adjust first for perpendicularity of the index mirror to the frame of the sextant. **To test for perpendicularity,** place the index arm at **about 35°** on the arc and hold the sextant on its side with the index mirror up and toward the eye. Observe the direct and reflected views of the sextant arc, **as illustrated below**. If the two views are not joined in a straight line, the index mirror is not perpendicular. If the **reflected image is above** the direct view, the mirror is inclined forward. If the **reflected image is below** the direct view, the mirror is **inclined backward**. Make the adjustment using two screws behind the index mirror.

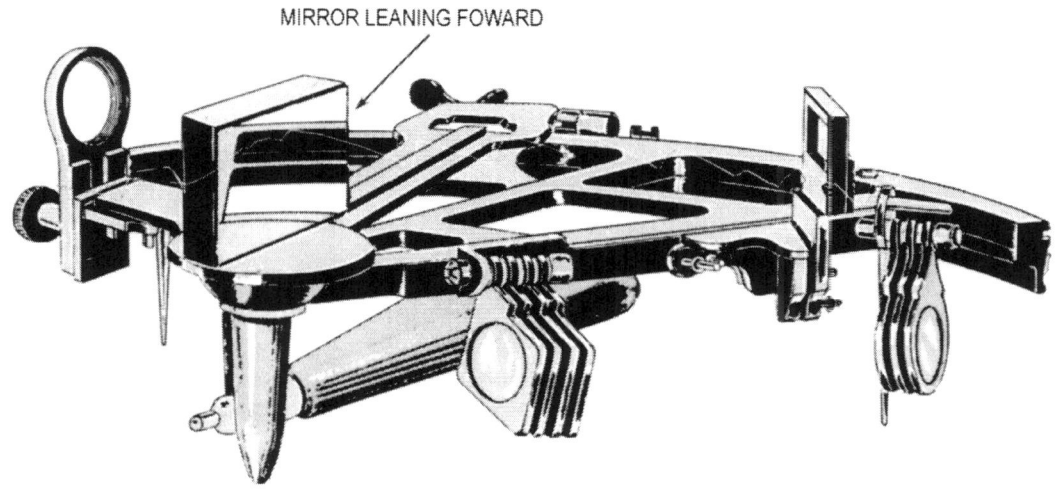

Testing the perpendicularity of the index mirror. Here the mirror is not perpendicular

2. **Side Error:** An error resulting from the horizon glass not being perpendicular is called **side error**. To test for side error, set the index arm at zero and direct the line of sight at a star. Then rotate the tangent screw back and forth so that the reflected image passes alternately above and below the direct view. If, in changing from one position to the other, the reflected image passes directly over the unreflected image, no side error exists. If it passes to one side, side error exists. **In the illustrate\ion below,** observations without side error (left) and with side error (right). Whether the sextant reads zero when the true and reflected images are in coincidence is immaterial for this test. An alternative method is to observe a vertical line, such as one edge of the mast of another vessel (or the sextant can be held on its side and the horizon used). If the direct and reflected portions do not form a continuous line, the horizon glass is not perpendicular to the frame of the sextant. A third method involves holding the sextant vertically, as in observing the altitude of a celestial body. Bring the reflected image of the horizon into coincidence with the direct view until it appears as a continuous line across the horizon glass. Then tilt the sextant right or left. If the horizon still appears continuous, the horizon glass is perpendicular to the frame, but if the reflected portion appears above or below the part seen directly, the glass is not perpendicular. **Make the appropriate adjustment using two screws behind the horizon glass.**

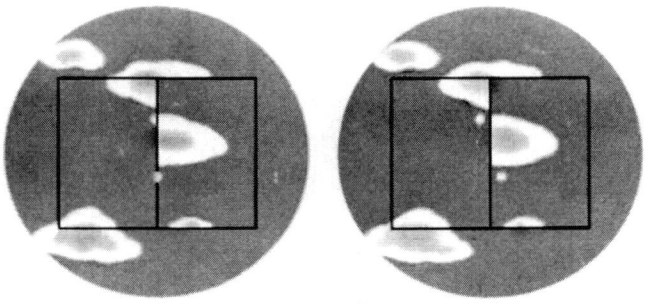

Testing the perpendicularity of the horizon glass. On the left,
side error does not exist. At the right, side error does exist.

3. **Collimation Error:** If the line of sight through the telescope is not parallel to the plane of the instrument, a **collimation error** will result. Altitudes measured will be greater than their actual values. To check for parallelism of the telescope, insert it in its collar and observe two stars 90° or more apart. Bring the reflected image of one into coincidence with the direct view of the other near either the right or left edge of the field of view (the upper or lower edge if the sextant is horizontal). Then tilt the sextant so that the stars appear near the opposite edge. If they remain in coincidence, the telescope is parallel to the frame; if they separate, it is not. An alternative method involves placing the telescope in its collar and then laying the sextant on a flat table. Sight along the frame of the sextant and have an assistant place a mark on the opposite bulkhead, in line with the frame. Place another mark above the first, at a distance equal to the distance from the center of the telescope to the frame. This second line should be in the center of the field of view of the telescope if the telescope is parallel to the frame. Adjust the collar to correct for non-parallelism.

4. **Index Error: Index error is the error remaining after the navigator has removed perpendicularity error, side error, and collimation error.** The index mirror and horizon glass not

being parallel when the index arm is set exactly at zero is the major cause of index error. To test for parallelism of the mirrors, set the instrument at zero and direct the line of sight at the horizon. Adjust the sextant reading as necessary to cause both images of the horizon to come into line. The sextant's reading when the horizon comes into line is the index error. If the index error is positive, subtract it from each sextant reading. If the index error is negative, add it to each sextant reading.

End-of-chapter questions

1. What is the principal function of a sextant in navigation?

   a. Measuring ranges to other ships
   b. Measuring the angle between a heavenly body and the visible horizon
   c. Determining the courses of the ships
   d. Determining the true bearings of navigational aids

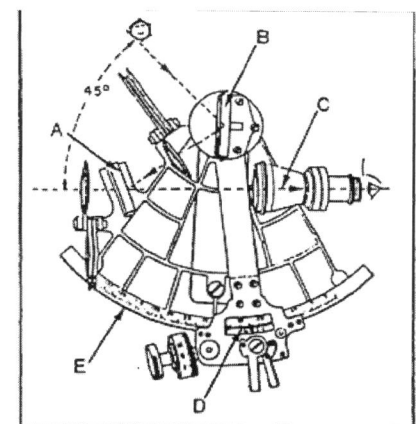

Diagram for Questions 2 through 4

2. The index arm of the sextant pivots about the exact center of curvature of the part of sextant marked:

   a. B
   b. E
   c. A
   d. C

3. What part of the sextant is the horizon glass:

   a. C
   b. E
   c. A
   d. C

4. What part of the sextant is parallel to the horizon glass when the index mark is at zero and there is no index correction?

   a. B
   b. C
   c. D
   d. E

5. How many degrees is the sextant index arm moved by one complete rotation of the micrometer drum?

   a. 10 degrees
   b. 5 degrees
   c. 2 degrees
   d. 1 degree

6. The micrometer drum of the sextant is graduated in:

    a. half seconds from 0 to 180
    b. half seconds from 0 to 20
    c. seconds from 0 to 60
    d. minutes from 0 to 60

7. You have sighted on the horizon to determine the index correction of a sextant. The index mark falls on the arc just to the left of the 0 degree line. If the drum and vernier read 9.4', what is the index correction?

    a. + 50.6'
    b. + 9.4'
    c. - 50.6'
    d. - 9.4'

8. Which of the following cleaning agents is used to clean the mirror or glass surface of a sextant?

    a. Saltwater
    b. Alcohol
    c. Ammonia
    d. Soapy water

9. Which of the following cleaning agents is used to clean the limb and the vernier of the sextant?

    a. Brass polish
    b. Alcohol
    c. Ammonia
    d. Soapy water

ANSWERS

1.   b
2.   a
3.   c
4.   a
5.   d
6.   d
7.   d
8.   b
9.   c

THE SAILINGS
BY CALCULATION

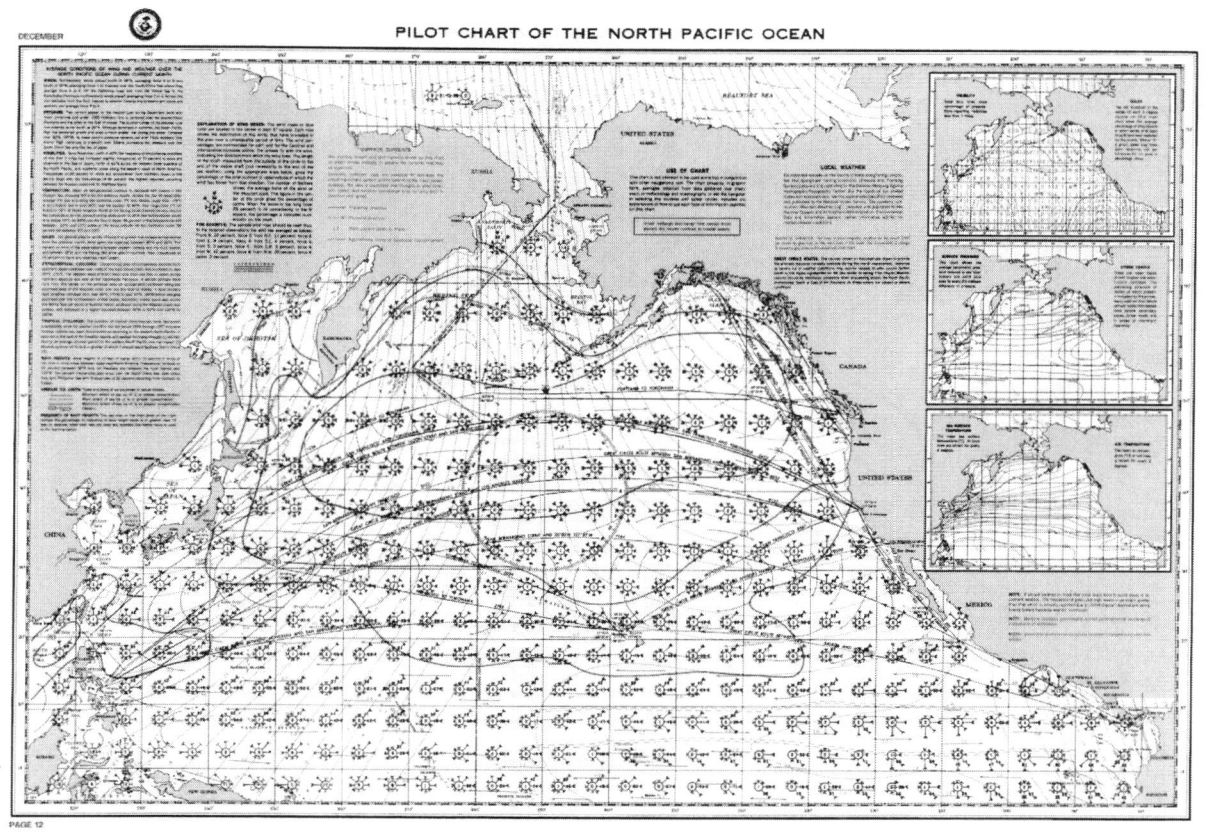

USCG SAILINGS WORKED-OUT
WITH EXCERPTS
AMERICAN PRACTICAL NAVIGATOR
CHAPTER 24

by
ALEXANDER F. HICKETHIER MBA
and
Dr. Hu Jia-Shen

THE SAILINGS

INTRODUCTION

Introduction

Dead reckoning involves the determination of one's present or future position by projecting the ship's course and distance run from a known position. A closely related problem is that of finding the course and distance from one known point to another known point. For short distances, these problems are easily solved directly on charts, but for long distances, a purely mathematical solution is often a better method. Collectively, these methods are called **The Sailings**.

Navigational computer programs and calculators commonly contain algorithms for computing all of the problems of the sailings.

Rhumb Lines And Great Circles

The principal advantage of a rhumb line is that it maintains constant true direction. A ship following the rhumb line between two places does not change true course. A rhumb line makes the same angle with all meridians it crosses and appears as a straight line on a Mercator chart. For any other case, the difference between the rhumb line and the great circle connecting two points increases (1) as the latitude increases, (2) as the difference of latitude between the two points decreases, and (3) as the difference of longitude increases. A great circle is the intersection of the surface of a sphere and a plane passing through the center of the sphere. It is the largest circle that can be drawn on the surface of the sphere, and is the shortest distance along the surface between any two points. Any two points are connected by only one great circle unless the points are **antipodal** (180° apart on the earth), and then an infinite number of great circles passes through them. Every great circle bisects every other great circle. Thus, except for the equator, every great circle lies exactly half in the Northern Hemisphere and half in the Southern Hemisphere. Any two points 180° apart on a great circle have the same latitude numerically, but contrary names, and are 180° apart in longitude. The point of greatest latitude is called the **vertex**. For each great circle, there is a vertex in each hemisphere, 180° apart in longitude.

At these points the great circle is tangent to a parallel of latitude, and its direction is due east-west. On each side of these vertices the direction changes progressively until the intersection with the equator is reached, 90° in longitude away, where the great circle crosses the equator at an angle equal to the latitude of the vertex. On a Mercator chart a great circle appears as a sine curve extending equal distances each side of the equator. The rhumb line connecting any two points of the great circle on the same side of the equator is a chord of the curve. Along any intersecting meridian the great circle crosses at a higher latitude than the rhumb line. If the two points are on opposite sides of the equator, the direction of curvature of the great circle relative to the rhumb line changes at the equator. The rhumb line and great circle may intersect each other, and if the points are equal distances on each side of the equator, the intersection takes place at the equator.

Great circle sailing takes advantage of the shorter distance along the great circle between two points, rather than the longer rhumb line. The arc of the great circle between the points is called the **great circle track**. If it could be followed exactly, the destination would be dead ahead throughout the voyage (assuming course and heading were the same). The rhumb line appears the more direct route on a Mercator chart because of chart distortion. The great circle crosses meridians at higher latitudes, where the distance between them is less. This is why the great circle route is shorter than the rhumb line.

The decision as to whether or not to use great-circle sailing depends upon the conditions. The saving in distance should be worth the additional effort, and of course the great circle route cannot cross land, nor should it carry the vessel into dangerous waters. **Composite sailing** may save time and distance over the rhumb line track without leading the vessel into danger. Since great circles other than a meridian or the equator are curved lines whose true direction changes continually, the navigator does not attempt to follow it exactly. Rather, he selects a number of points along the great circle, constructs rhumb lines between the points, and follows these rhumb lines from point to point.

Kinds Of Sailings

There are seven types of sailings:

1. **Plane sailing** solves problems involving a single course and distance, difference of latitude, and departure, in which the earth is regarded as a plane surface. This method, therefore, provides solution for latitude of the point of arrival, but not for longitude. To calculate the longitude, the spherical sailings are necessary. Do not use this method for distances of more than a few hundred miles.

2. **Traverse sailing** combines the plane sailing solutions when there are two or more courses and determines the equivalent course and distance made good by a vessel steaming along a series of rhumb lines.

3. **Parallel sailing** is the interconversion of departure and difference of longitude when a vessel is proceeding due east or due west.

4. **Middle- (or mid-) latitude sailing** uses the mean latitude for converting departure to difference of longitude when the course is not due east or due west.

5. **Mercator sailing** provides a mathematical solution of the plot as made on a Mercator chart. It is similar to plane sailing, but uses Meridional difference and difference of longitude in place of difference of latitude and departure.

6. **Great circle sailing** involves the solution of courses, distances, and points along a great circle between two points.

7. **Composite sailing** is a modification of great-circle sailing to limit the maximum latitude, generally to avoid ice or severe weather near the poles.

Terms And Definitions

In solutions of the sailings, the following quantities are used:

1. **Latitude (L)**. The latitude of the point of departure is designated L_1; that of the destination, L_2; middle (mid) or mean latitude, L_m; latitude of the vertex of a great circle, L_v; and latitude of any point on a great circle, L_x.

2. **Mean latitude (L_m)**. Half the arithmetical sum of the latitudes of two places on the same side of the equator.

3. **Middle or mid latitude (L_m)**. The latitude at which the arc length of the parallel separating the meridians passing through two specific points is exactly equal to the departure in proceeding from one point to the other. The mean latitude is used when there is no practicable means of determining the middle latitude.

4. **Difference of latitude (l or DLat.)**.

5. **Meridional parts (M)**. The Meridional parts of the point of departure are designated M_1, and of the point of arrival or the destination, M_2.

6. **Meridional difference (m)**.

7. **Longitude (Lo)**. The longitude of the point of departure is designated Lo_1; that of the point of arrival or the destination, Lo_2; of the vertex of a great circle, l_v; and of any point on a great circle, Lo_x

8. **Difference of longitude (DLo)**.

9. **Departure (p or Dep.)**.

10. **Course** or **course angle (Cn or C)**.

11. **Distance (D or Dist.)**.

GREAT CIRCLE SAILING

Great Circle Sailing By Chart

Navigators can most easily solve great-circle sailing problems graphically. DMAHTC publishes several gnomonic projections covering the principal navigable waters of the world. On these **great circle charts**, any straight line is a great circle. The chart, however, is not conformal; therefore, the navigator cannot directly measure directions and distances as on a Mercator chart. The usual method of using a gnomonic chart is to plot the route and pick points along the track every 5° of longitude using the latitude and longitude scales in the immediate vicinity of each point. These points are then transferred to a Mercator chart and connected by rhumb lines. The course and distance for each leg is measured on the Mercator chart.

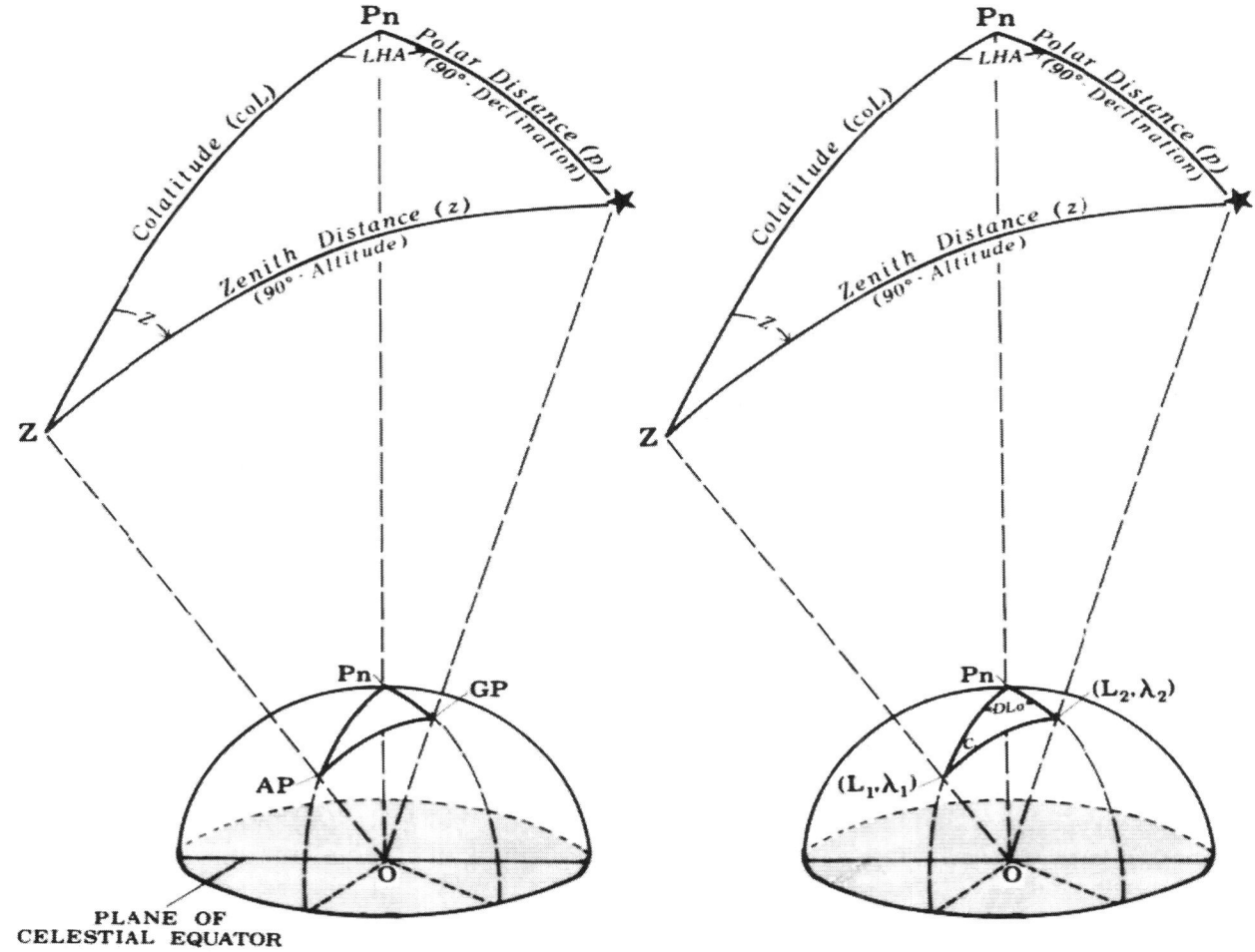

Figure 1 Adapting the astronomical triangle to the navigational triangle of great circle sailing.

Great Circle Sailing By Sight Reduction Tables

Any method of solving a celestial spherical triangle can be used for solving great circle sailing problems. The point of departure replaces the assumed position of the observer, the destination replaces the geographical position of the body, difference of longitude replaces meridian angle or local hour angle, initial course angle replaces azimuth angle, and great circle distance replaces zenith distance (90° - altitude). See Figure 1

Therefore, any table of azimuths (if the entering values are meridian angle, declination, and latitude) can be used for determining initial great-circle course. Tables which solve for altitude, such as *Pub. No. 229*, can be used for determining great circle distance. The required distance is 90°- altitude. In inspection tables such as *Pub. No. 229*, the given combination of L1, L2, and DLo may not be tabulated. In this case reverse the name of L2 and use 180° - DLo for entering the table. The required course angle is then 180° minus the tabulated azimuth, and distance is 90° plus the altitude. If neither combination can be found, solution cannot be made by that method. By interchanging L1 and L2, one can find the supplement of the final course angle. Solution by table often provides a rapid approximate check, but accurate results usually require triple interpolation. Except for *Pub. No. 229*, inspection tables do not provide a solution for points along the great circle. *Pub. No. 229* provides solutions for these points only if interpolation is not required.

Great Circle Sailing By *Pub. No. 229*

By entering *Pub. No. 229* with the latitude of the point of departure as latitude, latitude of destination as declination, and difference of longitude as LHA, the tabular altitude and azimuth angle may be extracted and converted to great-circle distance and course. As in sight reduction, the tables are entered according to whether the name of the latitude of the point of departure is the same as or contrary to the name of the latitude of the destination (declination). If the values correspond to those of a celestial body above the celestial horizon, 90° minus the arc of the tabular altitude becomes the distance; the tabular azimuth angle becomes the initial great-circle course angle. If the respondents correspond to those of a celestial body below the celestial horizon, the arc of the tabular altitude plus 90° becomes the distance; the supplement of the tabular azimuth angle becomes the initial great-circle course angle. When the Contrary/Same (CS) Line is crossed in either direction, the altitude becomes negative; the body lies below the celestial horizon. For example: If the tables are entered with the LHA (DLo) at the bottom of a right-hand page and declination (L2) such that the respondents lie above the CS Line, the CS Line has been crossed. Then the distance is 90° plus the tabular altitude; the initial course angle is the

supplement of the tabular azimuth angle. Similarly, if the tables are entered with the LHA (DLo) at the top of a right-hand page and the respondents are found below the CS Line, the distance is 90° plus the tabular altitude; the initial course angle is the supplement of the tabular azimuth angle. If the tables are entered with the LHA (DLo) at the bottom of a right-hand page and the name of L2 is contrary to L1, the respondents are found in the column for L1 on the facing page. In this case, the CS Line has been crossed; the distance is 90° plus the tabular altitude; the initial course angle is the supplement of the tabular azimuth angle. The tabular azimuth angle, or its supplement, is prefixed N or S for the latitude of the point of departure and Figure 2405. Adapting the astronomical triangle to the navigational triangle of great circle sailing. suffixed E or W depending upon the destination being east or west of the point of departure. If all entering arguments are integral degrees, the distance and course angle are obtained directly from the tables without interpolation. If the latitude of the destination is non-integral, interpolation for the additional minutes of latitude is done as in correcting altitude for any declination increment; if the latitude of departure or difference of longitude is non-integral, the additional interpolation is done graphically. Since the latitude of destination becomes the declination entry, and all declinations appear on every page, the great circle solution can always be extracted from the volume which covers the latitude of the point of departure.

Great Circle Sailing By Computation

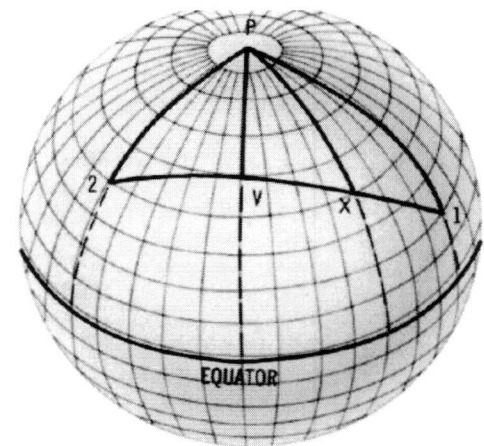

Figure 2. The navigational triangle and great circle sailing.

In Figure 2, 1 is the point of departure, 2 the destination, P the pole nearer 1, I-X-V-2 the great circle through 1 and 2, V the vertex, and X any point on the great circle. The arcs P1, PX, PV, and P2 are the colatitudes of points 1, X, V, and 2, respectively. If 1 and 2 are on opposite sides of the equator, P2 is 90°+L2. The length of arc 1-2 is the great circle distance between 1 and 2. Arcs 1-2, P1, and P2 form a spherical triangle. The angle at 1 is the initial great-circle course from 1 to 2, that at 2 the supplement of the final great-circle course (or the initial course from 2 to 1), and that at P the DLo between 1 and 2. Great circle sailing by computation usually involves solving for the initial great circle course; the distance; latitude and longitude, and sometimes the distance, of the vertex; and the latitude and longitude of various points (X) on the great circle. The computation for initial course and the distance involves solution of an oblique spherical triangle, and any method of solving such a triangle can be used. If 2 is the geographical position (GP) of a celestial body (the point at which the body is in the zenith), this triangle is solved in celestial navigation, except that 90° - D (the altitude) is desired instead of D. The solution for the vertex and any point X usually involves the solution of right spherical triangles.

Great Circle Formulae

$$\boldsymbol{cos\ D} =$$
$$(\cos L_1 \times \cos L_2 \times \cos DLo) \pm (\sin L_1 \times \sin L_2)$$

- Distance x 60
- Subtract (-) when crossing the Equator

$$\boldsymbol{tan\ C} =$$
$$\sin Dlo \div ((\cos L_1 \times \tan L_2) - (\sin L_1 \times \cos Dlo))$$

- Make L_2 (-) negative when crossing the Equator
- Label the initial course angle according the same name of L_1 and DLo
- Label the initial course angle according the same name of L_2 and DLo, when crossing the equator.

$$\cos L_v = \cos L_1 \times \sin C$$

- use Initial Course
- name L_v same name as L_1

$$\sin DLo_v = \cos C \div \sin L_v$$

- If the initial course angle is less than 90° then the vertex is ahead of you and in the direction of the original DLo.

- If the initial course angle is more than 90° then the vertex is behind you and in the direction of the away from original DLo

$$\tan L_x = \cos DLo_{vx} \times \tan L_v$$

Altering A Great Circle Track To Avoid Obstructions

Land, ice, or severe weather may prevent the use of great circle sailing for some or all of one's route. One of the principal advantages of solution by great circle chart is that the presence of any hazards is immediately apparent. The pilot charts are particularly useful in this regard. Often a relatively short run by rhumb line is sufficient to reach a point from which the great circle track can be followed. Where a choice is possible, the rhumb line selected should conform as nearly as practicable to the direct great circle. If the great circle route crosses a navigation hazard, change the track. It may be satisfactory to follow a great circle to the vicinity of the hazard, one or more rhumb lines along the edge of the hazard, and another great circle to the destination. Another possible solution is the use of composite sailing; still another is the use of two great circles, one from the point of departure to a point near the maximum latitude of unobstructed water and the second from this point to the destination.

Composite Sailing

When the great circle would carry a vessel to a higher latitude than desired, a modification of great circle sailing called **composite sailing** may be used to good advantage. The composite track consists of a great circle from the point of departure and tangent to the limiting parallel, a course line along the parallel, and a great circle tangent to the limiting parallel and through the destination. Solution of composite sailing problems is most easily made with a great circle chart. For this solution, draw lines from the point of departure and the destination, tangent to the limiting parallel. Then measure the coordinates of various selected points along the composite track and transfer them to a Mercator chart, as in great circle sailing. Composite sailing problems can also be solved by computation, using the equation:

$$\textbf{cos DLovx + tanLx cot Lv}$$

The point of departure and the destination are used successively as point X. Solve the two great circles at each end of the limiting parallel, and use parallel sailing along the limiting parallel. Since both great circles have vertices at the same parallel, computation for C, D, and DLo_x can be made by considering them parts of the same great circle with L_1, L_2, and L_v as given and $DLo = DLo_{v1} + DLo_{v2}$. The total distance is the sum of the great circle and parallel distances.

THE SAILING BY COMPUTATION

Plane Sailing

In plane sailing the figure formed by the meridian through the point of departure, the parallel through the point of arrival, and the course line is considered a plane right triangle. This is illustrated in Figure 3. P_1 and P_2 are the points of departure and arrival, respectively. The course angle and the three sides are as labeled. From this triangle:

From the first two of these formulas the following relationships can be derived:

$$DLat = D \times \cos C \qquad D = DLat \div \cos C$$

$$p = D \times \sin C$$

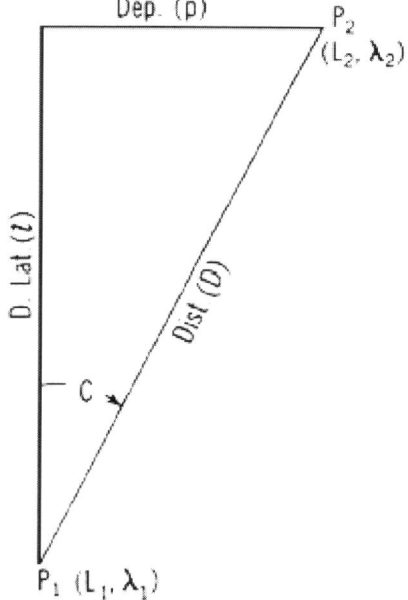

Figure 3. The plane sailing triangle.

Example 1
A ship has steamed 188.0 miles on a course of 005°
Required: (1)(a) Difference in Latitude and (b) departure

Solution:

(1) (a) DLat by computation:

$$Dlat = D \times \cos C$$

= 188.0 miles x cos (005°)
= 187.3 arc min / 60
= 3° 07.3' N

Draw the course vectors to determine the correct course. In this case the vessel has gone north 136 miles and west 203 miles. The course, therefore, must have been between 270° and 360°. No solution other than 304° is reasonable.

Parallel Sailing

Parallel sailing consists of the interconversion of departure and difference of longitude. It is the simplest form of spherical sailing. The formulas for these transformations are:

$$DLo = p \div \cos L \qquad p = DLo \times \cos L$$

Example 1: The DR latitude of a ship on course 090 is 49° 30' N. The ship steams on this course until the longitude changes 3° 30'.

Required: The departure by (1) computation

DLo = 3° 30' x 60
DLo = 210 arc min
$$p = DLo \times \cos L$$
p = 210 arc minutes x cos (49.5°)
p = 136.4 miles

Answer:
p = 136.4 miles

Example 2: The DR latitude of a ship on course 270° is 38° 15' S. The ship steams on this course for a distance of 215.5 miles.

Required: The change in longitude by (1) computation

$$DLo = p \div \cos L$$

Solution:
(1) Solution by computation

DLo = 215.5 arc min / cos (38.25°)
DLo = 215.5 arc min ÷ 0.7853
DLo = 274.4 minutes of arc (west)/ 60
DLo = 4° 34.4' W

Answer:
DLo = 4° 34.4' W

Middle-Latitude Sailing
Middle-latitude sailing combines plane sailing and parallel sailing. Plane sailing is used to find difference of latitude and departure when course and distance are known, or vice versa. Parallel sailing is used to interconvert departure and difference of longitude. The mean latitude (Lm) is normally used for want of a practicable means of determining the middle latitude, the latitude at which the arc length of the parallel separating the meridians passing through two specific points is exactly equal to the departure in proceeding from one point to the other. The formulas for these transformations are:

$$DLo = p \div \cos L_m \qquad p = DLo \times \cos L_m \text{ D}$$

The mean latitude (Lm) is half the arithmetical sum of the latitudes of two places on the same side of the equator. It is labeled N or S to indicate its position north or south of the equator. If a course line crosses the equator, solve each course line segment separately.

Example 1: A vessel steams 1,253 miles on course 070° from lat. 15° 17.0' N, long. 151°37.0' E.

Required: Latitude and longitude of the point of arrival by (1) computation.

Solution:

(1) Solution by computation:

$$DLat = D \times \cos C \qquad p = D \times \sin C$$

$$DLo = p \div \cos L_m$$

D = 1253.0 miles.
C = 070°

p = 1177.4 miles E

L1 = 15° 17.0' N
L2 = 22° 25.6' N
DLat = 7° 08.6' N
Dlat = 428.6' N

Lm = 18° 51.3' N

Lo1 = 151° 37.0' E
Lo2 = 172° 21.2' E
DLo = 20° 44.2' E
DLo = 1244.2' E

Answer:
L2 = 22° 25.6' N
L2 = 172° 21.2' E

Example 2: A vessel at lat. 8° 48.9' S, long. 89° 53.3' W is to proceed to lat. 17° 06.9' S, long. 104° 51.6' W.

Required: Course and distance by (1) Solution by computation:

$$p = DLo \times \cos L_m \qquad \tan C = p \div DLat$$
$$D = DLat \div \cos C$$

DLo = 14° 58.3'
DLo = 898.3'

Lm = 12° 57.9' S
p = 898.3 arc min x cos (12° 57.9')
p = 875.4 arc min
DLat = 17.1° - 8.8'
DLat = 8.3°
DLat l = 498 arc min

C = Tan⁻¹(875.4 DLat 498)
C = S 60.4° W
C = 240.4°

D = 498 arc min x DLat cos (60.4°)
D = 1008.2 miles

Answer:
C = 240.4°
D = 1008.2 miles

The labels (N, S, E, W) of l, p, DLo, and C are determined by noting the direction of motion or the relative positions of the two places.

Mercator Sailing

Mercator sailing problems can be solved graphically on a Mercator chart. For mathematical solution, the formulas of Mercator sailing are:

$$\tan C = DLo \div m \qquad DLo = m \times \tan C$$

After solving for course angle by Mercator sailing, solve for distance using the plane sailing formula:

$$D = DLat \div \cos C.$$

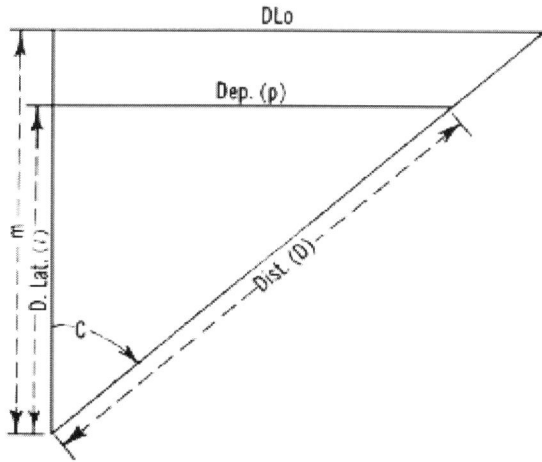

Figure 4 Mercator and plane sailing relationships.

Example 1: A ship at lat. 32°14.7' N, long. 66° 28.9' W is to head for a point near Chesapeake Light, lat. 36° 58.7' N, long. 75° 42.2' W.

Required: Course and distance by (1) computation

Solution:
(1) Solution by computation:

First calculate the meridional difference by entering Table 6 and interpolating for the meridional parts for the original and final latitudes. The meridional difference is the difference between these two values. (Except when crossing the equator the values are added.) Having calculated the meridional difference, simply solve for course and distance from the equations above.

M2 (36° 58.7' N) = 2377.5
M1 (32° 14.7' N) = 2032.9
m = 344.6

L2 = 075° 42.2' W
L1 = 066° 28.9' W
DLo = 9° 13.3' W
DLo = 553.3' W

C = arctan (553.3 ÷ 344.6')
C = N 58.1° W
C = 301.9°

L2 = 36° 58.7' N
L1 = 32° 14.7' N

DLat = 4° 44.0' N
DLal = 284.0'
D = 284.0 arc min x sec (58.1°)
D = 537.4 miles

Answer:
C = 301.9°
D = 537.4 miles

Example 2: A ship at lat. 75° 31.7' N, long. 79° 08.7' W, in Baffin Bay, steams 263.5 miles on course 155°.

Required: Latitude and longitude of point of arrival by (1) computation and (2) traverse table.
Solution:

(1) Solution by computation:

$$DLat = D \times \cos C \qquad DLo = m \times \tan C$$

and DLo = m tan C

= (263.5 x cos 155)÷60
= 3°58.8'

L1 = 75°31.7' N
DLat = 3° 58.8' S
L2 = 71° 32.9' N

M1 = 7072.4
M2 = 6226.1
m = 846.3

$= 846.3 \times \tan 155$

DLo $= 394.8'$ E $\div 60$

DLo $= 6°\ 34.8'$ E

L1 $= 79°\ 08.7'$ W

DLo $= 6°\ 34.8'$ E

L2 $= 072°\ 34.3'$ W

The labels (N, S, E, W) of L, DLo, and C are determined by noting the direction of motion or the relative positions of the two places.

Answer:

L2 $= 71°\ 32.9'$

L2 $= 072°\ 34.3'$

2-12

Parallel Sailings
Chapter 1, Advanced Subjects for Master/Mate Unlimited

Deterring Distance and Course

1. (00526) Your vessel receives a distress call from a vessel reporting her position as LAT 35° 01.0' S, LONG 18° 51.0' W. Your position is LAT 35° 01.0' S, LONG 21° 42,0' W. Determine the true course and distance from your vessel to the vessel in distress by parallel sailing.

A. 090° T, 140.0 miles
B. 090° T, 189.2 miles
C. 270° T, 140.0 miles
D. 270° T, 189.2 miles

2. (00532) You depart LAT 26° 03' S, LONG 10° 28' E, for LAT 26° 03' S, LONG 01° 16' W. What are the course and distance?

A. 090° T, 547.2 miles
B. 090° T, 632.5 miles
C. 270° T, 547.2 miles
D. 270° T, 632.5 miles

3. (00533) You depart LAT 38° 14' N, LONG 12° 42' W, for LAT 38° 14' N, LONG 46° 09' W. What are the course and distance?

A. 090° T, 1576.5 miles
B. 090° T, 2879.0 miles
C. 270° T, 1576.5 miles
D. 270° T, 2868.5 miles

4. (00534) You depart LAT 52° 01' N, LONG 176° 09' E, for LAT 52° 01' N, LONG 178° 46' W. What are the course and distance?

A. 090° T, 95 miles
B. 090° T, 188 miles
C. 270° T, 95 miles
D. 270° T, 188 miles

5. (00535) You depart LAT 49° 38' N, LONG 152° 49' E, for LAT 49° 38' N, LONG 176° 12' E. What are the course and distance?

A. 090° T, 909 miles
B. 090° T, 1204 miles
C. 270° T, 909 miles
D. 270° T, 1204 miles

6. (00536) Determine the distance from LAT 63° 54.0' N, LONG 04° 52.0' E to LAT 63° 54.0' N, LONG 18° 24.0' W.

A. 608.6 miles
B. 610.9 miles
C. 612.3 miles
D. 614.2 miles

7. (00537) Determine the distance from LAT 19° 54.0' N, LONG 166° 36.0' E to LAT 19° 54.0' N, LONG 157° 54.0' W.

A. 2204.6 miles
B. 2006.9 miles
C. 2002.8 miles
D. 1990.6 miles

8. (00538) Determine the distance from LAT 23° 24' S, LONG 13° 54.0' E to LAT 23° 24'S, LONG 42° 48' W.

A. 3119.3 miles
B. 3122.2 miles
C. 3124.5 miles
D. 3126.6 miles

9. (00539) Determine the distance from LAT 59° 12.0' N, LONG 14° 00' W to LAT 59° 12' N, LONG 03° 20' W.

A. 324.2 miles
B. 325.4 miles
C. 327.7 miles
D. 328.9 miles

10. (00540) Determine the distance from LAT 34° 18'S, LONG 172° 40' E to LAT 34° 18' S, LONG 152° 38' E.

A. 993.0 miles
B. 995.2 miles
C. 996.4 miles
D. 998.6 miles

Deterring Longitude of Arrival.

1. (00527) You depart LAT 25° 54' N, LONG 9° 38' E and steam 592 miles on course 270° . What is the LONG of arrival?

A. 1° 20' E
B. 0° 40' E
C. 0° 40' W
D. 1° 20' W

2. (00528) You depart LAT 38° 12' S, LONG 12° 06' W and steam 1543 miles on course 270° . What is the LONG of arrival?

A. 44° 49' W
B. 45° 12' W
C. 45° 37' W
D. 45° 42' W

3. (00529) You depart LAT 51° 48.0' S, LONG 178° 35.0' W and steam 179 miles on course 270° . What is the LONG of arrival?

A. 173° 47' W
B. 174° 27' E
C. 176° 36' E
D. 179° 52' W

4. (00530) You depart LAT 50° 06.0' N, LONG 153° 06.0' E and steam 879 miles on course 090° . What is the LONG of arrival?

A. 175° 56.0' E
B. 177° 24.0' E
C. 178° 36.0' W
D. 175° 04.0' W

5. (00531) You depart LAT 15° 48' N, LONG 174° 06' E and steam 905 miles on course 090° . What is the LONG of arrival?

A. 165° 41' W
B. 170° 13' W
C. 172° 47' W
D. 179° 06' E

PARALLEL SAILINGS
Required Course and Distance

1. (00526)

Date:				
L_1	35° 01.0′ S		Lo_1	021° 42.0′ W
L_2	35° 01.0′ S		Lo_2	018° 51.0′ W
DLat	0		DLo	2° 51′ E

Formulae   171'

$$p(D) = Dlo \times \cos L =$$
$$p(D) = 171 \times \cos 35° 01.0' = 140.04$$

Distance 140.0
Course 090
Answer A

---

2. (00532)

Date:				
L_1	26° 03.0′ S		Lo_1	010° 28.0′ E
L_2	26° 03.0′ S		Lo_2	001° 16.0′ W
DLat	0		DLo	11° 44.0′ W

Formulae   **704'**

$$p(D) = Dlo \times \cos L =$$
$$p(D) = 704 \times \cos 26° 03.0' = 632.48$$

Distance 632.5
Course 270
Answer D

---

3. (00533)

Date:				
L_1	38° 14.0′ N		Lo_1	012° 42.0′ W
L_2	38° 14.0′ N		Lo	046° 09.0′ W′
DLat	0		DLo	033° 27.0′ W

Formulae   **2007'**

$$p(D) = Dlo \times \cos L =$$
$$p(D) = 2007 \times \cos 38° 14.0' = 1576.49$$

Distance 1576.5
Course 270
Answer C

---

4. (00534)

Date:				
L_1	52° 01.0′ N		Lo_1	176° 09.0′ E
L_2	52° 01.0′ N		Lo	178° 46.0′ W
DLat	0		DLo	354° 55.0′

Formulae   **305' E**

$$p(D) = Dlo \times \cos L =$$
$$p(D) = 305 \times \cos 52° 01.0' = 187.71$$

Distance 187.71
Course 090
Answer B

NOTE: We cross the International Date Line going EAST. When crossing the International Date we find the DLo by adding the Longitudes and subtract the results from 360. 630 - 354° 55.0' = 5° 05' or 305' of arc.

5. (00535)				
Date:				
L_1	49° 38.0' N		Lo_1	152° 49.0' E
L_2	49° 38.0' N		Lo	176° 12.0' E
DLat	0		DLo	023° 23.0' E
		Formulae		**1403'**
Distance	908.69	$p(D) = Dlo \times \cos L =$		
Course	090	$p(D) = 1403 \times \cos 49° 38.0' = 908.6904752$		
Answer				

6. (00536)				
Date:				
L_1	63° 54.0' N		Lo_1	004° 52.0' E
L_2	63° 54.0' N		Lo	018° 24.0' W
DLat	0		DLo	023° 16.0' W
		Formulae		**1396'**
Distance	614.155	$p(D) = Dlo \times \cos L =$		
Course	270	$p(D) = 1396 \times \cos 63° 54.0' = 614.155$		
Answer D				

7. (00537)				
Date:				
L_1	19° 54.0' N		Lo_1	166° 36.0' E
L_2	19° 54.0' N		Lo	157° 54.0' W
DLat	0		DLo	035° 30.0' E
		Formulae		**2130'**
Distance	2002.8137	$p(D) = Dlo \times \cos L =$		
Course	090	$p(D) = 2130 \times \cos 19° 54.0' = 2002.8137$		
Answer C				

NOTE: We cross the International Date Line going EAST. When crossing the International Date we find the DLo by adding the Longitudes and subtract the results from 360 - 324° 30.0' = 35° 30' of arc.

8. (00538)				
Date:				
L_1	23° 24.0' S		Lo_1	013° 54.0' E
L_2	23° 24.0' S		Lo	042° 48.0' W
DLat	0		DLo	056° 42.0' W
		Formulae		**3402'**
Distance	3122.2012	$p(D) = Dlo \times \cos L =$		
Course	270	$p(D) = 3402 \times \cos 23° 24.0' = 3122.2012$		
Answer B				

Note: When we cross the Greenwich Meridian we add the Longitudes 13° 54' + 42° 48 = 56° 42' of arc.

9. (00539)				
Date:				
L$_1$	59° 12.0' N		Lc$_1$	014° 00.0' W
L$_2$	59° 12.0' N		Lc	003° 20.0' W
DLat	0		DLo	010° 40.0' E
		Formulae		**640'**
Distance	327.7074	$p(D) = Dlo \times \cos L =$		
Course	090	$p(D) = 640 \times \cos 59° 12.0' = 327.7074$		
Answer C				

10. (00540)				
Date:				
L$_1$	34° 18.0' S		Lo$_1$	172° 40.0' E
L$_2$	34° 18.0' S		Lo	152° 38.0' E
DLat	0		DLo	20° 02.0' W
		Formulae		**1202'**
Distance	992.970	$p(D) = Dlo \times \cos L =$		
Course	270	$p(D) = 1202 \times \cos 34° 18.0' = 992.970$		
Answer A				

PARALLEL SAILINGS
Required Longitude of Arrival

1. (00527)				
Date:				
L_1	25° 54.0' N		Lo_1	009° 38.0' E
±DLat	0		±DLo	+ 10° 58.1' W
L_2	25° 54.0' N		Lo	001° 20.0' W

Formulae

$$Dlo = \frac{p(D)}{\cos L} = \frac{592}{\cos 25° 54.0} = 658.1011/60 = 10° 58.1$$

Distance 592
Course 270
Answer D

2. (00528)				
Date:				
L_1	38° 12.0' N		Lo_1	012° 06.0' W
±DLat	0'		±DLo	+ 32° 43.5' W
L_2	38° 12.0' N		Lo	044° 49.5' W

Formulae

$$Dlo = \frac{p(D)}{\cos L} = \frac{1543}{\cos 38° 12.0} = 1963.46/60 = 32° 43.5$$

Distance 1543
Course 270
Answer A

3. (00529)				
Date:				
L_1	51° 48.0' S		Lo_1	178° 35.0' W
±DLat	0'		±DLo	+ 4° 49.5' W
L_2	51° 48.0' S		Lo	183° 24.5'
			360 - 183° 24.5 = **176° 35.5 E**	

Formulae

$$Dlo = \frac{p(D)}{\cos L} = \frac{179}{\cos 51° 48.0'} = 289.45/60 = 4° 49.5$$

Distance 179
Course 270
Answer C

4. (00530)				
Date:				
L_1	50° 06.0' N		Lo_1	153° 06.0' E
±DLat	0		±DLo	+ 22° 50.3' E
L_2	50° 06.0' N		Lo	175° 56.3' E

Formulae

$$Dlo = \frac{p(D)}{\cos L} = \frac{879}{\cos 50° 06.0} = 1370.33/60 = 22° 50.3$$

Distance 879
Course 090

ANSWER A

5. (00531)				
Date:				
L_1	15° 48.0' N		Lo$_1$	174° 06.0' E
±DLat	0'		±DLo	+ 15° 40.5' E
L_2	15° 48.0' N		Lo	189° 46.5' E
				360 - 189° 46.5' = **170° 13.5 W**

Formulae

$$Dlo = \frac{p(D)}{\cos L} = \frac{905}{\cos 15° 48.0} = 940.54/60 = 15° 40.5$$

Distance 905
Course 090
Answer B

Alexander F. Hickethier MBA © 1999-2013

MID-LATITUDE SAILINGS
Chapter 1, Advanced Subjects for Master/Mate Unlimited

Determining Course and Distance

1.
301. You depart LAT 28° 55.0' N, LONG 89° 10.0' W, enroute to LAT 24° 25.0' N, LONG 83° 00.0' W.
Determine the true course and distance by mid-latitude sailing.

A. 418 miles, 122° T
B. 427 miles, 129° T
C. 436 miles, 133° T
D. 442 miles, 122° T

2.
307. A vessel at LAT 28° 00.0' N, LONG 116° 00.0' E is to proceed to LAT 34° 00.0' N, LONG 123° 40.0' E.

Required. -- Course and distance by Mid-latitude sailing.

A. 045.0° T, 530.1 miles
B. 049.5° T, 525.8 miles
C. 047.6° T, 533.9 miles
D. 042.1° T, 527.7 miles

3.
308. A vessel at LAT 20° 00' N, LONG 107° 30' W is to proceed to LAT 24° 40' N, LONG 112° 30' W.

Required. -- Course and distance by Mid-latitude sailing.

A. 314.0° T, 389.0 miles
B. 315.3° T, 394.0 miles
C. 317.2° T, 397.0 miles
D. 318.3° T, 399.0 miles

4.
309. A vessel at LAT 14° 10' N, LONG 61° 00' W is to proceed to LAT 10° 00' N, LONG 53° 23' W.

Required. -- Course and distance by mid-latitude sailing.

A. 117.3° T, 503.0 miles
B. 117.9° T, 504.0 miles
C. 118.6° T, 508.0 miles
D. 119.2° T, 512.0 miles

5.
310. A vessel at LAT 28° 20' N, LONG 16° 00 W is to proceed to LAT 21° 00' N, LONG 18° 00' W.

Required. -- Course and distance by mid-latitude sailing.

A. 194.0° T, 453.0 miles
B. 195.2° T, 451.0 miles
C. 196.8° T, 450.0 miles
D. 197.3° T, 448.0 miles

6.
311. A vessel at LAT 20° 10' N, LONG 122° 00' E is to proceed to LAT 26° 18' N, LONG 128° 20' E.

Required. -- Course and distance by mid-latitude sailing.

A. 041.2° T, 501.0 miles
B. 041.9° T, 503.6 miles
C. 043.5° T, 507.3 miles
D. 044.7° T, 509.7 miles

THE SAILINGS Rev. 31 March 2013

7.

Answers

312.   A vessel at LAT 07° 05' N, LONG 81° 45' W is to proceed to LAT 08° 40' N, LONG 88° 00' W.

Required. -- Course and distance by mid-latitude sailing.

A. 283.1° T, 381.2 miles
B. 284.3° T, 383.4 miles
C. 285.6° T, 385.0 miles
D. 286.8° T, 387.4 miles

00301	B
00302	B
00303	D
00304	C
00305	B
00306	B
00307	C
00308	B
00309	D
00310	A
00311	C
00312	B

Mid-Latitude SAILINGS							
Required Course and Distance							
Problem # 1 (301)			Chapter				
Date:			Mid-Latitude				
L_1	28° 55.0' N	L_1	28° 55.0' N		Lo_1		089° 10.0' W
L_2	24° 25.0' N	±½ Dlat	2° 15.0' S		Lo		083° 00.0' W
DLat	4° 30.0' S	MidLat	26° 40'.0' N		DLo		6° 10.0' E
X 60	270				X 60		370

Formulae

$$\tan C = \frac{p}{DLat} = \tan^{-1}\left(\frac{330.64}{270}\right) = 50.77$$

	N
360 -	Same
180 +	180-
	S

Distance 426.92
Course 129.23

180- 50.77 = 129.23

$$p = DLo \times \cos L_m = 370 \times \cos 26° 40' = 330.64 \qquad D = \frac{DLat}{\cos C} = \left(\frac{270}{\cos 129.23}\right) = 426.92$$

Problem # 2 (307)			Chapter				
Date:			Mid-Latitude				
L_1	28° 00.0' N	L_1	28° 00.0' N		Lo_1		116° 00.0' E
L_2	34° 00.0' N	±½ Dlat	3° 00.0' N		Lo		123° 40.0' E
DLat	6° 00.0' N	MidLat	31° 00.0' N		DLo		7° 40.0' E
X 60	360				X 60		460

Formulae

$$\tan C = \frac{p}{DLat} = \tan^{-1}\left(\frac{394.3}{360}\right) = 47.6$$

	N
360 -	Same
180 +	180 -
	S

Distance 533.88
Course 047.6

$$p = DLo \times \cos L_m = 460 \times \cos 31 = 394.3 \qquad D = \frac{DLat}{\cos C} = \left(\frac{360}{\cos 047.6}\right) = 533.88$$

Problem # 3	(308)		Chapter				
Date:			Mid-Latitude				
L_1	20° 00.0' N	L_1	20° 00.0' N		Lo_1	107° 30.0' W	
L_2	24° 40.0' N	±½ Dlat	+ 2° 20.0' N		Lo	112° 30.0' W	
DLat	4° 40.0' N	MidLat	22° 20.0' N		DLo	5° 00.0' W	
X 60	280				X 60	300	

Formulae

$$\tan C = \frac{p}{DLat} = \tan^{-1}\left(\frac{277.5}{280}\right) = 44.7$$

$$360 - 44.7 = 315.3$$

Distance 393.9 Course 315.3

	N	
360 -		Same
180 +		180 -
	S	

$$p = DLo \times \cos L_m = 300 \times \cos 22°\,20' = 277.5$$

$$D = \frac{DLat}{\cos C} = \left(\frac{280}{\cos 315.3}\right) = 393.9$$

Problem # 4	(309)		Chapter				
Date:			Mid-Latitude				
L_1	14° 10.0' N	L_1	14° 10.0' N		Lo_1	061° 00.0' W	
L_2	10° 00.0' N	±½ Dlat	- 2° 05.0' S		Lo	053° 23.0' W	
DLat	4° 10.0' S	MidLat	12° 05.0' N		DLo	7° 37.0' W	
X 60	250				X 60	457	

Formulae

$$\tan C = \frac{p}{DLat} = \tan^{-1}\left(\frac{446.87}{250}\right) = 60.77$$

$$180 - 60.8 = 119.2$$

Distance 512.4 Course 119.2

	N	
360 -		Same
180 +		180 -
	S	

$$p = DLo \times \cos L_m = 457 \times \cos 12°\,05' = 446.87$$

$$D = \frac{DLat}{\cos C} = \left(\frac{250}{\cos 119.2}\right) = 512.4$$

Problem # 5	(310)		Chapter				
Date:			Mid-Latitude				
L_1	28° 20' N	L_1	28° 20' N		Lo_1	016° 00' W	
L_2	21° 00' N	±½ Dlat	- 3° 40' S		Lo	018° 00' W	
DLat	7° 20' S	MidLat	24° 40' N		DLo	2° 00' W	
X 60	440'				X 60	120	

			Formulae			N	
Distance	453.27		$\tan C = \dfrac{p}{DLat} = \tan^{-1}\left(\dfrac{109.05}{440}\right) = 13.9$		360 -	Same	
Course	193.9				180 +	180 -	
			$180 + 13.9 = 193.9$		S		

$$p = DLo \times \cos L_m = 120 \times \cos 24° 40' = 109.05 \qquad D = \dfrac{DLat}{\cos C} = \left(\dfrac{440}{\cos 193.9}\right) = 453.27$$

Problem # 6	(311)		Chapter				
Date:			Mid-Latitude				
L_1	20° 10' N	L_1	20° 10' N		Lo_1	122° 00' E	
L_2	26° 18' N	±½ Dlat	+ 3° 04' N		Lo	128° 20' E	
DLat	6° 08' N	MidLat	23° 14' N		DLo	6° 20' E	
X 60	368				X 60	380	

			Formulae			N	
Distance	507.3		$\tan C = \dfrac{p}{DLat} = \tan^{-1}\left(\dfrac{349.18}{368}\right) = 43.5$		360 -	Same	
Course	043.5		43.5		180 +	180 -	
					S		

$$p = DLo \times \cos L_m = 380 \times \cos 23° 14 = 349.18 \qquad D = \dfrac{DLat}{\cos C} = \left(\dfrac{368}{\cos 43.5}\right) = 507.3$$

Problem # 7	(312)		Chapter		
Date:			Mid-Latitude		
L_1	7° 05' N	L_1	7° 05' N	Lo_1	081° 45' W
L_2	8° 40' N	±½ Dlat	- 0° 47' N	Lo	088° 00' W
DLat	1° 35' N	MidLat	6° 17.5' N	DLo	6° 15' W
X 60	95			X 60	375

Formulae

$$\tan C = \frac{p}{DLat} = \tan^{-1}\left(\frac{372.74}{95}\right) = 75.7$$

$$360 - 75.7 = 284.3$$

	N
36 0 -	Same
18 0 +	180 -
	S

Distance 384.62

Course 284.3

$$p = DLo \times \cos L_m = 375 \times \cos 6°17.5' = 372.74 \qquad D = \frac{DLat}{\cos C} = \left(\frac{95}{\cos 284.3}\right) = 384.62$$

MID-LATITUDE SAILINGS
Chapter 1, Advanced Subjects for Master/Mate Unlimited

Determining Latitude and Longitude

1.
302.   A vessel steams 720 miles on course 058° T from LAT 30° 06.0' S LONG 31° 42.0' E.

Required. -- Latitude and longitude of the point of arrival by Mid-latitude sailing.

A. LAT 23° 46' S,   LONG 43° 11' E
B. LAT 23° 42' S,   LONG 43° 07' E
C. LAT 23° 38' S,   LONG 43° 03' E
D. LAT 23° 34' S,   LONG 43° 00' E

303.   A vessel steams 576 miles on course 260° T from LAT 40° 36' N, LONG 50° 24' W.

Required. -- Latitude and longitude of the point of arrival by Mid-latitude sailing.

A. LAT 39° 12' N,   LONG 62° 28' W
B. LAT 39° 06' N,   LONG 62° 34' W
C. LAT 39° 02' N,   LONG 62° 37' W
D. LAT 38° 56' N,   LONG 62° 42' W

304.   A vessel steams 580 miles on course 083° T from LAT 13° 12' N, LONG 71° 12' W.

Required. -- Latitude and longitude of the point of arrival by Mid-latitude sailing.

A. LAT 14° 17' N,   LONG 61° 23' W
B. LAT 14° 20' N,   LONG 61° 21' W
C. LAT 14° 23' N,   LONG 61° 19' W
D. LAT 14° 25' N,   LONG 61° 17' W

305.   A vessel steams 666 miles on course 295° T from LAT 24° 24' N, LONG 83° 00' W.

Required. -- Latitude and longitude of the point of arrival by Mid-latitude sailing.

A. LAT 29° 01' N,   LONG 94° 18' W
B. LAT 29° 06' N,   LONG 94° 16' W
C. LAT 29° 10' N,   LONG 94° 10' W
D. LAT 29° 13' N,   LONG 94° 06' W

306.   A vessel steams 640 miles on course 047° T from LAT 34° 45' N, LONG 140° 00' E.

Required. -- Latitude and longitude of the point of arrival by Mid-latitude sailing.

A. LAT 41° 57' N,   LONG 150° 02' E
B. LAT 42° 01' N,   LONG 149° 57' E
C. LAT 42° 06' N,   LONG 149° 53' E
D. LAT 42° 09' N,   LONG 149° 50' E

Answers

1.   302   B
2.   303   D
3.   304   C
4.   305   B
5.   306   B

MID-LATITUDE SAILINGS					
Required Latitude and Longitude of Arrival					
Problem # 1	(00302)		Chapter		
Date:			Mid-Latitude		
L_1	30° 06.0' S	L_1	3 0° 06' S	Lo_1	031° 42.0' E
±DLat	- 6° 21.5' N	±½ Dlat	+- 3° 10.5 N	±DLo	+ 11° 24.8' E
L_2	23° 44.5' S	Lm	26° 55.5' S	Lo	43° 06.8' E

		Formulae	
Distance	720		
Course	058	$DLat = D \times \cos C = 720 \times \cos 58 = 381.54 \div 60 = 6° \, 21.5'$	

$p = D \times \sin C = 720 \times \sin 58 = 610.59$

$$DLo = \frac{p}{\cos L_m} = \frac{610.59}{\cos 26° \, 55.5'} = 684.83$$

$$\div 60 = 11° \, 24.8'$$

Problem # 2	(00303)		Chapter		
Date:			Mid-Latitude		
L_1	40° 36.0' N	L_1	40° 36.0' N	Lo_1	050° 24.0' W
±DLat	- 1° 40.0' S	±½ Dlat	- 0° 50'0' S	±DLo	+ 12° 18.0' W
L_2	38° 56.0' N	Lm	39° 46.0' N	Lo_2	062° 42.0' W

		Formulae	
Distance	576		
Course	260	$DLat = D \times \cos C = 576 \times \cos 260 = 100.02 \div 60 = 1°40'$	

$p = D \times \sin C = 576 \times \sin 260 = 567.25$

$$DLo = \frac{p}{\cos L_m} = \frac{567.25}{\cos 39° \, 46'} = 737.98$$

$$\div 60 = 12°18.0'$$

Problem # 3	(00304)		Chapter			
Date:			Mid-Latitude			
L_1	13° 12' N	L_1	13° 12' N		Lo_1	071° 12' W
±DLat	+ 1° 11' N	±½ Dlat	+0° 36' N		±DLo	- 9° 53' E
L_2	14° 23' N	Lm	13° 48' N		Lo	061° 19' W

Distance 580

Course 083

Formulae

$$DLat = D \times \cos C = 580 \times \cos 83 = 70.68 \div 60 = 1°11'$$

$$p = D \times \sin C = 580 \times \sin 83 = 575.68$$

$$DLo = \frac{p}{\cos L_m} = \frac{575.68}{\cos 13° 48'} = 591.79$$

$$\div 60 = 9° 53'$$

Problem # 4	(00305)		Chapter			
Date:			Mid-Latitude			
L_1	24° 24.0' N	L_1	24° 24.0' N		Lo_1	083° 00.0' W
±DLat	+ 4° 41.5' N	±½ Dlat	+ 2° 11.5' N		±DLo	+ 11° 15.9' W
L_2	29° 05.5' N	Lm	26° 44.5' N		Lo	094° 15.9' W

Distance 666

Course 295

Formulae

$$DLat = D \times \cos C = 666 \times \cos 295 = 281.46 \div 60 = 4° 41.5'$$

$$p = D \times \sin C = 666 \times \sin 295 = 603.60$$

$$DLo = \frac{p}{\cos L_m} = \frac{603.60}{\cos 26° 44.5'} = 675.89$$

$$\div 60 = 11° 15.9'$$

Problem # 5	(00306)		Chapter			
Date:			Mid-Latitude			
L_1	34° 45.0' N	L_1	34°45.0' N		Lo_1	140° 00.0' E
±DLat	+ 7° 16.5' N	±½ Dlat	3° 38.2' N		±DLo	+ 9° 57.1' E
L_2	42° 01.5' N	Lm	38° 23.2' N		Lo	149° 57.1' E

Distance 640

Course 047

Formulae

$$DLat = D \times \cos C = 640 \times \cos 47 = 436.48 \div 60 = 7° 16.5'$$

$$p = D \times \sin C = 640 \times \sin 47 = 468.07$$

$$DLo = \frac{p}{\cos L_m} = \frac{468.07}{\cos 38° 23.2'} = 597.15$$

$$\div 60 = 9° 57.1' E$$

Mercator Sailings,
Chapter 1, Advanced subjects for Master/Mate Unlimited

1.
376. You depart LAT 40° 42.0' N, LONG 74° 01.0' W, and steam 3365.6 miles on course 118°T. What is the longitude of your arrival?

A. 10° 46.0' W
B. 22° 58.0' W
C. 17° 41.0' W
D. 24° 29.0' W

2.
377. You depart LAT 22° 35.0'N, LONG 157° 30.0'W, and steam 4505.0 miles on course 135° T. What are the latitude and longitude of your arrival?

A. 30° 30.5' S,   102°35.3' W
B. 30° 30.5' S,   104° 30.0' W
C. 32° 20.0' S,   102° 35.3' W
D. 32° 20.0' S,   104° 30.0' W

3.
405. You depart LAT 33° 45.0' N, LONG 118° 30.0' W, and steam 2216 miles on course 250° T. What is the longitude of your arrival by Mercator sailing?

A. LONG 156° 08.0' W
B. LONG 156° 36.0' W
C. LONG 157° 21.0' W
D. LONG 157° 31.0' W

4.
406. You depart LAT 49° 45.0' N, LONG 06° 35.0' W, and steam 3599 miles on course 246.5° T. What is the longitude of your arrival by Mercator sailing?

A. LONG 76° 36.2' W
B. LONG 77° 02.8' W
C. LONG 78° 14.0' W
D. LONG 78° 22.6' W

5.
407. You depart LAT 34° 22' S, LONG 18° 23' E, and steam 3174 miles on course 282° T. What is the longitude of your arrival by Mercator sailing?

A. LONG 40° 33.5' W
B. LONG 40° 19.5' W
C. LONG 40° 18.2' W
D. LONG 40° 17.3' W

6.
408. You depart LAT 37° 36' N, LONG 123° 00' W, and steam 2022 miles on course 241° T. What is the longitude of your arrival by Mercator sailing?

A. LONG 163° 28.2' W
B. LONG 163° 18.2' W
C. LONG 156° 51.7' W
D. LONG 154° 18.3' W

7.
409.   A vessel steams 1082 miles on course 047° T from LAT 37° 18.0' N, LONG 24° 40.0' W.

Required. -- Latitude and longitude of the point of arrival by Mercator sailing.

A. LAT 49° 30.0' N,   LONG 06° 22.0' W
B. LAT 49° 33.0' N,   LONG 06° 25.0' W
C. LAT 49° 36.0' N,   LONG 06° 28.0' W
D. LAT 49° 39.0' N,   LONG 06° 31.0' W

8.
410. A vessel steams 666 miles on course 135° T from LAT 40° 24.0' N, LONG 74° 30.0' W.

Required. -- Latitude and longitude of the point of arrival by Mercator sailing.

A. LAT 32° 30.0' N,   LONG 64° 41.0' W
B. LAT 32° 33.0' N,   LONG 64° 46.0' W
C. LAT 32° 36.0' N,   LONG 64° 49.0' W
D. LAT 32° 39.0' N,   LONG 64° 53.0' W

9.

00411.   A vessel steams 3312 miles on course 282° T from LAT 34° 24' S, LONG 18° 18' E.

Required. -- Latitude and longitude of the point of arrival by Mercator sailing.

A. LAT 22° 39.0' S,   LONG 43° 17.0' W
B. LAT 22° 42.0' S,   LONG 43° 14.0' W
C. LAT 22° 47.0' S,   LONG 43° 10.0' W
D. LAT 22° 55.0' S,   LONG 43° 05.0' W

10.

412.   A vessel steams 1650 miles on course 077° T from LAT 12° 47' N, LONG 45° 10' E.

Required. -- Latitude and longitude of the point of arrival by Mercator sailing.

A. LAT 18° 54' N,   LONG 72° 58' E
B. LAT 18° 58' N,   LONG 72° 52' E
C. LAT 19° 02' N,   LONG 72° 44' E
D. LAT 19° 06' N,   LONG 72° 36' E

11.

413.   A vessel steams 1106 miles on course 249° T from LAT 13° 30.0' N, LONG 144° 30.3' E.

Required. -- Latitude and longitude of the point of arrival by Mercator sailing.

A. LAT 07° 01.0' N,   LONG 127° 02.0' E
B. LAT 06° 54.0' N,   LONG 127° 08.0' E
C. LAT 06° 50.0' N,   LONG 127° 13.0' E
D. LAT 06° 46.0' N,   LONG 127° 17.0' E

12.

404. You depart LAT 18° 54' N, LONG 73° 00' E, and steam 1150 miles on course 253° T. What are the latitude and longitude of your arrival by Mercator sailing?

A. LAT 13° 16' N,   LONG 55° 18' E
B. LAT 13° 18' N,   LONG 54° 03' E
C. LAT 13° 19' N,   LONG 53° 46' E
D. LAT 13° 20' N,   LONG 53° 28' E

Answers
1.   376 C
2.   377 A
3.   405 D
4.   406 B
5.   407 A
6.   408 C
7.   409 C
8.   410 B
9.   411 D
10. 412 B
11. 413 B
12. 404 B

MERCATOR SAILINGS
Required Latitude and Longitude of Arrival

Problem # 1 (00376)			Chapter			
Date:			Meridional Parts			
L_1	40° 42.0' N	M_1	2662.8		Lo_1	074° 01.0' W
±DLat	- 26° 20.0' S				±DLo	- 56° 20.0' E
L_2	14° 22.0' N	M_2	865.5		Lo_2	017° 41.0' W
		m	1797.3			

Formulae

$$DLat = D \times \cos C = 3365.6 \times \cos 118 = 1580.05 \div 60 = 26°\,20.0'\,S$$

Distance	3365.6
Course	118

Notes:

$$DLo = m \times \tan C = 1797.3 \times \tan 118 = 3380.23 \div 60 = 56°20.0'E$$

Problem # 2 (00377)			Chapter			
Date:			Meridional Parts			
L_1	22° 35.0' N	M_1	1382.7		Lo_1	157° 30.0' W
±DLat	- 53° 06.0' S				±DLo	- 54° 55.3' E
L_2	30° 31.0' S	M_2	1912.6		Lo_2	102° 34.7' W
		m	3295.3			

Formulae

$$DLat = D \times \cos C = \times \cos = 4505 \times \cos 135 = 3185.5160 \div 60 = 53°\,05.5$$

Distance	4505.0
Course	135

Notes:

$$DLo = m \times \tan C = 3295.3 \times \tan 135 = 3295.3 \div 60 = 54°\,55.3'\,E$$

Problem # 3	(00405)		Chapter			
Date:			Meridional Parts			
L_1	33° 45.0' N	M_1	2140.6		Lo_1	118° 30.0' W
±DLat	- 12° 37.9' S				±DLo	+ 39° 01.1' W
L_2	21° 07.1' N	M_2	1288.5		Lo_2	157° 31.1 W
		m	852.1			
			Formulae			
Distance	2216		$DLat = D \times \cos C = 2216 \times \cos 250 = 757.91 \div 60 =$			
Course	250		$12° 37.9\,S$			
Notes:			$DLo = m \times \tan C = 852.1 \times \tan 250 = 2341.13 \div 60 =$			
			$39° 01.1\,W$			

Problem # 4	(00406)		Chapter			
Date:			Meridional Parts			
L_1	49° 45.0' N	M_1	3433.6		Lo_1	006° 35.0' W
±DLat	- 23° 55.1' S				±DLo	+ 70° 28.0' W
L_2	20° 49.9' N	M_2	1595.2		Lo_2	077° 03.0' W
		m	1838.4			
			Formulae			
Distance	3599		$DLat = D \times \cos C = 3599 \times \cos 246.5 = 1435.1 \div 60 =$			
Course	246.5		$23° 55.1'\,S$			
Notes:			$DLo = m \times \tan C = 1838.4 \times \tan 246.5 = 4228.03 \div 60 =$			
			$70° 28.0'\,W$			

Problem # 5	(00407)		Chapter			
Date:			Meridional Parts			
L_1	34° 22.0' S	M_1	2185.1		Lo_1	18° 23.0' E
±DLat	- 10° 59.9' N				±DLo	58° 26.5' W
L_2	23° 12.1' N	M_2	1433.4		Lo_2	40° 33.5 W
		m	751.7			
			Formulae			
Distance	3174.0		$DLat = D \times \cos C = 3174 \times \cos 282 = 659.91 \div 60 =$			
Course	282		$10° 59.9'\,N$			
Notes:			$DLo = m \times \tan C = 751.7 \times \tan 282 = 3536.47 \div 60 =$			
			$58° 56.5'\,W$			

2-32

Problem # 6	(00408)		Chapter			
Date:			Meridional Parts			
L_1	37° 36.0' N	M_1	2423.8		Lo_1	123° 00.0' W
±DLat	- 16° 20.3' S				±DLo	+ 33° 51.5' W
L_2	21° 15.7' N	M_2	1297.7		Lo_2	156° 51.5' W
		m	1126.1			
			Formulae			
Distance	2022					
Course	241		$DLat = D \times \cos C = 2022 \times \cos 241 = 980.29 \div 60 =$ $16° 20.3' S$			
Notes:			$DLo = m \times \tan C = 1126.1 \times \tan 241 = 2031.54 \div 60 =$ $33° 51.5' W$			

Problem # 7	(00409)		Chapter			
Date:			Meridional Parts			
L_1	37° 18.0' N	M_1	2401.3		Lo_1	024° 40.0' W
±DLat	+ 12° 17.9' N				±DLo	- 18° 12.1' E
L_2	49° 35.9' N	M_2	3419.7		Lo_2	006° 27.9' W
		m	1018.4			
			Formulae			
Distance	1082					
Course	047		$DLat = D \times \cos C = 1082 \times \cos 47 = 737.92 \div 60 =$ $12° 17.9' N$			
Notes:			$DLo = m \times \tan C = 1018.4 \times \tan 47 = 1092.10 \div 60 =$ $18° 12.1' E$			

Problem # 8	(00410)		Chapter			
Date:			Meridional Parts			
L_1	40° 24.0' N	M_1	2639.2		Lo_1	074° 30.0' W
±DLat	- 7° 53.9' S				±DLo	- 9° 44.2' E
L_2	32° 33.1' N	M_2	2055.0		Lo_2	064° 45.8' W
		m	584.2			
			Formulae			
Distance	666					
Course	135		$DLat = D \times \cos C = 666 \times \cos 135 = 470.93 \div 60 =$ $7° 55.9' S$			
Notes:			$DLo = m \times \tan C = 584.2 \times \tan 135 = 584.2 \div 60 =$ $9° 44.2' E$			

2-33

Problem # 9 (00411)			Chapter			
Date:			Meridional Parts			
L_1	34° 24.0' S	M_1	2187.5		Lo_1	018° 18.0' E
±DLat	- 11° 28.6' N				±DLo	- 61° 23.8' W
L_2	22° 55.4' S	M_2	1404.5		Lo_2	043° 05.8' W
		m	783.0			
			Formulae			
Distance	3312		$DLat = D \times \cos C = 3312 \times \cos 282 = 688.60 \div 60 =$			
Course	282		$11° 28.6' N$			
Notes:			$DLo = m \times \tan C = 783 \times \tan 282 = 3683.73 \div 60 =$			
			$61° 23.8' W$			

Problem # 10 (00412)			Chapter			
Date:			Meridional Parts			
L_1	12° 47.0' N	M_1	768.4		Lo_1	045° 10.0' E
±DLat	+ 6° 11.2' N				±DLo	+ 27° 42.0' E
L_2	18° 58.2' N	M_2	1152.1		Lo_2	072° 52.0' E
		m	383.7			
			Formulae			
Distance	1650		$DLat = D \times \cos C = 1650 \times \cos 77 = 371.17 \div 60 =$			
Course	077		$6° 11.2' N$			
Notes:			$DLo = m \times \tan C = 383.7 \times \tan 77 = 1661.99 \div 60 =$			
			$27° 42.0' E$			

Problem # 11 (00413)			Chapter			
Date:			Meridional Parts			
L_1	13° 30.0' N	M_1	812.2		Lo_1	144° 30.3' E
±DLat	- 6° 36.4' S				±DLo	- 17° 22.8' W
L_2	6° 53.6' N	M_2	411.9		Lo_2	127° 07.5' E
		m	400.3			
			Formulae			
Distance	1106		$DLat = D \times \cos C = \times 1106 \cos 249 = 396.35 \div 60 =$			
Course	249		$6° 53.6' N$			
Notes:			$DLo = m \times \tan C = 400.3 \times \tan 253 = 1042.82 \div 60 =$			
			$17° 22.8' W$			

Problem # 12	(00404)		Chapter			
Date:			Meridional Parts			
L_1	18° 54.0' N	M_1	1147.7		Lo_1	073° 00.0' E
±DLat	- 5° 36.2' S				±DLo	- 18° 58.3' W
L_2	13° 17.8' N	M_2	799.7		Lo_2	054° 01.7' E
		m	348.0			

		Formulae	
Distance	1150	$DLat = D \times \cos C = 1150 \times \cos 253 = 336.23 \div 60 = 5°36.2'S$	
Course	253		
Notes:		$DLo = m \times \tan C = 348 \times \tan 253 = 1138.26 \div 60 = 18°58.3'W$	

Mercator Sailings,
Chapter 1, Advanced subjects for Master/Mate Unlimited

1.
378. A vessel at LAT 37° 24.0' N, LONG 178° 15.0' W, heads for a destination at LAT 34° 18.0' N, LONG 178° 25.0' E. Determine the true course and distance by Mercator sailing.

A. 041° T, 273.9 miles
B. 047° T, 273.9 miles
C. 221° T, 247.2 miles
D. 227° T, 247.2 miles

2.
379. A vessel at LAT 32° 05.0' N, LONG 81° 06.0' W, heads for a destination at LAT 35° 57.0N, LONG 5° 45.0' W. Determine the distance by Mercator sailing.

A. 3128.2 miles
B. 3770.6 miles
C. 4126.1 miles
D. 4508.0 miles

3.
380. A vessel at LAT 21° 18.5' N, LONG 157° 52.2' W, heads for a destination at LAT 8° 53.0' N, LONG 79° 31.0' W. Determine the true course and distance by Mercator sailing.

A. 081° T, 4617.5 miles
B. 081° T, 4915.8 miles
C. 099° T, 4617.5 miles
D. 099° T, 4915.8 miles

4.
00390. A vessel at LAT 29° 38.0' N, LONG 93° 49.0' W heads for a destination at LAT 24° 38.0' N, LONG 82° 55.2' W. Determine the true course and distance by Mercator sailing.

A. 115° T, 637 miles
B. 117° T, 660 miles
C. 122° T, 648 miles
D. 126° T, 665 miles

5.
391. A vessel at LAT 40° 42.0' N, LONG 74° 01.0' W heads for a destination at LAT 14° 41.0' N, LONG 17° 26.0' W. Determine the true course and distance by Mercator sailing.

A. 123° T, 3066.5 miles
B. 123° T, 3065.6 miles
C. 118° T, 3066.5 miles
D. 118° T, 3365.0 miles

6.
393. A vessel at LAT 32° 14.7' N, LONG 66° 28.9' W, heads for a destination at LAT 36° 58.7' N, LONG 75° 42.2' W. Determine the distance by Mercator sailing.

A. 241.2 miles
B. 270.2 miles
C. 300.2 miles
D. 538.2 miles

7.
394. A vessel at LAT 38° 03.0' S, LONG 49° 38.0' W, heads for a destination at LAT 41° 26.0' S, LONG 38° 32.0' W. Determine the true course by Mercator sailing.

A. 111.5° T
B. 113.5° T
C. 158.5° T
D. 160.5° T

8.
395. A vessel is LAT 45° 36.0', LONG 11° 36.0' W, heads for a destination at LAT 24° 16.0' N, LONG 73° 52.0' W. Determine the true course and distance by Mercator sailing.

A. 247° T, 3299.3 miles
B. 247° T, 3951.6 miles
C. 251° T, 3298.5 miles
D. 251° T, 3951.6 miles

9.

396. A vessel at LAT 10° 22.0' S, LONG 7° 18.0' E, heads for a destination at LAT 6° 52.0' N, LONG 57° 23.0' W. Determine the true course and distance by Mercator sailing.

A. 285° T, 3825.3 miles
B. 285° T, 4025.7 miles
C. 296° T, 3825.3 miles
D. 296° T, 4025.7 miles

10.

398. You depart LAT 32° 16.6' N, LONG 68° 28.0' W. What is the course and distance as calculated by Mercator sailing to a position at LAT 43° 12.2' N, LONG 55° 39.0' W?

A. 042.8°, 896.2 miles
B. 049.1°, 955.1 miles
C. 132.8°, 896.2 miles
D. 136.6°, 955.1 miles

11.

399. A vessel at LAT 11° 22' S, LONG 009° 18' E heads for a destination at LAT 06° 52' N, LONG 57° 23' W. Determine the true course and distance by Mercator sailing.

A. 296° T, 3,825.3 miles
B. 296° T, 4,154.2 miles
C. 285° T, 3,825.3 miles
D. 285° T, 4,154.2 miles

12

401. Your vessel receives a distress call from a vessel reporting her position as LAT 35° 01' S, LONG 18° 51' W. Your position is LAT 30° 18' LONG 21° 42' W. Determine the true course from your vessel to the vessel in distress by Mercator sailing.

A. 135° T
B. 149° T
C. 153° T
D. 160° T

13.

402. A vessel at LAT 38° 36' N, LONG 11° 36' W, heads for a destination at LAT 24° 16' N, LONG 71° 52' W. Determine the true course and distance by Mercator sailing.

A. 236.4° T, 2,916.9 miles
B. 254.4° T, 2,916.9 miles
C. 254.4° T, 3,203.6 miles
D. 285.6° T, 3,203.6 miles

14.

403. You receive a d stress call from a vessel reporting her position as LAT 30° 21' N, LONG 88° 34' W. Your position is LAT 24° 30' N, LONG 83° 00' W. Determine the true course and distance to the distress scene by Mercator sailing.

A. 317° T, 470 miles
B. 320° T, 460 miles
C. 322° T, 455 miles
D. 324° T, 460 miles

15.

414. A vessel at LAT 49° 45' N, LONG 6° 35' W, heads for a destination at LAT 25° 50' N, LONG 77° 00' W. Determine the true course and distance by Mercator sailing.

A. 246.5°, 3597 miles
B. 253.0°, 3648 miles
C. 268.6°, 3483 miles
D. 066.4°, 3602 miles

16.

415. A vessel at LAT 33° 45' N, LONG 118° 30' W, heads for a destination at LAT 21° 15' N, LONG 157° 36' W. Determine the true course and distance by Mercator sailing.

A. 109.8°, 2196 miles
B. 236.3°, 2259 miles
C. 250.2°, 2216 miles
D. 289.2°, 2413 miles

17.

416. A vessel at LAT 18° 54' N, LONG 73° 00' E, heads for a destination at LAT 13° 12' N, LONG 54° 00' E.   Determine the true course and distance by Mercator sailing.

A. 247°,   1161 miles
B. 250°,   1172 miles
C. 253°,   1154 miles
D. 256°,   1136 miles

18

417. A vessel at LAT 21° 32' N, LONG 160° 30' W, heads for a destination at LAT 30° 00' N, LONG 150° 00' E.   Determine the true course and distance by Mercator sailing.

A. 273° T,   2645 miles
B. 273° T,   2692 miles
C. 281° T,   2733 miles
D. 284° T,   2762 miles

Answers

1.   00378 C
2.   00379 B
3.   00380 C
4.   00390 B
5.   00391 D
6.   00392 C
7.   00394 A
8.   00395 A
9.   00396 B
10. 00398 A
11. 00399 D
12. 00401 C
13. 00402 C
14. 00403 B
15. 00414 A
16. 00415 C
17. 00416 C
18. 00417 C

MERCATOR SAILINGS
Required Course and Distance

Problem 1. (00378)			Chapter			
Date:			Meridional Parts			
L_1	37° 24.0' N	M_1	2408.8		Lo_1	178° 15.0' W
L_2	34° 18.0' N	M_2	2180.3		Lo_2	178° 25.0' E
DLat	3 ° 06.0' S	m	228.5		DLo	003° 20.0' W
X 60	186 S				X 60	200 W

Formulae

$$\tan C = \frac{Dlo}{m} = \tan^{-1}\left(\frac{200}{228.5}\right) = 41.2$$

$$+\,180 = 221.2$$

Distance	247.2
Course	221.2

S41.2W

	N
360 -	Same
180 +	180 -
	S

Notes: crossing the dateline we add the longitudes and subtract from 360.
178 ° 15' - 178° 25' = 356 ° 40' - 360 = 3° 20'

$$D = \frac{DLat}{\cos C} = \left(\frac{186}{\cos 221.2}\right) = 247.204$$

Problem 2. (00379)			Chapter			
Date:			Meridional Parts			
L_1	32° 05.0' N	M_1	2022.1		Lo_1	081° 06.0' W
L_2	35° 57.0' N	M_2	2300.8		Lo_2	005° 45.0' W
DLat	3° 52.0' N	m	278.7		DLo	075 ° 21.0' E
X 60	232 N				X 60	4521 E

Formulae

$$\tan C = \frac{Dlo}{m} = \tan^{-1}\left(\frac{4521}{278.7}\right) = 86.47$$

N86.47E

Distance	3767.99
Course	86.5

	N
360 -	Same
180 +	180 -
	S

Notes:

$$D = \frac{DLat}{\cos C} = \left(\frac{232}{\cos 86.47}\right) = 3767.99$$

Problem 3. (00380)			Chapter			
Date:			Meridional Parts			
L_1	21° 18.5' N	M_1	1300.5		Lo_1	157° 52.2' W
L_2	8° 53.0' N	M_2	531.6		Lo_2	079° 31.0' W
DLat	12° 25.5' S	m	768.9		DLo	078° 21.2' E
X 60	745.5 S				X 60	4701.2 E

Formulae

$$\tan C = \frac{Dlo}{m} = \tan^{-1}\left(\frac{4701.2}{768.9}\right) = 80.7$$

$$180 - S80.7E = 99.3$$

Distance	4613.1
Course	99.3

	N
360 -	Same
180 +	180 -
	S

Notes:

$$D = \frac{DLat}{\cos C} = \left(\frac{745.5}{\cos 99.3}\right) = 4613.1$$

Alexander F. Hickethier MBA © 1990-2013

Problem 4. (0390)			Chapter			
Date:			Meridional Parts			
L_1	29° 38.0' N	M_1	1851.6		Lo_1	093° 49.0' W
L_2	24° 38.0' N	M_2	1516.2		Lo_2	082° 55.2' W
DLat	5-00.0' S	m	335.4		DLo	010° 53.8' E
X 60	300 S				X 60	653.8 E

		Formulae		N	
Distance	117	$$\tan C = \frac{Dlo}{m} = \tan^{-1}\left(\frac{653.8}{335.4}\right) = 62.8421$$ $$180 - S62.8E = 117.2$$		360 -	Same
Course	656.3			180 +	180 -
				S	

Notes:	
	$$D = \frac{DLat}{\cos C} = \left(\frac{300}{\cos 117.2}\right) = 656.3145056$$

Problem 5. (00391)			Chapter			
Date:			Meridional Parts			
L_1	40° 42.0' N	M_1	2662.8		Lo_1	074° 01.0' W
L_2	14° 41.0' N	M_2	885.0		Lo_2	017° 26.0' W
DLat	26 ° 01.0' S	m	1777.8		DLo	056 ° 35.0' E
X 60	1561 S				X 60	3395 E

		Formulae		N	
Distance	3369.3	$$\tan C = \frac{Dlo}{m} = \tan^{-1}\left(\frac{3395}{1777.8}\right) = 62.36$$ $$180 - S62.4E = 117.6$$		360 -	Same
Course	117.6			180 +	180 -
				S	

Notes:	
	$$D = \frac{DLat}{\cos C} = \left(\frac{1561}{\cos 117.6}\right) = 3369.34$$

Problem 6. (0392)			Chapter			
Date:			Meridional Parts			
L_1	32° 14.7' N	M_1	2033.3		Lo_1	066° 28.9' W
L_2	36° 58.7' N	M_2	2377.3		Lo_2	075° 42.2' W
DLat	4° 44.0'S	m	344		DLo	009° 13.3'
X 60	284 S				X 60	553.3 W

		Formulae		N	
Distance		$$\tan C = \frac{Dlo}{m} = \tan^{-1}\left(\frac{553.3}{344}\right) = 58.12$$ $$180 + 58.1 = 238.1$$		360 -	Same
Course				180 +	180 -
				S	

Notes:	
	$$D = \frac{DLat}{\cos C} = \left(\frac{284}{\cos 238.1}\right) = 537.43$$

Problem 7. (00394)			Chapter			
Date:			Meridional Parts			
L₁	38° 03.0' S	M₁	2457.9		Lo₁	049° 38.0' W
L₂	41° 26.0' S	M₂	2720.9		Lo₂	038° 32.0' W
DLat	3° 23.0' S	m	263		DLo	011° 36.0' E
X60	203 S				X60	666 E

L_1 = 38° 03.0' S, M_1 = 2457.9, Lo_1 = 049° 38.0' W
L_2 = 41° 26.0' S, M_2 = 2720.9, Lo_2 = 038° 32.0' W
$DLat$ = 3° 23.0' S, m = 263, DLo = 011° 36.0' E
X60 = 203 S, X60 = 666 E

Distance 553.9
Course 111.5

Formulae

	N
360 -	Same
180 +	180 -
	S

$$\tan C = \frac{Dlo}{m} = \tan^{-1}\left(\frac{666}{263}\right) = 68.45$$

$180 - S68.5E = 111.5$

Notes:

$$D = \frac{DLat}{\cos C} = \left(\frac{203}{\cos 111.5}\right) = 553.88$$

Problem 8. (0395)			Chapter			
Date:			Meridional Parts			
L₁	45° 36.0' N	M₁	3064.7		Lo₁	011° 36.0' W
L₂	24° 16.0' N	M₂	1492.1		Lo₂	073° 52.0' W
DLat	21° 20.0' S	m	1572.6		DLo	062° 16.0' W
X60	1280 S				X60	3736 W

Distance 3299
Course 247

Formulae

	N
360 -	Same
180 +	180 -
	S

$$\tan C = \frac{Dlo}{m} = \tan^{-1}\left(\frac{3736}{1572.6}\right) = 67.17$$

$180 + S67.2W = 247.2$

Notes:

$$D = \frac{DLat}{\cos C} = \left(\frac{1280}{\cos 247.17}\right) = 3298.98$$

Problem 9. (0396)			Chapter			
Date:			Meridional Parts			
L₁	10° 22.0' S	M₁	621.3		Lo₁	007° 18.0' E
L₂	6° 52.0' N	M₂	410.2		Lo₂	057° 23.0' W
DLat	17° 14.0' N	m	1031.5		DLo	064° 41.0' W
X60	1034 N				X60	3881 W

Distance
Course 285

Formulae

	N
360 -	Same
180 +	180 -
	S

$$\tan C = \frac{Dlo}{m} = \tan^{-1}\left(\frac{3881}{1031.5}\right) = 75.12$$

$360 - S75.1W = 284.9$

Notes: Notes: Crossing the Equator we add the Lat's and Meridional parts, crossing the 0 longitude we add the longitudes

$$D = \frac{DLat}{\cos C} = \left(\frac{1034}{\cos 284.9}\right) = 4021.28$$

Problem 10. (0398)			Chapter			
Date:			Meridional Parts			
L_1	32° 16.6' N	M_1	2035.7		Lo_1	068° 28.0' W
L_2	43° 12.2' N	M_2	2864.1		Lo_2	055° 39.0' W
DLat	10° 55.6' N	m	828.4		DLo	012 °49.0' E
X60	655.6 N				X60	769 E

Formulae

$$\tan C = \frac{Dlo}{m} = \tan^{-1}\left(\frac{769}{828.4}\right) = 42.87$$

	N	
360 -	Same	
180 +	180 -	
	S	

N42.87E = Same

Distance 894.5
Course 42.9

Notes:

$$D = \frac{DLat}{\cos C} = \left(\frac{655.6}{\cos 42.9}\right) = 894.52$$

Problem 11. (0399)			Chapter			
Date:			Meridional Parts			
L_1	11° 22.0' S	M_1	682.0		Lo_1	009° 18.0' E
L_2	6° 52.0' N	M_2	410.2		Lo_2	057° 23.0' W
DLat	18° 14.0' N	m	1092		DLo	066° 41.0' W
X60	1094 N				X60	4001 W

Formulae

$$\tan C = \frac{Dlo}{m} = \tan^{-1}\left(\frac{4001}{1092}\right) = 74.73$$

	N	
360 -	Same	
180 +	180 -	
	S	

360 − 74.73 = 285.26

Distance 4156.54
Course 285.26

Notes: Notes: Crossing the Equator we add the Lat's and Meridional parts, crossing the 0 longitude we add the longitudes

$$D = \frac{DLat}{\cos C} = \left(\frac{1094}{\cos 285.26}\right) = 4156.54$$

Problem 12. (0401)			Chapter			
Date:			Meridional Parts			
L_1	30° 18.0' S	M_1	1897.6		Lo_1	021° 42.0' W
L_2	35° 01.0' S	M_2	2232.3		Lo_2	018° 51.0' W
DLat	4° 43.0' S	m	334.7		DLo	002° 51.0' E
X60	283 S				X60	171 E

Formulae

$$\tan C = \frac{Dlo}{m} = \tan^{-1}\left(\frac{171}{334.7}\right) = 27.06$$

	N	
360 -	Same	
180 +	180 -	
	S	

180 − N27.06E = 152.94

Distance 320.5
Course 153

Notes:

$$D = \frac{DLat}{\cos C} = \left(\frac{283}{\cos 152}\right) = 320.5$$

Problem 13. (0402)			Chapter			
Date:			Meridional Parts			
L_1	38° 36.0' N	M_1	2499.8	Lo_1	011° 36.0' W	
L_2	24° 16.0' N	M_2	1492.1	Lo_2	071° 52.0' W	
DLat	14°-20.0' S	m	1007.7	DLo	060° 16.0' W	
x60	860 S			x60	3616 W	

		Formulae		N	
Distance				360 -	Same
Course	254.43	$\tan C = \dfrac{Dlo}{m} = \tan^{-1}\left(\dfrac{3616}{1007.7}\right) = 74.428$		180 +	180 -
		180 + S74.43W = 254.428		S	

Notes:	
	$D = \dfrac{DLat}{\cos C} = \left(\dfrac{860}{\cos 254.428}\right) = 3203.58$

Problem 14. (0403)			Chapter			
Date:			Meridional Parts			
L_1	24° 30.0' N	M_1	1507.4	Lo_1	083° 00.0' W	
L_2	30° 21.0' N	M_2	1901.0	Lo_2	088° 34.0' W	
DLat	5° 51.0' N	m	393.6	DLo	005° 34.0' W	
x60	351 N			x60	334 W	

		Formulae		N	
Distance	460			360 -	Same
Course	320	$\tan C = \dfrac{Dlo}{m} = \tan^{-1}\left(\dfrac{334}{393.6}\right) = 40.32$		180 +	180 -
		360 - S40.32E = 319.68		S	

Notes:	
	$D = \dfrac{DLat}{\cos C} = \left(\dfrac{351}{\cos 319.68}\right) = 460.36$

Problem 15. (0414)			Chapter			
Date:			Meridional Parts			
L_1	49° 45.0' N	M_1	3433.6	Lo_1	006° 35.0' W	
L_2	25° 50.0' N	M_2	1595.3	Lo_2	077° 00.0' W	
DLat	23° 55.0' S	m	1838.3	DLo	070° 25.0' W	
x60	1435 S			x60	4225 W	

		Formulae		N	
Distance	3598.75			360 -	Same
Course	246.5	$\tan C = \dfrac{Dlo}{m} = \tan^{-1}\left(\dfrac{4225}{1838.3}\right) = 66.49$		180 +	180 -
		180 + 66.49 = 246.49		S	

Notes:	
	$D = \dfrac{DLat}{\cos C} = \left(\dfrac{1435}{\cos 246.49}\right) = 3597.31$

Problem 16. (0415)			Chapter			
Date:			Meridional Parts			
L_1	33° 45.0' N	M_1	2140.6	Lo_1	118° 30.0' W	
L_2	21° 15.0' N	M_2	1296.9	Lo_2	157° 36.0' W	
DLat	12° 30.0' S	m	843.7	DLo	009° 06.0' W	
x60	750 S			x60	2346 W	
			Formulae		N	
Distance	2216.22		$\tan C = \dfrac{Dlo}{m} = \tan^{-1}\left(\dfrac{2346}{843.7}\right) = 70.22$		360 −	Same
Course	250.22				180 +	180 −
			$180 + 70.22 = 250.22$		S	
Notes:			$D = \dfrac{DLat}{\cos C} = \left(\dfrac{750}{\cos 250.22}\right) = 2216.22$			

Problem 17. (0416)			Chapter			
Date:			Meridional Parts			
L_1	18° 54.0' N	M_1	1147.7	Lo_1	073° 00.0' E	
L_2	13° 12.0' N	M_2	793.8	Lo_2	054° 00.0' E	
DLat	5° 42.0' S	m	353.2	DLo	019° 00.0' W	
x60	342 S			x60	1140 W	
			Formulae		N	
Distance	1155.62		$\tan C = \dfrac{Dlo}{m} = \tan^{-1}\left(\dfrac{1140}{353.2}\right) = 72.79$		360 −	Same
Course	252.79				180 +	180 −
			$180 + 72.79 = 252.79$		S	
Notes:			$D = \dfrac{DLat}{\cos C} = \left(\dfrac{342}{\cos 252.79}\right) = 1155.62$			

Problem 18. (0417)			Chapter			
Date:			Meridional Parts			
L_1	21° 32.0' N	M_1	1315.1	Lo_1	160° 30.0' W	
L_2	30° 00.0' N	M_2	1876.9	Lo_2	150° 00.0' E	
DLat	8° 28.0' N	m	561.8	DLo	049° 30.0' W	
x60	508 N			x60	2970 W	
			Formulae		N	
Distance	2733.2		$\tan C = \dfrac{Dlo}{m} = \tan^{-1}\left(\dfrac{2970}{561.8}\right) = 79.29$		360 −	Same
Course	280.71				180 +	180 −
			$360 - N79.29W = 280.71$		S	
Notes: crossing the dateline we add the longitudes and subtract from 360. 360 − (160° 30 + 150) = 49° 30'			$D = \dfrac{DLat}{\cos C} = \left(\dfrac{508}{\cos 280.71}\right) = 2733.20$			

GREAT CIRCLE SAILINGS
Chapter 1, Advanced Subjects for Master/Mate Unlimited

451.　　Given the following information:

1. Latitude of departure   (L1) 27° 51.0' N
2. Longitude of departure (LO1) 71° 41.0' W
3. Latitude of arrival   (L2) 49° 45.0' N
4. Longitude of arrival   (LO2) 06° 14.0' W

Determine the great circle distance (GCD) and initial course (Cn).

A. 3196 miles,   Cn 043.1° T
B. 3214 miles,   Cn 046.9° T
C. 3219 miles,   Cn 042.5° T
D. 3231 miles,   Cn 041.4° T

452. Given the following information:

1. Latitude of departure   (L1) 35° 17.6' N
2. Longitude of departure (LO1) 144° 23.0' E
3. Latitude of arrival   (L2) 47° 36.0' N
4. Longitude of arrival   (LO2) 124° 22.0' W

Determine the great circle distance (GCD) and initial course (Cn).

A. 3946 miles,   Cn 312 T
B. 3931 miles,   Cn 048° T
C. 3881 miles,   Cn 042° T
D. 3718 miles,   Cn 318° T

453.　　Given the following information:

1. Latitude of departure   (L1) 08° 36.0' N
2. Longitude of departure (LO1) 126° 17.0' E
3. Latitude of arrival   (L2) 02° 12.0' S
4. Longitude of arrival   (LO2) 81° 53.0' W

Determine the great circle distance (GCD) and initial course (Cn).

A. 9015 miles,   Cn 067° T
B. 9076 miles,   Cn 067° T
C. 9105 miles,   Cn 079° T
D. 9076 miles,   Cn 079° T

454. Given the following information:

1. Latitude of departure   (L1) 26° 00.0' S
2. Longitude of departure (LO1) 56° 00.0' W
3. Latitude of arrival   (L2) 34° 00.0' S
4. Longitude of arrival   (LO2) 18° 15.0' E

Determine the great circle distance (GCD) and initial course (Cn).

A. 3705 miles,   Cn 153° T
B. 3481 miles,   Cn 068° T
C. 3849 miles,   Cn 248° T
D. 3805 miles,   Cn 117° T

455. Given the following information:

1. Latitude of departure   (L1) 24° 52.0' N
2. Longitude of departure (LO1) 78° 27.0' W
3. Latitude of arrival   (L2) 47° 19.0' N
4. Longitude of arrival   (LO2) 06° 42.0' W

Determine the great circle distance (GCD) and initial course (Cn).

A. 3593 miles,   Cn 048.1° T
B. 3457 miles,   Cn 053.3° T
C. 3389 miles,   Cn 042.4° T
D. 3367 miles,   Cn 045.0° T

457. Given the following information:

1. Latitude of departure   (L1) 31° 57.0' S
2. Longitude of departure (LO1) 115° 52.0' E
3. Latitude of arrival   (L2) 24° 47.0' N
4. Longitude of arrival   (LO2) 66° 59.0' E

Determine the great circle distance (GCD) and initial course (Cn).

A. 4516 miles,   Cn 134.5° T
B. 4407 miles,   Cn 314.5° T
C. 4402 miles,   Cn 319.5° T
D. 4378 miles,   Cn 336.8° T

458. Given the following information:

1. Latitude of departure   (L1) 38° 42.0' N
2. Longitude of departure (L01) 09° 10.5' W
3. Latitude of arrival   (L2) 32° 05.0' N
4. Longitude of arrival   (L02) 81° 05.0' W

Determine the great circle distance (GCD) and initial course (Cn).

A. 3402.0 miles, Cn 072.5° T
B. 3412.6 miles, Cn 085.8° T
C. 3432.0 miles, Cn 278.3° T
D. 3449.4 miles, Cn 287.2° T

459. Given the following information:

1. Latitude of departure   (L1) 25° 47.0' N
2. Longitude of departure (L01) 79° 59.5' W
3. Latitude of arrival   (L2) 38° 42.0' N
4. Longitude of arrival   (L02) 09° 10.5' W

Determine the great circle distance (GCD) and initial course (Cn).

A. 3341.0 miles, Cn 063° T
B. 3347.0 miles, Cn 063° T
C. 3427.8 miles, Cn 061° T
D. 3588.6 miles, Cn 059° T

460. Given the following information:

1. Latitude of departure   (L1) 35° 27.0' N
2. Longitude of departure (L01) 140° 20.5' E
3. Latitude of arrival   (L2) 47° 51.0' N
4. Longitude of arrival   (L02) 122° 51.0' W

Determine the great circle distance (GCD) and initial course (Cn).

A. 4087 miles,   Cn 043° T
B. 4115 miles,   Cn 046° T
C. 4122 miles,   Cn 076° T
D. 4136 miles,   Cn 076° T

461. Given the following information:

1. Latitude of departure   (L1) 32° 43.0' N
2. Longitude of departure (L01) 121° 18.0' W
3. Latitude of arrival   (L2) 35° 27.0' N
4. Longitude of arrival   (L02) 140° 20.5' E

Determine the great circle distance (GCD) and initial course (Cn).

A. 4644 miles,   Cn 302°
B. 4659 miles,   Cn 304°
C. 4671 miles,   Cn 306°
D. 4683 miles,   Cn 308°

462. Given the following information:

1. Latitude of departure   (L1) 12° 45.2' N
2. Longitude of departure (L01) 124° 20.1' E
3. Latitude of arrival   (L2) 33° 48.8' N
4. Longitude of arrival   (L02) 120° 07.0' W

Determine the great circle distance (GCD) and initial course (Cn).

A. 6185.9 miles, Cn 050.3° T
B. 6231.3 miles, Cn 319.7° T
C. 6248.0 miles, Cn 048.3 T°
D. 6382.0 miles, Cn 311.7° t

463. Given the following information:

1. Latitude of departure   (L1) 37° 47.5' N
2. Longitude of departure (L01) 122° 27.8' W
3. Latitude of arrival   (L2) 33° 51.7' S
4. Longitude of arrival   (L02) 151° 12.7' E

Determine the great circle distance (GCD) and initial course (Cn).

A. 6324.2 miles, Cn 310.3° T
B. 6345.3 miles, Cn 301.7° T
C. 6398.0 miles, Cn 298.3° T
D. 6445.2 miles, Cn 240.3° T

464. Given the following information:

1. Latitude of departure   (L1) 33° 53.3' S
2. Longitude of departure (LO1) 18° 23.1' E
3. Latitude of arrival   (L2) 40° 27.0' N
4. Longitude of arrival   (LO2) 73° 49.4' W

Determine the great circle distance (GCD) and initial course (Cn).

A. 6648.0 miles, Cn 298.7° T
B. 6743.5 miles, Cn 302.7° T
C. 6750.8 miles, Cn 235.5° T
D. 6763.0 miles, Cn 305.4° T

465. Given the following information:

1. Latitude of departure   (L1) 34° 51.0' N
2. Longitude of departure (LO1) 115° 01.2' E
3. Latitude of arrival   (L2) 10° 16.0' S
4. Longitude of arrival   (LO2) 51° 42.6 E'

Determine the great circle distance (GCD) and initial course (Cn).

A. 4436 miles,   Cn 245.3° T
B. 4498 miles,   Cn 245.6° T
C. 4493 miles,   Cn 245.6° T
D. 4582 miles,   Cn 245.6° T

466. Given the following information:

1. Latitude of departure   (L1) 25° 50.0' N
2. Longitude of departure (LO1) 77° 00.0' W
3. Latitude of arrival   (L2) 35° 56.0' N
4. Longitude of arrival   (LO2) 06° 15.0' W

Determine the great circle distance (GCD) and initial course (Cn).

A. 3470 miles,   Cn 298° T
B. 3518 miles,   Cn 028° T
C. 3616 miles,   Cn 062° T
D. 3718 miles,   Cn 118° T

ANSWERS

451 B
452 B
453 D
454 D
455 A
457 B
458 D
459 D
460 B
461 B
462 A
463 D
464 D
465 C
466 C

Great Circle

Problem 451

L_1 27° 51.0' N

L_2 49° 45.0' N

Lo_1 071° 41.0' W

Lo_2 - 006° 14.0' W

Dlo 065° 27.0' E

$$cos\ D = (cos\ L_1 \times cos L_2 \times cos\ DLo) + (sin\ L_1 \times sin\ L_2)$$

$$COS^{-1}((cos\ 27°51.0' \times cos\ 49°45.0' \times cos\ 65°27.0') + (sin\ 27°51.0' \times sin\ 49°45.0'))$$
$$= 53.56486287 \times 60 = 3213.891772$$

$$tan\ C = sin\ DLo \div ((cos\ L_1 * tan\ L_2) - (sin\ L_1 * cos\ DLo))$$

$$tan^{-1}((Sin\ 65°27.0' \div ((cos\ 27°51.0' \times tan\ 49°\ 45') - (sin\ 27°51.0' \times cos\ 65°27.0')))$$
$$= 46.92882608$$

Course Angle $N46°.92882608E$

Rules to convert course angle to course:

IF:

L1 is N, DLo is E	CN = C
L1 is S, DLo is E	CN = 180 - C
L1 is S, DLo is W	CN = 180 + C
L1 is N, DLo is W	CN = 360 - C

Convert to True Course N 46.9° E

Problem 452

L_1 35° 17.6' N

Lo_1 144° 23.0' E
Lo_2 124° 22.0' W

L_2 47° 36.0' N

Dlo 091° 15.0' E

144°23.0' + 124°22.0' = 268°45.0' = (360° - 268°45.0') = 91°15.0'

Note: when crossing the Date Line (180 E/W), We add Lo1 and Lo2 and Subtract the sum from 360 to find Dlo.

$$cos\ D = (cos\ L_1 \times cosL_2 \times cos\ DLo) + (sin\ L_1 \times sin\ L_2)$$

$$COS^{-1}((\cos 35°\ 17.6' \times \cos 47°\ 36.0' \times \cos 91°15.0') + (\sin 35°17.6' \times \sin 47°36.0'))$$
$$= 65.50299428 \times 60 = 3930.179657$$

$$tan\ C = sin\ DLo \div ((cos\ L_1 * tan\ L_2) - (sin\ L_1 * cos\ DLo))$$

$$tan^{-1}((Sin\ 91°15.0' \div ((\cos 35°17.6' \times tan\ 47°36.0') - (\sin 35°17.6' \times \cos 91°15.0')))$$
$$= 47.80209747$$

Course Angle $N47.80209747°E$

Rules to convert course angle to course:

IF:

L1 is N, DLo is E	CN = C
L1 is S, DLo is E	CN = 180 - C
L1 is S, DLo is W	CN = 180 + C
L1 is N, DLo is W	CN = 360 - C

Convert to True Course   N 47.8° E

Problem 453

L$_1$ 08° 36.0' N   Lo$_1$ 126° 17.0' E

L$_2$ 02° 12.0' S   Lo$_2$ 081° 53.0' W

Dlo 151° 50.0' E

126°17.0' + 081°53.0' = 208°10.0' = (360° - 208°10.0') = 151°50.0'

Note: when crossing the Date Line (180 E/W), We add Lo1 and Lo2 and Subtract the sum from 360 to find Dlo.

$$cos\ D\ =\ (cos\ L_1\ \times\ cosL_2\ \times\ cos\ DLo)\ +\ (sin\ L_1\ \times\ sin\ L_2)$$

$$COS^{-1}((\cos 08°36.0' \times \cos 2°12.0' \times \cos 151°50.0') + (\sin 08°36.0' \times \sin 2°12.0'))$$
$$= 151.2544292 \times 60 = 9075.265753$$

$$tan\ C\ =\ sin\ DLo\ \div\ ((cos\ L_1\ *\ tan\ L_2)\ -\ (sin\ L_1\ *\ cos\ DLo))$$

$$tan^{-1}((Sin\ 151°50.0' \div ((\cos 8°36.0' \times \tan - 2°12.0') - (\sin 8°36.0' \times \cos 151°50.0')))$$
$$= 78.75598702$$

Course Angle $N78.5598702°E$

Rules to convert course angle to course:

IF:

L1 is N, DLo is E	CN = C
L1 is S, DLo is E	CN = 180 - C
L1 is S, DLo is W	CN = 180 + C
L1 is N, DLo is W	CN = 360 - C

Convert to True Course   N 78.6° E

Problem 454

L_1 26° 00.0' S Lo_1 056° 00.0' W
L_2 34° 00.0' S Lo_2 + 018° 15.0' E
                                          Dlo   074° 15.0' W

$$56°00.0' + 18°15.0' = 74°15.0'$$

Note: when crossing Greenwich (000 E/W), We add Lo1 and Lo2 and the sum is Dlo.

$$cos\ D\ =\ (cos\ L_1\ \times\ cosL_2\ \times\ cos\ DLo)\ +\ (sin\ L_1\ \times\ sin\ L_2)$$

$$COS^{-1}((\cos 26°00.0' \times \cos 34°00.0' \times \cos 74°15.0') + (\sin 26°00.0' \times \sin 34°00.0'))$$
$$= 63.42342048 \times 60 = 3805.405229$$

$$tan\ C\ =\ sin\ DLo \div ((cos\ L_1\ *\ tan\ L_2) - (sin\ L_1\ *\ cos\ DLo))$$

$$tan^{-1}((Sin\ 74°15.0' \div ((\cos 26°00.0' \times \tan 34°00.0') - (\sin 26°00.0' \times \cos 74°15.0')))$$
$$=\ 63.14873112$$

Course Angle $S63.14873112E$

Rules to convert course angle to course:

IF:
L1 is N, DLo is E   CN = C
L1 is S, DLo is E   CN = 180 - C
L1 is S, DLo is W   CN = 180 + C
L1 is N, DLo is W   CN = 360 - C

Convert to True Course $180 - 63.14 =$ S 116.86° E

Problem 455

L_1 24° 52.0' N

Lo_1 078° 27.0' W
Lo_2 - 006° 42.0' W

L_2 47° 19.0' N

Dlo 071° 45.0' E

$$cos\ D\ =\ (cos\ L_1\ \times\ cosL_2\ \times\ cos\ DLo)\ +\ (sin\ L_1\ \times\ sin\ L_2)$$

$$COS^{-1}((cos\ 24°52.0'\ \times\ cos\ 47°19.0'\ \times\ cos\ 71°45.0')\ +\ (sin\ 24°52.0'\ \times\ sin\ 47°19.0'))$$
$$=\ 59.88447054 \times 60\ =\ 3593.068232$$

$$tan\ C\ =\ sin\ DLo \div ((cos\ L_1\ *\ tan\ L_2)\ -\ (sin\ L_1\ *\ cos\ DLo))$$

$$tan^{-1}((Sin\ 71°45.0'\ \div ((cos\ 24°52.0'\ \times\ tan\ 47°19.0'\ )\ -\ (sin\ 24°52.0'\ \times\ cos\ 71°45.0')))$$
$$=\ 48.10035705$$

Course Angle $N48.10035705E$

Rules to convert course angle to course:

IF:

L1 is N, DLo is E	CN = C
L1 is S, DLo is E	CN = 180 - C
L1 is S, DLo is W	CN = 180 + C
L1 is N, DLo is W	CN = 360 - C

Convert to True Course   N 48.1° E

Problem 457

L$_1$ 31° 57.0' S   Lo$_1$ 115° 52.0' E
L$_2$ 24° 47.0' N   Lo$_2$ - 066° 59.0' E
                                                     Dlo   048° 53.0' W

$$cos\ D = (cos\ L_1 \times cosL_2 \times cos\ DLo) \mp (sin\ L_1 \times sin\ L_2)$$

Note: when crossing the Equator we SUBTRACT.

$$COS^{-1}((cos\ 31°57.0' \times cos\ 24°47.0 \times cos\ 48°53.0') - (sin\ 31°57.0' \times sin\ 24°47.0'))$$
$$= 73.45548256 \times 60 = 4407.328954$$

$$tan\ C = sin\ DLo \div ((cos\ L_1 * tan\ L_2) - (sin\ L_1 * cos\ DLo))$$

Note: when crossing the Equator L$_2$ is NEGATIVE.

$$tan^{-1}((sin\ 48°53.0' \div ((cos\ 31°\ 57.0' \times tan\ -24°47.0') - (sin\ 31°57.0' \times cos\ 48°53.0')))$$
$$= 45.5226151$$

Note: when crossing the Equator at an acute angle Label Course Angle with L$_2$

Course Angle $N45.5226151W$

Rules to convert course angle to course:

IF:
L1 is N, DLo is E   CN = C
L1 is S, DLo is E   CN = 180 - C
L1 is S, DLo is W   CN = 180 + C
L1 is N, DLo is W   CN = 360 - C

Convert to True Course   360 - 45.5 = N 314.5° W

Problem 458

L_1 38° 42.0' N

Lo_1 009°10.5' W

L_2 32° 05.0' N

Lo_2 081°05.0' W

Dlo 071°54.5' W

$$cos\ D\ =\ (cos\ L_1\ \times\ cosL_2\ \times\ cos\ DLo)\ \mp\ (sin\ L_1\ \times\ sin\ L_2)$$

$$COS^{-1}\big((\cos 38°42.0' \times \cos 32°05.0 \times \cos 471°54.5') - (\sin 38°42.0' \times \sin 32°05.0')\big)$$
$$= 57.49050696 \times 60 = 3449.4$$

$$tan\ C\ =\ sin\ DLo\ \div\ ((cos\ L_1\ *\ tan\ L_2) - (sin\ L_1\ *\ cos\ DLo))$$

$$tan^{-1}\big((\sin 71°54.5' \div \big((\cos 38°\ 42.0' \times \tan 32°05.0') - (\sin 38°42.0' \times \cos 71°54.5')\big)\big)$$
$$= 45.5226151$$

Course Angle $N72.75395526W$

Rules to convert course angle to course:

IF:

L1 is N, DLo is E	CN = C
L1 is S, DLo is E	CN = 180 - C
L1 is S, DLo is W	CN = 180 + C
L1 is N, DLo is W	CN = 360 - C

Convert to True Course $360 - 72.7539552 = N\ 287.24600447°\ W$

Problem 459

L$_1$ 25° 47.0' N	Lo$_1$	079° 59.5' W
L$_2$ 38° 42.0' N	Lo	009° 10.5' W
	Dlo	070° 49.0' E

$$cos\ D\ =\ (cos\ L_1\ \times\ cosL_2\ \times\ cos\ DLo)\ \mp\ (sin\ L_1\ \times\ sin\ L_2)$$

$$COS^{-1}\big((\cos\ 25°47.0'\times\cos 38°42.0\times\cos 70°49.0')+\ (\sin 25°47.0'\ \times\sin 38°42.0')\big)$$
$$=\ 59.80965419\times 60 = 3588.579251$$

$$tan\ C\ =\ sin\ DLo \div ((cos\ L_1\ *\ tan\ L_2)\ -\ (sin\ L_1\ *\ cos\ DLo))$$

$$tan^{-1}\big((sin\ 70°49.0' \div \big((\cos 25°\ 47.0'\times \tan 38°42.0')-\ (\sin 25°47.0'\times\cos 70°49.0')\big)\big)$$
$$=\ 58.70812972$$

Course Angle $N58.70812972E$

Rules to convert course angle to course:

IF:

L1 is N, DLo is E	CN = C
L1 is S, DLo is E	CN = 180 - C
L1 is S, DLo is W	CN = 180 + C
L1 is N, DLo is W	CN = 360 - C

Convert to True Course $N58.70812972E$

2-55

Problem 460

L_1 35° 27.0' N

L_2 47° 51.0' N

Lo_1 140° 20.5' E

Lo_2 122° 51.0' W

Dlo   096° 48.5' E

Note: when crossing the Date Line (180 E/W), We add Lo1 and Lo2 and Subtract the sum from 360 to find Dlo.

$$cos\ D\ =\ (cos\ L_1\ \times\ cosL_2\ \times\ cos\ DLo)\ \mp\ (sin\ L_1\ \times\ sin\ L_2)$$

$$COS^{-1}\big((cos\ 35°27.0'\ \times\ cos\ 47°51.0\ \times\ cos\ 96°48.5')\ +\ (sin\ 35°27.0'\ \times\ sin\ 47°51.0')\big)$$
$$=\ 68.58049344\ \times\ 60\ =\ 4114.829606$$

$$tan\ C\ =\ sin\ DLo\ \div\ ((cos\ L_1\ *\ tan\ L_2)\ -\ (sin\ L_1\ *\ cos\ DLo))$$

$$tan^{-1}\big((sin\ 96°48.5'\ \div\ \big((cos\ 35°\ 27.0'\ \times\ tan\ 47°51.0')\ -\ (sin\ 35°27.0'\ \times\ cos\ 96°\ 48.5')\big)\big)$$
$$=\ 45.70711155$$

Course Angle $N45.70711155E$

Rules to convert course angle to course:

IF:

L1 is N, DLo is E	CN = C
L1 is S, DLo is E	CN = 180 - C
L1 is S, DLo is W	CN = 180 + C
L1 is N, DLo is W	CN = 360 - C

Convert to True Course $N45.70711155E$

Problem 462

L$_1$ 12° 45.2'N

L$_2$ 33° 48.8'N

Lo$_1$	124° 20.1'E
Lo$_2$	120° 07.0'W
Dlo	115° 32.9'E

Note: when crossing the Date Line (180 E/W), We add Lo1 and Lo2 and Subtract the sum from 360 to find Dlo.

$$cos\ D\ =\ (cos\ L_1\ \times\ cosL_2\ \times\ cos\ DLo)\ +\ (sin\ L_1\ \times\ sin\ L_2)$$

$$(cos\ 12°45.2'\ \times\ cos\ 33°48.8\ \times\ cos\ 115°32.9')\ +\ (sin\ 12°45.2'\ \times\ sin\ 33°48.8)$$
$$=\ 103.0979383 \times 60\ =\ 6185.876034$$

$$tan\ C\ =\ sin\ DLo \div ((cos\ L_1\ *\ tan\ L_2)\ -\ (sin\ L_1\ *\ cos\ DLo))$$

$$tan^{-1}(Sin\ 115°32.9'$$
$$\div \left((cos\ 12°45.2'\ \times\ tan\ 33°48.8')\ -\ (sin\ 12°45.2'\ \times\ cos\ 115°32.9')\right))$$
$$=\ 50.32237839$$

Course Angle $N50.32237839°E$

Rules to convert course angle to course:

IF:

L1 is N, DLo is E	CN = C
L1 is S, DLo is E	CN = 180 - C
L1 is S, DLo is W	CN = 180 + C
L1 is N, DLo is W	CN = 360 - C

Convert to True Course   N 50.3° E

Alexander F. Hickethier MBA © 1990-2013

Problem 463

L_1 37° 47.5' N Lo_1 122° 27.8' W
L_2 33° 51.7' S Lo_2 151° 12.7' E
                          Dlo   086° 19.5' W

Note: when crossing the Date Line (180 E/W), We add Lo1 and Lo2 and Subtract the sum from 360 to find Dlo.

$$cos\ D\ =\ (cos\ L_1\ \times\ cosL_2\ \times\ cos\ DLo)\ \mp\ (sin\ L_1\ \times\ sin\ L_2)$$

Note: when crossing the Equator we SUBTRACT.

$$COS^{-1}((cos\ 37°\ 47.5'\ \times\ cos\ 33°\ 51.7\ \times\ cos\ 86°19.5')\ -\ (sin\ 37°\ 47.5'\ \times\ sin\ 33°\ 51.7'))$$
$$=\ 107.4204052\ \times\ 60\ =\ 6445.224313$$

$$tan\ C\ =\ sin\ DLo\ \div\ ((cos\ L_1\ *\ tan\ L_2)\ -\ (sin\ L_1\ *\ cos\ DLo))$$

Note: when crossing the Equator L_2 is NEGATIVE.

$$tan^{-1}((sin\ 86°\ 19.5'$$
$$\div\ ((cos\ 37°\ 47.5'\ \times\ tan\ -33°\ 51.7')\ -\ (sin\ 34°\ 47.5'\ \times\ cos\ 86°\ 19.5')))$$
$$=\ 60.40358889$$

Course Angle $S60.40358889W$

Note: when crossing the Equator at an acute angle Label Course Angle with L_2

Rules to convert course angle to course:

IF:
L1 is N, DLo is E	CN = C
L1 is S, DLo is E	CN = 180 - C
L1 is S, DLo is W	CN = 180 + C
L1 is N, DLo is W	CN = 360 - C

Convert to True Course   180 + 60.3 = S 240.3° W

Alexander F. Hickethier MBA © 1990-2013

Problem 464

L_1 33° 53.3' S		Lo_1	018° 23.1' E
L_2 40° 27.0' N		Lo_2	073° 49.4' W
		Dlo	092° 12.5' W

Note: when crossing Greenwich (000 E/W), We add Lo1 and Lo2 and the sum is Dlo.

$$cos\ D\ =\ (cos\ L_1\ \times\ cosL_2\ \times\ cos\ DLo)\ \mp\ (sin\ L_1\ \times\ sin\ L_2)$$

Note: when crossing the Equator we SUBTRACT.

$$COS^{-1}((cos\ 33° 53.3'\ \times\ cos\ 40° 27.0'\ \times\ cos\ 92° 12.5')\ -\ (sin\ 33° 53.3'\ \times\ sin\ 40° 27.0'))$$
$$=\ 112.4204052\ \times\ 60\ =\ 6762.678327$$

$$tan\ C\ =\ sin\ DLo\ \div\ ((cos\ L_1\ *\ tan\ L_2)\ -\ (sin\ L_1\ *\ cos\ DLo))$$

Note: when crossing the Equator L2 is NEGATIVE.

$$tan^{-1}((sin\ 92° 12.5'$$
$$\div\ ((cos\ 33° 53.3'\ \times\ tan\ -40° 27.0')\ -\ (sin\ 33° 53.3'\ \times\ cos\ 92° 12.5')))$$
$$=\ 55.51998925$$

Course Angle $N55.51998925W$

Note: when crossing the Equator an acute angle Label Course Angle with L_2

Rules to convert course angle to course:

IF:

L1 is N, DLo is E	CN = C
L1 is S, DLo is E	CN = 180 - C
L1 is S, DLo is W	CN = 180 + C
L1 is N, DLo is W	CN = 360 - C

Convert to True Course   360 - 55.5 = N 304.5° W

Problem 465

L_1 34° 51.0' N

L_2 10° 16.0' S

Lo_1 115° 01.2' E

Lo_2 051° 42.6' E

Dlo   063° 18.6' W

$$cos\ D\ =\ (cos\ L_1\ \times\ cos L_2\ \times\ cos\ DLo)\ \mp\ (sin\ L_1\ \times\ sin\ L_2)$$

Note: when crossing the Equator we SUBTRACT.

$$COS^{-1}((\cos\ 34°\ 51.0'\ \times \cos 10°\ 16.0'\ \times \cos 63°\ 18.6')\ -\ (\sin 34°\ 51.0'\ \times \sin 10°\ 16.0'))$$
$$=\ 74.87899546 \times 60\ =\ 4492.739728$$

$$tan\ C\ =\ sin\ DLo \div ((cos\ L_1\ *\ tan\ L_2) - (sin\ L_1\ *\ cos\ DLo))$$

Note: when crossing the Equator L_2 is NEGATIVE.

$$tan^{-1}((sin\ 63°\ 18.6'$$
$$\div \big((\cos 34°\ 51.0'\ \times \tan -10°\ 16.0') - (\sin 34°\ 51.0'\ \times \cos 63°\ 18.6')\big))$$
$$=\ 65.59878696$$

Course Angle $S65.59878696W$

Note: when crossing the Equator at an acute angle Label Course Angle with L_2

Rules to convert course angle to course:

IF:

L1 is N, DLo is E	CN = C
L1 is S, DLo is E	CN = 180 - C
L1 is S, DLo is W	CN = 180 + C
L1 is N, DLo is W	CN = 360 - C

Convert to True Course   180 + 65.6 = S 245.6° W

Problem 466

L$_1$ 25° 50.0' N   Lo$_1$ 077° 00.0' W
L$_2$ 35° 56.0' N   Lo$_2$ 006° 15.0' W
                                                     Dlo   070° 45.0' E

$$cos\ D\ =\ (cos\ L_1\ \times\ cos L_2\ \times\ cos\ DLo)\ \mp\ (sin\ L_1\ \times\ sin\ L_2)$$

$$COS^{-1}((cos\ 25°\ 50.0'\times cos\ 35°\ 56.0'\times cos\ 70°\ 45')+\ (sin\ 25°\ 50.0'\ \times sin\ 35°\ 56.0'))$$
$$=\ 60.264754\times 60\ =\ 3615.88254$$

$$tan\ C\ =\ sin\ DLo \div ((cos\ L_1\ *\ tan\ L_2)\ -\ (sin\ L_1\ *\ cos\ DLo))$$

$$tan^{-1}((sin\ 70°\ 45'\div \big((cos\ 25°\ 50.0'\times tan\ 35°\ 56.0')-\ (sin\ 25°\ 50.0'\times cos\ 70°\ 45')\big))$$
$$=\ 61.68432519$$

Course Angle $N61.68432519E$

Rules to convert course angle to course:

IF:
L1 is N, DLo is E   CN = C
L1 is S, DLo is E   CN = 180 - C
L1 is S, DLo is W   CN = 180 + C
L1 is N, DLo is W   CN = 360 - C

Convert to True Course   N 61.68° E

Great Circle

Determine the parallel of latitude (L_x)

4002212.
Given the following information:

1. L1 25° 50.0' N	LO$_1$ 077° 00.0' W
2. L2 36° 56.0' N	LO$_2$ 006° 15.0' W
3. Great circle distance (CGD)	3616 Miles
4. Initial great circle course (Cn)	61.7° T
5. Latitude of upper vertex (L_v) (V1)	37°35.6' N
6. Longitude of upper vertex (LO_v) (V1)	25°57.8' W

7. Difference of longitude from the upper vertex (V$_1$) to a point (X) on the great circle track (DLO$_{vx}$) 10°0' W.

Determine the parallel of latitude (L_x) which intersects the great circle track at point (X).

A. LAT 37° 02.5' N
B. LAT 37° 10.2' N
C. LAT 37° 15.6' N
D. LAT 37° 21.2' N

Formula:

$$tan\, L_x = cos\, DLo_{vx} \times tan\, L_v$$

Note: If Dlovx is given in Nautical Miles East or West of Vertex convert it to Degrees by dividing the distance by 60.

$$cos\, 10° \times tan\, 37°35.6' = tan\, 0.7582215386$$

$$tan^{-1}\, 0.75582215386 \times 37.17018789 = 37°10'12.68"\, or$$

<u>Ans. B   37°10.2</u>

Alexander F. Hickethier MBA © 1990-2013

Great Circle

Determine the longitude of the upper vertex (LO$_v$) (V1).

4002200.
Given the following information:

1. L1 35° 57.2' N   LO$_1$ 005° 45.7' W
2. L2 24° 25.3' N   LO$_2$ 083° 02.6' W
3. Great circle distance (GCD)   3966.5 miles
4. Initial great circle course (Cn)   076° 16.5' T
5. Latitude of upper vertex (L$_v$) (V1)   38° 09.4' N

Determine the longitude of the upper vertex (LO$_v$) (V1).

A. LONG 28° 12.6' W
B. LONG 28° 24.5' W
C. LONG 28° 36.3' W
D. LONG 28° 47.7' W

Formula:

$$sin\ Dlov\ =\ cos\ C\ \div\ sin\ L_v$$

$$cos\ 76°16.5'\ \div\ sin\ 38°09.4'\ =\ 0.3844922011\ sin^{-1}\ =\ 22.58383420\ =\ 22°35.1$$

	Lo$_1$	05°45.7
+ Dlo$_v$		22°35.1
		28°20.8

Great Circle

Determine the distance in miles (Dv)

4002203.
Given the following information:

1. Latitude of departure (L$_1$)	25° 50.0' N
2. Longitude of departure (LO$_1$)	77° 00.0' W
3. Latitude of vertex (Lv)	037° 35.6' N
4. Longitude of vertex (LOv)	025° 57.8' W
5. Initial course (Cn)	061.7° T

Determine the distance in miles (Dv) along the great circle track (GCT) between the point of departure (L$_1$, LO$_1$) and the vertex (V$_1$).

A. 2735.1 miles
B. 2664.9 miles
C. 2583.2 miles
D. 2420.0 miles

Formula:

$$sin\ Dv\ =\ cos\ L_1\ \times\ sin\ Dlov$$

$$cos\ 25°50'\ \times\ 51°02.2\ =\ 0.701650631 sin^{-1}\ =\ 44.4145332$$

$$44.4145332\ \times\ 60\ =\ 2664.871992\ NM$$

Example 5

Determine the latitude of the upper vertex (V_1)

4002204.

Given the following information:

1. L1 35° 08.0' S LO_1 19° 26.0' E
2. L2 33° 16.0' S LO_2 115° 36.0' E
3. Great circle distance (GCD)   4559 miles
4. Initial great circle course (Cn)   121° 02.4' T

Determine the latitude of the upper vertex (V_1).

A. LAT 44° 29.1' S
B. LAT 45° 30.9' S
C. LAT 46° 18.2' S
D. LAT 43° 41.8' S

Formula:

$$cos\ Lvx\ =\ cos\ L_1\ \times\ sin\ C$$

$$cos\ 35°08'\ \times\ sin\ 121°02.4'\ =\ 0.7007710094\ cos^{-1}\ =\ 45.5159972$$

$$45°30.9'\ S$$

Alexander F. Hickethier MBA © 1990-2013

USCG AMPLITUDE PROBLEMS WORKED-OUT

With
EXTRACTS FROM THE
AMERICAN PRACTICAL NAVIGATOR
CHAPTER 17 - AMPLITUDE

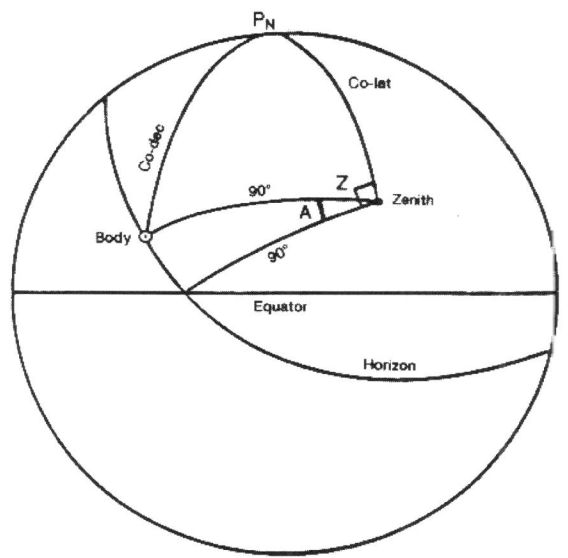

The amplitude angle (A) subtends the arc of the horizon between the body and the point where the prime vertical and the equator intersect the horizon. Note that it's the compliment of the azimuth angle (Z).

Alexander F. Hickethier, MBA
and
Dr. Hu Jia-Shen

AMPLITUDES
Chapter 20,

A celestial body's amplitude angle is the complement of its azimuth angle. At the moment that a body rises or sets, the amplitude angle is the arc of the horizon between the body and the East/West point of the horizon where the observer's prime vertical intersects the horizon (at 90°), which is also the point where the plane of the equator intersects the horizon (at an angle numerically equal to the observer's co-latitude). See Figure 1.

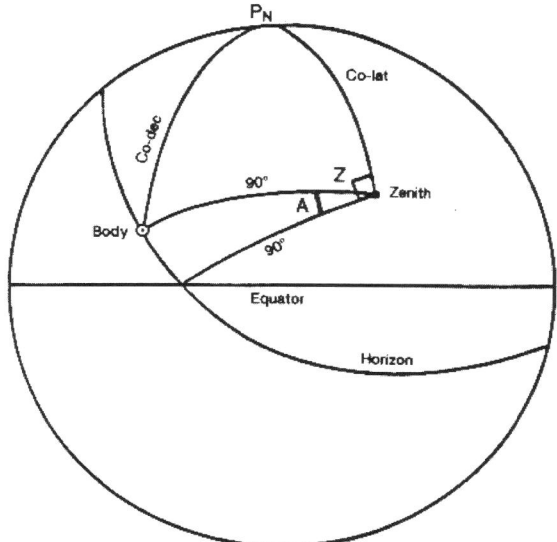

Figure 1. The amplitude angle (A) subtends the arc of the horizon between the body and the point where the prime vertical and the equator intersect the horizon. Note that it s the compliment of the azimuth angle (Z).

In practical navigation, a bearing (psc or pgc) of a body can be observed when it is on either the **celestial or the visible horizon**. To determine compass error, simply convert the computed amplitude angle to true degrees and compare it with the observed compass bearing.

The angle is computed by the formula:

sin A = sin Dec / cos Lat.

This formula gives the angle at the instant the body is on the celestial horizon. It does not contain an altitude term because the body's computed latitude is zero at this instant.

The angle is prefixed **E** if the body is rising and **W** if it is setting. This is the only angle in celestial navigation referenced FROM East or West, i.e. from the prime vertical. A body with northerly declination will rise and set **North** of the prime vertical. Likewise, a body with southerly declination will rise and set **South** of the prime vertical. Therefore, the angle is suffixed N or S to agree with the name of the body's declination. A body, whose declination is zero rises and sets exactly on the prime vertical.

The Sun is on the celestial horizon when its lower limb is approximately two thirds of a diameter above the visible horizon. The Moon is on the celestial horizon when its upper limb is on the visible horizon. Stars and planets are on the celestial horizon when they are approximately one Sun diameter above the visible horizon.

When observing a body on the visible horizon, a correction from Table 23 **(Figure 3)** must be applied. This correction accounts for the slight change in bearing as the body moves between the visible and celestial horizons. It reduces the bearing on the visible horizon to the celestial horizon, from which the table is computed.

For the Sun, stars, and planets, apply this correction to **the observed bearing in the direction away from the elevated pole.** For the moon, apply one half of the correction toward the elevated pole. Note that the algebraic sign of the correction does not depend upon the body's declination, but only on the observer's latitude. Assuming the body is the Sun the rule for applying the correction can be outlined as follows:

North Rising Add to
North Setting Subtract from
South Rising Subtract from
South Setting Add to

The following two examples demonstrate the procedure for obtaining the amplitude of the Sun on both the celestial and visible horizons.

Observer's Lat. Rising/Setting Observed bearing

TABLE 22 Amplitudes													
Latitude	Declination													Latitude
	18°0	18°5	19°0	19°5	20°0	20°5	21°0	21°5	22°0	22°5	23°0	23°5	24°0	
°	°	°	°	°	°	°	°	°	°	°	°	°	°	°
0	18.0	18.5	19.0	19.5	20.0	20.5	21.0	21.5	22.0	22.5	23.0	23.5	24.0	0
10	18.3	18.8	19.3	19.8	20.3	20.8	21.3	21.8	22.4	22.9	23.4	23.9	24.4	10
15	18.7	19.2	19.7	20.2	20.7	21.3	21.8	22.3	22.8	23.3	23.9	24.4	24.9	15
20	19.2	19.7	20.3	20.8	21.3	21.9	22.4	23.0	23.5	24.0	24.6	25.1	25.6	20
25	19.9	20.5	21.1	21.6	22.2	22.7	23.3	23.9	24.4	25.0	25.5	26.1	26.7	25
30	20.9	21.5	22.1	22.7	23.3	23.9	24.4	25.0	25.6	26.2	26.8	27.4	28.0	30
32	21.4	22.0	22.6	23.2	23.8	24.4	25.0	25.6	26.2	26.8	27.4	28.0	28.7	32
34	21.9	22.5	23.1	23.7	24.4	25.0	25.6	26.2	26.9	27.5	28.1	28.7	29.4	34
36	22.5	23.1	23.7	24.4	25.0	25.7	26.3	26.9	27.6	28.2	28.9	29.5	30.2	36
38	23.1	23.7	24.4	25.1	25.7	26.4	27.1	27.7	28.4	29.1	29.7	30.4	31.1	38
40	23.8	24.5	25.2	25.8	26.5	27.2	27.9	28.6	29.3	30.0	30.7	31.4	32.1	40
41	24.2	24.9	25.6	26.3	26.9	27.6	28.3	29.1	29.8	30.5	31.2	31.9	32.6	41
42	24.6	25.3	26.0	26.7	27.4	28.1	28.8	29.5	30.3	31.0	31.7	32.5	33.2	42
43	25.0	25.7	26.4	27.2	27.9	28.6	29.3	30.1	30.8	31.6	32.3	33.0	33.8	43
44	25.4	26.2	26.9	27.6	28.4	29.1	29.9	30.6	31.4	32.1	32.9	33.7	34.4	44
45	25.9	26.7	27.4	28.2	28.9	29.7	30.5	31.2	32.0	32.8	33.5	34.3	35.1	45
46	26.4	27.2	27.9	28.7	29.5	30.3	31.1	31.8	32.6	33.4	34.2	35.0	35.8	46
47	26.9	27.7	28.5	29.3	30.1	30.9	31.7	32.5	33.3	34.1	35.0	35.8	36.6	47
48	27.5	28.3	29.1	29.9	30.7	31.6	32.4	33.2	34.0	34.9	35.7	36.6	37.4	48
49	28.1	28.9	29.8	30.6	31.4	32.3	33.1	34.0	34.8	35.7	36.6	37.4	38.3	49
50	28.7	29.6	30.4	31.3	32.1	33.0	33.9	34.8	35.6	36.5	37.4	38.3	39.3	50
51	29.4	30.3	31.2	32.0	32.9	33.8	34.7	35.6	36.5	37.5	38.4	39.3	40.3	51
52	30.1	31.0	31.9	32.8	33.7	34.7	35.6	36.5	37.5	38.4	39.4	40.4	41.3	52
53	30.9	31.8	32.8	33.7	34.6	35.6	36.5	37.5	38.5	39.5	40.5	41.5	42.5	53
54	31.7	32.7	33.6	34.6	35.6	36.6	37.6	38.6	39.6	40.6	41.7	42.7	43.8	54

Figure 2

TABLE 23
Correction of Amplitude as Observed on the Visible Horizon

Latitude	Declination													Latitude
	0°	2°	4°	6°	8°	10°	12°	14°	16°	18°	20°	22°	24°	
°	°	°	°	°	°	°	°	°	°	°	°	°	°	°
0	0.0	0.0	0.0	0.0	0.0	0.0	0.0	0.0	0.0	0.0	0.0	0.0	0.0	0
10	0.1	0.1	0.1	0.1	0.1	0.1	0.1	0.1	0.1	0.1	0.1	0.1	0.1	10
15	0.2	0.2	0.2	0.2	0.2	0.2	0.2	0.2	0.2	0.2	0.2	0.2	0.2	15
20	0.3	0.3	0.3	0.3	0.3	0.3	0.3	0.3	0.3	0.3	0.3	0.3	0.3	20
25	0.3	0.3	0.3	0.3	0.3	0.4	0.3	0.3	0.3	0.3	0.3	0.3	0.3	25
30	0.4	0.4	0.4	0.4	0.5	0.4	0.4	0.4	0.4	0.4	0.4	0.5	0.5	30
32	0.4	0.4	0.4	0.4	0.5	0.4	0.4	0.4	0.4	0.4	0.5	0.5	0.5	32
34	0.5	0.5	0.5	0.5	0.5	0.5	0.5	0.5	0.5	0.5	0.5	0.5	0.5	34
36	0.5	0.5	0.5	0.5	0.5	0.5	0.5	0.5	0.6	0.5	0.6	0.6	0.6	36
38	0.6	0.6	0.6	0.6	0.6	0.6	0.6	0.6	0.6	0.6	0.6	0.6	0.6	38
40	0.6	0.6	0.6	0.6	0.6	0.6	0.6	0.6	0.6	0.6	0.7	0.7	0.7	40
42	0.6	0.6	0.6	0.6	0.7	0.7	0.7	0.7	0.7	0.7	0.7	0.7	0.7	42
44	0.7	0.7	0.7	0.6	0.6	0.7	0.7	0.7	0.8	0.8	0.8	0.8	0.9	44
46	0.7	0.7	0.7	0.7	0.7	0.8	0.8	0.8	0.8	0.8	0.8	0.9	0.9	46
48	0.8	0.8	0.8	0.8	0.8	0.8	0.8	0.8	0.9	0.9	1.0	1.0	1.0	48
50	0.8	0.8	0.8	0.8	0.9	0.9	0.9	0.9	0.9	1.0	1.0	1.1	1.0	50
51	0.8	0.8	0.8	0.8	0.9	0.9	0.9	0.9	0.9	1.0	1.1	1.1	1.1	51
52	0.9	0.9	0.9	0.9	0.9	0.9	1.0	1.0	1.0	1.1	1.1	1.1	1.3	52
53	0.9	0.9	0.9	0.9	0.9	0.9	1.0	1.0	1.0	1.1	1.2	1.2	1.3	53
54	1.0	1.0	1.0	1.0	1.0	1.0	1.1	1.1	1.1	1.2	1.2	1.3	1.3	54

Figure 3

Examples

Example 1 - Amplitude of the Sun on the Celestial Horizon

The DR latitude of a ship is 51° 24.6' N. The navigator observes the setting Sun on the celestial horizon. Its AZIMUTHS AND AMPLITUDES declination is N 19° 40.4'. Its observed bearing is 303° pgc.

Required:

Gyro error.

Solution:

*Interpolate in Table 22 for the Sun's calculated amplitude as follows. **See Figure 2** The actual values for latitude and*

declination are L = 51.4° N and dec. = N 19.67°. Find the tabulated values of latitude and declination closest to these actual values. In this case, these tabulated values are L = 51° and dec. = 19.5°. Record the amplitude corresponding to these base values, 32.0°, as the base amplitude.

Next, holding the base declination value constant at 19.5°, increase the value of latitude to the next tabulated value: N 52°. Note that this value of latitude was increased because the actual latitude value was greater than the base value of latitude. Record the tabulated amplitude for L = 52° and dec. = 19.5°: 32.8°. Then, holding the base latitude value constant at 51°, increase the declination value to the next tabulated

3-5

value: 20°. Record the tabulated amplitude for L = 51° and dec. = 20°: 32.9°.

The latitude's actual value (51.4°) is 0.4 of the way between the base value (51°) and the value used to determine the tabulated amplitude (52°). The declination's actual value (19.67°) is 0.3 of the way between the base value (19.5°) and the value used to determine the tabulated amplitude (20.0°). To determine the total correction to base amplitude, multiply these increments (0.4 and 0.3) by the respective difference between the base and tabulated values (+0.8 and +0.9, respectively) and sum the products. The total correction is +0.6°. Add the total correction (+0.6°) to the base amplitude (32.0°) to determine the final amplitude (32.6°) which will be converted to a true bearing. Because of its northerly declination (in this case), the Sun was 32.6° north of west when it was on the celestial horizon. Therefore its true bearing was 302.6° (270° + 32.6°) at this moment. Comparing this with the gyro bearing of 303° gives an error of 0.4°W, which can be rounded to 1/2°W.

Example - 2 Amplitude of the Sun on the Visible Horizon

In higher latitudes, amplitude observations should be made when the body is on the visible horizon because the value of the correction is large enough to cause significant error if the observer misjudges the exact position of the celestial horizon. The observation will yield precise results whenever the visible horizon is clearly defined.

Example:

Observer's DR latitude is 59°47'N, Sun's declination is 5°11.3'S. At sunrise the Sun is observed on the visible horizon bearing 098.5° pgc.

Required:
Compass error.

Solution:

Given this particular latitude and declination, the amplitude angle is E100.4°S, so that the Sun's true bearing is 100.4° at the moment it is on the celestial horizon, that is, when its Hc is precisely 0°. The Sun would have been bearing 099.7° pgc had the observation been made when the Sun was on the celestial horizon. Therefore, the gyro error is 0.7°E.

Example - 3 Amplitude by Calculation

As an alternative to using Table 22 and Table 23, a visible horizon amplitude observation can be solved by the "altitude azimuth" formula, because azimuth and amplitude angles are complimentary, and the co-functions of complimentary angles are equal; i.e., cosine Z = sine A. Sine A = [Sin D - (sin L sin H)] / (cos L cos H)

For shipboard observations, the Sun's (computed) altitude is negative 0.7° when it is on the visible horizon.

Using the same entities as in **Example 2** the amplitude angle is computed as follows: Sin A = [sin 5.2°- (sin 59.8° X sin -0.7°)] / (cos 59.8° X cos 0.7°)

COMPASS ERROR BY AMPLITUDE (any Body)
Chapter 20, Upon Oceans for Limited Master

01651. On 23 October 1981, in DR position LAT 21° 13.0' N, LONG 152° 18.0 E, you observe an amplitude of the Sun. The Sun's center is on the visible horizon and bears 259° psc. The chronometer reads 07h 21m 46s and is 01m 32s slow. Variation in the area is 5° E. What is the deviation of the magnetic compress?

A. 0.9° E
B. 1.5° W
C. 5.9° W
D. 6.5° E

01652. On 22 October 1981, in DR position LAT 21° 51.0' S, LONG 76° 24.0 E, you observe the amplitude of the Sun. The Sun's center is on the visible horizon and bears 256° psc. The chronometer reads 01h 01m 25s and is 01m 15s fast. Variation for the area is 2° E. What is the deviation of the magnetic compass?

A. 0.3° E
B. 0.3° W
C. 2.0° E
D. 2.0° W

01653. On 28 Sept., 1981, in DR position LAT 24° 12.0' S, LONG 85° 25.0' E, you observe an amplitude of the Sun. The Sun's center is on the visible horizon and bears 094° psc. The chronometer reads 11h 29m 42s and is 03m 30s slow. Variation in the area is 4° W. What is the deviation of the magnetic compass?

A. 1.5° W
B. 2.1° W
C. 2.4° E
D. 4.2° E

01654. On 28 September 1981, in DR position LAT 27° 16.7' S, LONG 113° 27.2' W, you observe an

amplitude of the Sun. The Sun's center is on the celestial horizon and bears 273° psc. The chronometer reads 01h 17m 26s and is 01m 49s slow. Variation in the area is 6° W. What is the deviation of the magnetic compass?

A. 0.2° W
B. 0.4° E
C. 0.8° E
D. 0.6° W

01655. On 22 October 1981, in DR position LAT 21° 51.0' S, LONG 76° 24.0' E, you observe the amplitude of the Sun. The Sun's center is on the visible horizon and bears 256° psc. The chronometer reads 01h 01m 25s and is 01m 15s fast. Variation in the area is 2° E. What is the deviation of the magnetic compass?

A. 0.3° E
B. 0.3° W
C. 2.0° E
D. 2.3° W

01656. On 5 September 1981 in DR position LAT 23° 17.0' S, LONG 154° 35.0' E, you observe an amplitude of the Sun. The Sun's center is on the visible horizon and bears 275° psc. The chronometer reads 07h 49m 26s and is 01m 52s fast. Variation in the area is 3° W. What is the deviation of the magnetic compass?

A. 2.1° E
B. 2.4° W
C. 5.4° E
D. 5.1° W

01657. On 24 August 1981, in DR position LAT 26° 49.4' N, LONG 146° 19.4' E, you observe an amplitude of the Sun. The Sun's center is on the celestial horizon and bears 084° psc. The chronometer reads 07h 55m 06s and is 01m 11s fast. Variation in the area is 15° W. What is the deviation of the magnetic compass?

A. 2.3° W
B. 3.6° E
C. 6.6° W
D. 8.5° E

01658. On 23 August 1981, in DR position LAT 24° 07.0' N, LONG 136° 16'0 E, you observe the amplitude of the Sun. The Sun's center is on the visible horizon and bears 074.5° psc. The chronometer reads 08h 56m 19s and is 02m 34s fast. Variation in the area is 2° W. What is the deviation of the magnetic compass?

A. 2.5° E
B. 2.8° W
C. 4.5° E
D. 4.8° W

01659. On 15 July 1981, in DR position LAT 22° 19.0' N, LONG 154° 37.0' W, you observe the amplitude of the Sun. The Sun's center is on the visible horizon and bears 298° psc. The chronometer reads 04h 45m 19s and is 01m 56s slow. Variation in the area is 7.5° W. What is the deviation of the magnetic compass?

A. 2.7° W
B. 3.0° E
C. 3.6° W
D. 3.9° E

01660. On 23 June 1981, in DR position LAT 21° 39.0' S, LONG 106° 28.0' W, you observe an amplitude of the Sun. The Sun's center is on the celestial horizon and bears 078° psc. The chronometer reads 02h 14m 39s and is 01m 43s slow. Variation in the area is 9° W. What is the deviation of the magnetic compass?

A. 2.8° E
B. 3.9° W
C. 4.3° W
D. 4.6° E

01661. On 11 May 1981, in DR position LAT 28° 13.7' N, LONG 168° 36.3' E, you observe the amplitude of the Sun. The Sun's center is on the celestial horizon and bears 283° psc. The chronometer reads 07h 13m 19s and is 02m 56s slow. Variation in the area is 13° E. What is the deviation of the magnetic compass?

A. 5.2° W
B. 5.6° W
C. 7.4° E
D. 7.8° E

01663. On 7 April 1981, in DR position LAT 27° 42.0' N, LONG 114° 03.0' W, you observe an amplitude of the Sun. The Sun's center is on the celestial horizon and bears 076° psc. The chronometer reads 02h 10m 17s and is 01m 52s slow. Variation in the area is 8° E. What is the deviation of the magnetic compass?

A. 1.8° W
B. 2.3° E
C. 6.2° E
D. 7.8° W

01664. On 10 February 1981, in DR position LAT 25° 32.0' N, LONG 135° 15.0' E, you observe an amplitude of the Sun. The Sun's center is on the celestial horizon and bears 109° psc. The chronometer reads 09h 43m 25s and is 03m 20s fast. Variation in the area is 4.5° W. What is the deviation of the magnetic compass?

A. 1.6° E
B. 2.9° W
C. 10.5° E
D. 30.5° W

01665. On 11 January 1981, your vessel's 0655 zone time DR position is LAT 24° 30' N, LONG 122° 02' W, when an amplitude of the Sun is observed. The Sun's center is on the celestial horizon and bears 101.0° per standard compass. Variation in the area is 11.6° E. The chronometer reads 02h 52m 48s and is 02m 12s slow. What is the deviation of the standard compass?

A. 1.4° E
B. 1.4° W
C. 4.6° E
D. 4.6° W

01666. On 23 October 1981, your vessel's 1722 zone time DR position is LAT 27° 36' S, LONG 096° 16' W, when an amplitude of the Sun is observed. The Sun's lower limb is about 20 minutes of arc above the visible horizon and bears 246° per standard compass. Variation in the area is 14.0° E. The chronometer reads 11h 24m 19s and is 01m 43s fast. What is the deviation of the standard compass?

A. 2.3° E
B. 2.7° E
C. 2.7° W
D. 3.1° W

1667. On Sunday 8 November 1981, your ship is enroute from Texas City, TX, to Portland, ME. At 0632 zone time, you fix your position by loran at LAT 27° 06' N, LONG 90° 36' W. When the lower limb of the Sun was two-thirds of a diameter above the visible horizon, the Sun bore 105° per standard magnetic compass. Given the following information, determine the deviation of the standard compass?

Chronometer time: 12h 39m 20s
Chronometer error: slow 3m 20s
Variation: 3.0° E

A. 0.8° E
B. 0.8° W
C. 3.8° E
D. 3.8° W

01668. On 20 June 1981, your vessel's 1955 ZT, DR position is LAT 52° 38.9' N, LONG 03° 42.7' E, when an amplitude of the Sun is observed. The Sun's

center is on the vis ble horizon and bears 311° per gyrocompass. Variation in the area is 6° W. At the time of the observation, the helmsman noted that he was heading 352° per gyrocompass and 358° per steering compass. What is the gyro error and deviation for that heading?

A. 1.3° W GE   1.3° E DEV
B. 0°   GE   0°   DEV
C. 1.3° W GE   1.3° W DEV
D. 1.3° E GE   1.3° E DEV

01669. On 19 June 1981, your vessel's 0523 ZT DR position is LAT 25° 12.0' N, LONG 123° 14.0' W, when an amplitude of the Sun is observed. The Sun's center is on the visible horizon and bears 052.0° per standard compass. Variation in the area is 15° E. The chronometer reads 01h 21m 58s and is 01m 18s slow. What is the deviation of the standard compass?

A. 1.4° E
B. 1.4° W
C. 1.7° W
D. 3.3° W

01670. On 10 August 1981, your vessel's 0426 zone time DR position is LAT 52° 07' N, LONG 142° 16' E, when an amplitude of the Sun is observed. The Sun's lower limb is abou: 20 minutes of arc above the visible horizon and bears 074.5° per standard compass. Variation in the area is 12° W. The chronometer reads 07h 24m 19s and is 02m 34s fast. Which of the following is the deviation of the standard compass?

A. 0.0°
B. 1.3° W
C. 1.3° E
D. 2.3° W

01671. On 9 May 1981, your vessel's 1809 ZT, DR position is LAT 48° 13.7' N, LONG 168° 36.3' E, when an amplitude of the Sun is observed. The Sun's center is on the celestial horizon and bears 283.7° per standard compass. Variation in the area is 13.0° E. The chronometer reads 07h 13m 19s and is 02m 56s fast. What is the deviation of the standard compass?

A. 0.1° E
B. 1.1° W
C. 1.1° E
D. 1.9° W

01672. On 11 May 1981, your vessel's 1839 zone time position is LAT 17° 30' N, LONG 63° 55' W, when an amplitude of the Sun's center is observed on the celestial horizon bearing 301° per standard compass. Variation for this area is 10.5° W. The chronometer reads 10h 37m 10s and is 02m 08s slow. Which of the following is the deviation of the compass?

A. 2.5° W
B. 2.0° W
C. 1.5° W
D. 2.0° E

1673. On 17 April 1981, your vessel's position is LAT 21° 00' S, LONG 78° 30'W, when an amplitude of the Sun is observed. The Sun's center is on the celestial horizon and bears 082.7° per standard compass. Variation in the area is 2.0° W. The chronometer reads 10h 59m 24s and is 01m 24s fast. What is the deviation of the compass?

A. 2.0° W
B. 3.0° W
C. 2.5° E
D. 3.0° E

01674. On 4 July 1981, your vessel's 1722 zone time DR position is LAT 34° 30' S, LONG 174° 48' E, when an amplitude of the Sun is observed. The Sun's center is on the visible horizon and bears 282° per standard magnetic compass. Variation in the area is 17.2° E. The chronometer reads 05h 21m 48s and is 02m 01s fast. What is the deviation of the compass?

A. 1.6° W
B. 2.0° W
C. 1.5° E
D. 2.0° E

01675. On 28 November 1981, your vessel's 0652 DR position is LAT 37° 30' N, LONG 124° 12' W, when an amplitude of the Sun is observed. The Sun's center is on the visible horizon and bears 103° per standard magnetic compass. Variation in the area is 16.3° E. The chronometer reads 14h 54m 18s and is 02m 06s fast. What is the deviation of the compass?

A. 2.5° W
B. 3.0° W
C. 2.0° E
D. 3.0° E

01676. On 10 June 1981, your vessel's 0519 zone time DR position is LAT 27° 07.0' N, LONG 92° 10.0' W, when an amplitude of the Sun is observed. The Sun's center is on the visible horizon and bears 063.6° per standard magnetic compass. The variation in the area is 4.8° E. The chronometer reads 11h 17m 32s and is 01m 18s slow. What is the deviation of the compass?

A. 5.6° E
B. 4.8° E
C. 4.2° W
D. 4.8° W

01677. At 0604 ZT on 23 August 1981, in DR position AT 16° 42.3' S. LONG 28° 19.3' W, you observed an amplitude of the Sun. The lower limb was about 20' of arc above the horizon, and the Sun bore 076.0° pgc. At the time of the observation, the helmsman reported that he was heading 143° pgc and 167° per magnetic compass. The variation in the area was 23° W. What were the gyro error and deviation for that heading?

A. 1° W GE,   2° W DEV
B. 1° E GE,   1° E DEV
C. 2° W GE,   1° E DEV
D. 2° E GE,   1° E DEV

01678. On 2 January 1981, your vessel's 1822 zone time loran position is LAT 21° 42' S, LONG 39° 12' W, when an amplitude of the Sun is observed. The Sun's center is on the celestial horizon and bears 260° per standard magnetic compass. Variation in the area is 19° W. The chronometer reads 10h 44m 36s and is 03m 24s slow. What is the deviation of the standard magnetic compass?

A. 4.3° E
B. 4.3° W
C. 5.1° E
D. 5.1° W

Answers to the USCG Amplitude Questions

01651 C
01652 B
01653 C
01654 B
01655 B
01656 C
01657 D
01658 C
01659 B
01660 C
01661 B
01663 A
01664 A
01665 A
01666 D
01667 A
01668 D

01669 D
01670 C
01671 A
01672 C
01673 A
01674 A
01675 A
01676 D
01677 D
01678 A
01679 B
01680 B
01681 D
01682 B
01776 D
01777 A
01778 C

Celestial Problems
Sight Reduction Amplitude

Problem # (USCG) (1651)				Chapter		

Date 23 Oct		**Time**			**LAT 21° 13.0' N**		
	ZT	17	**CT**	07:21:46	**LONG 152° 18.0' E**		
	ZD	- 10	**CE**	+ 1:32	**GYRO**		**COMPASS**
	GMT	07	**CCT**	07:28:20		**T**	257.8
DECLINATION			**GMT**	07:28:20	**T**	**V**	- 5.0 E
DEC		S 11° 23.8'			**E**	**M**	252.8
d (+0.9)		+0.5'			**G**	**D**	**5.9 W**
DEC		S 11° 24.3'				**C**	258.7

Calculating True Bearing	Table 28 or

$$\sin^{-1}\left(\frac{\sin Dec}{\cos Lat}\right) = Amplitude$$

$$\sin^{-1}\left(\frac{\sin 11 - 24.3}{\cos 21 - 13}\right) = 12.246$$

pcs/pgc	259
Correction (±)	-0.3
psc/pgc	258.7

Correcting Amplitude to TRUE	
270 / 090	270
± Amplitude	S 12.2 W
TRUE	**257.8**

```
        N
    -   |   +
270 ――――――――――― 090
    +   |   -
        S
```

```
      +   |   -
270 ――――――――――― 090
      -   |   +
```

NOTE:

Alexander F. Hickethier MBA © 2012

Celestial Problems
Sight Reduction Amplitude

Problem # (USCG) (1652)		Chapter	

Date 22 October 1981 Time

			LAT	21° 51.0' S		
ZT	1800	**CT**	01:01:25	**LONG** 076° 24.0' E		
ZD	-5	**CE**	- 1:15	**GYRO**		**COMPASS**
GMT	1300	**CCT**	01:00:10		**T**	258.0
DECLINATION		**GMT**	13:00:10	**T**	**V**	- 2.0E
DEC	S 11° 08.0'			**E**	**M**	256.0
d (+0.9)	0			**G**	**D**	0.3W
DEC	S 11° 08.0'				**C**	256.3

Calculating True Bearing	**Table 28 or**

$$\sin^{-1}\left(\frac{\sin Dec}{\cos Lat}\right) = Amplitude$$

pcs/pgc	256.0
Correction (±)	+0.3
psc/pgc	256.3

$$\sin^{-1}\left(\frac{\sin 11-08}{\cos 21-51}\right) = 12.007$$

Correcting Amplitude to TRUE

270 / 090	270
± Amplitude	S 12.0 W
TRUE	**258.0**

```
            N
       -  |  +
270  -------------  090
       +  |  -
            S
```

NOTE:

```
       +  |  -
270  -------------  090
       -  |  +
```

Celestial Problems
Sight Reduction Amplitude

Problem #	**(USCG)**	**(1653)**		Chapter	

Date 28 Sep		**Time**			**LAT** 24° 12.0' S

					LONG 085° 25.0' E
	ZT	0500	**CT**	11:29:42	
	ZD	6	**CE**	+ 3:30	**GYRO**	**COMPASS**
	GMT	2300	**CCT**	11:33:12		**T** 092.1
	DECLINATION		**GMT**	23:33:12	**T**	**V** + 4.0 W
DEC		S 1° 52.9'	27 SEP		**E**	**M** 096.1
d (+1.0)		+0.5'			**G**	**D** 2.4 E
DEC		S 1° 53.4'				**C** 093.7

Calculating True Bearing	Table 28 or

$$\sin^{-1}\left(\frac{\sin Dec}{\cos Lat}\right) = Amplitude$$

pcs/pgc	094
Correction (±)	-0.3
psc/pgc	093.7

$$\sin^{-1}\left(\frac{\sin 1-53.4}{\cos 24-12}\right) = 2.072$$

Correcting Amplitude to TRUE

270 / 090	90
± Amplitude	S 52.1 E
TRUE	**092.1**

```
        N
      - | +
270  ---+---  090
      + | -
        S
```

```
      + | -
270  ---+---  090
      - | +
```

NOTE:

Celestial Problems
Sight Reduction Amplitude

Problem # (USCG) (1654)			Chapter		

Date 28 Sep		**Time**			

LAT 27° 16.7' S
LONG 113° 27.2' W

	ZT	1700	CT	01:17:26	
	ZD	+8	CE	+ 01:49	**GYRO** / **COMPASS**
	GMT	2500	CCT	01:19:15	T — 267.4
	DECLINATION		GMT	01:19:15	T / V + 6.0 W
DEC		S 2° 18.2'			E / M 273.4
d (+ 1.0)		+.3'			G / D 0.4 E
DEC		S 2° 18.5'			C 273.0

Calculating True Bearing

$$\sin^{-1}\left(\frac{\sin Dec}{\cos Lat}\right) = Amplitude$$

$$\sin^{-1}\left(\frac{\sin 2 - 18.5}{\cos 27.16.7}\right) = 2.597$$

Table 28 or

pcs/pgc

Correction (±) _____

psc/pgc

Correcting Amplitude to TRUE

270 / 090	270
± Amplitude	S 52.6 W
TRUE	**267.4**

270 + / - | - / + 090

270 - / + | + / - 090 N ... S

NOTE:

Alexander F. Hickethier MBA © 2012

Celestial Problems
Sight Reduction Amplitude

Problem # (USCG) (1655)					Chapter		

Date 22 Oct		Time			LAT 21° 51.0' S		
	ZT	1800	CT	01:01{25	LONG 076-24.0' E		
	ZD	-5	CE	- 01:15	GYRO	COMPASS	
	GMT	1300	CCT	01:00:10		T	258.0
	DECLINATION		GMT	13:00:10	T	V	- 2.0 E
DEC		S 11° 08.0'			E	M	256.0
d (+.9)		0			G	D	0.3 W
DEC		S 11° 08.0'				C	256.3

Calculating True Bearing	Table 28 or

$$\sin^{-1}\left(\frac{\sin Dec}{\cos Lat}\right) = Amplitude$$

$$\sin^{-1}\left(\frac{\sin 11 - 08.0}{\cos\ 21 - 51}\right) = 12.00$$

pcs/pgc	256.0
Correction (±)	+0.3
psc/pgc	256.3

Correcting Amplitude to TRUE

270 / 090	270
± Amplitude	S12.0 W
TRUE	**258.0**

```
        N
      - | +
270 ——————— 090
      + | -
        S
```

```
      + | -
270 ——————— 090
      - | +
```

NOTE:

Celestial Problems
Sight Reduction Amplitude

Problem # (USCG) (1656)				Chapter		

Date 5 Sep		**Time**			**LAT** 23° 17.0' S	
	ZT	1700	**CT**	07:49:26	**LONG** 154° 35.0' E	

	ZT	1700	**CT**	07:49:26	**GYRO**		**COMPASS**	
	ZD	-10	**CE**	- 1:52			**T**	277.4
	GMT	0700	**CCT**	07:47:34			**V**	+ 3.0 W
DECLINATION			**GMT**	07:47:34	**T**		**V**	+ 3.0 W
DEC		N 6° 49.3'			**E**		**M**	280.4
d (-0.9)		-0.6'			**G**		**D**	5.1 E
DEC		N 6° 48.7'					**C**	275.3

Calculating True Bearing	**Table 28 or**

$$\sin^{-1}\left(\frac{\sin Dec}{\cos Lat}\right) = Amplitude$$

pcs/pgc	275.0
Correction (±)	+0.3
psc/pgc	275.3

$$\sin^{-1}\left(\frac{\sin 6 - 48.7}{\cos 23 - 17}\right) = 7.42$$

Correcting Amplitude to TRUE

270 / 090	270
± Amplitude	N 7.4 W
TRUE	**277.4**

270 $\dfrac{\quad + \quad | \quad - \quad}{\quad - \quad | \quad + \quad}$ 090

270 $\dfrac{\quad - \quad | \quad + \quad}{\quad + \quad | \quad - \quad}$ 090

N / S

NOTE:

CG=5.4 E

Celestial Problems
Sight Reduction Amplitude

Problem # (USCG) (1657)	Chapter

Date 24 Aug	Time			LAT 26° 49.4' N

	ZT	0400	CT	07:55:06	LONG 146° 19.4' E

	ZD	-9	CE	- 1:11	GYRO		COMPASS
	GMT	1900	CCT	07:53:55		T	067.3
DECLINATION			GMT	19:54:05	T	V	+ 15.0 W
DEC		N 11° 17.0'	23 Aug		E	M	082.3
d (-0.9)		-0.8'			G	D	1.7 W
DEC		N 11° 16.2'				C	084.0

Calculating True Bearing	Table 28 or

$$\sin^{-1}\left(\frac{\sin Dec}{\cos Lat}\right) = Amplitude$$

$$\sin^{-1}\left(\frac{\sin 11 - 16.2}{\cos 26 - 49.4}\right) = 16.650$$

pcs/pgc

Correction (±) _____

psc/pgc

Correcting Amplitude to TRUE

270 / 090	90
± Amplitude	N 12.7 E
TRUE	**067.3**

```
       +  |  -
270 ------|------ 090
       -  |  +
```

```
        N
     -  |  +
270 ----|---- 090
     +  |  -
        S
```

NOTE:

Celestial Problems
Sight Reduction Amplitude

Problem # (USCG) (1658)	Chapter

Date 23 Aug	Time			LAT 24° 07.0' N

				LAT	24° 07.0' N		
	ZT	0600	CT	08:56:19	LONG 136° 16.0' E		
	ZD	-9	CE	- 2:34	GYRO	COMPASS	
	GMT	2100	CCT	08:55:45		T	077.3
DECLINATION			GMT	20:55:45	T	V	+ 2.0 W
DEC		N 11° 36.5'			E	M	079.3
d (-0.8)		-0.7'	22 Aug		G	D	4.8 E
DEC		N 11° 35.8'				C	074.5

Calculating True Bearing	Table 28 or

$$\sin^{-1}\left(\frac{\sin Dec}{\cos Lat}\right) = Amplitude$$

$$\sin^{-1}\left(\frac{\sin 11 - 35.8}{\cos\ 24 - 07}\right) = 12.723$$

pcs/pgc

Correction (±) _____

psc/pgc

Correcting Amplitude to TRUE

270 / 090	90
± Amplitude	N 12.7 E
TRUE	**077.3**

```
        +  |  -
270 ———————————— 090
        -  |  +
```

```
        N
        -  | +
270 ———————————— 090
        +  | -
        S
```

NOTE:

Alexander F. Hickethier MBA © 2012

Celestial Problems
Sight Reduction Amplitude

Problem #	(USCG) (1659)			Chapter	

Date 15 July		**Time**				

					LAT	**22° 19.0' N**	
					LONG	**154° 37.0' W**	

	ZT	1800	**CT**	04:45:19			
	ZD	+10	**CE**	+ 1:56	**GYRO**		**COMPASS**
	GMT	0400	**CCT**	04:47:15		**T**	293.3
DECLINATION			**GMT**	04:47:15	**T**	**V**	+ 7.5 W
DEC		N 21° 28.6'			**E**	**M**	300.8
d (-0.4)		-0.3'	16 July		**G**	**D**	3.1 E
DEC		N 21° 28.3'				**C**	297.7

Calculating True Bearing	**Table 28 or**

$$\sin^{-1}\left(\frac{\sin Dec}{\cos Lat}\right) = Amplitude$$

pcs/pgc	298.0
Correction (±)	-0.3
psc/pgc	297.7

$$\sin^{-1}\left(\frac{\sin\ 21-28.3}{\cos\ \ 22-19}\right) = 23.3.8$$

Correcting Amplitude to TRUE	

270 / 090	270
± Amplitude	N 23.3 W
TRUE	**293.3**

```
        +    -
270 ---------+--------- 090
        -    +
```

```
         N
        -  +
270 ---------+--------- 090
        +  -
         S
```

NOTE:

Celestial Problems
Sight Reduction Amplitude

Problem # (USCG) (1660)					Chapter		

Date 23 June   **Time**

	ZT	0700	CT	02:14:39	**LAT 21° 39.0' S** **LONG 106° 28.0' W**		
	ZD	+ 7	CE	+ 1:43	**GYRO**		**COMPASS**
	GMT	1400	CCT	02:16:22		T	064.7
	DECLINATION		GMT	14:16:22	T	V	+ 9.0 W
DEC		N 23° 25.5'			E	M	073.7
d (0)		0'			G	D	4.3 W
DEC		N 23° 25.5'				C	078.0

Calculating True Bearing	**Table 28 or**

$$\sin^{-1}\left(\frac{\sin Dec}{\cos Lat}\right) = Amplitude$$

pcs/pgc

Correction (±) _____

psc/pgc

$$\sin^{-1}\left(\frac{\sin 23 - 25.5}{\cos 21 - 34}\right) = 25.323$$

Correcting Amplitude to TRUE

270 / 090	90
± Amplitude	N 25.3 E
TRUE	**064.7**

270 + / - 090 (diagram, top), - / + (bottom)

270 −|+ 090 (diagram) +|−

N / S diagram: 270 − + / + − 090

NOTE:

Alexander F. Hickethier MBA © 2012

Celestial Problems
Sight Reduction Amplitude

Problem # (USCG) (1661)	Chapter

Date 11 May   **Time**

LAT   28° 13.7' N
LONG   168° 36.3' E

ZT	1800	CT	07:13:19	**GYRO**		**COMPASS**
ZD	-11	CE	+ 2:56		T	290.4
GMT	0700	CCT	07:16:15	T	V	- 13.0 E
DECLINATION		GMT	07:16:15	E	M	277.4
DEC	N 17° 52.5'			G	D	5.6 W
d (+0.6	+0.2'				C	283.0
DEC	N 17° 52.7'					

Calculating True Bearing	Table 28 or

$$\sin^{-1}\left(\frac{\sin Dec}{\cos Lat}\right) = Amplitude$$

pcs/pgc

Correction (±) _____

psc/pgc

$$\sin^{-1}\left(\frac{\sin 17 - 52.7}{\cos\ 28 - 13.7}\right) = 20.391$$

Correcting Amplitude to TRUE

270 / 090	270
± Amplitude	N 20.4 W
TRUE	**290.4**

```
          N
        - | +
270  -------------  090
        + | -
          S
```

```
        + | -
270  -------------  090
        - | +
```

NOTE:

Alexander F. Hickethier MBA © 2012

Celestial Problems
Sight Reduction Amplitude

Problem # (USCG) (1663)				Chapter	

Date 7 Apr		Time			**LAT 27° 42.0' N**	

	ZT	0600	**CT**	02:10:17	**LONG 114° 03.0' W**	
	ZD	+8	**CE**	+ 1:52	**GYRO**	**COMPASS**
	GMT	1400	**CCT**	02:12:09		**T** 082.2
	DECLINATION		**GMT**	14:12:09	**T**	**V** - 8.0 E
DEC		N 6° 55.9'			**E**	**M** 074.2
d (+0.9		+0.2'			**G**	**D** 1.8 W
DEC		N 6° 56.1'				**C** 076.0

Calculating True Bearing	**Table 28 or**

$$\sin^{-1}\left(\frac{\sin Dec}{\cos Lat}\right) = Amplitude$$

pcs/pgc

Correction (±) _____

psc/pgc

$$\sin^{-1}\left(\frac{\sin 6 - 56.1}{\cos 27 - 42}\right) = 7.837$$

Correcting Amplitude to TRUE

270 / 090   090

± Amplitude   N 7.8 E

TRUE

```
            N
        -   |   +
 270  ———————————  090
        +   |   -
            S
```

NOTE:

```
        +   |   -
 270  ———————————  090
        -   |   +
```

Celestial Problems
Sight Reduction Amplitude

Problem #	(USCG)	(1664)		Chapter	

Date	**10 Feb**		**Time**			**LAT**	**25° 32.0' N**		

	ZT	0600	**CT**	09:43:25	**LONG**	**135° 15.0' E**		

	ZD	-9	**CE**	- 3:20	**GYRO**		**COMPASS**	
	GMT	2100	**CCT**	09:40:05		**T**	106.1	
DECLINATION			**GMT**	21:40:05	**T**	**V**	+ 4.5 W	
DEC		S 14° 29.1'			**E**	**M**	110.6	
d (-0.8		-0.5'	9 FEB		**G**	**D**	1.6 E	
DEC		S 14° 28.6'				**C**	109.0	

Calculating True Bearing	**Table 28 or**

$$\sin^{-1}\left(\frac{\sin Dec}{\cos Lat}\right) = Amplitude$$

pcs/pgc

Correction (±) _____

psc/pgc

$$\sin^{-1}\left(\frac{\sin 17 - 28.6}{\cos \ 25 - 32}\right) = 16.083$$

Correcting Amplitude to TRUE

270 / 090   090

± Amplitude   S 16.1 E

TRUE   **106.1**

```
        N
     -  |  +
270 ───┼─── 090
     +  |  -
        S
```

```
     +  |  -
270 ───┼─── 090
     -  |  +
```

NOTE:

Celestial Problems
Sight Reduction Amplitude

Problem # (USCG) (1665)			Chapter		

Date 11 Jan		Time			LAT 24° 30.0' N

LONG 122° 02.0' W

	ZT	0656	CT	02:52:48	GYRO	COMPASS
	ZD	+ 8	CE	+ 2:12		T 114.0
	GMT	1455	CCT	02:55:00	T	V - 11.6 E
	DECLINATION		GMT	14:55:00		M 102.4
DEC		S 21°-45.4'			E	D 1.4 E
d (-0.4)		-0.4'			G	C 101.0
DEC		S 21° 45.0'				

Calculating True Bearing

$$\sin^{-1}\left(\frac{\sin Dec}{\cos Lat}\right) = Amplitude$$

$$\sin^{-1}\left(\frac{\sin 21-45}{\cos 24-30}\right) = 24.030$$

Table 28 or

pcs/pgc

Correction (±) _____

psc/pgc

Correcting Amplitude to TRUE

270 / 090	90
± Amplitude	S 24 E
TRUE	**114**

NOTE:

Alexander F. Hickethier MBA © 2012

Celestial Problems
Sight Reduction Amplitude

Problem # (USCG) (1666)				Chapter			

Date 23 Oct		Time			LAT 27° 36.0' S		

LONG 96° 16.0' W

	ZT	1722	CT	11:24:19			
	ZD	+6	CE	+ 1:43	**GYRO**		**COMPASS**
	GMT	2322	CCT	11:22:36		T	256.8
DECLINATION			GMT	23:22:36	T	V	- 14.0 E
DEC		S 11° 37.8'			E	M	242.8
d (+0.9)		+0.3'			G	D	3.2 W
DEC		S 11° 38.1'				C	246.0

Calculating True Bearing	**Table 28 or**

$$\sin^{-1}\left(\frac{\sin Dec}{\cos Lat}\right) = Amplitude$$

pcs/pgc

Correction (±) _____

$$\sin^{-1}\left(\frac{\sin 11-38.1}{\cos 27-36}\right) = 13.154$$

psc/pgc

Correcting Amplitude to TRUE		
270 / 090	270	
± Amplitude	S 13.2 W	
TRUE	**256.8**	

```
        N
      - | +
270 ------|------ 090
      + | -
        S
```

NOTE:

```
      + | -
270 ------|------ 090
      - | +
```

Alexander F. Hickethier MBA © 2012

Celestial Problems
Sight Reduction Amplitude

Problem # (USCG) (1667)					Chapter		

Date 8 Nov		**Time 0632**			**LAT 27° 06.0' N**		
	ZT	0632	**CT**	12:39:20	**LONG 90° 36.0' W**		
	ZD	+06	**CE**	+ 3:20	**GYRO**		**COMPASS**
	GMT	1232	**CCT**	12:42:50		**T**	108.8
	DECLINATION		**GMT**	12:42:50	**T**	**V**	- 3.0 E
DEC		S 16° 37.6'			**E**	**M**	105.8
d (+7)		+.5'			**G**	**D**	.8 E
DEC		S 16° 38.1'				**C**	105.0

Calculating True Bearing	**Table 28 or**

$$\sin^{-1}\left(\frac{\sin Dec}{\cos Lat}\right) = Amplitude$$

$$\sin^{-1}\left(\frac{\sin\ 16-38.1}{\cos\ 20-06}\right) = 18.75$$

pcs/pgc

Correction (±) _____

psc/pgc

Correcting Amplitude to TRUE

270 / 090	090
± Amplitude	S 18.8 E
TRUE	**108.8**

```
        +  |  -
270  ---------  090
        -  |  +
```

```
        N
        -  |  +
270  ---------  090
        +  |  -
        S
```

NOTE:

Alexander F. Hickethier MBA © 2012

Celestial Problems
Sight Reduction Amplitude

Problem # (USCG) (1668)			Chapter		

Date 20 Jun		Time 1955		LAT 52° 38.9' N	
	ZT	1955	CT	19:55:00	LONG 003° 42.7' E
	ZD	0	CE	0	**GYRO** / **COMPASS**
	GMT	1955	CCT	19:55:00	T
	DECLINATION		GMT	19:55:00	T 311.0 / V
DEC		N 23° 26.3'			E - 1.3 E / M
d (0)		0			G 309.7 / D
DEC		N 23° 26.3'			C

Calculating True Bearing	Table 28 or

$$\sin^{-1}\left(\frac{\sin Dec}{\cos Lat}\right) = Amplitude$$

$$\sin^{-1}\left(\frac{\sin 23 - 26.3}{\cos 52 - 38.9}\right) = 40.96$$

pcs/pgc	311.0
Correction (±)	-1.3
psc/pgc	309.7

Correcting Amplitude to TRUE

270 / 090	270
± Amplitude	N 41 W
TRUE	**311**

```
         N
     -  |  +
270 ─────────── 090
     +  |  -
         S
```

NOTE: Comparing Gyro to Compass

```
G  352.0        T  353.3
E     1.3 E     V     6.0 W
T  353.3        M  359.3
                D     1.3 E
                C  358.0
```

```
        +  |  -
270 ─────────── 090
        -  |  +
```

Alexander F. Hickethier MBA © 2012

Celestial Problems
Sight Reduction Amplitude

Problem # (USCG) (1669)					Chapter		

Date 19 Jun			Time 0523		LAT 25° 12.0' N		
	ZT	0523	**CT**	01:21:58	**LONG 123° 14.0' W**		
	ZD	+08	**CE**	+ 01:18	**GYRO**		**COMPASS**
	GMT	1323	**CCT**	01:23:16		**T**	063.9
	DECLINATION		**GMT**	13:23:16	**T**	**V**	- 15.0 E
DEC		N 23° 25.6'			**E**	**M**	048.9
d (0)		0			**G**	**D**	3.4 W
DEC		N 23° 25.6'				**C**	052.3

Calculating True Bearing	Table 28 or

$$\sin^{-1}\left(\frac{\sin Dec}{\cos Lat}\right) = Amplitude$$

pcs/pgc	052.0
Correction (±)	.3
psc/pgc	052.3

$$\sin^{-1}\left(\frac{\sin 23° 25.6}{\cos 25° 12}\right) = 26.06518$$

Correcting Amplitude to TRUE

270 / 090	090
± Amplitude	N 26.1 E
TRUE	**63.9**

```
        N
    -  |  +
270 ――――――――― 090
    +  |  -
        S
```

```
      +  |  -
270 ――――――――― 090
      -  |  +
```

NOTE:

Celestial Problems
Sight Reduction Amplitude

Problem # (USCG) (1670)					Chapter		

Date 10 Aug		Time			LAT 52° 07.0' N		
	ZT	0426	CT	07:24:19	LONG 142° 16.0' E		
	ZD	-9	CE	- 2:34	GYRO	COMPASS	
	GMT	1926	CCT	07:21:45		T	063.8
	DECLINATION		GMT	19:21:45	T	V	+ 12.0 W
DEC		N 15° 43.1'	9 Aug.		E	M	075.8
d (-0.7)		-0.3'			G	D	1.3 E
DEC		N 15° 42.9'				C	074.5

Calculating True Bearing	Table 28 or

$$\sin^{-1}\left(\frac{\sin Dec}{\cos Lat}\right) = Amplitude$$

$$\sin^{-1}\left(\frac{\sin 15 - 42.9}{\cos 52 - 07}\right) = 26.173$$

pcs/pgc

Correction (±) _____

psc/pgc

Correcting Amplitude to TRUE		
270 / 090	90	
± Amplitude	N 26.2 E	
TRUE	**063.8**	

```
        +   -
270  ─────┼─────  090
        -   +
```

```
        -   +
270  ─────┼─────  090
        +   -
```

N

S

NOTE:

Alexander F. Hickethier MBA © 2012

Celestial Problems
Sight Reduction Amplitude

Problem # (USCG) (1671)					Chapter	

Date 9 May		Time 1809				

					LAT 48° 13.7' N	
	ZT	1809	CT	07:13:10	LONG 168° 36.3' E	
	ZD	-11	CE	- 2:56	GYRO	COMPASS
	GMT	0709	CCT	07:10:23		T	296.6
	DECLINATION		GMT	07:10:23	T	V	- 13.0E
DEC		N 17° 21.1'			E	M	283.6
d (+0.7)		+ 0.1'			G	D	.1 W
DEC		N 17° 21.2'				C	283.7

Calculating True Bearing	Table 28 or

$$\sin^{-1}\left(\frac{\sin Dec}{\cos Lat}\right) = Amplitude$$

pcs/pgc

Correction (±) _____

psc/pgc

$$\sin^{-1}\left(\frac{\sin 17 - 21.2}{\cos 48 - 13.7}\right) = \text{N 26.6 W}$$

Correcting Amplitude to TRUE

270 / 090	270
± Amplitude	N 26.6 W
TRUE	**296.6**

```
         +    -
270 ───────┼─────── 090
         -    +
```

```
          N
       -  │  +
270  ─────┼───── 090
       +  │  -
          S
```

NOTE:

Note: USCG answer is .1

Celestial Problems
Sight Reduction Amplitude

Problem # (USCG) (1672)	Chapter

Date 11 May			Time 1839		LAT 17° 30.0' N

LONG 063° 55.0' W

	ZT	1839	CT	10:37:10	
	ZD	+4	CE	+ 2:08	**GYRO**
	GMT	2239	CCT	10:39:18	

	GYRO		COMPASS	
		T	288.9	

	DECLINATION		GMT	22:39:18	T		V	+ 10.5 W
DEC		N 18° 02.1'			E		M	299.4
d (+0.6)		+0.4'			G		D	1.6 W
DEC		N 18° 02.5'					C	301.0

Calculating True Bearing	Table 28 or

$$\sin^{-1}\left(\frac{\sin Dec}{\cos Lat}\right) = Amplitude$$

$$\sin^{-1}\left(\frac{\sin 18 - 02.5}{\cos 17 - 30}\right) = 18.949$$

pcs/pgc

Correction (±) _____

psc/pgc

Correcting Amplitude to TRUE

270 / 090	270
± Amplitude	N 18.9 W
TRUE	**288.9**

```
        N
     -  |  +
270 ---------- 090
     +  |  -
        S
```

NOTE:

```
      +  |  -
270 ---------- 090
      -  |  +
```

Alexander F. Hickethier MBA © 2012

Celestial Problems
Sight Reduction Amplitude

Problem # (USCG) (1673)			Chapter		

Date 17 Apr		**Time**		**LAT** 21° 00.0' S	

				LAT 21° 00.0' S **LONG** 078° 30.0' W	
	ZT	0500	**CT**	10:59:24	

				GYRO		**COMPASS**	
	ZD	+5	**CE**	- 1:24		**T**	078.2
	GMT	10.00	**CCT**	10:58:00		**V**	+2.0 W
DECLINATION			**GMT**	10:58:00	**T**	**M**	080.7
DEC		N 10° 30.8'			**E**	**D**	2.0 W
d (+0.9)		+0.9'			**G**	**C**	082.7
DEC		N 10° 31.7'					

Calculating True Bearing	Table 28

$$\sin^{-1}\left(\frac{\sin Dec}{\cos Lat}\right) = Amplitude$$

pcs/pgc

Correction (±) _____

psc/pgc

$$\sin^{-1}\left(\frac{\sin 10 - 31.7}{\cos 21 - 00}\right) = 11.3$$

Correcting Amplitude to TRUE

270 / 090   090

± Amplitude   N 11.3 E

TRUE   **078.7**

N
```
        -  |  +
270  ————————  090
        +  |  -
        S
```

```
        +  |  -
270  ————————  090
        -  |  +
```

NOTE:

Celestial Problems
Sight Reduction Amplitude

Problem #   (USCG)   (1674) | Chapter

Date	4 July		Time	1722			LAT	34° 30.0' S

LAT   34° 30.0' S
LONG: 174° 48.0' E

	ZT	1722	CT	05:21:48				
	ZD	-12	CE	- 2:01		**GYRO**		**COMPASS**
	GMT	05-22	**CCT**	05:19:47			**T**	298.2
	DECLINATION		**GMT**	05:19:47	**T**		**V**	- 7.2 E
DEC		N 22° 53.2'			**E**		**M**	281.0
d (-0.2)		-0.1'			**G**		**D**	1.5 W
DEC		N 22° 53.1'					**C**	282.5

Calculating True Bearing	Table 28 or

$$\sin^{-1}\left(\frac{\sin Dec}{\cos Lat}\right) = Amplitude$$

$$\sin^{-1}\left(\frac{\sin 22-53.1}{\cos 34-30}\right) = 28.2$$

pcs/pgc   282
Correction (±)   +0.5
psc/pgc   282.5

Correcting Amplitude to TRUE

270 / 090   270
± Amplitude   N 28.2 W
TRUE   **298.2**

```
        N
      -  |  +
270  ---+---  090
      +  |  -
        S
```

```
      +  |  -
270  ---+---  090
      -  |  +
```

NOTE:

Celestial Problems
Sight Reduction Amplitude

Problem # (USCG) (1675)					Chapter	

Date 28 Nov   **Time 0652**

LAT   37° 30.0' N
LONG   124° 12.0' W

	ZT	0652	CT	14:54:18			
	ZD	+8	CE	- 2:06	**GYRO**		**COMPASS**
	GMT	1452	CCT	14:52:12		T	117.3
	DECLINATION		GMT	14:52:12	T	V	- 16.3 E
DEC		S 21° 21.1'			E	M	101.0
d (+0.4)		+ 0.4'			G	D	2.6 W
DEC		S 21° 21.2'				C	103.6

Calculating True Bearing	**Table 28 or**

$$\sin^{-1}\left(\frac{\sin Dec}{\cos Lat}\right) = Amplitude$$

$$\sin^{-1}\left(\frac{\sin 21-21.2}{\cos 37-30}\right) = 27.3$$

pcs/pgc	103.0
Correction (±)	+0.6
psc/pgc	103.6

Correcting Amplitude to TRUE

270 / 090	90
± Amplitude	S 27.3 E
TRUE	**117.3**

```
          N
       -  |  +
270  ———————  090
       +  |  -
          S
```

NOTE:

```
       +  |  -
270  ———————  090
       -  |  +
```

Alexander F. Hickethier MBA © 2012

Celestial Problems
Sight Reduction Amplitude

Problem # (USCG) (1676)					Chapter		

Date	10 Jun		Time				
					LAT	27° 07.0' N	
					LONG	092° 10.0' W	
	ZT	0519	**CT**	11:17:32			
	ZD	+6	**CE**	+ 1:18	**GYRO**		**COMPASS**
	GMT	1119	**CCT**	11:18:50		**T**	063.9
	DECLINATION		**GMT**	11:18:50	**T**	**V**	- 4.8 E
DEC		N 23-01.3'			**E**	**M**	059.1
d (+0.2)		+0.1'			**G**	**D**	4.9 W
DEC		N 23-01.4'				**C**	064.0

Calculating True Bearing	Table 28 or

$$\sin^{-1}\left(\frac{\sin Dec}{\cos Lat}\right) = Amplitude$$

pcs/pgc	063.6
Correction (±)	+0.4
psc/pgc	064.0

$$\sin^{-1}\left(\frac{\sin 23 - 01.4}{\cos 27 - 07}\right) = 26.1$$

Correcting Amplitude to TRUE	

270 / 090   090

± Amplitude   N 26.1 E

TRUE   **063.9**

```
        +   |   -
270  ------+------  090
        -   |   +
```

```
            N
        -   |   +
270  ------+------  090
        +   |   -
            S
```

NOTE:

Celestial Problems
Sight Reduction Amplitude

Problem # (USCG) (1677)		Chapter	

Date 23 Aug   **Time 0604**

					LAT 16° 42.3' S	
	ZT	0604	CT	08:04:00	LONG 028° 19.3' W	
	ZD	+2	CE		**GYRO**	**COMPASS**
	GMT	0804	CCT	08:04:00	T 078.0	T
	DECLINATION		GMT	08:04:00	E - 2.0 E	V
DEC		N 11° 27.2'			G 076.0	M
d (-0.9))		-0.1'				D
DEC		N 11° 27.1'				C

Calculating True Bearing	**Table 28 or**

$$\sin^{-1}\left(\frac{\sin Dec}{\cos Lat}\right) = Amplitude$$

$$\sin^{-1}\left(\frac{\sin 11-27.1}{\cos 16-42.3}\right) = 11.963$$

pcs/pgc

Correction (±) _____

psc/pgc

Correcting Amplitude to TRUE

270 / 090	090
± Amplitude	N 12 E
TRUE	**078**

```
        N
     -  |  +
270 ――――――――― 090
     +  |  -
        S
```

270 $\dfrac{+\ \ |\ \ -}{-\ \ |\ \ +}$ 090

NOTE: Comparison of Gyro to Compass

T 145.0	T 145.0
E - 2.0 E	V + 23.0 W
G 143.0	M 168.0
	D - 1.0 E
	C 167.0

Celestial Problems
Sight Reduction Amplitude

Problem # (USCG) (1678)	Chapter

Date 2 Jan.		Time 1822			LAT 21° 42.0' S

LONG 039° 12.0' W

	ZT	1822	CT	10:44:36		
	ZD	+3	CE	+ 03:24	GYRO	COMPASS
	GMT	2122	CCT	10:48:00		T	245.3
	DECLINATION		GMT	22:48:00	T	V	+ 19.0 W
DEC		S 22° 51.5'			E	M	264.3
d (-0.2)		-0.2'			G	D	5.7 W
DEC		S 22° 51.3'				C	260.0

Calculating True Bearing	Table 28 or

$$\sin^{-1}\left(\frac{\sin Dec}{\cos Lat}\right) = Amplitude$$

$$\sin^{-1}\left(\frac{\sin 22 - 51.3}{\cos 21 - 42.5}\right) = 24.71$$

pcs/pgc

Correction (±) _____

psc/pgc

Correcting Amplitude to TRUE

270 / 090	270
± Amplitude	S 24.7 W
TRUE	245.3

```
        N
     -  |  +
270 ───────── 090
     +  |  -
        S
```

```
      +  |  -
270 ───────── 090
      -  |  +
```

NOTE:

Alexander F. Hickethier MBA © 2012

Rev. December 19, 2012

USCG AZIMUTH PROBLEMS WORKED-OUT

With

EXTRACTS FROM THE AMERICAN PRACTICAL NAVIGATOR (CHAPTER 17 – AZIMUTH)

By Alexander F. Hickethier MBA

and

DR. Hu Jia-Shen

3-1

AZIMUTH

Mariners may use Pub 229, Sight Reduction Tables for Marine Navigation to compute the Sun's azimuth. They compare the computed azimuth to the azimuth measured with the compass to determine compass error. In computing an azimuth, interpolate the tabular azimuth angle for the difference between the table arguments and the actual values of declination, latitude, and local hour angle. Do this triple interpolation of the azimuth angle as follows:

1. Enter the Sight Reduction Tables with the nearest integral values of declination, latitude, and local hour angle. For each of these arguments, extract a base azimuth angle.

2. Reenter the tables with the same latitude and LHA arguments but with the declination argument 1° greater or less than the base declination argument, depending upon whether the actual declination is greater or less than the base argument. Record the difference between the respondent azimuth angle and the base azimuth angle and label it as the azimuth angle difference (Z Diff.).

3. Reenter the tables with the base declination and LHA arguments, but with the latitude argument 1^0 greater or less than the base latitude argument, depending upon whether the actual (usually DR) latitude is greater or less than the base argument. Record the Z Diff. for the increment of latitude.

4. Reenter the tables with the base declination and latitude arguments, but with the LHA argument $1°$ greater or less than the base LHA argument, depending upon whether the actual LHA is greater or less than the base argument. Record the Z Diff. for the increment of LHA.

5. Correct the base azimuth angle for each increment.

Example:

In DR latitude 33° 24.0 'N, the azimuth of the Sun is 096.5° pgc. At the time of the observation, the declination of the Sun is 20° 13.8'N; the local hour angle of the Sun is 316° 41.2'. Determine compass error.

Example Worked-out

LHA	316° 41.2'	DEC	N 20° 13.8'	LAT	33°24.0' N

T	097.7
E	1.2 E
G	096.5°

LHA	316° 41.2'	DEC	N 20° 13.8'	LAT	33° 24.0' N
		Publication 229			
Z (316)	097.1°	Z (20)	097.1°	Z (33)	097.1°
Z (317)	097.8 °	Z (21)	095.7°	Z (34)	098.2°
d	+ .7	d	−1.4°	d	+1.1°
Inc Dec (X)	41.2'	Inc Dec (X)	13.8'	Inc Dec (X)	24.0'
Inv	60	Inv	60	Inv	60
correction	- .5	correction	- .3	correction	+ .4
Base Z	097.1°	Z to ZN	097.7		
tcorr	+ .6	ZN = Z			
Z	097.7				

Note: SAME

Figure 1 Azimuth by Pub. No. 229

Solution:

See Figure 1 Enter the actual value of declination, DR latitude, and LHA. Round each argument to the Next Lower whole degree. Enter the Sight Reduction Tables with these whole degree arguments and extract the base azimuth value for these rounded off arguments. Record the base azimuth value in the table.

As the first step in the triple interpolation process, increase the value of declination by 1° (to 21°) because the actual declination value was greater than the base declination. Enter the Sight Reduction Tables with the following arguments:

    (1)Declination =   21°;
    (2)DR Latitude =   33°;
    (3)LHA =   316°.

Record the tabulated azimuth for these arguments.

3-4

As the second step in the triple interpolation process, increase the value of latitude by 1° to 34° because the actual DR latitude was greater than the base latitude. Enter the Sight Reduction Tables with the following arguments:

(1)   Declination =   20°;
(2)   DR Latitude =   34°;
(3)   LHA =   316°.

Record the tabulated azimuth for these arguments.

As the third and final step in the triple interpolation process, increase the value of LHA to 317° because the actual LHA value was smaller than the base LHA. Enter the Sight Reduction Tables with the following arguments:

(1)   Declination =   20°;
(2)   DR Latitude =   33°;
(3)   LHA =   316°.

Record the tabulated azimuth for these arguments.

Calculate the Z Difference by subtracting the base azimuth from the tabulated azimuth. Be careful to carry the correct sign.

Z Difference = Tab Z - Base Z

Next, determine the increment for each argument by taking the difference between the actual values of each argument and the base argument. Calculate the correction for each of the three argument interpolations by multiplying the increment by the Z difference and dividing the resulting product by 60.

The sign of each correction is the same as the sign of the corresponding Z difference used to calculate it. In the above example, the total correction sums to **+0.6'**. Apply this value to the base azimuth of **97.1°** to obtain the true azimuth 97.7°. Compare this to the compass reading of **096.5°** pgc. The compass error is **1.2°E**, which can be rounded to 1° for steering and logging purposes.

Deviation by Azimuth (Any Body)
Chapter 21, Upon Oceans for Limited Master

01451. On 11 December 1981, your 1816 zone time DR position is LAT 26° 30.0' N, LONG 140° 35.0' E. At that time, you observe Venus bearing 230° pgc. The chronometer reads 09h 14m 52s, and the chronometer error is 01m 02s slow. The variation is 3.5° E. What is the gyro error?

A. 2.2° E
B. 3.3° E
C. 3.2° W
D. 4.2° W

01452. On 6 November 1981, your 0752 zone time DR position is LAT 25° 11.0' N, LONG 76° 07.0' W. At that time, you observe the Sun bearing 119° psc. The chronometer reads 00h 53m 07s, and the chronometer error is 01m 19s fast. The variation is 3° W. What is the deviation of the standard compass?

A. 2.2° W
B. 3.8° W
C. 2.8° E
D. 3.2° E

01453. On 15 October 1981, your 0325 zone time DR position is LAT 26° 51.0' N, LONG 138° 17.0' W. At that time, you observe Canopus bearing 167° pgc. The chronometer reads 00h 25m 36s, and the chronometer error is 00m 20s slow. The variation is 2° E. What is the gyro error?

A. 1.2° W
B. 3.2° W
C. 3.2° E
D. 4.1° W

01454. On 4 October 1981, your 0734 zone time DR position is LAT 24° 11.0' N, LONG 162° 34.0' E. At that time, you observe the Sun bearing 105.5° psc. The chronometer reads 08h 36m 11s, and the chronometer error is 01m 46s fast. The variation is 7° W. What is the deviation of the standard compass?

A. 1.2° W
B. 1.9° E
C. 5.3° W
D. 5.8° E

01455. On 4 October 1981, your 1907 zone time DR position is LAT 25° 15.0'S, LONG 105° 44.0' E. At that time, you observe Deneb bearing 011.5° psc. The chronometer reads 00h 07m 42s, and the chronometer error is 00m 36s fast. The variation is 7.5° W. What is the deviation of the standard compass?

A. 3.2° E
B. 4.3° W
C. 2.1° E
D. 2.1° W

01456. On 12 September 1981, your 0736 zone time DR position is LAT 28° 34.0' S, LONG 174° 49.0' E. At that time, you observe the Sun bearing 084° psc. The chronometer reads 07h 38m 11s, and the chronometer error is 01m 46s fast. The variation is 11° W. What is the deviation of the standard compass?

A. 2.9° W
B. 3.3° E
C. 3.9° E
D. 4.7° W

01457. On 25 August 1981, your 1926 zone time DR position is LAT 24° 17.0' S, LONG 05° 47.0' W. At that time, you observe Fomalhaut bearing 117° psc. The chronometer reads 07h 26m 52s, and the chronometer error is 00m 15s fast. The variation is 1.5° E. What is the deviation of the standard compass?

A. 0.2° W
B. 0.4° E
C. 1.3° W
D. 2.8° W

01458. On 6 August 1981, your 1552 zone time DR position is LAT 24° 26.0' S, LONG 73° 19.0' E. At that time, you observe the Sun bearing 302° psc. The chronometer reads 10h 55m 07s, and the chronometer error is 02m 38s fast. The variation is 6° E. What is the deviation of the standard compass?

A. 4.1° W
B. 4.6° E
C. 5.9° E
D. 6.1° W

01459. On 28 July 1981, your 1937 zone time DR position is LAT 26° 13.0' N, LONG 78° 27.0' E. At that time, you observe Deneb bearing 048.7° pgc. The chronometer reads 02h 37m 42s, and the chronometer error is 00m 15s fast. The variation is 4° W. What is the gyro error?

A. 2.4° W
B. 2.8° E
C. 3.6° W
D. 3.6° E

01460. On 27 June 1981, your 1905 zone time DR position is LAT 24° 35.0' N, LONG 50° 15.0' W. At that time, you observe Saturn bearing 211° pgc. The chronometer reads 10h 04m 26s, and the chronometer error is 01m 20s slow. The variation is 4.5° E. What is the gyro error?

A. 1.1° W
B. 3.4° E
C. 3.4° W
D. 5.6° W

01461. On 27 June 1981, your 0734 zone time DR position is LAT 22° 14.0' N, LONG 53° 52.0' W. At that time, you observe the Sun bearing 069.5° psc. The chronometer reads 11h 32m 51s, and the chronometer error is 01m 26s slow. The variation is 5° E. What is the deviation of the standard compass?

A. 1.6° E
B. 2.9° W
C. 2.9° E
D. 3.2° E

01462. On 17 June 1981, your 0815 zone time DR position is LAT 25° 27.0' N, LONG 47° 16.0' W. At that time, you observe the Sun bearing 079.5° psc. The chronometer reads 11h 15m 03s, and the chronometer error is 01m 15s fast. The variation is 3° E. What is the deviation of the standard compass?

A. 0.7° W
B. 3.5° W
C. 3.7° E
D. 2.3° E

01463. On 26 May 1981, your 0723 zone time DR position is LAT 24° 50.0' N, LONG 38° 11.0' W. At that time, you observe the Sun bearing 076.5° psc. The chronometer reads 10h 25m 43s, and the chronometer error is 02m 57s fast. The variation is 7° W. What is the deviation of the standard compass?

A. 3.3° E
B. 3.7° W
C. 8.3° W
D. 10.7° E

01464. On 17 May 1981, your 1554 zone time DR position is LAT 26° 33.0' N, LONG 65° 46.0' W. At that time, you observe the Sun bearing 269° psc. The chronometer reads 07h 55m 47s, and the chronometer error is 01m 14s fast. The variation is 3° W. What is the deviation of the standard compass?

A. 0.6° E
B. 1.6° W
C. 4.6° W
D. 7.6° E

01465. On 22 April 1981, your 0344 zone time DR position is LAT 21° 16.0' N, LONG 107° 32.0' W. At that time, you observe Spica bearing 236° psc. The chronometer reads 10h 45m 16s, and the chronometer error is 00m 25s fast. The variation is 7.5° E. What is the deviation of the standard compass?

A. 1.1° W
B. 5.2° E
C. 5.2° W
D. 6.1° W

01466. On 21 April 1981, your 1542 zone time DR position is LAT 28° 54.0' S, LONG 19° 07.0' W. At that time, you observe the Sun bearing 299° psc. The chronometer reads 04h 44m 11s, and the chronometer error is 01m 54s fast. The variation is 3° E. What is the deviation of the standard compass?

A. 0.3° W
B. 0.4° E
C. 2.7° W
D. 2.7° E

01467. On 17 April 1981, your 1610 zone time DR position is LAT 22° 07.0' N, LONG 158° 16.0' W. At that time, you observe the Sun bearing 271° psc. The chronometer reads 03h 08m 52s, and the chronometer error is 01m 16s slow. The variation is 4° E. What is the deviation of the standard compass?

A. 1.1° W
B. 1.7° E
C. 2.3° W
D. 2.9° E

01468. On 17 April 1981, your 1516 zone time DR position is LAT 27° 24.0' N, LONG 115° 24.0' E. At that time, you observe the Sun bearing 247° psc. The chronometer reads 07h 16m 26s, and the chronometer error is 00m 32s slow. The variation is 4.5° E. What is the deviation of the standard compass?

A. 4.5° W
B. 5.4° E
C. 6.2° E
D. 6.2° W

01469. On 2 March 1981, your 2216 zone time DR position is LAT 21° 20.0' S, LONG 17° 10.0' W. At that time, you observe Saturn bearing 078° psc. The chronometer reads 11h 14m 04s, and the chronometer error is 02m 20s slow. The variation is 4.5° W. What is the deviation of the standard compass?

A. 1.5° W
B. 1.6° E
C. 2.9° W
D. 3.6° E

01470. On 1 March 1981, your 2135 zone time DR position is LAT 23° 54.0' N, LONG 63° 22.0' W. At that time, you observe Schedar bearing 328° psc. The chronometer reads 01h 35m 16s, and the chronometer error is 00m 07s slow. The variation is 3.5° E. What is the deviation of the standard compass?

A. 2.3° E
B. 2.5° W
C. 3.2° W
D. 4.2° E

01471. On 21 February 1981, your 0823 zone time DR position is LAT 21° 44.0' S, LONG 80° 14.0' E. At that time, you observe the Sun bearing 096° psc. The chronometer reads 03h 25m 19s, and the chronometer error is 01m 52s fast. The variation is 5° W. What is the deviation of the standard compass?

A. 2.2° E
B. 4.8° W
C. 5.7° E
D. 6.3° W

01472. On 9 February 1981, your 0739 zone time DR position is LAT 23° 31.0' N, LONG 143° 41.0' E. At that time, you observe the Sun bearing 104.5° psc. The chronometer reads 09h 37m 12s, and the chronometer error is 01m 52s slow. The variation is 3.5° W. What is the deviation of the standard compass?

A. 1.6° E
B. 2.3° W
C. 5.1° W
D. 8.6° E

01473. On 26 January 1981, your 1615 zone time DR position is LAT 27° 14.0' S, LONG 57° 22.0' W. At that time, you observe the Sun bearing 266° psc. The chronometer reads 08h 13m 19s, and the chronometer error is 01m 46s slow. The variation is 4° E. What is the deviation of the standard compass?

A. 4.9° W
B. 4.8° E
C. 5.9° W
D. 7.8° E

01474. On 14 January 1981, your 0746 zone time DR position is LAT 26° 37.0' N, LONG 153° 19.0' W. At that time, you observe the Sun bearing 123° psc. The chronometer reads 05h 49m 16s, and the chronometer error is 02m 29s fast. The variation is 3° W. What is the deviation of the standard compass?

A. 1.4° W
B. 1.6° E
C. 3.4° E
D. 4.4° W

01475. On 26 February 1981, your vessel's 1615 ZT DR position is LAT 25° 14' S, LONG 57° 22' W, when an azimuth of the Sun is observed. The chronometer time of the sight is 8h 13m 19s, and the Sun is bearing 266.0° per standard compass. The chronometer error is 01m 46s slow, and the variation in the area is 6° E. What is the deviation of the standard compass?

A. 1.7° E
B. 3.4° W
C. 7.7° E
D. 13.7° E

01476. On 16 September 1981, your vessel's 0736 zone time DR position is LAT 27° 34' S, LONG 174° 49' E, when an azimuth of the Sun is observed. The chronometer time of the sight is 07h 38m 11s, and the Sun is bearing 079.8° per gyrocompass. The chronometer error is 01m 46s fast, and the variation in the area is 11.0° W. At the time of the sight, the helmsman reports that he was heading 252° pgc and 258° per magnetic compass. What is the deviation of the magnetic compass?

A. 2° W
B. 3° W
C. 3° E
D. 8° W

01477. On 27 June 1981, your vessel's 0816 ZT DR position is LAT 22° 14' S, LONG 53° 52' W, when an azimuth of the Sun is observed. The chronometer time of the sight is 12h 15m 02s, and the Sun is bearing 047.5° per standard compass. The chronometer error is 00m 46s slow, and the variation in the area is 6.0° E. What is the deviation of the standard compass?

A. 1.5° E
B. 1.9° W
C. 3.0° W
D. 3.0° E

01478. At 0906 zone time on 12 June 1981, your position is LAT 26° 52' N, LONG 84° 34' W. The chronometer reads 03h 17m 00s. Chronometer error is 01m 40s slow. At that time, an azimuth of the Sun is obtained. The bearing is 089.5° per standard compass. Variation for this area is 4.5° E. What is the deviation of the standard compass?

A. 9.5° E
B. 9.5° W
C. 5.0° E
D. 5.0° W

01479. On 6 November 1981, your vessel's 0706 zone time DR position is LAT 25° 30.0' N, LONG 85° 35.0' W, when an azimuth of the Sun is observed. The chronometer time of the sight is 01h 03m 30s, and the Sun is bearing 114.0° pgc. The chronometer error is 02m 30s slow, and the variation in the area is 2° E. What is the gyro error?

A. 0.8° E
B. 0.8° W
C. 1.8° W
D. 1.8° E

1480. On 28 November 1981, your vessel's 0712 zone time DR position is LAT 26° 54' S, LONG 45° 18' W, when an azimuth of the Sun is taken:

Chronometer time: 10h 09m 18s
Chronometer error: slow 02m 54s
Gyro bearing   102°

What is the gyro error?

A. 1.7° W
B. 0.6° W
C. 1.1° E
D. 0.8° E

1481. On 24 May 1981, your vessel's 1000 ZT position is LAT 25° 36.0' N, LONG 118° 39.5' W, when an azimuth of the Sun is taken:

Chronometer   06h 21m 48s
Chronometer error: fast 01m 36s
Gyro bearing: 099.4°
Variation: 11.1' E

What is the gyro error?

A. 0.3° W
B. 1.3° W
C. 1.8° E
D. 2.4° E

1482. On 20 July 1981, your vessel's 1626 zone time DR position is LAT 27° 13.0' N, LONG 63° 42.0' W, when an azimuth of the Sun is taken:

Chronometer time: 08h 24m 18s
Chronometer error: slow 02m 12s
Gyro bearing: 279.5°
Variation: 15° W

What is the gyro error?

A. 1.9° W
B. 2.6° W
C. 1.4° E
D. 2.6° E

01483. On 31 May 1981, your vessel's 1420 zone time DR position is LAT 29° 06' N, LONG 120° 06' W, when an azimuth of the Sun is observed. The bearing of the Sun per standard compass was 255.3° . The chronometer time of the observation is 10h 17m 24s. The chronometer error is 02m 32s slow. The variation for this area is 12.9° E. What is the deviation of the standard compass?

A. 2.5° W
B. 2.9° W
C. 2.9° E
D. 3.2° E

01484. On 7 December 1981, your vessel's 0835 zone time DR position is LAT 28° 30.0' N, LONG 125° 39.3' W, when an azimuth of the Sun is observed. The chronometer time of the sight is 04h 34m 48s, and the Sun is bearing 113° per standard compass. The chronometer error is 01m 24s slow, and the variation in the area is 13.0° E. What is the deviation of the standard compass?

A. 2.0° E
B. 2.0° W
C. 2.3° E
D. 2.3° W

01485. On 6 October 1981, your 0416 zone time DR position is LAT 25° 16.0' N, LONG 130° 25.0' E. At that time, you observe Mars bearing 083° psc. The chronometer reads 07h 16m 22s, and the chronometer error is 00m 10s fast. The variation is 1.5° E. What is the deviation of the standard compass?

A. 0.4° E
B. 1.2° W
C. 3.5° E
D. 19.0° E

01486. On 1 September 1981, your 1115 zone time DR position is LAT 25° 20.0' N, LONG 28° 24.0' W. At that time, you observe the Sun bearing 160.5° psc. The chronometer reads 01h 14m 58s, and the chronometer error is 01m 17s fast. The variation is 13.5° W. What is the deviation of the standard compass?

A. 2.1° E
B. 4.1° E
C. 11.0° W
D. 11.0° E

01487. On 5 June 1981, your 0420 zone time DR position is LAT 26° 47.0' N, LONG 133° 19.5' W. At that time, you observe Vega bearing 298.1° psc. The chronometer reads 01h 21m 17s, and the chronometer error is 02m 25s fast. The variation is 3.5° E. What is the deviation of the standard compass?

A. 1.8° E
B. 5.2° E
C. 1.8° W
D. 5.2° W

01488. At 2326 zone time on 22 June 1981, your vessel's position is LAT 28° 30' N, LONG 150° 04' W. An azimuth of the planet Jupiter is observed, and the standard compass bearing is 250.4°. The chronometer reads 09h 24m 36s and is 01m 12s slow. The variation of this area is 13.5° E. What is the deviation of the standard compass?

A. 3.0° W
B. 3.5° W
C. 1.5° E
D. 2.3° E

Azimuth Answers

01451	B
01452	D
01453	A
01454	D
01455	A
01456	B
01457	D
01458	D
01459	B
01460	A
01461	A
01462	B
01463	D
01464	D
01465	B
01466	A
01467	C
01468	B
01469	D
01470	C
01471	B
01472	D
01473	C
01474	A
01475	A
01476	C
01477	C
01478	D
01479	D
01480	B
01481	B
01482	A
01483	A
01484	C
01485	B
01486	A
01487	C
01488	D

Celestial Problems							
Sight Reduction Azimuth							

Problem #	**(USCG)**	**(1451)**		**VENUS**		Chapter 21	

Date:	**11 Dec**		Time		**LAT:**	26° 30.0' N	
					LONG	140° 35.0' E	
	ZT	1816	**CT**	09:14:52	**S-**		
	ZD	- 9	**CE**	+ 1:02	**C-**		
	GMT	0916	**CCT**	09 15:54			
			GMT	09:15:54	**DR**		
					Time		
					LAT		
					LONG		

Almanac							
	GHA	270° 35.6'	**DEC**	S 21° 47.4'			
	M/S	3° 58.5'	**d**	- .6 - .2'	**T**	233.7	
	GHA	274° 34.1'	**DEC**	S 21° 47.2'	**E**	3.3 E	
	LONG	+140° 35.0'			**G**	239.0	
	± v (+.8)	+ .2'					
	LHA	415° 09.3'					
		55° 09.3'					

LHA	55° 09.3'	**DEC**	S 21° 47.2'	**LAT**	26° 30.0' **N**
Publication 229					
Z (55)	126.1	**Z** (21)	126.1	**Z** (26)	126.1
Z (56)	125.4	**Z** (22)	126.9	**Z** (27)	126.3
d	- .7	**d**	+ .8	**d**	+ .2
Inc Dec (X)	09.3	**Inc Dec (X)**	47.2	**Inc Dec (X)**	30.0
Inv	60	**Inv**	60	**Inv**	60
correction	- .1	**correction**	+ .6	**correction**	+ .1
Base Z	126.1	**Z to ZN**		360 – 126.7 = **233.7**	
tcorr	+ .6	**ZN = 360 -Z**			
Z	126.7				

Note: CONTRARY

Celestial Problems			
Sight Reduction Azimuth			

Problem # (USCG) (1452)			**SUN**		Chapter 21	

Date:	**6 Nov**		Time		**LAT:**	25° 11.0' N
					LONG	076° 07.0' W
	ZT	0752	**CT**	00:53:07	**S-**	
	ZD	+ 5	**CE**	- 1:19	**C-**	
	GMT	1252	**CCT**	00:51:48		
			GMT	12:51:48	**DR**	
					Time	
					LAT	
					LONG	

Almanac					
GHA	4° 05.0'	**DEC**	S 16° 02.3'		
M/S	12° 57.0'	**d**	+.7 +.6'	**T**	119.2
GHA	17° 02.0'	**DEC**	S 16° 02.9'	**V**	3 W
LONG ±	- 76° 07.0'			**M**	121.2
LHA	300° 55.0'			**D**	3.2 E
				C	119.0

LHA	300° 55.0'	**DEC**	S 16° 02.9'	**LAT**	25° 11.0' **N**
Publication 229					
Z (300)	118.5	**Z (16)**	118.5	**Z (25)**	118.5
Z (301)	119.1	**Z (17)**	119.4	**Z (26)**	118.8
d	+ .6	**d**	+ .9	**d**	+ .3
Inc Dec (X)	55.0	**Inc Dec (X)**	2.9	**Inc Dec (X)**	11.0
Inv	60	**Inv**	60	**Inv**	60
correction	+ .6	**correction**	0	**correction**	+ .1

Base Z	118.5	**Z to ZN**		
tcorr	+ .7	**ZN = Z**	**119.2**	
Z	119.2			

Note: CONTRARY

3-14

Celestial Problems					
Sight Reduction Azimuth					
Problem # (USCG) (1453)		**CANOPUS**		Chapter 21	

Date:	**15 OCT**	Time		**LAT:**	26° 51.0' N
				LONG	138° 17.0' W
	ZT	0325	**CT** 00:25:36	**S-**	
	ZD	+9	**CE** + 00:20	**C-**	
	GMT	1225	**CCT** 00:25:56		
			GMT 12:25:56		

Almanac

GHA Υ	203° 55.8'	**DEC**	S 52° 40.9'		
M/S	6° 30.1'	**d**		**T**	165.7
GHA Υ	210° 25.9'	**DEC**	S 52° 40.9'	**E**	1.3 W
SHA *	264° 06.7'			**G**	167.0
GHA *	474° 32.6'				
LONG	- 138° 17.0'				
LHA *	336° 15.6'				

LHA	336° 15.6'	**DEC**	S 52° 40.9'	**LAT**	26° 51.0' **N**
Publication 229					
Z (336)	165.3	**Z** (52)	165.3	**Z** (26)	165.3
Z (337)	165.9	**Z** (53)	165.7	**Z** (27)	165.3
d	+ .6	**d**	+ .4	**d**	0
Inc Dec (X)	15.6	**Inc Dec (X)**	40.9	**Inc Dec (X)**	51.0
Inv	60	**Inv**	60	**Inv**	60
correction	+ .2	**correction**	+ .3	**correction**	0

Base Z	165.3	**Z to ZN**		165.7	
tcorr	+ .5	**ZN = Z**			
Z	165.7				

Note: CONTRARY

Celestial Problems
Sight Reduction Azimuth

Problem # (USCG) (1454)			SUN	Chapter 21	
Date: 4 Oct		Time		**LAT:**	24° 11.0' N
				LONG	162° 34.0' E
	ZT	0734	**CT**	08:36:11	**S-**
	ZD	- 11	**CE**	- 1:46	**C-**
	GMT	2034	**CCT**	08:34:25	
2043 3 Oct			**GMT**	20:34:25	

Almanac

GHA	122° 46.1'	**DEC**	S	4° 04.8'		
M/S	8° 36.3'	**d**	+.1	+ .1'	**T**	104.4
GHA	131° 22.4'	**DEC**	S	4° 09.0'	**V**	7 W
LONG	162° 34.0'				**M**	111.4
LHA	293° 56.4'				**D**	5.9 E
					C	105.5

LHA	293° 56.4'	**DEC**	S 4° 09.0'	**LAT**	24° 11.0' **N**
		Publication 229			
Z (293)	103.6	**Z (4)**	103.6	**Z (24)**	103.6
Z 294()	104.1	**Z (5)**	104.5	**Z (25)**	103.9
d	+ .5	**d**	+ .9	**d**	+ .3
Inc Dec (X)	56.4	**Inc Dec (X)**	9.0	**Inc Dec (X)**	11.0
Inv	60	**Inv**	60	**Inv**	60
correction	+ .5	**correction**	+ .2	**correction**	+ .1

Base Z	103.6	**Z to ZN**		101.4	
tcorr	+ .8	**ZN = Z**			
Z	104.4				

Note: CONTRARY

3-16

Alexander F. Hickethier MBA © 1990-2012

Celestial Problems						
Sight Reduction Azimuth						
Problem #	**(USCG)**	(1455)	**DENEB**			Chapter 21

Date:	**4 OCT**		Time		**LAT:**	25° 15.0' S
					LONG	105° 44.0' E
	ZT	1907	**CT**	00:07:42	S-	
	ZD	-7	**CE**	- 00:36	C-	
	GMT	1207	**CCT**	00:07:06		
			GMT	12:07:06		

Almanac						
GHA Y	193° 05.3'	**DEC**	N 45° 13.2'			
M/S	1° 46.8'	**d**		**T**	007.2	
GHA Y	194° 52.1'	**DEC**	N 45° 13.2'	**V**	7.5 W	
SHA *	49° 47.8'			**M**	014.7	
GHA *	244° 33.9'			**D**	3.2 E	
LONG	+ 105° 44.0'			**C**	011.5	
LHA *	350° 23.9'					

LHA	350° 22.4'	**DEC**	N 45° 13.2'	**LAT**	25° 15.0' **S**
Publication 229					
Z (350)	172.5	**Z (45)**	172.5	**Z (25)**	172.5
Z (351)	173.3	**Z (46)**	172.7	**Z (26)**	172.6
d	+ .8	**d**	+ .2	**d**	+ .1
Inc Dec (X)	22.4	**Inc Dec (X)**	13.2	**Inc Dec (X)**	15.0
Inv	60	**Inv**	60	**Inv**	60
correction	+ .3	**correction**	0	**correction**	0

Base Z	172.5	**Z to ZN**		
tcorr	+ .3	**ZN = 180 -Z**	180 – 172.8 = **007.2**	
Z	172.8			

Note: CONTRARY

Celestial Problems
Sight Reduction Azimuth

Problem # (USCG) (1456)	**SUN**	Chapter 21

Date: **12 Nov**	Time		LAT:	28° 34.0' S
			LONG	174° 49.0' E
ZT 0736	**CT** 07:38:11		S-	
ZD -12	**CE** - 1:40		C-	
GMT 1936	**CCT** 07:36:25			
	GMT 19:36:25			
1936 11 Sept				

		Almanac			
GHA	105° 52.6'	**DEC**	N 4° 22.6'		
M/S	9° 06.3'	**d**	-.1 -.1'	**T**	76.4
GHA	114° 58.9'	**DEC**	N 4° 22.5'	**V**	11 W
LONG	174° 49.0'			**M**	87.4
LHA	289° 47.9'			**D**	3.4 E
				C	084.0

LHA	289° 47.9'	**DEC**	N 4° 22.5'	**LAT**	28° 24.0' **S**
		Publication 229			
Z (289)	102.8	Z (4)	102.8	Z (28)	102.8
Z (290)	103.3	Z (5)	103.7	Z (29)	103.0
d	+ .5	d	+ .9	d	+ .2
Inc Dec (X)	47.9	Inc Dec (X)	22.5	Inc Dec (X)	24.0
Inv	60	Inv	60	Inv	60
correction	+.4	correction	+ .3	correction	+ .1

Base Z	102.8	Z to ZN		ZN= 180 - 103.6 = **76.4**
tcorr	+ .8	ZN = 180 -Z		
Z	103.6			

Note: CONTRARY

			Celestial Problems					
			Sight Reduction Azimuth					
Problem #	**(USCG)**	(1457)	**FOMALHAUT**			Chapter 21		

Date:	**25 AUG**		Time				**LAT:**	24° 17.0' S
							LONG	005° 47.0' W
	ZT	1926	**CT**	07:26:52			**S-**	
	ZD	0	**CE**	- 00:15			**C-**	
	GMT	1926	**CCT**	07:26:37				
			GMT	19:26:37				

Almanac

GHA Υ	258° 57.0'	**DEC**	S 29° 43.1'				
M/S	6° 39.3'	**d**			**T**	115.7	
GHA Υ	265° 36.3'	**DEC**	S 29° 43.1'		**V**	1.5 E	
SHA *	15° 50.3'				**M**	114.2	
GHA *	281° 26.6'				**D**	2.8 W	
LONG	- 5° 47.0'				**C**	117	
LHA *	275° 39.6'						

LHA	274° 39.6'	**DEC**	S 29° 43.1'	**LAT**	24° 17.0' **S**
		Publication 229			
Z (275)	064.7	**Z (29)**	064.7	**Z (24)**	064.7
Z (276)	065.0	**Z (30)**	063.7	**Z (25)**	065.0
d	+ .3	**d**	- 1.0	**d**	+ .3
Inc Dec (X)	39.6	**Inc Dec (X)**	43.1	**Inc Dec (X)**	17.0 S
Inv	60	**Inv**	60	**Inv**	60
correction	+ .2	**correction**	- .7	**correction**	+ .1

Base Z	064.7	**Z to ZN**		
tcorr	- .4	**ZN = 180 -Z**	180 – 064.3 = **115.7**	
Z	064.3			

Note: SAME

Celestial Problems Sight Reduction Azimuth					
Problem # (USCG) (1458)			**SUN**	Chapter 21	

Date:	6 Aug		Time		LAT:	24° 26.0 S
					LONG	073° 19.0 E
	ZT	1552	**CT**	10:55:07	**S-**	
	ZD	- 5	**CE**	- 2:38	**C-**	
	GMT	1052	**CCT**	10:52:29		
			GMT	10:52:29		

Almanac						
GHA	328° 032.6'	**DEC**	N 16° 40.4'			
M/S	13° 07.3'	**d**	-.7 -.6'	**T**	301. 8	
GHA	341° 39.6'	**DEC**	N 16° 39.8'	**V**	6 E	
LONG	+73° 19.0'			**M**	295.8	
LHA	414° 58.9'			**D**	6.2 W	
	- 360° 00.0'			**C**	302	
	54° 58.9					

LHA	54° 58.9'	**DEC**	N 16° 39.4'	**LAT**	24° 26.0' **S**
Publication 229					
Z (54)	121.8	**Z (16)**	121.8	**Z (24)**	121.8
Z (55)	121.2	**Z (17)**	122.6	**Z (24)**	122.1
d	-.6	**d**	+.8	**d**	+.3
Inc Dec (X)	58.9	**Inc Dec (X)**	39.8	**Inc Dec (X)**	26.0
Inv	60	**Inv**	60	**Inv**	60
correction	-.6	**correction**	+.5	**correction**	+.1

Base Z	121.8	**Z to ZN**		ZN=180 + 121.8 = **301.8**
tcorr	0	**ZN = 180 +Z**		
Z	121.8			

Note: CONTRARY

Celestial Problems Sight Reduction Azimuth				
Problem # **(USCG)** (1459)		**DENEB**	Chapter 21	

Date:	**28 JULY**	Time		**LAT:**	26° 13.0' N
				LONG	078° 27.0' E
	ZT	1937	**CT**	02:37:42	**S-**
	ZD	- 5	**CE**	- 00:15	**C-**
	GMT	1437	**CCT**	02:37:27	
			GMT	14:37:27	

Almanac

GHA Y	156° 08.8'	**DEC**	N 45° 13.2'			
M/S	9° 23.3'	**d**		**T**	051.5	
GHA Y	165° 32.1'	**DEC**	N 45° 13.2'	**E**	2.8 E	
SHA *	49° 47.8'			**G**	048.7	
GHA *	215° 19.9'					
LONG	+ 78° 27.0'					
LHA *	293° 46.9'					

LHA	293° 46.9'	**DEC**	N 45° 13.2'	**LAT**	26° 13.0' N
Publication 229					
Z (293)	051.7	**Z (45)**	051.7	**Z (26)**	051.7
Z (294)	051.7	**Z (46)**	050.5	**Z (27)**	052.2
d	0	**d**	- 1.2	**d**	+ .5
Inc Dec (X)	46.9	**Inc Dec (X)**	13.2	**Inc Dec (X)**	13.0
Inv	60	**Inv**	60	**Inv**	60
correction	0	**correction**	- .3	**correction**	+ .1
Base Z	051.7	**Z to ZN**		051.5	
tcorr	- .2	**ZN = Z**			
Z	051.5				

Note: SAME

Celestial Problems					
Sight Reduction Azimuth					
Problem # (USCG) (1460)		**SATURN**		Chapter 21	

Date:	**27 JUNE**	Time		LAT:	24° 35.0' N
				LONG	050° 15.0' W
	ZT	1905	**CT** 10:04:26	S-	
	ZD	+ 3	**CE** + 01:20	C-	
	GMT	2205	**CCT** 10:05:46		
			GMT 22:05:46		

Almanac

GHA SAT	61° 48.7'	**DEC**	N 0° 51.1'		
M/S PL	01° 26.5'	**d**		**T**	209.9
GHA SAT	63° 15.2'	**DEC**	N 0° 51.1'	**E**	1.1 W
± v (+ 2.4)	+ .2'			**G**	211.0
GHA SAT	63° 15.4'				
LONG	50° 15.0'				
LHA SAT	13° 00.4'				

LHA	13° 00.4'	DEC	N 0° 51.1'	LAT	24° 35.0' N
Publication 229					
Z (13)	150.4	**Z** (0)	150.4	**Z** (24)	150.4
Z 14()	148.5	**Z** (1)	149.4	**Z** (25)	151.4
d	- 1.9	**d**	+ 1.0	**d**	+ 1.0
Inc Dec (X)	00.4	**Inc Dec (X)**	51.1	**Inc Dec (X)**	35.0
Inv	60	**Inv**	60	**Inv**	60
correction	0	**correction**	- .9	**correction**	+ .6

Base Z	150.4	**Z to ZN**	360 – 150.1 = **209.9**	
tcorr	- .3	**ZN = 360 -Z**		
Z	150.1			

Note: SAME

Celestial Problems Sight Reduction Azimuth						
Problem # (USCG) (1461)			**SUN**		Chapter 21	

Date: **27 JUNE**		Time			**LAT:**	22° 14.0' N
					LONG	053° 52.0' W
	ZT	0734	**CT**	11:32:51	**S-**	
	ZD	+ 4	**CE**	+ 1:26	**C-**	
	GMT	1134	**CCT**	11:34:17		
			GMT	11:34:17	**DR**	
					Time	
					LAT	
					LONG	

Almanac							
	GHA	344° 15.9'	**DEC**	N 23° 19.1'			
	M/S	8° 34.3'	**d**	-.1 -.1'	**T**	076.3	
	GHA	352° 50.2'	**DEC**	N 23° 19.0'	**V**	5.0 E	
	LONG	- 53° 52.0'			**M**	071.3	
	LHA	298° 58.2'			**D**	1.8 E	
					C	069.5	

LHA	298° 58.2'	**DEC**	N 23° 19.0'	**LAT**	22° 14.0' **N**
Publication 229					
Z (298)	76.1	**Z** (23)	76.1	**Z** (22)	76.1
Z (299)	76.4	**Z** (24)	75.0	**Z** (23)	76.8
d	+ .3	**d**	- 1.1	**d**	+ .7
Inc Dec (X)	58.2	**Inc Dec (X)**	19.0	**Inc Dec (X)**	14.0
Inv	60	**Inv**	60	**Inv**	60
correction	+ .3	**correction**	- .3	**correction**	+ .2

Base Z	76.1	**Z to ZN**		076.3	
tcorr	- .2	**ZN = Z**			
Z	76.3				

Note: SAME

Celestial Problems Sight Reduction Azimuth				
Problem # (USCG) (1462)		SUN		Chapter 21

Date:	20 July		Time		LAT:		27° 18.0' N
					LONG		063° 42.0' W
	ZT	1626	CT	08:24:18	S-		
	ZD	+ 4	CE	+ 2:12	C-		
	GMT	2026	CCT	08:26:30			
			GMT	20:26:30	DR		
					Time		
					LAT		
					LONG		

Almanac					
GHA	118° 25.8'	DEC	N 20° 33.9'		
M/S	6° 37.5'	d	- .5 - .2'	T	277.3
GHA	125° 03.3'	DEC	N 20° 33.7'	E	2.2 W
LONG	63° 03.3'			G	279.5
LHA	61° 21.3'				

LHA	61° 21.3'	DEC	N 20° 33.7'	LAT	27° 18.0' N
Publication 229					
Z (61)	083.2	Z (20)	083.2	Z (27)	083.2
Z (62)	082.8	Z (21)	082.1	Z (28)	83.9
d	- .4	d	- 1.1	d	+ .7
Inc Dec (X)	21.3	Inc Dec (X)	33.7	Inc Dec (X)	13.0
Inv	60	Inv	60	Inv	60
correction	- .1	correction	- .6	correction	+ .2

Base Z	083.2	Z to ZN		
tcorr	- .5	ZN = 360 -Z	360 – 82.7 = **277.3**	
Z	082.7			

Note: SAME

Celestial Problems						
Sight Reduction Azimuth						
Problem # (USCG) (1463)			**SUN**		Chapter 21	
Date: 26 May		Time		**LAT:**	24° 50.0' N	
				LONG	38° 11.0' W	
	ZT	0723	**CT** 10:25:43	**S-**		
	ZD	+ 3	**CE** + 02:57	**C-**		
	GMT	1023	**CCT** 10:22:46			
			GMT 10:22:46			

Almanac						
	GHA	330° 46.0'	**DEC**	N 21° 08.6'		
	M/S	5° 41.5'	**d**	+ .4 + .2'	**T**	080.2
	GHA	336° 27.5'	**DEC**	N 21° 08.8'	**V**	7.0 W
	LONG	- 38° 11.0'			**M**	087.2
	LHA	298° 16.5'			**D**	10.7 E
					C	076.5

LHA	298° 16.5'	**DEC**	N 21° 08.8'	**LAT**	24° 50.0' N
Publication 229					
Z (298)	079.7	**Z (21)**	079.7	**Z (24)**	079.7
Z (299)	080.0	**Z (22)**	078.6	**Z (25)**	080.4
d	+ .3	**d**	- 1.1	**d**	+ .7
Inc Dec (X)	16.5	**Inc Dec (X)**	8.8	**Inc Dec (X)**	50.0
Inv	60	**Inv**	60	**Inv**	60
correction	+ .1	**correction**	- .2	**correction**	+ .6
Base Z	079.7	**Z to ZN**		080.2	
tcorr	+ .5	**ZN = Z**			
Z	080.2				
Note: SAME					

Celestial Problems
Sight Reduction Azimuth

Problem # (USCG) (1464)	SUN	Chapter 21

Date:	17 MAY		Time			LAT:	26° 33.0' N
						LONG	065° 46.0' W
	ZT	1554	CT	07:55:47		S-	
	ZD	+ 4	CE	- 01:14		C-	
	GMT	1954	CCT	07:54:33			
			GMT	19:54:33			

Almanac

GHA	105° 55.1'	DEC	N 19° 26.1'				
M/S	13° 38.3'	d	+ .6 + .5'	T	273.6		
GHA	119° 33.4'	DEC	N 19° 26.6'	V	3.0 W		
LONG	- 65° 46.0'			M	276.6		
LHA	53° 47.4'			D	7.6 E		
				C	269.0		

LHA	53° 47.4'	DEC	N 19° 26.6'	LAT	26° 33.0' N
		Publication 229			
Z (53)	086.7	Z (19)	086.7	Z (26)	086.7
Z (54)	086.3	Z (20)	085.5	Z (27)	087.6
d	- .4	d	- 1.2	d	+ .9
Inc Dec (X)	47.4	Inc Dec (X)	26.6	Inc Dec (X)	33.0
Inv	60	Inv	60	Inv	60
correction	- .3	correction	- .5	correction	+ .5

Base Z	086.7	Z to ZN		360 – 086.4 = **273.6**
tcorr	- .3	ZN = 360 -Z		
Z	086.47			

Note: SAME

Alexander F. Hickethier MBA © 1990-2012

Celestial Problems					
Sight Reduction Azimuth					
Problem # (USCG) (1465)		**SPICA**		Chapter 21	

Date: **22 APRIL**		Time			**LAT:**	21° 16.0' N
					LONG	107° 32.0' W
	ZT	0344	**CT**	10:45:16	S-	
	ZD	+ 7	**CE**	- 00:25	C-	
	GMT	1044	**CCT**	10:44:51		
			GMT	10:44:51		

Almanac

GHA Υ	0° 22.5'	**DEC**	S 11° .03.8'				
M/S	11° 14.6'	**d**			**T**	248.8	
GHA Υ	11° 37.1'	**DEC**	S 11° .03.8'		**V**	7.5 E	
SHA *	158° 56.1'				**M**	241.2	
GHA *	170° 33.9'				**D**	5.3 E	
LONG	-107° 32.0'				**C**	236.0	
LHA *	63° 01.9'						

LHA	63° 01.9'	**DEC**	S 11° .03.8'	**LAT**	21° 16.0' **N**
Publication 229					
Z (63)	111.1	**Z (11)**	111.1	**Z (21)**	111.1
Z (64)	112.1	**Z (12)**	110.6	**Z (22)**	111.5
d	+ 1.0	**d**	- .5	**d**	+ .4
Inc Dec (X)	01.9	**Inc Dec (X)**	03.8	**Inc Dec (X)**	16.0
Inv	60	**Inv**	60	**Inv**	60
correction	0	**correction**	0	**correction**	+ .1

Base Z	111.1	**Z to ZN**		
tcorr	+ .1	**ZN = 360 -Z**	360 – 111.2 = **248.8**	
Z	111.2			

Note: CONTRARY

Celestial Problems Sight Reduction Azimuth					
Problem # (USCG) (1466)			**SUN**	Chapter 21	

Date:	**21 APRIL**	Time			LAT:	28° 54.0' S
					LONG	019° 07.0' W
	ZT	1542	**CT**	04:44:11	S-	
	ZD	+ 1	**CE**	- 1:54	C-	
	GMT	1642	**CCT**	04:42:17		
			GMT	16:42:17		

Almanac						
GHA	60° 20.3'	**DEC**	N 11° 58.8'			
M/S	10° 34.3'	**d**	+ .9 + .6'	**T**	301.7	
GHA	70° 54.6'	**DEC**	N 11° 59.4'	**V**	3.0 E	
LONG	-19° 07.0'			**M**	297.7	
LHA	51° 47.6'			**D**	.3 W	
				C	299.0	

LHA	51° 47.6'	**DEC**	N 11° 59.4'	**LAT**	28° 54.0' **S**
Publication 229					
Z (51)	121.0	**Z** (11)	121.0	**Z** (28)	121.0
Z (52)	120.3	**Z** (12)	121.9	**Z** (29)	121.4
d	- .7	**d**	+ .9	**d**	+ .4
Inc Dec (X)	47.6	**Inc Dec (X)**	59.4	**Inc Dec (X)**	54.0
Inv	60	**Inv**	60	**Inv**	60
correction	- .6	**correction**	+ .9	**correction**	+ .4

Base Z	121.0	**Z to ZN**		
tcorr	+ .7	**ZN = 180 +Z**	180 + 121.7 = **301.7**	
Z	121.7			

Note: CONTRARY

Alexander F. Hickethier MBA © 1990-2012

			Celestial Problems				
			Sight Reduction Azimuth				

Problem # (USCG) (1467)		SUN		Chapter 21	

Date: 17 APRIL		Time			LAT:	27° 07.0' N
					LONG	158° 16.0' W
	ZT	1610	CT	03:08:52	S-	
	ZD	+ 11	CE	+ 01:16	C-	
	GMT	2710	CCT	03:10:08		
0310 18 APRIL			GMT	03:10:08		

			Almanac				

	GHA	225° 08.8'	DEC	N 10° 45.7'			
	M/S	2° 32.0'	d	+ .9 + .2'	T	272.8	
	GHA	227° 40.8'	DEC	N 10° 45.9'	V	4.0 W	
	LONG	-158° 16.0'			M	268.8	
	LHA	69° 24.8'			D	**2.2 W**	
					C	271.0	

LHA	69° 24.8'	DEC	N 10° 45.9'	LAT	27° 07.0' N
		Publication 229			
Z (69)	088.2	Z (10)	088.2	Z (27)	088.2
Z (70)	087.8	Z (11)	087.2	Z (28)	088.6
d	- .4	d	- 1.0	d	+ .4
Inc Dec (X)	24.8	Inc Dec (X)	45.9	Inc Dec (X)	07.0
Inv	60	Inv	60	Inv	60
correction	- .2	correction	- .8	correction	0

Base Z	088.2	Z to ZN		360 − 087.2 = **272.8**	
tcorr	- 1.0	ZN =360 -Z			
Z	087.2				

Note: SAME

Alexander F. Hickethier MBA © 1990-2012

Celestial Problems				
Sight Reduction Azimuth				
Problem # (USCG) (1468)		**SUN**		Chapter 21

Date:	**17 APRIL**	Time		**LAT:**	27° 24.0 N
				LONG	115° 24.0 E
	ZT 1516	**CT**	07:16:26	**S-**	
	ZD - 8	**CE**	+ 00:32	**C-**	
	GMT 0716	**CCT**	07:16:58		
		GMT	07:16:58		

Almanac

GHA	285° 05.9	**DEC**	N 10° 28.1'		
M/S	4° 14.5	**d**	+ .9 + .2'	**T**	256.9
GHA	289° 20.4	**DEC**	N 10° 28.3'	**V**	4.5 E
LONG	+115° 24.0			**M**	252.4
LHA	404° 44.4			**D**	5.4 W
-360	44° 44.0			**C**	247.0

LHA	44° 44.0'	**DEC**	N 10° 28.3'	**LAT**	27° 24.0' **N**
Publication 229					
Z (44)	103.7	**Z (10)**	103.7	**Z (27)**	103.7
Z (45)	103.1	**Z (11)**	102.5	**Z (28)**	104.7
d	- .6	**d**	- 1.2	**d**	+ 1.0
Inc Dec (X)	44.0	**Inc Dec (X)**	28.3	**Inc Dec (X)**	24.0
Inv	60	**Inv**	60	**Inv**	60
correction	- .4	**correction**	- .6	**correction**	+ .4

Base Z	103.7	**Z to ZN**	360 − 103.1 = **256.9**	
tcorr	- .6	**ZN = 360 -Z**		
Z	103.1			

Note: SAME

Celestial Problems				
Sight Reduction Azimuth				
Problem # (USCG) (1469)		**SATURN**		Chapter 21

Date:	**2 MARCH**	Time		**LAT:**	21° 20.0' S
				LONG	017° 10.0' W
	ZT	2216	**CT** 11:14:04	**S-**	
	ZD	+ 1	**CE** + 02:20	**C-**	
	GMT	2316	**CCT** 11:16:24		
			GMT 23:16:24		

			Almanac			
	GHA SAT	317° 03.3'	**DEC**	S 0° 51.8'		
	M/S	4° 06.0'	**d**		**T**	077.1
	GHA SAT	321° 09.3'	**DEC**	S 0° 51.8'	**V**	4.5 W
	± v (+2.6)	+ .7'			**M**	081.6
	GHA SAT	321° 10.0'			**D**	**3.6** E
	LONG	- 17° 10.0'			**C**	078
	LHA	304° 00.0'				

LHA	304° 00.0'	**DEC**	S 0° 51.8'	**LAT**	21° 20.0' **S**
		Publication 229			
Z (304)	102.6	**Z (0)**	102.6	**Z (21)**	102.6
Z (305)		**Z (1)**	102.5	**Z (22)**	104.2
d		**d**	- 1.1	**d**	+ .6
Inc Dec (X)	00.0	**Inc Dec (X)**	51.8	**Inc Dec (X)**	20.0
Inv	60	**Inv**	60	**Inv**	60
correction	0	**correction**	- .9	**correction**	+ .2

Base Z	102.6	**Z to ZN**	180 − 102.9 = **077.1**
tcorr	- .7	**ZN = 180 -Z**	
Z	102.9		

Note: SAME

Celestial Problems					
Sight Reduction Azimuth					
Problem # (USCG) (1470)			**SCHEDAR**	Chapter 21	
Date: **1 MARCH**		Time	**LAT:**	23° 54.0' N	
			LONG	063° 22.0' W	
ZT	2135	**CT**	01:35:16	**S-**	
ZD	+ 4	**CE**	+ 00:07	**C-**	
GMT	2535	**CCT**	01:35:23		
0135 2 MARCH		**GMT**	01:35:23		

Almanac					
GHA Y	174° 44.2'	**DEC**	N 56° 26.0'		
M/S	8° 52.2'	**d**		**T**	328.3
GHA Y	183° 36.4'	**DEC**	N 56° 26.0'	**V**	+3.5 E
SHA *	350° 09.1'			**M**	324.8
GHA *	533°5.5'			**D**	**3.2 W**
LONG	-63° 22.0'			**C**	328.0
LHA *	470° 23.5'				
	- 360° 00.0'				
LHA *	110° 23.5'				

LHA	110° 23.5'	DEC	N 56° 26.0'	LAT	23° 54.0' N
Publication 229					
Z (110)	032.1	**Z (56)**	032.1	**Z (23)**	032.1
Z (111)	031.8	**Z (57)**	031.2	**Z (24)**	032.2
d	- .3	**d**	1.0	**d**	+ .1
Inc Dec (X)	23.5	**Inc Dec (X)**	26.0	**Inc Dec (X)**	54.0
Inv	60	**Inv**	60	**Inv**	60
correction	- .1	**correction**	- .4	**correction**	+ .1

Base Z	032.1		360 – 031.7 = **328.3**
tcorr	- .4	**ZN = 360 -Z**	
Z	031.7		

Note: SAME

Celestial Problems
Sight Reduction Azimuth

Problem # (USCG) (1471)	**SUN**	Chapter 21

Date: **21 FEB**	Time			**LAT:**	21° 44.0' S

					LONG	080° 14.0' E
	ZT	0823	**CT**	03:25:19	**S-**	
	ZD	- 5	**CE**	- 1:52	**C-**	
	GMT	0323	**CCT**	03:23:27		
			GMT	03:23:27	**DR**	
					Time	
					LAT	
					LONG	

Almanac						
GHA	221° 34.5'	**DEC**	S 10° 37.2'			
M/S	+ 5° 51.8'	**d**	- .9 - .4'	**T**	086.2	
GHA	227° 26.3'	**DEC**	S 10° 36.3'	**V**	5 W	
LONG	80° 14.0'			**M**	091.2	
LHA	307° 40.3'			**D**	4.5 W	
				C	096.0	

LHA	307° 40.3'	**DEC**	S 10° 36.3'	**LAT**	21° 44.0' **S**
Publication 229					
Z (307)	093.7	**Z (10)**	093.7	**Z (21)**	093.7
Z (308)	094.1	**Z (11)**	092.5	**Z (22)**	094.4
d	+ .4	**d**	- 1.2	**d**	+ .7
Inc Dec (X)	40.3	**Inc Dec (X)**	36.3	**Inc Dec (X)**	44.0
Inv	60	**Inv**	60	**Inv**	60
correction	+ .3	**correction**	- .7	**correction**	+ .5

Base Z	093.7	**Z to ZN**	180 – 93.8 = **086.2**	
tcorr	+ .1	**ZN = 180 -Z**		
Z	093.8			

Note: SAME

Celestial Problems Sight Reduction Azimuth				

Problem # (USCG) (1472) **SUN** Chapter 21

Date:	9 FEB	Time		LAT:	23° 31.0' N
				LONG	143° 41.0' E
	ZT	0739	CT	09:37:12	S-
	ZD	- 10	CE	+ 01:52	C-
	GMT	2139	CCT	09:38:04	
8 FEB			GMT	21:38:04	

Almanac

.	GHA	131° 26.2'	DEC	S 14° 48.4'		
	M/S	9° 31.0'	d	- .8 - .5'	2	109.6
	GHA	140° 57.2'	DEC	S 14° 47.9'	V	3.5 W
	LONG	+143° 41.0'			M	113.1
	LHA	284° 38.2'			D	8.6 E
					C	104.5

LHA	284° 38.2'	DEC	S 14° 47.9'	LAT	23° 31.0' N
Publication 229					
Z (284)	108.5	Z (14)	108.5	Z (23)	108.5
Z (285)	108.9	Z (15)	109.4	Z (24)	108.6
d	+ .4	d	+ .9	d	+ .1
Inc Dec (X)	38.2	Inc Dec (X)	47.9	Inc Dec (X)	31.0
Inv	60	Inv	60	Inv	60
correction	+ .3	correction	+ .7	correction	+ .1

Base Z	108.5	Z to ZN		109.6
tcorr	+ 1.1	ZN = Z		
Z	109.6			

Note: CONTRARY

Alexander F. Hickethier MBA © 1990-2012

Celestial Problems						
Sight Reduction Azimuth						
Problem # (USCG) (1473)			**SUN**		Chapter 21	
Date: **26 JAN**	Time			**LAT:**	27° 14.0' S	
				LONG	057° 22.0' W	
ZT	1615	**CT**	08:13:19	**S-**		
ZD	+4	**CE**	+ 01:46	**C-**		
GMT	2015	**CCT**	08:15:05			
		GMT	20:15:05			

Almanac						
GHA	116° 49.8'	**DEC**	S 18°°4.5'			
M/S	3° 46.3'	**d**	- .6 - .2'	**T**	264.1	
GHA	120° 36.1'	**DEC**	S 18° 34.3'	**V**	4.0 E	
LONG	-57° 22.0'			**M**	260.1	
LHA	63° 14.6'			**D**	5.9 W	
				C	266.0	

LHA	63° 14.6'	**DEC**	S 18° 34.3'	**LAT**	27° 14.0' **S**
Publication 229					
Z (63)	084.7	**Z (18)**	084.7	**Z (27)**	084.7
Z (64)	084.3	**Z (19)**	083.6	**Z (28)**	085.3
d	- .4	**d**	- 1.1	**d**	+ .6
Inc Dec (X)	14.6	**Inc Dec (X)**	34.3	**Inc Dec (X)**	14.0
Inv	60	**Inv**	60	**Inv**	60
correction	- .1	**correction**	- .6	**correction**	+ .1

Base Z	084.7	**Z to ZN**		180 + 084.1 = **264.1**
tcorr	- .6	**ZN = 180 +Z**		
Z	084.1			

Note: SAME

Celestial Problems				
Sight Reduction Azimuth				

Problem # (USCG) (1474)		SUN		Chapter 21

Date:	14 JAN		Time		LAT:	26° 37.0' N
					LONG	153° 19.0' W
	ZT	0746	CT	05:49:16	S-	
	ZD	+ 10	CE	- 02:29	C-	
	GMT	1746	CCT	05:46:47		
			GMT	17:46:47		

Almanac						
GHA	72° 41.6'	DEC	S 21° 13.7'			
M/S	11° 41.8'	d	- .4 - .3'	T	118.6
GHA	84° 23.4'	DEC	S 21° 13.4'	V	3.0 W
LONG	-153° 19.0'			M	122.6
LHA	291° 04.4'			D	1.4 W
				C	123.0

LHA	291° 04.4'	DEC	S 21° 13.4'	LAT	26° 37.0' N
Publication 229					
Z (291)	118.3	Z (21)	118.3	Z (26)	118.3
Z (292)	118.8	Z (22)	119.1	Z (27)	118.4
d	+ .5	d	+ .8	d	+ .1
Inc Dec (X)	04.4	Inc Dec (X)	13.4	Inc Dec (X)	37.0
Inv	60	Inv	60	Inv	60
correction	0	correction	+ .2	correction	+ .1

Base Z	118.3	Z to ZN		
tcorr	+. 3	ZN = Z	118.6	
Z	118.6			

Note: CONTRARY

Celestial Problems					
Sight Reduction Azimuth					
Problem # (USCG) (1475)		**SUN**		Chapter 21	

Date: **26 FEB**		Time		LAT:	25° 14.0' S
				LONG	057° 22.0' W
	ZT	1615	CT	08:13:19	S-
	ZD	+4	CE	+ 01:46	C-
	GMT	2015	CCT	08:15:05	
			GMT	20:15:05	

Almanac						
GHA	116° 47.0'	DEC	S 8° 51.0'			
M/S	3° 46.3'	d	-.9 -.2'	T	273.6	
GHA	120° 33.3'	DEC	S 8° 30.8'	V	6.0 E	
LONG	-57° 22.0'			M	267.6	
LHA	63° 11.3'			D	1.6 E	
				C	266.0	

LHA	63° 11.3'	DEC	S 8° 30.8'	LAT	25° 14.0' **S**
Publication 229					
Z (63)	094.1	Z (8)	094.1	Z (25)	094.1
Z (64)	093.7	Z (9)	093.1	Z (26)	094.7
d	- .4	d	- 1.0	d	+ .6
Inc Dec (X)	11.3	Inc Dec (X)	30.8	Inc Dec (X)	14.0
Inv	60	Inv	60	Inv	60
correction	- .1	correction	- .5	correction	+ .1

Base Z	094.1	Z to ZN	180 + 093.6 = **273.6**	
tcorr	- .5	ZN = 180 + Z		
Z	093.6			

Note: SAME

Celestial Problems					
Sight Reduction Azimuth					
Problem # (USCG) (1476)			**SUN**	Chapter 21	

Date: **17 April**		Time		LAT:	22° 07.0' N
				LONG	158° 16.0' W
ZT	1610	**CT**	03:08:52	S-	
ZD	+ 11	**CE**	+ 1:16	C-	
GMT	2710	**CCT**	03:10:08		
		GMT	03:10:08	**DR**	
0310 18 April				**Time**	
				LAT	
				LONG	

Almanac					
GHA	225° 08.8'	**DEC**	N 10° 45.7'		
M/S	2° 32.0'	**d**	+ .9 + .2'	**T**	272.7
GHA	227° 40.8'	**DEC**	N 10° 45.9'	**V**	4.0 E
LONG	158° 16.0'			**M**	268.7
LHA	69° 24.8'			**D**	2.3 W
				C	271.0

LHA	69° 24.8'	DEC	N 10° 45.9'	LAT	22° 07.0' **N**
Publication 229					
Z (69)	88.2	**Z (10)**	88.2	**Z (22)**	88.2
Z (70)	87.8	**Z (11)**	87.2	**Z (23)**	88.6
d	- .4	**d**	- 1.0	**d**	+ .4
Inc Dec (X)	24.8	**Inc Dec (X)**	45.0	**Inc Dec (X)**	7.0
Inv	60	**Inv**	60	**Inv**	60
correction	- .2	**correction**	- .8	**correction**	+.1

Base Z	88.2	**Z to ZN**	360- 87.2 + **272.7**	
tcorr	- .9	**ZN = 360 -Z**		
Z	87.3			

Note: SAME

Celestial Problems
Sight Reduction Azimuth

Problem # (USCG) (1477)	SUN	Chapter 21

Date:	27 JUNE		Time			LAT:	22° 14.0' S
						LONG	053° 52.0' W
	ZT	0816	CT	12:15:02		S-	
	ZD	+ 4	CE	+ 00:46		C-	
	GMT	1216	CCT	12:15:48			
			GMT	12:15:48			

Almanac

GHA	359° 15.8'	DEC	N 23° 19.0'				
M/S	3° 57.0'	d	- .1	0'	T	050.4	
GHA	363° 12.8'	DEC	N 23° 19.0'		V	6.0 E	
LONG	-53° 52.0'				M	044.4	
LHA	309° 20.8'				D	3.0 W	
					C	047.5	

LHA	309° 20.8'	DEC	N 23° 19.0'	LAT	22° 14.0' S
Publication 229					
Z (309)	129.0	Z (23)	129.0	Z (22)	129.0
Z (310)	129.6	Z (24)	129.8	Z (23)	129.3
d	+ .6	d	+ .8	d	+ .3
Inc Dec (X)	20.8	Inc Dec (X)	19.0	Inc Dec (X)	14.0
Inv	60	Inv	60	Inv	60
correction	+ .2	correction	+ .3	correction	+ .1

Base Z	129.0	Z to ZN	180 – 129.6 = **050.4**	
tcorr	+ .6	ZN = 180 -Z		
Z	129.6			

Note: CONTRARY

Celestial Problems				
Sight Reduction Azimuth				
Problem # (USCG) (1478)		**SUN**	Chapter 21	

Date:	**12 JUNE**	Time			**LAT:**	26° 52.0' N
					LONG	084° 34.0' W
	ZT	0906	**CT**	03:17:00	**S-**	
	ZD	+ 6	**CE**	+ 01:40	**C-**	
	GMT	1506	**CCT**	03:18:40		
			GMT	15:18:40		

Almanac						
GHA	45° 03.3'	**DEC**	N 23° 10.2'			
M/S	4° 40.0'	**d**	+ .1 0'	**T**	068.9	
GHA	49° 43.3'	**DEC**	N 23° 10.3'	**V**	4.5 E	
LONG	- 84° 34.0'			**M**	084.4	
LHA	325° 09.3'			**D**	5.1 W	
				C	089.5	

LHA	325° 09.3'	**DEC**	N 23° 10.3'	**LAT**	26° 52.0' N
Publication 229					
Z (325)	087.8	**Z (23)**	087.8	**Z (26)**	087.8
Z (326)	088.1	**Z (24)**	085.9	**Z (27)**	089.4
d	+ .3	**d**	- 1.9	**d**	+ 1.6
Inc Dec (X)	09.3	**Inc Dec (X)**	10.3	**Inc Dec (X)**	52.0
Inv	60	**Inv**	60	**Inv**	60
correction	0	**correction**	- .3	**correction**	+ 1.4

Base Z	087.8	**Z to ZN**		088.9
tcorr	+ 1.1	**ZN = Z**		
Z	088.9			

Note: SAME

Celestial Problems					
Sight Reduction Azimuth					
Problem # (USCG) (1479)			**SUN**	Chapter 21	
Date: 6 NOV	Time			**LAT:** 25° 30.0' N	
				LONG 085° 35.0' W	
ZT	0706	**CT**	01:03:30	**S-**	
ZD	+ 6	**CE**	+ 02:30	**C-**	
GMT	1306	**CCT**	01:06:00		
		GMT	13:06:00		

Almanac					
GHA	19° 05.0'	**DEC**	S 16° 02.3		
M/S	1° 30.0'	**d**	+.7 0	**T**	115.9
GHA	20° 35.0'	**DEC**	S 16° 02.3	**E**	1.9 E
LONG	-85° 35.0'			**G**	114.0
LHA	295° 00.0'				

LHA	295° 00'	**DEC**	S 16° 02.3'	**LAT**	25° 30.0' **N**
Publication 229					
Z (295)	115.8	**Z (16)**	115.8	**Z (25)**	115.8
Z (296)	115.8	**Z (17)**	116.7	**Z (26)**	116.0
d	0	**d**	+ .9	**d**	+ .2
Inc Dec (X)	00	**Inc Dec (X)**	02.3	**Inc Dec (X)**	30.0
Inv	60	**Inv**	60	**Inv**	60
correction	0	**correction**	0	**correction**	+ .1

Base Z	115.8	**Z to ZN**			
tcorr	+ .1	**ZN = Z**	115.9		
Z	115.9				

Note: CONTRARY

Celestial Problems
Sight Reduction Azimuth

Problem # (USCG) (1480)			**SUN**		Chapter 21	
Date: **28 NOV**		Time		**LAT:**	26° 54.0' S	
				LONG	045° 18.0' W	
ZT	0715	**CT**	10:09:18	**S-**		
ZD	+ 3	**CE**	+ 02:54	**C-**		
GMT	1015	**CCT**	10:12:12			
		GMT	10:12:12			

Almanac						
GHA	333° 00.4'	**DEC**	S 21° 19.5'			
M/S	3° 03.0'	**d**	+ .4 + .1'	**T**	101.4	
GHA	336° 02.4'	**DEC**	S 21° 19.6'	**E**	.6 W	
LONG	-45° 18.0'			**G**	102.0	
LHA	290° 44.4'					

LHA	290° 44.4'	**DEC**	S 21° 19.6'	**LAT**	26° 54.0' S
		Publication 229			
Z (290)	078.3	**Z (21)**	078.3	**Z (26)**	078.3
Z (291)	078.6	**Z (22)**	077.2	**Z (27)**	078.8
d	+ .3	**d**	- 1.1	**d**	+ .5
Inc Dec (X)	44.4	**Inc Dec (X)**	19.6	**Inc Dec (X)**	54.0
Inv	60	**Inv**	60	**Inv**	60
correction	+. 2	**correction**	- .4	**correction**	+ .5
Base Z	078.3	**Z to ZN**		180 – 078.6 = **101.4**	
tcorr	+.3	**ZN = 180 -Z**			
Z	078.6				

Note: SAME

3-42

Celestial Problems Sight Reduction Azimuth						

Problem #   (USCG)   (1481)   **SUN**   Chapter 21

Date:	24 MAY	Time			LAT:	25° 36.0' N
					LONG	118° 39.5' W
	ZT	1000	CT	06:21:48	S-	
	ZD	+ 8	CE	- 01:36	C-	
	GMT	1800	CCT	06:20:12		
			GMT	18:20:36		

Almanac

	GHA	90° 48.5'	DEC	N 20° 50.8'		
	M/S	5° 03.0'	d	+ .5 + .2'	T	098.1
	GHA	95° 51.5'	DEC	N 20° 51.0'	E	1.3 W
	LONG	-118° 39.5'			G	099.4
	LHA	337° 12.0'				

LHA	337° 12.0'	DEC	N 20° 51.0'	LAT	25° 36.0' **N**
Publication 229					
Z (337)	098.6	Z (20)	098.6	Z (25)	098.6
Z (338)	099.4	Z (21)	096.0	Z (26)	101.1
d	+ .8	d	- 2.6	d	+ 2.5
Inc Dec (X)	12.0	Inc Dec (X)	51.0	Inc Dec (X)	36.0
Inv	60	Inv	60	Inv	60
correction	+ .2	correction	- 2.2	correction	+ 1.5

Base Z	098.6	Z to ZN		098.1	
tcorr	- .5	ZN = Z			
Z	098.1				

Note: SAME

Celestial Problems Sight Reduction Azimuth					
Problem # (USCG) (1482)			**SUN**	Chapter 21	
Date: 20 JULY		Time		**LAT:** 27° 13.0' N	
				LONG 063° 42.0' W	
	ZT 1626	**CT**	08:24:18	S-	
	ZD + 4	**CE**	+ 02:12	C-	
	GMT 2026	**CCT**	08:26:30		
		GMT	20:26:30		

Almanac

GHA	118° 25.8'	**DEC**	N 20° 33.9'		
M/S	6° 37.5'	**d**	- .5 -.2'	**T**	277.3
GHA	125° 03.3'	**DEC**	N 20° 33.7'	**E**	2.2 W
LONG	-63° 42.0'			**G**	279.5
LHA	63° 21.3'				

LHA	63° 21.3'	**DEC**	N 20° 33.7'	**LAT**	27° 13.0' **N**
Publication 229					
Z (63)	083.2	**Z (20)**	083.2	**Z (27)**	083.2
Z (64)	082.8	**Z (21)**	083.1	**Z (28)**	083.9
d	- .4	**d**	- 1.1	**d**	+ .7
Inc Dec (X)	21.3	**Inc Dec (X)**	33.7	**Inc Dec (X)**	13.0
Inv	60	**Inv**	60	**Inv**	60
correction	- .1	**correction**	- .6	**correction**	+ .2
Base Z	083.2	**Z to ZN**			
tcorr	- .5	**ZN = 360 -Z**	$360 - 082.7 = \mathbf{277.3}$		
Z	082.7				

Note: SAME

Celestial Problems Sight Reduction Azimuth						
Problem # (USCG)	(1483)		**SUN**		Chapter 21	

Date:	**31 MAY**		Time		LAT:	29° 06.0' N
					LONG	120° 06.0' W
	ZT	1420	**CT**	10:17:24	S-	
	ZD	+ 8	**CE**	+ 02:32	C-	
	GMT	2220	**CCT**	10:19:56		
			GMT	22:19:56		

Almanac							
	GHA	150° 35.3'	**DEC**	N 21° 59.9'			
	M/S	4° 59.0'	**d**	+ .9 + .3'	**T**	265.2	
	GHA	155° 34.3'	**DEC**	N 22° 00.2'	**V**	12.9 E	
	LONG	-120° 06.0'			**M**	252.8	
	LHA	35° 28.5'			**D**	2.5 W	
					C	255.3	

LHA	35° 28.5'	**DEC**	N 22° 00.2'	**LAT**	29° 06.0' N
Publication 229					
Z (35)	094.4	**Z (22)**	094.4	**Z (29)**	094.4
Z (36)	093.8	**Z (23)**	092.6	**Z (30)**	095.9
d	- 6	**d**	- 1.8	**d**	+ 1.5
Inc Dec (X)	28.5	**Inc Dec (X)**	00.2	**Inc Dec (X)**	06.0
Inv	60	**Inv**	60	**Inv**	60
correction	- .3	**correction**	0	**correction**	+ .2

Base Z	094.4	**Z to ZN**		
tcorr	- .1	**ZN = 360 -Z**	360 – 094.3 = **265.7**	
Z	094.3			

Note: SAME

Celestial Problems					
Sight Reduction Azimuth					

Problem # (USCG) (1484)			SUN		Chapter 21

Date: 7 DEC		Time		LAT:	28° 30.0' N
				LONG	125° 39.3' W
	ZT	0835	CT	04:34:48	S-
	ZD	+ 8	CE	+ 01:24	C-
	GMT	1635	CCT	04:36:12	
			GMT	16:36:12	

Almanac						
GHA	62° 06.3'	DEC	S 22° 38.9'			
M/S	9° 03.0'	d	+ .9 + .5'	T	128.3
GHA	71° 09.3'	DEC	S 22° 39.4'	V	13.0 E
LONG	-125° 39.3'			M	115.3
LHA	305° 30.0'			D	2.3 E
				C	113.0

LHA	305° 30.0'	DEC	S 22° 39.4'	LAT	28° 30.0' N
Publication 229					
Z (305)	127.4	Z (22)	127.4	Z (28)	127.4
Z (306)	128.0	Z (23)	128.2	Z (29)	127.6
d	+ .6	d	+ .8	d	+ .2
Inc Dec (X)	30.0	Inc Dec (X)	39.4	Inc Dec (X)	30.0
Inv	60	Inv	60	Inv	60
correction	+ .3	correction	+ .5	correction	+ .1

Base Z	127.4	Z to ZN		
tcorr	+ .9	ZN = Z	128.3	
Z	128.3			

Note: CONTRARY

Celestial Problems
Sight Reduction Azimuth

Problem # (USCG) (1485)	**MARS**	Chapter 21

Date: 6 OCT	Time			**LAT:**	25° 16.0' N
				LONG	130° 25.0' E
ZT	0416	**CT**	07:16:22	S-	
ZD	- 9	**CE**	- 00:10	C-	
GMT	1916	**CCT**	07:16:12		
1916 Oct 5		**GMT**	19:16:12		

Almanac						
GHA MAR	155° 37.0'	**DEC**	N 15° 45.7'			
M/S	4° 03.0'	**d**	- .5 - .1'	**T**	083.4	
GHA MAR	159° 40.4'	**DEC**	N 15° 45.6''	**V**	1.5 E	
± v	+ 1.0 + .3'			**M**	081.9	
GHA MAR	159° 40.7'			**D**	1.1 W	
LONG	+130° 25.0'			**C**	083.0	
LHA MAR	290° 15.7'					

LHA	290° 05.7'	**DEC**	N 15° 45.6'	**LAT**	25° 16.0' N
Publication 229					
Z (290)	084.0	Z (15)	084.0	Z (25)	084.0
Z (291)	084.4	Z (16)	083.0	Z (26)	084.5
d	+ .4	d	- 1.0	d	+ .5
Inc Dec (X)	15.7	Inc Dec (X)	45.6	Inc Dec (X)	16.0
Inv	60	Inv	60	Inv	60
correction	+.1	correction	- .8	correction	+ .1

Base Z	084.0	Z to ZN	083.4
tcorr	- .6	ZN = Z	
Z	083.4		

Note: SAME

Celestial Problems				
Sight Reduction Azimuth				
Problem # (USCG) (1486)		**SUN**		Chapter 21

Date:	**1 SEPT**	Time			**LAT:**	25° 20.0' N
					LONG	028° 24.0' W
	ZT	1115	**CT**	01:14:58	**S-**	
	ZD	+ 2	**CE**	- 01:17	**C-**	
	GMT	1315	**CCT**	01:13:41		
			GMT	13:13:41		

Almanac						
GHA	15° 00.8'	**DEC**	N 8° 11.9'			
M/S	3° 25.3'	**d**	- .9 -.6'	**T**	149.3	
GHA	18° 26.1'	**DEC**	N 8° 11.7'	**V**	13.5 W	
LONG	-28° 24.0'			**M**	162.8	
LHA	350° 02.1'			**D**	2.3 E	
				C	160.5	

LHA	350° 02.1'	**DEC**	N 8° 11.7'	**LAT**	25° 20.0' **N**
Publication 229					
Z (350)	149.0	**Z (8)**	149.0	**Z (25)**	149.0
Z (351)	151.7	**Z (9)**	147.5	**Z (26)**	150.4
d	+ 2.7	**d**	- 1.5	**d**	+ 1.4
Inc Dec (X)	02.1	**Inc Dec (X)**	11.7	**Inc Dec (X)**	20.0
Inv	60	**Inv**	60	**Inv**	60
correction	+ .1	**correction**	- .3	**correction**	+ .5

Base Z	149.0	**Z to ZN**		
tcorr	+ .3	**ZN = Z**	149.3	
Z	149.3			

Note: SAME

Celestial Problems				
Sight Reduction Azimuth				
Problem # (USCG) (1487)		**VEGA**	Chapter 21	

Date:	**5 JUNE**		Time			LAT:	26° 47.0' N	
						LONG	133° 19.5' W	
	ZT	0420	**CT**	01:21:17		**S-**		
	ZD	+ 9	**CE**	- 02:25		**C-**		
	GMT	1320	**CCT**	01:18:52				
			GMT	13:18:52				

Almanac						
GHA Y	88° 52.0'	**DEC**	N 38° 45.9'			
M/S	4° 43.0'	**d**		**T**	299.9	
GHA Y	93° 35.0'	**DEC**	N 38° 45.9'	**V**	3.5 E	
SHA *	80° 55.1'			**M**	296.4	
GHA *	194° 20.1'			**D**	1.7 W	
LONG	-133° 19.5'			**C**	298.1	
LHA *	41° 00.6'					

LHA	41° 00.6'	**DEC**	N 38° 45.9'	**LAT**	26° 47.0' N
Publication 229					
Z (41)	060.5	**Z (38)**	060.5	**Z (26)**	060.5
Z (42)	060.6	**Z (39)**	058.5	**Z (27)**	061.7
d	+ .1	**d**	- 1.7	**d**	+ 1.2
Inc Dec (X)	00.6	**Inc Dec (X)**	45.9	**Inc Dec (X)**	47.0
Inv	60	**Inv**	60	**Inv**	60
correction	0	**correction**	- 1.3	**correction**	+ .9

Base Z	060.5	**Z to ZN**		
tcorr	- .4	**ZN = 360 -Z**	360 − 060.1 = **299.9**	
Z	060.1			

Note: SAME

Celestial Problems				
Sight Reduction Azimuth				

Problem # (USCG) (1488)		**JUPITER**		Chapter 21

Date:	**22 JUNE**	Time			**LAT:**	28° 30.0' N
					LONG	150° 04.0' W
	ZT	2326	CT	09:24:36	S-	
	ZD	+10	CE	+ 01:12	C-	
	GMT	3326	CCT	09:25:48		
0926 23 JUNE			GMT	09:25:48		

Almanac						
GHA JUP	224° 33.4'	**DEC**	N 0° 37.7'			
M/S	6° 27.0'	**d**	.+1 0	**T**	266.2	
GHA JUP	231° 00.4'	**DEC**	N 0° 37.7'	**V**	13.5 E	
± v	+2.3 1.0'			**M**	252.7	
GHA JUP	231° 01.4'			**D**	+2.3 E	
LONG	-150° 04.0'			**C**	250.4	
LHA JUP	80° 57.4'					

LHA	80° 57.4'	DEC	N 0° 37.7'	LAT	28° 30.0' N
Publication 229					
Z (80)	094.7	**Z (0)**	094.7	**Z (28)**	094.7
Z (81)	094.3	**Z (1)**	093.8	**Z (29)**	0949
d	- .4	**d**	- .9	**d**	+ .2
Inc Dec (X)	57.4	**Inc Dec (X)**	37.7	**Inc Dec (X)**	30.0
Inv	60	**Inv**	60	**Inv**	60
correction	- .4	**correction**	- .6	**correction**	+ .1

Base Z	094.7	**Z to ZN**		
tcorr	-.9	**ZN = 360 -Z**	360 – 093.8 = **266.2**	
Z	093.8			

Note: SAME

DEVIATION BY POLARIS

Compass Error By Azimuth Of Polaris

The Polaris tables in the *Nautical Almanac* list the azimuth of Polaris for latitudes between the equator and 65° N. Compare a compass bearing of Polaris to the tabular value of Polaris to determine compass error. The entering arguments for the table are LHA of Aries and observer latitude.

Alexander F. Hickethier MBA
and
DR. HU JIA-SHEN

Deviation by POLARIS
Chapter 16, Upon Oceans for Limited Master

1. 01489. On 23 July 1981, your 2100 ZT position is LAT 36° 43.0' N, LONG 16° 09.8' W, when you observed an azimuth of POLARIS to determine the compass error. POLARIS bears 359.0 per gyrocompass. At the time of the observation, the helmsman noted that he was heading 319.0° per gyrocompass and 331.0° per standard compass. Variation is 12.0° W. Which of the following statements is true?

A. The gyro error is 0.7° E.
B. The gyro error is 1.7° W.
C. The deviation is 1.7° E.
D. The compass error is 13.7° W

2. 01490. On 11 January 1981, your 0450 ZT position is LAT 38° 42' N, LONG 14° 16' W. You observe Polaris bearing 358.5° pgc. At the time of the observation the helmsman noted that he was heading 160° pgc and 173° psc. The variation is 9° W. What is the deviation for that heading?

A. 1° E
B. 1° W
C. 3° W
D. 13° W

3. 01491. On 5 February 1981, your 2320 ZT position is LAT 52° 28' N, LONG 23° 48' W. You observe Polaris bearing 000.2° pgc. At the time of the observation the helmsman noted that he was heading 224° pgc and 244° psc. The variation is 20° W. What is the deviation for that heading?

A. 0°
B. 1.5° W
C. 3.0° W
D. 4.5° W

4. 01492. On 22 February 1981, your 2045 ZT position is LAT 33° 19' N, LONG 52° 06' W. You observe Polaris bearing 358.1° pgc. At the time of the observation the helmsman noted that he was heading 048° pgc and 065° psc. The variation is 19° W. What is the deviation for that heading?

A. 1° E
B. 3° E
C. 1° W
D. 3° W

5. 01493. On 11 July 1981, your 0240 ZT position is LAT 14° 52' N, LONG 34° 23' W. You observe Polaris bearing 359.8° pgc. At the time of the observation the helmsman noted that he was heading 279° pgc and 299° psc. The variation is 19° W. What is the deviation for that heading?

A. 0°
B. 1° E
C. 1° W
D. 3° W

6. 01494. On 5 August 1981, your 0310 ZT position is LAT 09° 02' N, LONG 21° 08' W. You observe Polaris bearing 002° pgc. At the time of the observation the helmsman noted that he was heading 316° pgc and 329° psc. The variation is 15° W. What is the deviation for that heading?

A. 0°
B. 1.5° W
C. 3.0° W
D. 0.5° E

7. 01495. On 9 September 1981, your 2043 ZT position is LAT 24° 18' N, LONG 66° 46' W. You observe Polaris bearing 001° pgc. At the time of the observation the helmsman noted that he was heading 031° pgc and 040° psc. The variation is 11° W. What is the deviation for that heading?

A. 0°
B. 1° W
C. 3° W
D. 2° E

8. 01496. On 3 October 1981, your 2122 ZT position is LAT 26° 32' N, LONG 84° 26' W. You observe Polaris bearing 359.8° pgc. At the time of the observation the helmsman noted that he was heading 106° pgc and 107° psc. The variation is 0°. What is the deviation for that heading?

A. 1° E
B. 0°
C. 1° W
D. 2° W

9. 01497. On 19 November 1981, your 0146 ZT position is LAT 33° 48' N, LONG 25° 22° E. You observe Polaris bearing 359.8° pgc. At the time of the observation the helmsman noted that he was heading 224° pgc and 222.5° psc. The variation is 2° E. What is the deviation for that heading?

A. 2.0° E
B. 0.5° E
C. 1.0° W
D. 1.5° W

10. 01498. On 7 December 1981, your 0350 ZT position is LAT 35° 42' N, LONG 17° 38' E. You observe Polaris bearing 359.7° pgc. At the time of the observation the helmsman noted that he was heading 016° pgc and 014° psc. The variation is 1° E. What is the deviation for that heading?

A. 0.5° E
B. 0°
C. 0.5° W
D. 1.5° W

Answers

1.   01489 C
2.   01490 C
3.   01491 B
4.   01492 B
5.   01493 A
6.   01494 D
7.   01495 D
8.   01496 B
9.   01497 C
10. 01498 A
11. 01499 C

Celestial Problems
Compass Deviation By Polaris

Problem # 1 (USCG)   (01489)   Chapter

Date:	23 July		Time	21:00 ZT	LAT:		36° 43.0' N
			CT		LONG		16° 09.8' W
	ZT	21:00	CE		S-		
	ZD	+1	CCT		C-		
	GMT	22:00	GMT				

Almanac			Compass Correction		Deviation				
GHA		271° 32.8'							
M/S			T	000.7	T	320.7	T		320.7
GHA		271° 32.8'	E	1.7 E	E	1.7 E	V		12.0 W
±SHA/v			G	359.0	G	319.0	M		332.7
Sum		271° 32.8'	Polaris bearing from Almanac				D		1.7 E
Long		- 16° 09.8'					C		331.0
LHA		255° 23.0'		000.7					

Notes:

Celestial Problems
Compass Deviation By Polaris

Problem # 2 (USCG)   (01490)   Chapter

Date:	11 Jan.		Time	04:50 ZT	LAT:		38° 42' N
			CT		LONG		14° 16' W
	ZT	04:50	CE		S-		
	ZD	+1	CCT		C-		
	GMT	05:50	GMT				

Almanac			Compass Correction		Deviation				
GHA		185° 37.1'							
M/S		+12° 32.1'	T	359.5	T	161.0	T		161.0
GHA		198° 09.2'	E	1.0 E	E	1.0 E	V		9 W
±SHA/v			G	358.5	G	160	M		170
Sum		198° 09.2'	Polaris bearing from Almanac				D		3.0 W
Long		- 14° 16'					C		173.0
LHA		183° 53.2'		359.5					

Notes:

Celestial Problems
Compass Deviation By Polaris

Problem # 3 (USCG) (01491) — Chapter

Date:	**5 Feb.**		Time	23:20 ZT	**LAT:**	52° 28' N
	ZT	23:20	**CT**		**LONG**	23° 48' W
	ZD	+2	**CE**			**S-**
	GMT	25:20	**CCT**			**C-**
	6 Oct	01:20	**GMT**			

Almanac		Compass Correction		Deviation			
GHA	151° 04.9'						
M/S	5° 00.8'	**T**	358.7	**T**	222.5	**T**	222.5
GHA	156° 05.7'	**E**	1.5 W	**E**	1.5 W	**V**	20° W
±SHA/v		**G**	000.2	**G**	224°	**M**	242.5
Sum	156° 05.7'	Polaris bearing from Almanac				**D**	1.5 W
Long	- 23° 48.0'					**C**	244
LHA	132° 17.7'		358.7				

Notes:

Celestial Problems
Compass Deviation By Polaris

Problem # 4 (USCG) (01492) — Chapter

Date:	**22 Feb**		Time	20:45 ZT	**LAT:**	33-19' N
			CT		**LONG**	52° 06' W
	ZT	20:45	**CE**			**S-**
	ZD	+3	**CCT**			**C-**
	GMT	23:45	**GMT**			

Almanac		Compass Correction		Deviation			
GHA	122° 42.9'						
M/S	11° 16.8'	**T**	359.0	**T**	048.9	**T**	048.9
GHA	133° 59.7'	**E**	1.0 E	**E**	1.0 W	**V**	19 W
±SHA/v		**G**	358.0	**G**	048.0	**M**	067.9
Sum	133° 59.7'	Polaris bearing from Almanac				**D**	2.9 E
Long	- 52° 06.0'					**C**	065
LHA	81° 53.7'		359				

Notes:

3-94

Alexander F. Hickethier © 2008-2013

Celestial Problems
Compass Deviation By Polaris

Problem # 5 (USCG) (01493) Chapter

Date:	11 July	Time		02:40 ZT	LAT:	14° 52' N
		CT			**LONG**	34° 23' W
ZT	02:40	**CE**			**S-**	
ZD	+2	**CCT**			**C-**	
GMT	04:40	**GMT**				

Almanac		Compass Correction		Deviation		
GHA	348° 58.8'					
M/S	10° 01.6'	**T**	000.8	**T**	280.0	**T**	280.0
GHA	359° 00.4'	**E**	1.0 E	**E**	1.0 E	**V**	19° W
±SHA/v		**G**	359.8°	**G**	279°	**M**	299.
Sum	359° 00.4'	Polaris bearing from Almanac		**D**	0.0 E
Long	- 34° 23.0'			**C**	299°
LHA	309° 39.9'		000.8		

Notes:

Celestial Problems
Compass Deviation By Polaris

Problem # 6 (USCG) (01494) Chapter

Date:	5 Aug	Time		03:10 ZT	LAT:	09° 02' N
		CT			**LONG**	21° 08' W
ZT	03:10	**CE**			**S-**	
ZD	+1	**CCT**			**C-**	
GMT	04:10	**GMT**				

Almanac		Compass Correction		Deviation		
GHA	13° 37.2'					
M/S	2° 30.4'	**T**	000.5	**T**	314.5	**T**	314.5
GHA	16° 07.6'	**E**	1.5 W	**E**	1.5 W	**V**	15° W
±SHA/v		**G**	002.0	**G**	316°	**M**	329.5
Sum	16° 07.6'	Polaris bearing from Almanac		**D**	0.5 E
Long	- 21° 08.0'			**C**	329°
LHA	354° 59.6'		000.5		

Notes:

Deviation by Polaris Rev. 4 April 2013

Celestial Problems
Compass Deviation By Polaris

Problem # 7 (USCG) (01495) — Chapter

Date:	9 Sep	Time	20:43 ZT	LAT:	24° 18' N
ZT	20:43	CT		LONG	66° 46' W
ZD	+4	CE		S-	
GMT	24:43	CCT		C-	
10 Sept	00:43	GMT			

Almanac		Compass Correction		Deviation			
GHA	348° 56.4'						
M/S	10° 46.8'	T	001.0	T	031.0	T	031.0
GHA	359° 43.2'	E	0.0 W	E	0.0	V	11° W
±SHA/v		G	001°	G	031°	M	042.0
Sum	359° 43.2'	Polaris bearing from Almanac				D	2.0 E
Long	- 66° 46.0'					C	040°
LHA	292° 57.0'	001.0					

Notes: Interpolate 000.9 to 001.1 = 001.0

Celestial Problems
Compass Deviation By Polaris

Problem # 8 (USCG) (01496) — Chapter

Date:	3 Oct	Time	21:22 ZT	LAT:	26° 32' N
ZT	21:22	CT		LONG	84° 26' W
ZD	+6	CE		S-	
GMT	27:22	CCT		C-	
4 Oct	03:22	GMT			

Almanac		Compass Correction		Deviation			
GHA	57° 43.1'						
M/S	5° 30.9'	T	000.8	T	107.0	T	107.0
GHA	63° 14.0'	E	1.0 E	E	1.0 E	V	0
±SHA/v		G	359.8	G	106°	M	107.0
Sum	63° 14.0'	Polaris bearing from Almanac				D	0.0 W
Long	- 84° 26.0'					C	107°
LHA	278° 48.0'	000.8					

Notes: Interpolate 000.7 to 000.9 = 000.8

Celestial Problems
Compass Deviation By Polaris

Problem # 9 (USCG) (01497) Chapter

Date:	19 Nov		Time		01:46 ZT	LAT:		33° 48' N
			CT			LONG		25° 22' E
	ZT	01:46	CE				S-	
	ZD	-2	CCT				C-	
	GMT	23:46	GMT					

Almanac		Compass Correction		Deviation				
GHA	42° 53.6'							
M/S	11° 31.9'	T	359.3	T	223.5	T		223.5
GHA	54° 25.5'	E	0.5 W	E	0.5 W	V		2° E
±SHA/v		G	359.8	G	224°	M		221.5
Sum	54° 15.5'	Polaris bearing from Almanac				D		1.0 W
Long	+ 25° 22.0'					C		222.5°
LHA	79° 37.5'		359.3					

Notes:

Celestial Problems
Compass Deviation By Polaris

Problem # 10 (USCG) (01498) Chapter

Date:	7 Dec.		Time		03:50 ZT	LAT:		35° 42' N
			CT			LONG		17° 38' E
	ZT	03:50	CE				S-	
	ZD		CCT				C-	
	GMT	02:50	GMT					

Almanac		Compass Correction		Deviation				
GHA	105° 45.5'							
M/S	12° 32.1'	T	359.0	T	015.3	T		015.3
GHA	118° 17.6'	E	0.7 W	E	0.7 W	V		1° E
±SHA/v		G	359.7	G	016.0°	M		014.3
Sum	118° 17.6'	Polaris bearing from Almanac				D		0.3 E
Long	+ 17° 38.0'					C		014.0°
LHA	135° 55.6'		359.0					

Notes:

USCG SUN RISING AND SETTING,
PROBLEMS WORKED-OUT
Chapter 18, Celestial (Upon Oceans Endorsement)
WITH EXTRACTS FROM THE NAUTICAL ALMANAC

ALEXANDER F. HICKETHIER, MBA
and
DR. HU JIA-SHEN

SUN AND MOON RISING, SETTING, AND TWILIGHT

Rising, Setting, and Twilight

In both *Air* and *Nautical Almanacs*, the times of sunrise, sunset, moonrise, moonset, and twilight information, at various latitudes between 72°N and 60°S, is listed to the nearest whole minute. By definition, rising or setting occurs when the upper limb of the body is on the visible horizon, assuming standard refraction for zero height of eye. Because of variations in refraction and height of eye, computation to a greater precision than 1 minute of time is not justified.

In high latitudes, some of the phenomena do not occur during certain periods. Symbols are used in the almanacs to indicate:

1. Sun or Moon does not set, but remains continuously above the horizon, indicated by an open rectangle.

2. Sun or Moon does not rise, but remains continuously below the horizon, indicated by a solid rectangle.

3. Twilight lasts all night, indicated by 4 slashes (/////).

The *Nautical Almanac* makes no provision for finding the times of rising, setting, or twilight in Polar Regions. The *Air Almanac* has graphs for this purpose.

In the *Nautical Almanac*, sunrise, sunset, and twilight tables are given only once for the middle of the three days on each page opening. For navigational purposes this information can be used for all three days. Both almanacs have moonrise and moonset tables for each day.

Lat.	Twilight Naut.	Twilight Civil	Sunrise
°	h m	h m	h m
N 72	////	////	01 33
N 70	////	////	02 22
68	////	00 23	02 53
66	////	01 45	03 15
64	////	02 20	03 33
62	00 21	02 45	03 47
60	01 34	03 04	03 59
N 58	02 06	03 20	04 10
56	02 29	03 33	04 19
54	02 48	03 45	04 27
52	03 03	03 54	04 34
50	03 15	04 03	04 40
45	03 41	04 21	04 54
N 40	04 00	04 36	05 06
35	04 15	04 48	05 15
30	04 28	04 58	05 24
20	04 48	05 15	05 38
N 10	05 03	05 29	05 50
0	05 16	05 41	06 02
S 10	05 26	05 52	06 13
20	05 36	06 03	06 26
30	05 46	06 14	06 39
35	05 51	06 21	06 47
40	05 55	06 28	06 56
45	06 01	06 35	07 06
S 50	06 06	06 45	07 19
52	06 08	06 49	07 25
54	06 11	06 53	07 31
56	06 13	06 58	07 38
58	06 16	07 03	07 46
S 60	06 19	07 09	07 55

Lat.	Sunset	Twilight Civil	Twilight Naut.
°	h m	h m	h m
N 72	22 29	////	////
N 70	21 44	////	////
68	21 15	23 24	////
66	20 53	22 21	////
64	20 36	21 47	////
62	20 22	21 23	23 29
60	20 10	21 04	22 32
N 58	20 00	20 49	22 01
56	19 51	20 36	21 39
54	19 43	20 25	21 21
52	19 36	20 15	21 06
50	19 29	20 06	20 54
45	19 16	19 48	20 29
N 40	19 05	19 34	20 10
35	18 55	19 22	19 55
30	18 47	19 12	19 43
20	18 33	18 56	19 23
N 10	18 20	18 42	19 08
0	18 09	18 30	18 55
S 10	17 58	18 19	18 44
20	17 46	18 08	18 35
30	17 32	17 57	18 25
35	17 24	17 51	18 21
40	17 15	17 44	18 16
45	17 05	17 36	18 11
S 50	16 53	17 27	18 05
52	16 47	17 23	18 03
54	16 40	17 19	18 01
56	16 33	17 14	17 58
58	16 25	17 08	17 56
S 60	16 16	17 03	17 53

The tabulations are in LMT. On the zone meridian, this is the zone time (ZT). For every 15' of longitude the observer's position differs from the zone meridian, the zone time of the phenomena differs by 1m, being later if the observer is west of the zone meridian, and earlier if east of the zone meridian. The LMT of the phenomena varies with latitude of the observer, declination of the body, and hour angle of the body relative to the mean Sun.

The UT of the phenomenon is found from LMT by the formula:

UT = LMT + W Longitude.
UT = LMT - E Longitude.

To use this formula, convert the longitude to time using the table on page i or by computation, and add or subtract as indicated. Apply the zone description (ZD) to find the zone time of the phenomena. Sunrise and sunset are also tabulated in the tide tables (from 76°N to 60°S).

Finding Times of Sunrise and Sunset

To find the time of sunrise or sunset in the *Nautical Almanac*, enter the table on the daily page, and extract the LMT for the latitude next smaller than your own (unless it is exactly the same). Apply a correction from Table I on almanac page xxxii to interpolate for altitude, determining the sign by inspection. Then convert LMT to ZT using the difference of longitude between the local and zone meridians.

For the *Air Almanac*, the procedure is the same as for the *Nautical Almanac*, except that the LMT is taken from the tables of sunrise and sunset instead of

from the daily page, and the latitude correction is by linear interpolation. The tabulated times are for the Greenwich meridian. Except in high latitudes near the time of the equinoxes, the time of sunrise and sunset varies so little from day to day that no interpolation is needed for longitude. In high latitudes interpolation is not always possible. Between two tabulated entries, the Sun may in fact cease to set. In this case, the time of rising and setting is greatly influenced by small variations in refraction and changes in height of eye.

Twilight

Morning twilight ends at sunrise, and evening twilight begins at sunset. The time of the darker limit can be found from the almanacs. The time of the darker limits of both civil and nautical twilights (center of the Sun 6° and 12°, respectively, below the celestial horizon) is given in the *Nautical Almanac*.

The *Air Almanac* provides tabulations of civil twilight from 60°S to 72°N. The brightness of the sky at any given depression of the Sun below the horizon may vary considerably from day to day, depending upon the amount of cloudiness, haze, and other atmospheric conditions. In general, the most effective period for observing stars and planets occurs when the center of the Sun is between about 3° and 9° below the celestial horizon.

4-4

Hence, the darker limit of civil twilight occurs at about the mid-point of this period. At the darker limit of nautical twilight, the horizon is generally too dark for good

The Almanac Observations.

At the darker limit of astronomical twilight (center of the Sun 18° below the celestial horizon), full night has set in. The time of this twilight is given in the *Astronomical Almanac*. Its approximate value can be determined by extrapolation in the *Nautical Almanac*, noting that the duration of the different kinds of twilight is proportional to the number of degrees of depression for the center of the Sun. More precise determination of the time at which the center of the Sun is any given number of degrees below the celestial horizon can be determined by a large-scale diagram on the plane of the celestial meridian, or by computation. Duration of twilight in latitudes higher than 65°N is given in a graph in the *Air Almanac*.

In both *Nautical* and *Air Almanacs*, the method of finding the darker limit of twilight is the same as that for sunrise and sunset.

Sometimes in high latitudes the Sun does not rise but twilight occurs. This is indicated in the *Air Almanac* by a solid black rectangle symbol in the sunrise and sunset column. To find the time of beginning of morning twilight, subtract half the duration of twilight as obtained from the duration of twilight graph from the time of meridian transit of the Sun; and for the time of ending of evening twilight, add it to the time of meridian

transit. The LMT of meridian transit never differs by more than 16.4m (approximately) from 1200. The actual time on any date can be determined from the almanac.

Rising, Setting, and Twilight on a Moving Craft

Instructions to this point relate to a fixed position on the Earth. Aboard a moving craft the problem is complicated somewhat by the fact that time of occurrence depends upon the position of the craft, which itself depends on the time. At ship speeds, it is generally sufficiently accurate to make an approximate mental solution and use the position of the vessel at this time to make a more accurate solution. If greater accuracy is required, the position at the time indicated in the second solution can be used for a third solution. If desired, this process can be repeated until the same answer is obtained from two consecutive solutions. However, it is generally sufficient to alter the first solution by 1m for each 15' of longitude that the position of the craft differs from that used in the solution, adding if west of the estimated position, and subtracting if east of it. In applying this rule, use both longitudes to the nearest 15'. The first solution is the **first estimate**; the second solution is the **second estimate.**

A navigation team keeping an appropriate DR needs only make one calculation for the approximate position at estimated Rising, Setting, and Twilight for that day.

SUNRISE AND SUNSET
Chapter 18, Celestial for Master/Mate limited Upon Oceans

01251. On 16 August 1981, your 1600 ZT DR position is LAT 26° 17.0' N, LONG 165° 17.0' E. You are on course 301° T at a speed of 15 knots. What will be the zone time of sunset at your vessel?

A. 1827
B. 1832
C. 1838
D. 1845

01252. On 13 August 1981, your 0345 ZT DR position is LAT 21° 35.0' N, LONG 135° 26.0' W. You are on course 052° T at a speed of 14 knots. What will be the zone time of sunset at your vessel?

A. 0443
B. 0449
C. 0536
D. 0540

01253. On 8 August 1981, your 0400 ZT DR position is LAT 23° 16.0' S, LONG 105° 33.0' W. You are on course 295° T at a speed of 25 knots. What will be the zone time of sunrise at your vessel?

A. 0623
B. 0629
C. 0636
D. 0654

01254. On 19 July 1981, your 1500 ZT DR position is LAT 28° 15.0' N, LONG 120° 28.0' W. You are on course 233° at a speed of 10 knots. What will be the zone time of sunset at your vessel?

A. 1842
B. 1853
C. 1901
D. 1909

01255. On 12 June 1981, your 0400 ZT DR position is LAT 22° 31.0' N, LONG 31° 45.0'' W. You are on course 240° T at a speed of 16.5 knots. What will be the zone time of sunrise at your vessel?

A. 0507
B. 0515
C. 0523
D. 0645

01256. On 17 May 1981, your 0300 ZT DR position is LAT 27° 21.0' N, LONG 146° 14.0' E. You are on course 107° T at a speed of 18 knots. What will be the zone time of sunrise at your vessel?

A. 0457
B. 0511
C. 0519
D. 0522

01257. On 5 May 1981, your 1300 ZT DR position is LAT 25° 16.0' S, LONG 12° 30.0' W. You are on course 012° T at a speed of 14 knots. What will be the zone time of sunset at your vessel?

A. 1702
B. 1719
C. 1730
D. 1741

01258. On 28 April 1981, your 1600 ZT DR position is LAT 26° 21.0' S, LONG 68° 42.0' E. You are on course 072° T at a speed of 17 knots. What will be the zone time of sunset at your vessel?

A. 1706
B. 1730
C. 1739
D. 1756

01259. On 10 April 1981, your 1630 ZT DR position is LAT 21° 03.0' N, LONG 63° 11.0' W. You are on course 324° T at a speed of 22 knots. What will be the zone time of sunset at your vessel?

A. 1805
B. 1814
C. 1818
D. 1833

01260. On 16 March 1981, your 0330 ZT DR position is LAT 22° 36.0' S, LONG 76° 16.0' E. You are on course 098° T at a speed of 16 knots. What will be the zone time of sunrise at your vessel?

A. 0545
B. 0553
C. 0600
D. 0608

01261. On 16 February 1981, your 0300 ZT DR position is LAT 28° 32.0' S, LONG 176° 49.0' E. You are on course 082° T at a speed of 21 knots. What will be the zone time of sunrise at your vessel?

A. 0534
B. 0552
C. 0631
D. 0645

01262. On 27 September 1981, your 0345 ZT DR position is LAT 26° 18.0' S, LONG 4° 18.0' W. You are on course 271° T at a speed of 15 knots. What will be the zone time of sunrise at your vessel?

A. 0525
B. 0545
C. 0555
D. 0605

01263. On 18 October 1981, your 1330 ZT DR position is LAT 27° 32.0' N, LONG 154° 47.0' W.

You are on course 115° T at a speed of 20 knots. What will be the zone time of sunset at your vessel?

A. 1715
B. 1729
C. 1742
D. 1751

01264. On 17 November 1981, your 1530 ZT DR position is LAT 27° 13.0' S, LONG 153° 21.0' W. You are on course 261° T at a speed of 14 knots. What will be the zone time of sunset at your vessel?

A. 1813
B. 1830
C. 1842
D. 1847

01265. On 22 November 1981, your 1400 ZT DR position is LAT 22° 16.0' N, LONG 136° 37.0' E. You are on course 038° T at a speed of 22 knots. What will be the zone time of sunset at your vessel?

A. 1705
B. 1710
C. 1714
D. 1718

01266. On 1 December 1981, your 1600 ZT DR position is LAT 22° 48.0' S, LONG 91° 26.0' E. You are on course 327° T at a speed of 16 knots. What will be the zone time of sunset at your vessel?

A. 1823
B. 1827
C. 1831
D. 1847

4-8

01267. On 10 December 1981, your 1300 ZT DR position is LAT 26° 27.0' S, LONG 79° 04.0' E. You are on course 068° T at a speed of 14 knots. What will be the zone time of sunset at your vessel?

A. 1824
B. 1846
C. 1854
D. 1908

01268. On 25 December 1981, your 0330 ZT DR position is LAT 25° 15.0' N, LONG 32° 16.0' W. You are on course 145° T at a speed of 20 knots. What will be the zone time of sunrise at your vessel?

A. 0623
B. 0635
C. 0641
D. 0647

01269. At 1400 zone time on 11 April 1981, your DR position is LAT 25° 40' N, LONG 91° 00' W. You are steering 180° T at a speed of 10.0 knots. What is your zone time of sunset?

A. 1812
B. 1816
C. 1820
D. 1825

01270. At 0500 zone time on 21 August 1981, your DR position is LAT 47° 00' N, LONG 125° 15' W. You are steering 000° T at a speed of 9.8 knots. What is the zone time of sunrise?

A. 0525
B. 0529
C. 0531
D. 0535

01271. At 0400 zone time on 24 June 1981, your DR position is LAT 23° 10.0' N, LONG 085° 33' W. You are steering 295° T at a speed of 10.0 knots. What is the zone time of sunrise?

A. 0452
B. 0458
C. 0504
D. 0510

01272. At 1800 zone time on 7 December 1981, your DR position is LAT 22° 48' S, LONG 91° 26' W. You are steering 320° T at a speed of 14.0 knots. What is the zone time of sunset?

A. 1830
B. 1836
C. 1842
D. 1852

01273. At 1544 zone time on 5 October 1981, your DR position is LAT 25° 00' N, LONG 60° 15' W. You are steering 270° T at a speed of 6.8 knots. What is the zone time of sunset?

A. 1728
B. 1737
C. 1741
D. 1745

01274. At 0325 zone time on 13 February 1981, your DR position is LAT 23° 20' N, LONG 155° 15' W. You are steering 240° T at a speed of 13.6 knots. What is the zone time of sunrise?

A. 0652
B. 0657
C. 0706
D. 0711

01275. At 1730 zone time on 3 March 1981, your DR position is LAT 16° 00' S, LONG 80° 00' W. You are steering 000° T at a speed of 7.5 knots. What is the zone time of sunset?

A. 1829
B. 1834
C. 1843
D. 1852

01276. Your 0000 zone time on 13 June 1981 is LAT 24° 35' N, LONG 142° 26' E. Your vessel is on course 245° T, speed of 13.5 knots. What is the zone time of sunrise?

A. 0442
B. 0447
C. 0503
D. 0528

01277. On 22 June 1981, your 0400 zone time DR position is LAT 23° 00' N, LONG 81° 45' W. You are steaming on course 110° T at a speed of 8.6 knots. What will be the zone time of sunrise at your vessel?

A. 0537
B. 0541
C. 0545
D. 0547

01278. On 17 April 1981, your vessel is enroute from the Panama Canal to Kobe, Japan. Your 0400 zone time DR position is LAT 26° 12.0' N, LONG 126° 12.0' W. Your vessel is on course 285° T at a speed of 18 knots. What will be the zone time of sunrise at your vessel?

A. 0535
B. 0541
C. 0552
D. 0602

01279. At 0327 zone time on 29 May 1981, your DR position is LAT 25° 00' N, LONG 64° 15' W. You are steering 270° T at a speed of 13.6 knots. What is the zone time of sunrise?

A. 0521
B. 0529
C. 0536
D. 0548

01280. On 27 March 1981, your 0330 zone time DR position is LAT 23° 32' N, LONG 154° 47' E. Your vessel is on a course of 105° T at a speed of 20 knots. What will be the zone time of sunrise at your vessel?

A. 0534
B. 0557
C. 0612
D. 0624

01281. On 2 January 1981, you on a course of 094° T at a speed of 20 knots. At 0430, your DR position is LAT 24° 12' N, LONG 71° 24' W. Determine the zone time of sunrise.

A. 0627
B. 0636
C. 0644
D. 0701

01282. On 1 November 1981, your 1600 zone time DR position is LAT 27° 48' S, LONG 91° 26' E. Your vessel is on a course of 327° T at a speed of 16 knots. What will be the zone time of sunset at your vessel?

A. 1813
B. 1817
C. 1821
D. 1826

01283. On 5 May 1981, your 1800 zone time DR position is LAT 26° 11.5' N, LONG 65° 35.0' W. You are on course 270° T at a speed of 12 knots. What will be the zone time of sunset at your vessel?

A. 1825
B. 1840
C. 1857
D. 1901

01284. On 10 November 1981, your 1630 zone time DR position is LAT 25° 10.0' N, LONG 71° 12.0' W. You are on course 335° T at a speed of 24 knots. What will be the zone time of sunset at your vessel?

A. 1650
B. 1700
C. 1715
D. 1730

01285.   On 28 June 1981, your 1820 ZT DR position is LAT 16° 00.0' N, LONG 31° 00.0' W. You are on course 310° T at a speed of 18 knots. What will be the zone time of sunset at your vessel?

A. 1828
B. 1832
C. 1836
D. 1840

Answers for USCG Problems

01251 C
01252 C
01253 C
01254 C
01255 C
01256 D
01257 B
01258 D
01259 D
01260 B
01261 B
01262 D
01263 C
01264 D
01265 A
01266 B
01267 A
01268 D
01269 D
01270 A
01271 B
01272 C
01273 D
01274 B
01275 C
01276 B
01277 B
01278 D
01279 B
01280 A
01281 A
01282 A
01283 C
01284 B
01285 D

Celestial Problems
Sunrise and Sunset

Problem # (USCG) (1251)		Chapter 18	
Date: 16 Aug		**FIX TIME**	16:00
Required		**LAT**	26° 17' N
Sunset		**LONG**	165° 17' E
		C-	301°
		S-	15

LATITUDE CORRECTION		LONGITUDE CORRECTION		DR AT PREDICTED TIME OF SUNRISE OR SUNSET	
				TIME	16:30
LAT (20)	18:29	**STD MER**	165°	**LAT**	26° 37' N
LAT (30)	18:41	**LONG**	164° 41'	**LONG**	164° 41' E
d	+ 12	**Dlo**	0° 19'		
Inc LAT (x)	397	**dtime (E)**	− 1.2	**Base Time**	18:29
Inv Lat (÷)	600			**tcorr**	+0:07
Correction	+ 7.9			**Time of S/R - S/S**	18:36

NOTE:

Celestial Problems
Sunrise and Sunset

Problem # (USCG) (1252)		Chapter 18	
Date: 13 Aug		**FIX TIME**	03:45
Required		**LAT**	21° 35' N
Sunrise		**LONG**	135° 26' W
		C-	052°
		S-	14

LATITUDE CORRECTION		LONGITUDE CORRECTION		DR AT PREDICTED TIME OF SUNRISE OR SUNSET	
				TIME	05:30
LAT (20)	05:39	**STD MER**	135°	**LAT**	21° 50' N
LAT (30)	05:25	**LONG**	135° 05'	**LONG**	135° 05' W
d	- 14	**Dlo**	0° 05'		
Inc LAT (x)	110	**dtime (W)**	+ 0	**Base Time**	05:39
Inv Lat (÷)	600			**tcorr**	0:03
Correction	- 2.6 (3)			**Time of S/R - S/S**	05:36

NOTE: Problem States sunset vise sunrise

Celestial Problems
Sunrise and Sunset

Problem # (USCG) (1253)		Chapter 18		
Date: 8 Aug 81			**FIX TIME**	04:00
Required			**LAT**	23° 16' S
Sunrise			**LONG**	105° 33' W
			C-	295°
			S-	25

LATITUDE CORRECTION		LONGITUDE CORRECTION		DR AT PREDICTED TIME OF SUNRISE OR SUNSET	
				TIME	06:30
LAT (20)	06:26	**STD MER**	105°	**LAT**	22° 50' S
LAT (30)	06:39	**LONG**	106° 35'	**LONG**	106° 35' W
d	+ 0:13	**Dlo**	1° 35'		
Inc LAT (x)	170	**dtime (W)**	+ 6.3	**Base Time**	06:26
Inv Lat (÷)	600			**tcorr**	+0:10
Correction	+ 3.7			**Time of S/R - S/S**	06:36

NOTE:

Celestial Problems
Sunrise and Sunset

Problem # (USCG) (1254)		Chapter 18		
Date: 19 July			**FIX TIME**	15:00
Required			**LAT**	28° 15' N
Sunset			**LONG**	120° 28' W
			C-	233°
			S-	10

LATITUDE CORRECTION		LONGITUDE CORRECTION		DR AT PREDICTED TIME OF SUNRISE OR SUNSET	
				TIME	19:00
LAT (20)	18:42	**STD MER**	120°	**LAT**	27° 50' N
LAT (30)	19:01	**LONG**	121° 06'	**LONG**	121° 06' W
d	+ 19	**Dlo**	1° 06'		
Inc LAT (x)	470	**Dtime (W)**	+ 4	**Base Time**	18:42
Inv Lat (÷)	600			**tcorr**	+ 19
Correction	14.9			**Time of S/R - S/S**	19:01
	+ 15				

NOTE:

Celestial Problems Sunrise and Sunset			
Problem # (USCG) (1255)		Chapter 18	
Date: 12 June		**FIX TIME**	04:00
Required		**LAT**	22° 31' N
Sunrise		**LONG**	031° 45' W
		C-	240°
		S-	16.5
LATITUDE CORRECTION		**LONGITUDE CORRECTION**	**DR AT PREDICTED TIME OF SUNRISE OR SUNSET**

LATITUDE CORRECTION		**LONGITUDE CORRECTION**		**DR AT PREDICTED TIME OF SUNRISE OR SUNSET**	
				TIME	05:20
LAT (20)	05:20	**STD MER**	30°	**LAT**	22° 20' N
LAT (30)	04:58	**LONG**	32° 06'	**LONG**	032° 06' W
d	- 0:22	**Dlo**	2°06'		
Inc LAT (x)	140	**dtime (W)**	+ 8	**Base Time**	05:20
Inv Lat (÷)	600			**tcorr**	+0:03
Correction	- 5.1			**Time of S/R - S/S**	05:23
NOTE:					

Celestial Problems Sunrise and Sunset			
Problem # (USCG) (1256)		Chapter 18	
Date: 17 May		**FIX TIME**	03:00
Required		**LAT**	27° 21' N
Sunrise		**LONG**	146° 14' E
		C-	107°
		S-	18

LATITUDE CORRECTION		**LONGITUDE CORRECTION**		**DR AT PREDICTED TIME OF SUNRISE OR SUNSET**	
				TIME	05:20
LAT (20)	05:23	**STD MER**	150°	**LAT**	27° 10' N
LAT (30)	05:05	**LONG**	146° 54'	**LONG**	146° 54' E
d	- 18	**Dlo**	-3° 06'		
Inc LAT (x)	430	**dtime (W)**	+ 12.4	**Base Time**	05:23
Inv Lat (÷)	600			**tcorr**	-0:01
Correction	- 12.9			**Time of S/R - S/S**	05:22
NOTE:					

Celestial Problems Sunrise and Sunset					
Problem # (USCG) (1257			Chapter 18		
Date: 5 May			**FIX TIME**	13:00	
Required			LAT	25° 16' S	
Sunset			LONG	012° 30' W	
			C-	012°	
			S-	14	
LATITUDE CORRECTION		**LONGITUDE CORRECTION**		**DR AT PREDICTED TIME OF SUNRISE OR SUNSET**	
				TIME	17:15
LAT (20)	17:36	**STD MER**	15°	LAT	24° 20' S
LAT (30)	17:22	**LONG**	12° 11'	LONG	012° 11' W
d	- 14	**Dlo**	2° 49'		
Inc LAT (x)	260	**dtime** (E)	− 11.3	**Base Time**	17:36
Inv Lat (÷)	600			**tcorr**	-0:17
Correction	- 6			**Time of S/R - S/S**	17:19
NOTE:					

Celestial Problems Sunrise and Sunset					
Problem # (USCG) (1258)			Chapter 18		
Date: 28 Apr			**FIX TIME**	16:00	
Required			LAT	26° 21' S	
Sunset			LONG	068° 42' E	
			C-	072°	
			S-	17	
LATITUDE CORRECTION		**LONGITUDE CORRECTION**		**DR AT PREDICTED TIME OF SUNRISE OR SUNSET**	
				TIME	17:30
LAT (20)	17:39	**STD MER**	75°	LAT	26° 13' S
LAT (30)	17:27	**LONG**	69° 08'	LONG	069° 08' E
d	- 12	**Dlo**	5° 52'		
Inc LAT (x)	373	**dtime** (W)	+ 23	**Base Time**	17:39
Inv Lat (÷)	600			**tcorr**	+0:16
Correction	- 7.5			**Time of S/R - S/S**	17:55
NOTE:					

Celestial Problems Sunrise and Sunset		
Problem # (USCG) (1259)		Chapter 18
Date: 10 Apr **Required** Sunset		**FIX TIME** 16:30 LAT 21° 03' N LONG 063° 10' W C- 324° S- 22

LATITUDE CORRECTION		**LONGITUDE CORRECTION**		**DR AT PREDICTED TIME OF SUNRISE OR SUNSET**	
				TIME	18:20
LAT (20)	18:17	STD MER	60°	LAT	21° 39' N
LAT (30)	18:25	LONG	63° 38'	LONG	063° 38' N
d	+8	Dlo	3° 38'		
Inc LAT (x)	99	dtime (W)	+ 14.5	**Base Time**	18:17
Inv Lat (÷)	600			**tcorr**	+0:16
Correction	+ 1.3			**Time of S/R - S/S**	18:33

NOTE:

Celestial Problems Sunrise and Sunset		
Problem # (USCG) (1260)		Chapter 18
Date: 16 March Required Sunrise		**FIX TIME** 03:30 LAT 22° 36' S LONG 076° 16' E C- 098° S- 16

LATITUDE CORRECTION		**LONGITUDE CORRECTION**		**DR AT PREDICTED TIME OF SUNRISE OR SUNSET**	
				TIME	06:00
LAT (20)	06:02	STD MER	75°	LAT	22° 42' S
LAT (30)	06:00	LONG	76° 42'	LONG	076° 58' E
d	+ 0:02	Dlo	1° 42'		
Inc LAT (x)	162	dtime (E)	- 6.8	**Base Time**	06:02
Inv Lat (÷)	600			**tcorr**	-0:06
Correction	+ 0.5			**Time of S/R - S/S**	05:56

NOTE:

Celestial Problems Sunrise and Sunset			
Problem # (USCG) (1261)		Chapter 18	
Date: 16 Feb **Required** Sunrise		**FIX TIME** 03:00' LAT 28° 32' S LONG 176° 49' E C- 082° S- 21	

LATITUDE CORRECTION		**LONGITUDE CORRECTION**		**DR AT PREDICTED TIME OF SUNRISE OR SUNSET**	
				TIME	05:50
LAT (20)	05:52	**STD MER**	180°	LAT	28° 26' S
LAT (30)	05:41	**LONG**	177° 37'	LONG	177° 37' E
d	- 0:11	**Dlo**	2° 3'		
Inc LAT (x)	506	**dtime (W)**	+ 9.5	**Base Time**	05:52
Inv Lat (÷)	600			**tcorr**	0
Correction	- 9.3			**Time of S/R - S/S**	05:52
NOTE:					

Celestial Problems Sunrise and Sunset			
Problem # (USCG) (1262)		Chapter 18	
Date: 27 Sep Required Sunrise		**FIX TIME** 03:45 LAT 26° 18' S LONG 004° 18' W C- 271 S- 15	

LATITUDE CORRECTION		**LONGITUDE CORRECTION**		**DR AT PREDICTED TIME OF SUNRISE OR SUNSET**	
				TIME	05:45
LAT (20)	05:46	**STD MER**	0	LAT	26° 17' S
LAT (30)	05:45	**LONG**	4° 52'	LONG	004° 52' W
d	- 0:01	**Dlo**	4° 52'		
Inc LAT (x)	377	**dtime (W)**	+ 8.9	**Base Time**	05:46
Inv Lat (÷)	600			**tcorr**	+0:08
Correction	- 0.6			**Time of S/R - S/S**	05:54
NOTE:					

Celestial Problems Sunrise and Sunset					
Problem # (USCG) (1263))			Chapter 18		
Date: 18 Oct			**FIX TIME**	13:30	
Required			LAT	27° 32′ N	
Sunset			LONG	154° 47′ W	
			C-	115°	
			S-	20	
LATITUDE CORRECTION		**LONGITUDE CORRECTION**		**DR AT PREDICTED TIME OF SUNRISE OR SUNSET**	
				TIME	18:10
LAT (20)	17:35	**STD MER**	150°	LAT	26° 51′ N
LAT (30)	17:27	**LONG**	153° 12′	LONG	153° 12′ W
d	- 0:08	**Dlo**	3° 12′		
Inc LAT (x)	411	**dtime (W)**	+ 12.8	**Base Time**	17:35
Inv Lat (÷)	600			**tcorr**	+0:07
Correction	- 5.5			**Time of S/R - S/S**	17:42
NOTE:					

Celestial Problems Sunrise and Sunset					
Problem # (USCG) (1264)			Chapter 18		
Date: 17 Nov			**FIX TIME**		
Required			LAT	27° 13.0' S	
Sunset			LONG	153° 21.0' W	
			C-	261°	
			S-	14	
LATITUDE CORRECTION		**LONGITUDE CORRECTION**		**DR AT PREDICTED TIME OF SUNRISE OR SUNSET**	
				TIME	18:30
LAT (20)	18:17	**STD MER**	150°	LAT	27° 20′ N
LAT (30)	18:34	**LONG**	154° 07′	LONG	154° 07′ W
d	+0:17	**Dlo**	4° 07′		
Inc LAT (x)	440	**dtime (W)**	+16.5	**Base Time**	18:17
Inv Lat (÷)	600			**tcorr**	+0:29
Correction	+12.5			**Time of S/R - S/S**	18:46
NOTE:					

Celestial Problems
Sunrise and Sunset

Problem # (USCG) (1265)		Chapter 18	
Date: 22 Nov		**FIX TIME**	14:00
Required		LAT	22° 16' N
Sunset		LONG	136° 37' E
		C-	038°
		S-	22

LATITUDE CORRECTION		LONGITUDE CORRECTION		DR AT PREDICTED TIME OF SUNRISE OR SUNSET	
				TIME	17:00
LAT (20)	17:19	**STD MER**	135°	LAT	23° 10' N
LAT (30)	17:01	**LONG**	137° 23'	LONG	137° 23' E
d	- 0:18	**Dlo**	2° 23'		
Inc LAT (x)	190	**dtime (E)**	− 9.5	**Base Tim**	17:19
Inv Lat (÷)	600			**tcorr**	-0:15
Correction	- 5.7			**Time of S/R - S/S**	17:03

NOTE:

Celestial Problems
Sunrise and Sunset

Problem # (USCG) (1266)		Chapter 18	
Date: 1 Dec.		**FIX TIME**	16:00
Required		LAT	22° 4'8 S
Sunset		LONG	091° 26' E
		C-	327°
		S-	16

LATITUDE CORRECTION		LONGITUDE CORRECTION		DR AT PREDICTED TIME OF SUNRISE OR SUNSET	
				TIME	18:30
LAT (20)	18:27	**STD MER**	90°	LAT	22° 13' S
LAT (30)	18:47	**LONG**	91° 02'	LONG	091° 02' E
d	+ 20	**Dlo**	1° 02'		
Inc LAT (x)	133	**dtime (E)**	− 4	**Base Time**	18:27
Inv Lat (÷)	600			**tcorr**	0:00
Correction	+ 4.4			**Time of S/R - S/S**	18:27

NOTE:

Celestial Problems Sunrise and Sunset				
Problem # (USCG) (1269)			Chapter 18	
Date: 11 Apr			FIX TIME	14:00
Required			LAT	25° 40' N
Sunset			LONG	091° 00' W
			C-	180°
			S-	10
LATITUDE CORRECTION		**LONGITUDE CORRECTION**	**DR AT PREDICTED TIME OF SUNRISE OR SUNSET**	
			TIME	18:20
LAT (20)	18:17	**STD MER** 90°	LAT	24° 57' N
LAT (30)	18:25	**LONG** 91° 00'	LONG	091° 00' W
d	+ :08	**Dlo** 1° 00'		
Inc LAT (x)	297	**dtime (W)** + 4	**Base Time**	18:17
Inv Lat (÷)	600		**tcorr**	+0:08
Correction	+ 4		**Time of S/R - S/S**	18:25
NOTE:				

Celestial Problems Sunrise and Sunset				
Problem # (USCG) (1270)			Chapter 18	
Date: 21 Aug			FIX TIME	05:00
Required			LAT	47° 00' N
Sunrise			LONG	125° 15' W
			C-	000°
			S-	9.8
LATITUDE CORRECTION		**LONGITUDE CORRECTION**	**DR AT PREDICTED TIME OF SUNRISE OR SUNSET**	
			TIME	05:30
LAT (45)	05:08	**STD MER** 120°	LAT	47° 05' N
LAT (50)	04:58	**LONG** 125° 15'	LONG	125° 15' W
d	- 0:10	**Dlo** 5° 15'		
Inc LAT (x)	125	**dtime (W)** +21	**Base Time**	05:08
Inv Lat (÷)	600		**tcorr**	0:17
Correction	- 4		**Time of S/R - S/S**	05:25
NOTE:				

Celestial Problems Sunrise and Sunset					
Problem # (USCG) (1271)			Chapter 18		

Date: 24 Jun			**FIX TIME**	04:00	
Required			**LAT**	23° 10' N	
Sunrise			**LONG**	085° 33' W	
			C-	295°	
			S-	10	

LATITUDE CORRECTION		LONGITUDE CORRECTION		DR AT PREDICTED TIME OF SUNRISE OR SUNSET	
				TIME	05:15
LAT (20)	05:22	**STD MER**	90°	**LAT**	23° 16' N
LAT (30)	05:00	**LONG**	85° 47'	**LONG**	085° 47' W
d	- 0:22	**Dlo**	4° 13'		
Inc LAT (x)	196	**dtime (E)**	- 17	**Base Time**	05:22
Inv Lat (÷)	600			**tcorr**	-0:24
Correction	- 7			**Time of S/R - S/S**	04:58

NOTE:

Celestial Problems Sunrise and Sunset					
Problem # (USCG) (1272)			Chapter 18		

Date: 7 Dec			**FIX TIME**	18:00	
Required			**LAT**	22° 48' S	
Sunset			**LONG**	091° 26' W	
			C-	320°	
			S-	14	

LATITUDE CORRECTION		LONGITUDE CORRECTION		DR AT PREDICTED TIME OF SUNRISE OR SUNSET	
				TIME	18:45
LAT (20)	18:30	**STD MER**	90°	**LAT**	22° 38' S
LAT (30)	18:52	**LONG**	91° 34'	**LONG**	091° 34' W
d	+ 0:22	**Dlo**	1° 34'		
Inc LAT (x)	158	**dtime (W)**	+ 6	**Base Time**	18:30
Inv Lat (÷)	600			**tcorr**	0:12
Correction	+ 5.8			**Time of S/R - S/S**	18:42

NOTE:

Celestial Problems Sunrise and Sunset			
Problem # (USCG) (1273)		Chapter 18	

Date: 5 Oct			FIX TIME	15:44
Required			LAT	25° 00' N
Sunset			LONG	060° 15' W
			C-	270°
			S-	6.8

LATITUDE CORRECTION		LONGITUDE CORRECTION		DR AT PREDICTED TIME OF SUNRISE OR SUNSET	
				TIME	17:44
LAT (20)	17:45	STD MER	60° 00'	LAT	25° 00' N
LAT (30)	17:41	LONG	60° 30'	LONG	060° 30' W
d	- 0:04	Dlo	0° 30'		
Inc LAT (x)	300	dtime (W)	+2	Base Time	17:45
Inv Lat (÷)	600			tcorr	+ :00
Correction	- 2			Time of S/R - S/S	17:45

NOTE:

Celestial Problems Sunrise and Sunset			
Problem # (USCG) (1274)		Chapter 18	

Date: 13 Feb			FIX TIME	0325
Required			LAT	23° 20' N
Sunrise			LONG	155° 15' W
			C-	240°
			S-	13.6

LATITUDE CORRECTION		LONGITUDE CORRECTION		DR AT PREDICTED TIME OF SUNRISE OR SUNSET	
				TIME	06:30
LAT (20)	06:30	STD MER	150°	LAT	23° 20' N
LAT (30)	06:42	LONG	155° 27'	LONG	155° 27' W
d	+ 0:12	Dlo	5° 27'		
Inc LAT (x)	200	dtime (W)	+ 22	Base Time	06:30
Inv Lat (÷)	600			tcorr	+0:26
Correction	+ 4			Time of S/R - S/S	06:56

NOTE:

Celestial Problems		
Sunrise and Sunset		
Problem # (USCG) (1275)		Chapter 18

Date:	3 March		FIX TIME	17:30	
	Required		LAT	16° 00' S	
	Sunset		LONG	080° 00' W	
			C-	000°	
			S-	7.5	

LATITUDE CORRECTION		LONGITUDE CORRECTION		DR AT PREDICTED TIME OF SUNRISE OR SUNSET	
				TIME	18:30
LAT (20)	18:20	**STD MER**	75°	LAT	15° 52.5' S
LAT (30)	18:25	**LONG**	80° 00'	LONG	080° 00' W
d	+ 0:05	**Dlo**	5° 00'		
Inc LAT (x)	352.5	**dtime (W)**	+ 20	Base Time	18:20
Inv Lat (÷)	600			tcorr	0:23
Correction	+ 2.9			Time of S/R - S/S	18:43

NOTE:

Celestial Problems		
Sunrise and Sunset		
Problem # (USCG) (1276)		Chapter 18

Date:	13 June		FIX TIME	0000	
	Required		LAT	24° 35' N	
	Sunrise		LONG	142° 26' E	
			C-	245°	
			S-	13.5	

LATITUDE CORRECTION		LONGITUDE CORRECTION		DR AT PREDICTED TIME OF SUNRISE OR SUNSET	
				TIME	05:00
LAT (20)	05:20	**STD MER**	135°	LAT	24° 07' N
LAT (30)	04:58	**LONG**	141° 19'	LONG	141° 19' E
d	- 0:22	**Dlo**	6°19'		
Inc LAT (x)	247	**dtime (W)**	- 25	Base Time	05:20
Inv Lat (÷)	600			tcorr	- 0:34
Correction	- 9			Time of S/R - S/S	04:46

NOTE:

Celestial Problems Sunrise and Sunset					
Problem # (USCG) (1277)			Chapter 18		
Date: 22 June			**FIX TIME**	04:00	
Required			LAT	23° 00' N	
Sunrise			LONG	081°45' W	
			C-	110	
			S-	8.6	
LATITUDE CORRECTION		**LONGITUDE CORRECTION**		**DR AT PREDICTED TIME OF SUNRISE OR SUNSET**	
				TIME	05:15
LAT (20)	05:22	**STD MER**	75°	LAT	22° 56' N
LAT (30)	04:59	**LONG**	81° 32'	LONG	081° 32' W
d	- 0:23	**Dlo**	6° 32'		
Inc LAT (x)	176	**dtime (W)**	+ 26	Base Time	05:22
Inv Lat (÷)	600			tcorr	0:19
Correction	- 6.7			Time of S/R - S/S	05:41
NOTE:					

Celestial Problems Sunrise and Sunset					
Problem # (USCG) (1278)			Chapter 18		
Date: 17 Apr			**FIX TIME**	04:00	
Required			LAT	26°12' N	
Sunrise			LONG	126° 12' W	
			C-	285°	
			S-	18	
LATITUDE CORRECTION		**LONGITUDE CORRECTION**		**DR AT PREDICTED TIME OF SUNRISE OR SUNSET**	
				TIME	05:30
LAT (20)	05:41	**STD MER**	120°	LAT	26° 29' N
LAT (30)	05:31	**LONG**	126° 50'	LONG	126° 50' W
d	- 0:10	**Dlo**	6° 50'		
Inc LAT (x)	389	**dtime (W)**	+ 27.3	Base Time	05:41
Inv Lat (÷)	600			tcorr	+0:21
Correction	- 6.5			Time of S/R - S/S	06:02
NOTE:					

Celestial Problems		
Sunrise and Sunset		
Problem # (USCG) (1279)		Chapter 18

Date: 29 May		FIX TIME	03:27
Required		LAT	25° 00' N
Sunrise		LONG	064° 15' W
		C-	270°
		S-	13.6

LATITUDE CORRECTION		LONGITUDE CORRECTION		DR AT PREDICTED TIME OF SUNRISE OR SUNSET	
				TIME	05:15
LAT (20)	05:20	STD MER	60°	LAT	25° 00' N
LAT (30)	05:00	LONG	64° 43'	LONG	064° 43' W
d	- 0:20	Dlo	4° 43'		
Inc LAT (x)	300	dtime (W)	+ 19	Base Time	05:20
Inv Lat (÷)	600			tcorr	+0:09
Correction	- 10			Time of S/R - S/S	05:29

NOTE:

Celestial Problems		
Sunrise and Sunset		
Problem # (USCG) (1280)		Chapter 18

Date: 27 March		FIX TIME	03:30
Required		LAT	23° 32' N
Sunrise		LONG	154° 47' E
		C-	105°
		S-	20

LATITUDE CORRECTION		LONGITUDE CORRECTION		DR AT PREDICTED TIME OF SUNRISE OR SUNSET	
				TIME	06:00
LAT (20)	05:58	STD MER	150°	LAT	23° 19' N
LAT (30)	05:56	LONG	155° 40'	LONG	155° 40' E
d	-0:02	Dlo	5° 40'		
Inc LAT (x)	199	dtime (E)	- 22.7	Base Time	05:58
Inv Lat (÷)	600			tcorr	-0:23
Correction	-0.7			Time of S/R - S/S	05:35

NOTE:

Celestial Problems Sunrise and Sunset					
Problem # (USCG) (1281)			Chapter 18		
Date: 2 Jan			**FIX TIME**	04:30	
Required			LAT	24° 12' N	
Sunrise			LONG	071° 24' W	
			C-	094°	
			S-	20	
LATITUDE CORRECTION		**LONGITUDE CORRECTION**	**DR AT PREDICTED TIME OF SUNRISE OR SUNSET**		
			TIME	06:45	
LAT (20)	06:36	**STD MER**	75°'	LAT	24° 08' N
LAT (30)	06:56	**LONG**	70° 34'	LONG	070° 34' W
d	+0:20	**Dlo**	4° 26'		
Inc LAT (x)	248	**dtime (E)**	- 17.7	**Base Time**	06:36
Inv Lat (÷)	600			**tcorr**	-0:09
Correction	+8.3			**Time of S/R - S/S**	06:27
NOTE:					

Celestial Problems Sunrise and Sunset					
Problem # (USCG) (1282)			Chapter 18		
Date: 1 Nov			**FIX TIME**	16:00	
Required			LAT	27° 48' S	
Sunset			LONG	091° 26' E	
			C-	327°	
			S-	16	
LATITUDE CORRECTION		**LONGITUDE CORRECTION**	**DR AT PREDICTED TIME OF SUNRISE OR SUNSET**		
			TIME	18:15	
LAT (20)	18:09	**STD MER**	90°	LAT	26° 58' S
LAT (30)	18:22	**LONG**	91° 14'	LONG	091° 14' E
d	+0:13	**Dlo**	1° 14'		
Inc LAT (x)	418	**dtime (E)**	- 5	**Base Time**	18:09
Inv Lat (÷)	600			**tcorr**	+0:04
Correction	+9			**Time of S/R - S/S**	18:13
NOTE:					

Celestial Problems Sunrise and Sunset				
Problem # (USCG) (1283)		Chapter 18		
Date: 5 May		**FIX TIME**	18:00	
Required		LAT	26°11.5 N	
Sunset		LONG	065° 35' W	
		C-	270°	
		S-	12	
LATITUDE CORRECTION		**LONGITUDE CORRECTION**		**DR AT PREDICTED TIME OF SUNRISE OR SUNSET**

LATITUDE CORRECTION		**LONGITUDE CORRECTION**		**DR AT PREDICTED TIME OF SUNRISE OR SUNSET**	
				TIME	18:25
LAT (20)	18:25	**STD MER**	60°	LAT	26° 11.5' N
LAT (30)	18:40	**LONG**	65° 40'	LONG	065° 40' W
d	+ 0:15	**Dlo**	5-40		
Inc LAT (x)	11.5	**dtime (W)**	+ 226	**Base Time**	18:25
Inv Lat (÷)	600			**tcorr**	+0:32
Correction	+9.3			**Time of S/R - S/S**	18:57

NOTE:

Celestial Problems Sunrise and Sunset				
Problem # (USCG) (1284)		Chapter 18		
Date: 10 Nov		**FIX TIME**	16:30	
Required		LAT	25° 10' N	
Sunset		LONG	071° 12' W	
		C-	335°	
		S-	24	

LATITUDE CORRECTION		**LONGITUDE CORRECTION**		**DR AT PREDICTED TIME OF SUNRISE OR SUNSET**	
				TIME	17:15
LAT (20)	17:22	**STD MER**	75°	LAT	25° 27' N
LAT (30)	17:07	**LONG**	71° 23'	LONG	071° 23' W
d	-0:15	**Dlo**	3° 37'		
Inc LAT (x)	327	**dtime (E)**	− 14.5	**Base Time**	17:32
Inv Lat (÷)	600			**tcorr**	-0:23
Correction	-8.2			**Time of S/R - S/S**	16:59

NOTE:

Celestial Problems Sunrise and Sunset				
Problem # (USCG) (1285)			Chapter 18	
Date: 28 June			**FIX TIME**	18:20
Required			LAT	16°00' N
Sunset			LONG	031°00' W
			C-	310°
			S-	18
LATITUDE CORRECTION		**LONGITUDE CORRECTION**	**DR AT PREDICTED TIME OF SUNRISE OR SUNSET**	
			TIME	18:20
LAT (10)	18:24	**STD MER**	30°	LAT	16° 00' N
LAT (20)	18:43	**LONG**	31° 00'	LONG	031° 00' W
d	+0:19	**Dlo**	1° 00'		
Inc LAT (x)	360	**dtime (W)**	+ 4	**Base Time**	18:24
Inv Lat (÷)	600			**tcorr**	0:15
Correction	+11.4			**Time of S/R - S/S**	18:39
NOTE:				

CHRONOMETER ERROR CALCULATIONS
CELESTIAL NAVIGATION

Chapter 6, Celestial Navigation (Upon Oceans Endorsement)

by

Alexander F. Hickethier MBA
and
Dr. Hu Jia-Shen

Chronometer time (CT) is time indicated by a chronometer. Since a chronometer is set approximately to GMT and not reset until it is overhauled and cleaned about every 3 years, there is nearly always a **chronometer error (CE)**, either fast (F) or slow (S). The change in chronometer error in 24 hours is called **chronometer rate**, or **daily rate**, and designated gaining or losing. With a consistent rate of 1s per day for three years, the chronometer error would total approximately 18m. Since chronometer error is subject to change, it should be determined from time to time, preferably daily at sea. Chronometer error is found by radio time signal, by comparison with another timepiece of known error, or by applying chronometer rate to previous readings of the same instrument. It is recorded to the nearest whole or half second. Chronometer rate is recorded to the nearest 0.1 second.

CRONOMETER ERROR (TIME TICK)
Chapter 7, Upon Oceans for Master Limited

02578. On 12 November, you are taking a time tick using the 1600 GMT BBC Broadcast. You hear four pulses followed by a longer pulse. At the start of the longer pulse you start a stopwatch. You stop the stopwatch at the same time reading the chronometer with the following results: stopwatch 03m 19s, chronometer 15h 59m 46s. What is the chronometer error?

A. 01m 14s slow
B. 3m 19s fast
C. 3m 33s slow
D. 6m 54s slow

02579. You take a time tick using the 2000 signal from Montevideo, Uruguay. You hear a 10 second dash, a 5 second silent period, and then six dots. At the sixth dot, your comparing watch reads 08h 00m 12s. When compared to the chronometer, the comparing watch reads 08h 01m 22s, and the 0hronometer reads 07h 59m 39s. What is the chronometer error?

A. 0m 12s fast
B. 1m 10s fast
C. 0m 21s slow

D. 1m 31s slow

02580. You take a time tick using the 2000 GMT signal from Montevideo, Uruguay. You hear a 10 second dash, a 5 second silent period, and then six dots. At the sixth dot your comparing watch reads 07h 58m 18s. When compared to the chronometer, the watch reads 07h 59m 56s, and the chronometer reads 08h 00m 02s. What is the chronometer error?

A. 1m 42s slow
B. 1m 36s slow
C. 0m 02s fast
D. 1m 38s fast

02582. You take a time tick using the 2000 GMT signal from Montevideo, Uruguay. You hear a 10 second dash, a 5 second silent period, and then six dots. At the sixth dot, your comparing watch reads 7h 57m 38s. When compared to the chronometer, the comparing watch reads 7h 59m 18s and the chronometer reads 8h 00m 02s. What is the chronometer error?

A. 1m 38s slow
B. 2m 22s slow
C. 0m 02s fast
D. 1m 40s fast

02583. You take a time tick using the 2000 GMT signal from Montevideo, Uruguay. You hear a 10 second dash, a 5 second silent period, and then six dots. At the sixth dot, your comparing watch reads 8h 01m 16s. When compared to the chronometer, the comparing watch reads 8h 02m 48s and the chronometer reads 8h 02 48s. What is the chronometer error?

A. 1m 16s slow
B. 1m 32s slow
C. 1m 16s fast
D. 2m 48s fast

02584. You take a time tick using the 2000 GMT signal from Montevideo, Uruguay. You hear a 10 second dash, a 5 second silent period, and then six dots. At the sixth dot, your comparing watch reads 7h 59m 48s. When compared to the chronometer, the comparing watch reads 8h 01m 24s and the chronometer reads 8h 02m 13s. What is the chronometer error?

A. 0m 37s fast
B. 1m 36s fast
C. 2m 13s fast
D. 0m 12s slow

02585. You take a time tick using the 2000 GMT signal from Montevideo, Uruguay. You hear a 10 second dash, a 5 second silent period, and then six dots. At the sixth dot, your comparing watch reads 07h 57m 42s. When compared to the chronometer, the comparing watch reads 07h 59m 03s and the chronometer reads 07h 58m 16s. What is the chronometer error?

A. 1m 44s slow
B. 2m 18s slow
C. 3m 05s slow
D. 1m 21s fast

02586. You take a time tick using the 2000 GMT signal from Montevideo, Uruguay. You hear a 10 second dash, a 5 second silent period, and then six dots. At the sixth dot, your comparing watch reads 8h 03m 26s. When compared to the chronometer, the comparing watch reads 8h 05m 02s and the chronometer reads 08h 09m 27s. What is the chronometer error?

A. 1m 46s fast
B. 3m 26s fast
C. 7m 51s fast
D. 9m 37s fast

02587. You take a time tick using the 2000 GMT signal from Montevideo, Uruguay. You hear a 10 second dash, a 5 second silent period, and then six dots. At the sixth dot, your comparing watch reads 07h 58m 49s. When compared to the chronometer, the comparing watch reads 07h 59m 53s and the chronometer reads 08h 00m 53s. What is the chronometer error?

A. 1m 11s slow
B. 0m 11s slow
C. 0m 53s fast
D. 1m 04s fast

02588. You take a time tick using the 2000 GMT signal from Montevideo, Uruguay. You hear a 10 second dash, a 5 second silent period, and then six dots. At the sixth dot, your comparing watch reads 07h 56m 42s. When compared to the chronometer, the comparing watch reads 07h 58m 15s and the chronometer reads 08h 01m 39s. What is the chronometer error?

A. 3m 18s slow
B. 0m 06s fast
C. 1m 33s fast
D. 1m 39s fast

02589. You take a time tick using the 2000 GMT signal from Montevideo, Uruguay. You hear a 10 second dash, a 5 second silent period, and then six dots. At the sixth dot, your comparing watch reads 08h 02m 29s. When compared to the chronometer, the comparing watch reads 08h 03m 43s and the chronometer reads 08h 02m 01s. What is the chronometer error?

A. 0m 47s fast
B. 1m 14s fast
C. 2m 01s fast
D. 2m 29s fast

02590. You take a time tick using the 2000 GMT signal from Montevideo, Uruguay. You hear a 10 second dash, a 5 second silent period, and then six dots. At the sixth dot, your comparing watch reads 07h 58m 53. When compared to the chronometer, the comparing watch reads 08h 00m 09s and the chronometer reads 08h 01m 15s. What is the chronometer error?

A. 1m 07s slow
B. 0m 01s slow
C. 0m 09s fast
D. 1m 16s fast

02591. You take a time tick using the 2000 GMT signal from Montevideo, Uruguay. You hear a 10 second dash, a 5 second silent periods, and then six dots. At the sixth dot, your comparing watch reads 07h 57m 44s. When compared to the chronometer, the comparing watch reads 07h 59m 07s and the chronometer reads 08h 01m 21s. What is the chronometer error?

A. 1m 33s fast
B. 1m 21s fast
C. 2m 16s slow
D. 0m 02s slow

Answers to the Chronometer Questions

02578 C
02579 D
02580 B
02582 A
02583 C
02584 A
02585 C
02586 C
02587 B
02588 B
02589 A
02590 B
02591 D

USCG # 02578	12 Nov
GMT	16-00-00
Stop Watch	+03-19
GMT	16-03-19
CT	15-59-46
CE	(Slow) 3-33

USCG # 02579	
GMT	20-00-00
CWatch	20-00-12
WE	(Fast) 0-12
CWatch	20-01-22
WE	-12
GMT	20-01-10
CT	19-59-39
CE	(Slow) 1-31

USCG # 02580	
GMT	20-00-00
CWatch	19-58-18
WE	(Slow) 1-42
CWatch	19-59-56
WE	+1-42
GMT	20-01-38
CT	20-00-02
CE	(Slow) 1-36

USCG # 02582	
GMT	20-00-00
CWatch	19-57-38
WE	(Slow) 2-22
CWatch	19-59-18
WE	+2-22
GMT	20-01-40
CT	20-00-02
CE	(Slow) 1-38

USCG # 02583	
GMT	20-00-00
CWatch	20-01-16
WE	(Fast) 1-16
CWatch	20-02-48
WE	-1-16
GMT	20-01-32
CT	20-02-48
CE	(Fast) 1-16

USCG # 02584	
GMT	20-00-00
CWatch	19-59-48
WE	(Slow) 12
CWatch	20-01-24
WE	+12
GMT	20-01-36
CT	20-02-13
CE	(Fast) 37

USCG # 02585	
GMT	20-00-00
CWatch	19-57-42
WE	(Slow) 2-18
CWatch	19-59-03
WE	+2-18
GMT	20-01-21
CT	19-58-16
CE	(Slow) 3-05

USCG # 02586	
GMT	20-00-00
CWatch	20-03-26
WE	(Fast) 3-26
CWatch	20-05-02
WE	-3-26
GMT	20-01-36
CT	20-09-27
CE	(Fast) 7-51

USCG # 02587	
GMT	20-00-00
CWatch	19-58-49
WE	(Slow) 1-11
CWatch	19-59-53
WE	+1-11
GMT	20-01-04
CT	20-00-53
CE	(Slow) 11

USCG # 02588	
GMT	20-00-00
CWatch	19-56-42
WE	(Slow) 3-18
CWatch	19-58-15
WE	+3-18
GMT	20-01-33
CT	20-01-39
CE	(Fast) 06

USCG # 02589	
GMT	20-00-00
CWatch	20-02-29
WE	(Fast) 2-29
CWatch	20-03-043
WE	-2-29
GMT	20-01-14
CT	20-02-01
CE	(Fast) 46

USCG # 02590	
GMT	20-00-00
CWatch	19-58-53
WE	(Slow) 1-07
CWatch	20-00-09
WE	+1-07
GMT	20-01-16
CT	20-01-15
CE	(Slow) 01

USCG # 02591		
GMT		20-00-00
CWatch		19-57-44
WE	(Slow)	2-16
CWatch		19-59-07
WE		+2-16
GMT		20-01-23
CT		20-01-01
CE	(Slow)	01

Watch Time of Local Apparent Noon

Chapter 17, Celestial Navigation (Upon Oceans Endorsement)

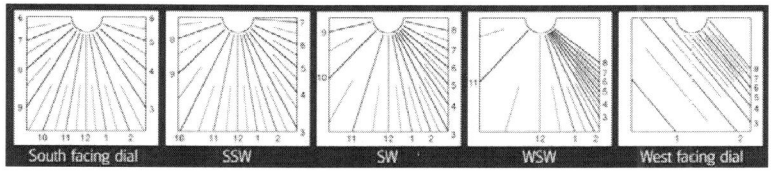

By
Alexander F. Hickethier MBA
and
Dr. Hu Jia-Shen

Watch Time of LAN
Chapter 15, Celestial Navigation for Master/Mate limited Upon Oceans

01175. On 12 February 1981, your 0900 zone time DR position is LAT 16° 43.0' N, LONG 51° 42.0' W. Your vessel is on course 093° T at a speed of 18.5 knots. What is the zone time of local apparent noon (LAN)?

A. 1237
B. 1233
C. 1230
D. 1226

01176. On 24 January 1981, your 0700 zone time DR position is LAT 22° 25.0' N, LONG 46° 10.0' W. Your vessel is on course 110° T at a speed of 12.0 knots. What is the zone time of local apparent noon (LAN)?

A. 1203
B. 1208
C. 1212
D. 1215

01177. On 2 April 1981, your 0900 zone time DR position is LAT 28° 04.0' S, LONG 94° 14.0' E. Your vessel is on course 316° T at a speed of 18.5 knots. What is the zone time of local apparent noon (LAN)?

A. 1138
B. 1143
C. 1146
D. 1149

01178. On 27 August 1981, your 0900 zone time DR position is LAT 24° 25.0' N, LONG 94° 20.0' W. Your vessel is on course 071° T at a speed of 20.0 knots. What is the zone time of local apparent noon (LAN)?

A. 1214
B. 1208
C. 1206
D. 1158

01179. On 26 September 1981, your 0830 zone time DR position is LAT 26° 04.0' N, LONG 129° 16.0' W. Your vessel is on course 119° T at a speed of 20.0 knots. What is the zone time of local apparent noon (LAN)?

A. 1124
B. 1127
C. 1130
D. 1133

01180. On 3 May 1981, your 1009 zone time DR position is LAT 30° 01.0' N, LONG 123° 15.0' W. Your vessel is on course 330° T at a speed of 8.6 knots. What is the zone time of local apparent noon (LAN)?

A. 1206
B. 1208
C. 1211
D. 1214

01181. On 4 January 1981, your 0800 zone time DR position is LAT 25° 25.0 S, LONG 16° 09.0' W. Your vessel is on course 290° T at a speed of 13.5 knots. What is the zone time of local apparent noon (LAN)?

A. 1157
B. 1205
C. 1209
D. 1213

01182. On 10 July 1981, your 1030 zone time DR position is LAT 20° 31.0' S, LONG 24° 41.0' W. Your vessel is on course 038° T at a speed of 22.0 knots. What is the zone time of local apparent noon (LAN)?

A. 1139
B. 1143
C. 1147
D. 1151

4-41

01183. On 25 June 1981, your 0900 zone time DR position is LAT 24° 10.0' S, LONG 148° 30.0' W. Your vessel is on course 230° T at a speed of 18.0 knots. What is the zone time of local apparent noon (LAN)?

A. 1154
B. 1156
C. 1200
D. 1204

01184. On 8 April 1981, your 0830 zone time DR position is LAT 22° 49.0' N, LONG 84° 37.0' W. Your vessel is on course 228° T at a speed of 19.0 knots. What is the zone time of local apparent noon (LAN)?

A. 1144
B. 1147
C. 1150
D. 1154

01185. On 31 January 1981, your 0920 zone time DR position is LAT 24° 16.0' S, LONG 151° 33.0' E. Your vessel is on course 258° T at a speed of 18.5 knots. What is the zone time of local apparent noon (LAN)?

A. 1202
B. 1207
C. 1211
D. 1215

01186. On 16 November 1981, your 0800 zone time DR position is LAT 25° 11.0' N, LONG 117° 41.0' W. Your vessel is on course 252° T at a speed of 14.5 knots. What is the zone time of local apparent noon (LAN)?

A. 1131
B. 1135
C. 1139
D. 1144

01187. On 17 March 1981, your 0800 zone time DR position is LAT 21° 27.0' N, LONG 65° 25.0' W. Your vessel is on course 105° T at a speed of 17.5 knots. What is the zone time of local apparent noon (LAN)?

A. 1210
B. 1218
C. 1225
D. 1231

01188. On 9 February 1981, your 0830 zone time DR position is LAT 22° 19.0' N, LONG 64° 37.0' E. Your vessel is on course 128° T at a speed of 19.0 knots. What is the zone time of local apparent noon (LAN)?

A. 1152
B. 1156
C. 1201
D. 1205

01189. On 7 February 1981, your 0800 zone time DR position is LAT 22° 16.0' N, LONG 92° 26.0' W. Your vessel is on course 270° T at a speed of 20.0 knots. What is the zone time of local apparent noon (LAN)?

A. 1218
B. 1222
C. 1226
D. 1230

01190. On 12 February 1981, your 0930 zone time DR position is LAT 25° 20.0' N, LONG 30° 40.0' W. Your vessel is on course 135° T at a speed of 11.2 knots. What is the zone time of local apparent noon (LAN)?

A. 1210
B. 1215
C. 1220
D. 1224

4-42

01191. On 14 October 1981, your 0800 zone time DR position is LAT 28° 22.0' N, LONG 161° 17.0' E. Your vessel is on course 116° T at a speed of 17.5 knots. What is the zone time of local apparent noon (LAN)?

A. 1142
B. 1148
C. 1152
D. 1156

01192. On 3 October 1981, your 0830 zone time position is LAT 26° 15.0' S, LONG 73° 16.0' E. Your vessel is on course 280° T at a speed of 19.0 knots. What is the zone time of local apparent noon (LAN)?

A. 1151
B. 1154
C. 1158
D. 1201

01193. On 26 September 1981, your 0830 zone time DR position is LAT 23° 04.0' N, LONG 129° 16.0' E. Your vessel is on course 119° T at a speed of 20.0 knots. What is the zone time of local apparent noon (LAN)?

A. 1158
B. 1205
C. 1210
D. 1214

01194. On 16 January 1981, your 0930 zone time DR position is LAT 26° 07.0'S, LONG 51° 43.0' E. Your vessel is on course 238° T at a speed of 17.0 knots. What is the zone time of local apparent noon (LAN)?

A. 1145
B. 1148
C. 1152
D. 1156

01195. On 23 June 1981, your 0900 zone time DR position is LAT 21° 26.0' N, LONG 137° 46.0' W. Your vessel is on course 059° T at a speed of 19.0 knots. What is the zone time of local apparent noon (LAN)?

A. 1159
B. 1205
C. 1210
D. 1214

01196. On 14 October 1981, your 0800 zone time DR position is LAT 28° 22.0' N, LONG 161° 17.0' E. Your vessel is on course 116° T at a speed of 17.5 knots. What is the zone time of local apparent noon (LAN)?

A. 1148
B. 1151
C. 1156
D. 1202

01197. On 16 November 1981, your 0800 zone time DR position is LAT 25° 11.0' N, LONG 117° 41.0' W. Your vessel is on course 252° T at a speed of 14.5 knots. What is the zone time of local apparent noon (LAN)?

A. 1135
B. 1139
C. 1143
D. 1146

01198. On 3 October 1981, your 0830 zone time DR position is LAT 26° 15.0' S, LONG 73° 16.0' E. Your vessel is on course 280° T at a speed of 19.0 knots. What is the zone time of local apparent noon (LAN)?

A. 1152
B. 1155
C. 1158
D. 1201

4-43

01199. On 20 June 1981, your 0800 zone time DR position is LAT 21° 02.0' N, LONG 152° 50.0' E. Your vessel is on course 265° T at a speed of 15.0 knots. What is the zone time of local apparent noon (LAN)?

A. 1149
B. 1154
C. 1159
D. 1203

01200. On 26 September 1981, your 0830 DR position is LAT 26° 04.0' N, LONG 129° 16.0' W. Your vessel is on a course of 119' T at a speed of 20.0 knots. What is the zone time of local apparent noon (LAN)?

A. 1124
B. 1128
C. 1142
D. 1146

01201. On 10 October 1981, your 0930 zone time position is LAT 25° 00.0' S, LONG 164° 38.6' W. Your vessel is on course 180° T at a speed to 10.0 knots. What is the zone time of local apparent noon (LAN)?

A. 1145
B. 1151
C. 1203
D. 1206

01202. Your 0830 DR position is LAT 27° 33' S, LONG 79° 17' E. Your vessel is on a course of 066° T, at a speed of 19.5 knots. Determine the time of LAN on 10 December 1981.

A. 1131
B. 1136
C. 1153
D. 1215

01203. On 21 June 1981, at 0906 EDT (ZD+4), Loran fixes your position at LAT 30° 48.0' N, LONG 71° 00.0' W. You are on a course of 167° T at 15.2 knots. What is the zone time of local apparent noon (LAN)?

A. 1145
B. 1202
C. 1218
D. 1245

01204. On 25 April 1981, your 0930 zone time position is LAT 28° 35' S, LONG 82° 30' W. Your vessel is on course 300 ° T at a speed of 20.0 knots. Determine the time of LAN.

A. 1131
B. 1158
C. 1211
D. 1225

01205. On 25 April 1981, your 1130 DR position is LAT 24° 50.0' N, LONG 61° 25.0' W. Your vessel is on a course of 300° T at a speed of 16.0 knots. Determine the zone time of (LAN) for your vessel.

A. 1154
B. 1156
C. 1202
D. 1204

4-44

Answers for Watch Time of LAN

01175	A		01192	D
01176	C		01193	C
01177	D		01194	A
01178	A		01195	C
01179	A		01196	C
01180	C		01197	B
01181	D		01198	D
01182	B		01199	B
01183	C		01200	A
01184	A		01201	A
01185	C		01202	A
01186	C		01203	D
01187	C		01204	A
01188	A		01205	D
01189	D			
01190	B			
01191	D			

4-45

Celestial Problems
Watch Time of LAN

Problem # (USCG) (1175)		Chapter 19	
Date: 12 Feb		**FIX TIME**	09:00
Required Watch Time of LAN		**LAT** **LONG** **C-** 093° **S-** 18.5	16° 43.0′ N 016° 43.0′ W

LONGITUDE CORRECTION		Time of Meridian Passage		DR AT PREDICTED TIME OF LAN	
STD MER	45° 00.0′	**Base Time of** **Mer. Pass.**	12:14	**TIME** **LAT** **LONG**	12:14 16° 40.0′ 050° 38.0′
LONG	50° 38.0′	**Correction**	+ 24		
Dlo	5° 38.0′	**Mer. Pass.**	12:38		
dtime (W)	+ 23.8				

NOTE:

Celestial Problems
Watch Time of LAN

Problem # (USCG) (1176)		Chapter 19	
Date: 24 Jan		**FIX TIME**	07:00
Required Watch Time of LAN		**LAT** **LONG** **C-** 110° **S-** 12.0	22° 25.0′ N 046°0.0′ W

LONGITUDE CORRECTION		Time of Meridian Passage		DR AT PREDICTED TIME OF LAN	
STD MER	45° 00.0′	**Base Time of** **Mer. Pass.**	12:12	**TIME** **LAT** **LONG**	12:12 22° 04.0′ N 045° 02.0′ W
LONG	45° 02.0′	**Correction**	0		
Dlo	02.0′	**Mer. Pass.**	12:12		
dtime (W)	0				

NOTE:

Celestial Problems
Watch Time of LAN

Problem # (USCG) (1177)			Chapter 19	
Date: 2 Apr			**FIX TIME**	09:00
Required			**LAT**	28° 04.0' S
Watch Time of LAN			**LONG**	094° 14.0' E
			C- 316°	
			S- 18.5	

LONGITUDE CORRECTION		**Time of Meridian Passage**		**DR AT PREDICTED TIME OF LAN**	
STD MER	90° 00.0'	**Base Time of Mer. Pass.**	12:04	**TIME**	12:04
LONG	93° 27.0'			**LAT**	27° 23.0' S
Dlo	3° 27'	**Correction**	- 14	**LONG**	093° 27.0' E
dtime (E)	- 14.0	**Mer. Pass.**	11:50		

NOTE:

Celestial Problems
Watch Time of LAN

Problem # (USCG) (1178)			Chapter 19	
Date: 27 Aug			**FIX TIME**	**09:00**
Required			**LAT**	24° 25.0' N
Watch Time of LAN			**LONG**	094° 20.0' W
			C- 071°	
			S- 20.0	

LONGITUDE CORRECTION		**Time of Meridian Passage**		**DR AT PREDICTED TIME OF LAN**	
STD MER	090° 00.0'	**Base Time of Mer. Pass.**	12:01	**TIME**	12:01
LONG	093° 15.0'			**LAT**	24° 45.0' N
Dlo	3° 15.0'	**Correction**	+ 13	**LONG**	093° 15.0' W
dtime (E)	+ 13.0	**Mer. Pass.**	12:14		

NOTE:

Celestial Problems
Watch Time of LAN

Problem # (USCG) (1179)		Chapter 19	

Date: 26 Sep

Required
Watch Time of LAN

FIX TIME	08:30	
LAT	26° 04.0' N	
LONG	129° 16.0" W	
C- 119°		
S- 20.0		

LONGITUDE CORRECTION		Time of Meridian Passage		DR AT PREDICTED TIME OF LAN	
STD MER	135° 00.0'	Base Time of Mer. Pass.	11:51	**TIME**	11:51
LONG	128° 12.0'	Correction	- 27	**LAT**	25° 32.0' N
Dlo	6° 48.0'	Mer. Pass.	11:24	**LONG**	128° 12.0' W
dtime (E)	- 27.2				

NOTE:

Celestial Problems
Watch Time of LAN

Problem # (USCG) (1180)		Chapter 19	

Date: 3 May

Required
Watch Time of LAN

FIX TIME	10:09	
LAT	30° 01.0' N	
LONG	123° 15.0' W	
C- 330°		
S- 8.6		

LONGITUDE CORRECTION		Time of Meridian Passage		DR AT PREDICTED TIME OF LAN	
STD MER	120° 00.0'	Base Time of Mer. Pass.	11:57	**TIME**	11:57
LONG	123° 24.0'	Correction	+ 14	**LAT**	30° 15.0' N
Dlo	3° 24.0'	Mer. Pass.	12:11	**LONG**	123° 24.0' W
dtime (W)	+ 13.6				

NOTE:

Alexander F. Hickethier MBA © 1988-2012

Celestial Problems
Watch Time of LAN

Problem # (USCG) (1181)	Chapter 19

Date: 4 Jan

Required
Watch Time of LAN

FIX TIME 08:00
LAT 25° 25.0 S
LONG 016° 09.0' W
C- 290°
S- 13.5

LONGITUDE CORRECTION		Time of Meridian Passage		DR AT PREDICTED TIME OF LAN	
STD MER	15° 00.0'	Base Time of Mer. Pass.	12:05	**TIME**	12:05
LONG	17° 04.0'			**LAT**	25° 05.0' S
Dlo	2° 04.0'	**Correction**	+ 8	**LONG**	017° 04.0' W
dtime (W)	+ 8.0	**Mer. Pass.**	12:13		

NOTE:

Celestial Problems
Watch Time of LAN

Problem # (USCG) (1182)	Chapter 19

Date: 10 Jul

Required
Watch Time of LAN

FIX TIME 10:30
LAT 20° 31.0' S
LONG 024° 41.0' W
C- 038°
S- 22.0

LONGITUDE CORRECTION		Time of Meridian Passage		DR AT PREDICTED TIME OF LAN	
STD MER	30° 00.0'	Base Time of Mer. Pass.	12:05	**TIME**	12:05
LONG	24° 17.0'			**LAT**	20° 03.0' S
Dlo	5° 43.0'	**Correction**	- 23	**LONG**	024° 17.0' W
dtime (E)	- 23.0	**Mer. Pass.**	11:42		

NOTE:

4-49

Celestial Problems
Watch Time of LAN

Problem # (USCG) (1183)		Chapter 19	

Date: 25 Jun		**FIX TIME**	09:00
Required		**LAT**	24° 10.0′ S
Watch Time of LAN		**LONG**	148° 30.0′ W
		C- 230°	
		S- 18.0	

LONGITUDE CORRECTION		Time of Meridian Passage		DR AT PREDICTED TIME OF LAN	
STD MER	150° 00.0′	Base Time of Mer. Pass.	12:03	**TIME**	12:03
LONG	149° 17.0′	Correction	- 3	**LAT**	24° 45.0′ S
Dlo	0° 43.0′	Mer. Pass.	12:00	**LONG**	149° 17.0′ W
dtime (E)	- 3.0				

NOTE:

Celestial Problems
Watch Time of LAN

Problem # (USCG) (1184)		Chapter 19	

Date: 8 Apr		**FIX TIME**	08:30
Required		**LAT**	22° 49.0′ N
Watch Time of LAN		**LONG**	084° 37.0′ W
		C- 228°	
		S- 19.0	

LONGITUDE CORRECTION		Time of Meridian Passage		DR AT PREDICTED TIME OF LAN	
STD MER	90° 00.0′	Base Time of Mer. Pass.	12:02	**TIME**	12:02
LONG	85° 32.0′	Correction	- 18	**LAT**	22° 05.0′ N
Dlo	4° 28.0′	Mer. Pass.	11:44	**LONG**	85° 32.0′ W
dtime (E)	- 18.0				

NOTE:

Celestial Problems
Watch Time of LAN

Problem # (USCG) (1185)		Chapter 19

Date: 31 Jan		**FIX TIME**	09:20
Required		**LAT**	24° 16.0' S
Watch Time of LAN		**LONG**	151° 33.0' E
		C- 258°	
		S- 18.5	

LONGITUDE CORRECTION		Time of Meridian Passage		DR AT PREDICTED TIME OF LAN	
STD MER	150° 00.0'	Base Time of Mer. Pass.	12:14	**TIME**	12:14
LONG	151° 36.0'			**LAT**	24° 27.0' S
Dlo	36.0	Correction	- 2	**LONG**	015° 36.0' E
dtime (E)	- 2.0	Mer. Pass.	12:12		

NOTE:

Celestial Problems
Watch Time of LAN

Problem # (USCG) (1186)		Chapter 19

Date: 16 Nov		**FIX TIME**	08:00
Required		**LAT**	25° 11.0' N
Watch Time of LAN		**LONG**	117° 41.0' W
		C- 252°	
		S- 14.5	

LONGITUDE CORRECTION		Time of Meridian Passage		DR AT PREDICTED TIME OF LAN	
STD MER	120° 00.0'	Base Time of Mer. Pass.	11:45	**TIME**	11:45
LONG	118° 38.0'			**LAT**	24° 54.0' N
Dlo	1° 22.0'	Correction	- 6	**LONG**	118° 38.0' W
dtime (E)	- 5.5	Mer. Pass.	11:39		

NOTE:

4-51

Celestial Problems
Watch Time of LAN

Problem # (USCG) (1187)	Chapter 19

Date: 17 Mar				**FIX TIME**	08:00
Required				**LAT**	21° 27.0' N
Watch Time of LAN				**LONG**	065° 25.0' W
				C- 105°	
				S- 17.5	

LONGITUDE CORRECTION		Time of Meridian Passage		DR AT PREDICTED TIME OF LAN	
STD MER	60° 00.0'	**Base Time of Mer. Pass.**	12:08	**TIME**	12:08
LONG	64° 10.0'	**Correction**	+ 17	**LAT**	21° 18.0' N
Dlo	4° 10.0'	**Mer. Pass.**	12:25	**LONG**	064° 10.0' W
dtime (W)	+ 17.0				

NOTE:

Celestial Problems
Watch Time of LAN

Problem # (USCG) (1188)	Chapter 19

Date: 9 Feb				**FIX TIME**	08:30
Required				**LAT**	22° 19.0'
Watch Time of LAN				**LONG**	064° 37.0' E
				C- 128°	
				S- 19.0	

LONGITUDE CORRECTION		Time of Meridian Passage		DR AT PREDICTED TIME OF LAN	
STD MER	60° 00.0'	**Base Time of Mer. Pass.**	12:14	**TIME**	12:14
LONG	65° 38.0'	**Correction**	- 22	**LAT**	21° 33.0' N
Dlo	5° 38'	**Mer. Pass.**	12:52	**LONG**	065° 38.0' E
dtime (E)	- 22.5				

NOTE:

Alexander F. Hickethier MBA © 1988-2012

Celestial Problems
Watch Time of LAN

Problem # (USCG) (1189)		Chapter 19	
Date: 7 Feb		**FIX TIME**	08:00
Required		**LAT**	22° 16.0' N
Watch Time of LAN		**LONG**	092° 26.0' W
		C- 270°	
		S- 20.0	

LONGITUDE CORRECTION		**Time of Meridian Passage**		**DR AT PREDICTED TIME OF LAN**	
		Base Time of Mer. Pass.	12:14	**TIME**	12:14
STD MER	90° 00.0'	Correction	+ 16	**LAT**	22° 16.0' N
LONG	93°56.0' W	Mer. Pass.	12:30	**LONG**	093° 56.0' W
Dlo	3° 56.0				
dtime (W)	+ 16.0				

NOTE:

Celestial Problems
Watch Time of LAN

Problem # (USCG) (1190)		Chapter 19	
Date: 12 Feb		**FIX TIME**	09:30
Required		**LAT**	25° 20.0' N
Watch Time of LAN		**LONG**	030° 40.0' W
		C- 135°	
		S- 11.2	

LONGITUDE CORRECTION		**Time of Meridian Passage**		**DR AT PREDICTED TIME OF LAN**	
		Base Time of Mer. Pass.	12:14	**TIME**	12:14
STD MER	30° 00.0'	Correction	+ 1	**LAT**	24° 59.0' N
LONG	30° 16.0'	Mer. Pass.	12:15	**LONG**	030° 16.0' W
Dlo	0° 16.0'				
dtime (W)	+ 1.0				

NOTE:

Alexander F. Hickethier MBA © 1988-2012

Celestial Problems
Watch Time of LAN

Problem # (USCG) (1191)	Chapter 19

Date: 14 Oct

Required
Watch Time of LAN

FIX TIME	08:00
LAT	28° 22.0' N
LONG	161° 17.0' E
C- 116°	
S- 17.5	

LONGITUDE CORRECTION		Time of Meridian Passage		DR AT PREDICTED TIME OF LAN	
STD MER	165° 00.0'	Base Time of Mer. Pass.	11:46	**TIME**	11:47
LONG	162° 23.0'	Correction	+ 11	**LAT**	27° 52.0' N
Dlo	2° 37.0'	Mer. Pass.	11:57	**LONG**	162° 23.0' E
dtime (W)	+ 10.5				

NOTE:

Celestial Problems
Watch Time of LAN

Problem # (USCG) (1192)	Chapter 19

Date: 3 Oct

Required
Watch Time of LAN

FIX TIME	08:30
LAT	26° 15.0' S
LONG	073° 16.0' E
C- 280°	
S- 19.0	

LONGITUDE CORRECTION		Time of Meridian Passage		DR AT PREDICTED TIME OF LAN	
STD MER	75° 00.0'	Base Time of Mer. Pass.	11:49	**TIME**	11:49
LONG	72° 07.0'	Correction	+ 12	**LAT**	26° 03.0' S
Dlo	2° 53.0'	Mer. Pass.	12:01	**LONG**	073° 07.0' E
dtime (W)	+ 11.5				

NOTE:

Alexander F. Hickethier MBA © 1988-2012

Celestial Problems
Watch Time of LAN

Problem # (USCG) (1193)		Chapter 19	
Date: 26 Sep		**FIX TIME**	08:30
Required		**LAT**	23° 04.0' N
Watch Time of LAN		**LONG**	129° 16.0' E
		C- 119°	
		S- 20.0	

LONGITUDE CORRECTION		**Time of Meridian Passage**		**DR AT PREDICTED TIME OF LAN**	
		Base Time of Mer. Pass.	11:51	**TIME**	11:51
STD MER	135° 00.0'			**LAT**	23° 34.0' N
LONG	130° 20.0'	Correction	+ 19	**LONG**	130° 20.0' E
Dlo	4° 46.0'	Mer. Pass.	12:10		
dtime (W)	+ 19.0				

NOTE:

Celestial Problems
Watch Time of LAN

Problem # (USCG) (1194)		Chapter 19	
Date: 16 Jan		**FIX TIME**	**09:30**
Required		**LAT**	26° 07.0' S
Watch Time of LAN		**LONG**	051° 43.0' E
		C- 238°	
		S- 17.0	

LONGITUDE CORRECTION		**Time of Meridian Passage**		**DR AT PREDICTED TIME OF LAN**	
		Base Time of Mer. Pass.	12:10	**TIME**	12:10
STD MER	45° 00.0'			**LAT**	26° 31.0' S
LONG	51° 00.0'	Correction	- 24	**LONG**	051° 00.0' E
Dlo	6° 00.0'	Mer. Pass.	11:46		
dtime (E)	- 24.0				

NOTE:

Alexander F. Hickethier MBA © 1988-2012

Celestial Problems
Watch Time of LAN

Problem # (USCG) (1195)		Chapter 19	

Date: 23 Jun

Required

Watch Time of LAN

FIX TIME	09:00
LAT	21° 26.0' N
LONG	137° 46.0' W
C- 059°	
S- 19.0	

LONGITUDE CORRECTION		Time of Meridian Passage		DR AT PREDICTED TIME OF LAN	
STD MER	135° 00.0'	**Base Time of Mer. Pass.**	12:02	**TIME**	12:02
LONG	137° 00.0'	**Correction**	+ 10	**LAT**	21° 57.0' N
Dlo	2° 00.0'	**Mer. Pass.**	12:10	**LONG**	137° 00.0' W
dtime (W)	+ 8.0				

NOTE:

Celestial Problems
Watch Time of LAN

Problem # (USCG) (1196)		Chapter 19	

Date: 14 Oct

Required

Watch Time of LAN

FIX TIME	08:00
LAT	28° 22.0' N
LONG	161° 17.0' E
C- 116°	
S- 17.5	

LONGITUDE CORRECTION		Time of Meridian Passage		DR AT PREDICTED TIME OF LAN	
STD MER	165° 00.0'	**Base Time of Mer. Pass.**	11:46	**TIME**	11:46
LONG	162° 27.0'	**Correction**	+ 10	**LAT**	27° 53.0' N
Dlo	2° 33.0'	**Mer. Pass.**	11:56	**LONG**	162° 27.0' E
dtime (W)	+ 10.0				

NOTE:

4-56

Celestial Problems
Watch Time of LAN

Problem # (USCG) (1197)		Chapter 19	

Date: 14 Oct		**FIX TIME**	08:00
Required		**LAT**	25° 11.0' N
Watch Time of LAN		**LONG**	117° 41.0' W
		C- 252°	
		S- 14.5	

LONGITUDE CORRECTION		**Time of Meridian Passage**		**DR AT PREDICTED TIME OF LAN**	
		Base Time of Mer. Pass.	11:45	**TIME**	**11:45**
STD MER	120° 00.0'	**Correction**	- 6	**LAT**	25° 00.0' N
LONG	118° 37.0'	**Mer. Pass.**	11:39	**LONG**	118° 37.0' W
Dlo	1° 23.0'				
dtime (E)	- 5.5				

NOTE:

Celestial Problems
Watch Time of LAN

Problem # (USCG) (1198)		Chapter 19	

Date: 3 October		**FIX TIME**	08:30
Required		**LAT**	26° 15.0' S
Watch Time of LAN		**LONG**	073° 16.0' E
		C- 280°	
		S- 19.0	

LONGITUDE CORRECTION		**Time of Meridian Passage**		**DR AT PREDICTED TIME OF LAN**	
		Base Time of Mer. Pass.	11:49	**TIME**	11:49
STD MER	75° 00.0'	**Correction**	+ 12	**LAT**	26° 04.0' S
LONG	72° 08.0'	**Mer. Pass.**	12:01	**LONG**	072° 08.0' E
Dlo	2° 52'				
dtime (W)	+ 11.5				

NOTE:

4-57

Celestial Problems
Watch Time of LAN

Problem # (USCG) (1199)	Chapter 19

Date: 20 Jun		FIX TIME	08:00
Required		LAT	21° 02.0' N
Watch Time of LAN		LONG	152° 50.0' E
		C- 265°	
		S-15.0	

LONGITUDE CORRECTION		Time of Meridian Passage		DR AT PREDICTED TIME OF LAN	
		Base Time of Mer. Pass.	12:01	TIME	12:01
STD MER	150° 00.0'			LAT	20° 57.0' N
LONG	151° 50.0'	Correction	- 07	LONG	151° 50.0'
Dlo	1° 50.5'	Mer. Pass.	11:54		
dtime (E)	- 7.4				

NOTE:

Celestial Problems
Watch Time of LAN

Problem # (USCG) (1200)	Chapter 19

Date: 26 Sep		FIX TIME	08:30
Required		LAT	26° 04.0' N
Watch Time of LAN		LONG	129° 16.0' W
		C-	
		S-	

LONGITUDE CORRECTION		Time of Meridian Passage		DR AT PREDICTED TIME OF LAN	
		Base Time of Mer. Pass.	11:51	TIME	11:51
STD MER	135° 00.0'			LAT	25° 30.0' N
LONG	128° 10.0'	Correction	- 27	LONG	128° 10.0' W
Dlo	6° 50.0'	Mer. Pass.	11:24		
dtime (E)	- 27.0				

NOTE:

Celestial Problems
Watch Time of LAN

Problem # (USCG) (1201)		Chapter 19

Date: 10 Oct

Required
Watch Time of LAN

FIX TIME	09:30
LAT	25° 00.0' S
LONG	164° 38.6' W
C- 180°	
S- 10.0	

LONGITUDE CORRECTION		Time of Meridian Passage		DR AT PREDICTED TIME OF LAN	
STD MER	165° 00.0'	Base Time of Mer. Pass.	11:47	TIME	11:47
LONG	164° 38.6'	Correction	- 1	LAT	25° 23.0' S
Dlo	0° 21.4'	Mer. Pass.	11:46	LONG	164° 33.6' W
dtime (E)	- 1.4				

NOTE:

Celestial Problems
Watch Time of LAN

Problem # (USCG) (1202)		Chapter 19

Date: 10 Dec

Required
Watch Time of LAN

FIX TIME	08:30
LAT	27° 33.0' S
LONG	079° 17.0' E
C- 066°	
S- 19.5	

LONGITUDE CORRECTION		Time of Meridian Passage		DR AT PREDICTED TIME OF LAN	
STD MER	75° 00.0'	Base Time of Mer. Pass.	11:53	TIME	
LONG	80° 24.0'	Correction	- 22	LAT	27° 07.0' S
Dlo	5° 24.0'	Mer. Pass.	11:31	LONG	
dtime (E)	- 21.6				

NOTE:

4-59

Celestial Problems
Watch Time of LAN

Problem # (USCG) (1203)		Chapter 19	

Date: 21 Jun			**FIX TIME**	09:06
Required			**LAT**	30° 48.0' N
Watch Time of LAN			**LONG**	071° 00.0' W
			C-167°	
			S-15.2	

LONGITUDE CORRECTION		**Time of Meridian Passage**		**DR AT PREDICTED TIME OF LAN**	
		Base Time of Mer. Pass.	12:02	**TIME**	12:02
STD MER	75° 00.0'			**LAT**	30° 04.0' N
LONG	70° 49.0'	**Correction**	- 17	**LONG**	070° 49.0' W
Dlo	4° 11.0'	**Mer. Pass.**	11:45		
dtime (E)	- 16.7				

NOTE:

Celestial Problems
Watch Time of LAN

Problem # (USCG) (1204)		Chapter 19	

Date: 25 Apr			**FIX TIME**	09:30
Required			**LAT**	28° 35.0' S
Watch Time of LAN			**LONG**	082° 30.0' W
			C- 300°	
			S- 20.0	

LONGITUDE CORRECTION		**Time of Meridian Passage**		**DR AT PREDICTED TIME OF LAN**	
		Base Time of Mer. Pass.	11:58	**TIME**	11:58
STD MER	90° 00.0'			**LAT**	28° 10.0' S
LONG	83° 19.0'	**Correction**	- 27	**LONG**	083° 19.0' W
Dlo	6° 41.0'	**Mer. Pass.**	11:31		
dtime (E)	- 26.7				

NOTE:

4-60

Celestial Problems
Watch Time of LAN

Problem # (USCG) (1205)	Chapter 19

Date: 25 Apr	**FIX TIME** 11:30
Required	**LAT** 24° 50.0' N
Watch Time of LAN	**LONG** 061° 25.0' W
	C- 300
	S-

LONGITUDE CORRECTION		Time of Meridian Passage		DR AT PREDICTED TIME OF LAN	
STD MER	60° 00.0'	**Base Time of Mer. Pass.**	1158	**TIME**	11:58
LONG	61° 36.0'	**Correction**	+ 6	**LAT**	24° 55.0' N
Dlo	1° 36.0'	**Mer. Pass.**	12: 04	**LONG**	61° 36.0' W
dtime (W)	+ 6.4				

NOTE:

4-61

ESTIMATED TIME OF ARRIVAL PROBLEMS
WORKED-OUT

CHAPTER 4, CELESTIAL NAVIGATION (Upon Oceans Endorsement)

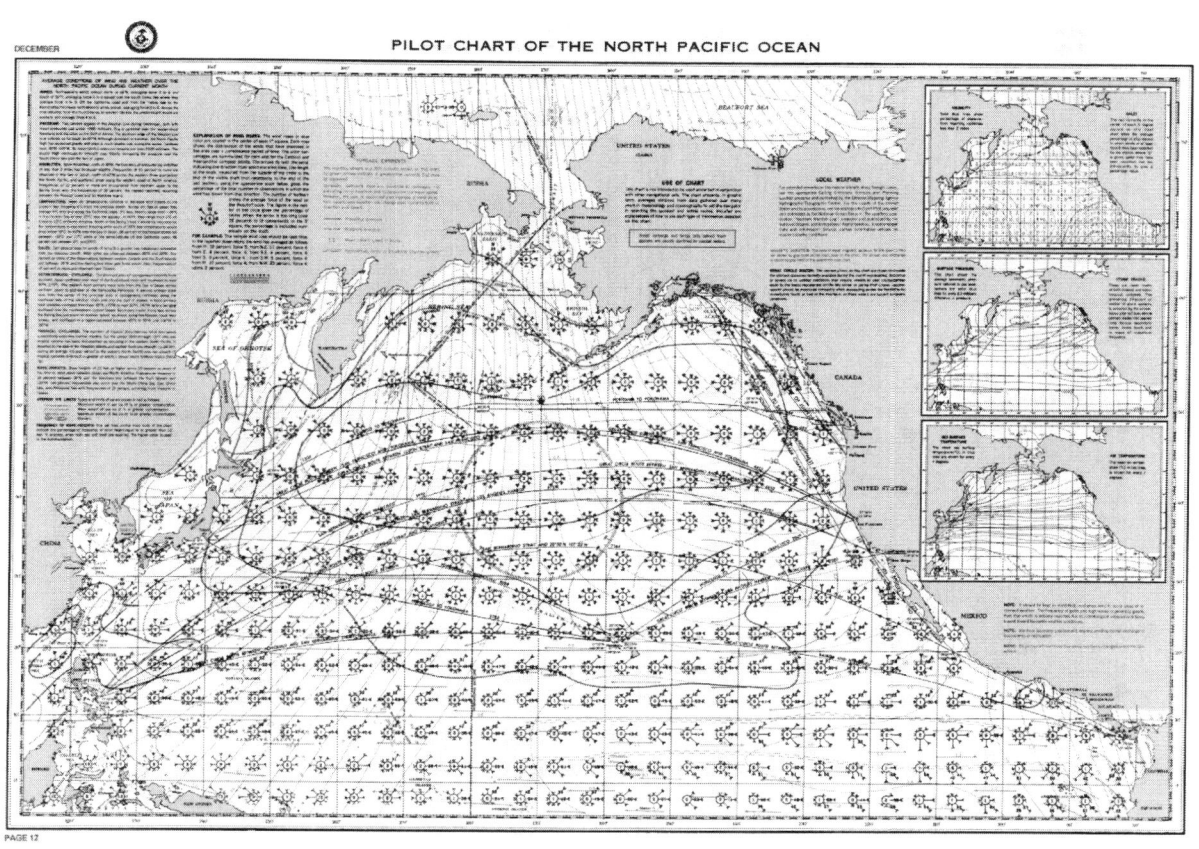

by
Alexander F. Hickethier, MBA
and
Dr. Hu Jia Shen

ESTIMATED TIME OF ARRIVAL (ETA)

In Marine Navigation, we are continually determining our ETA to insure safe navigation. We use the: time, speed, distance calculation **(ETA = Distance/Speed)** to find our DR position, the time we will sight a light or the time of an upcoming turn. These ETA's are normally for a few minutes to several hours, but with Ocean going vessels that make world voyages we must determine ETA's taking into consideration great distances which may cross several time zones.

As in the other chapters of this textbook we will use an actual USCG. question below to explain a method of calculating this type of ETA.

You are on a voyage from Valdez, AK to Panama Canal Zone. The distance from pilot to pilot is 4950 miles. The speed of advance is 15.0 knots. You estimate a layover in San Francisco, CA of 36.0 hours. If you take departure at 0800 (ZD +10) 29, October, what is your ETA (ZD +5) at Panama Canal Zone.

   A. 1900, 13 November
   B. 1400, 13 November
   C. 1400, 14 November
   D. 0900, 13 November

Our first step is to change our departure time from local zone time to Greenwich Mean Time (GMT). (For more information on Time Zones see Chapter 7)

0800 (ZD + 10)= 1800 29 October

Next, we calculate the time required to transit the 4950 miles between Valdez, AK to the Panama Canal Zone at 15 knots with a 36 hour layover in San Francisco.

First, we divide the distance to be traveled (4950 NM) by our speed of 15 kts.

4950/15 = 330 hours

Then, we convert this to days by dividing the 330 hours by 24.

330/24 = 13.75 Days

Next, we multiply the 3/4 (.75) of a day back to hours by 24.

.75 x 24 = 18 Hours.

This gives us the number of days and hours for our transit not including our 36 hour layover.

To 13 days 18 hours of transit we add the 1 day 12 hours of layover. Thus we have 16 day and 06 hours. Adding this to our departure time of 29 October, 1800., we have an arrival date and time of November 14, 0000 GMT. (Remember: October has 31 days)

We must now convert this to local time in Panama (ZD + 5). This is done by applying the reverse of the destination zone description (ZD - 5).

November 14 0000 − 5 Hours = <u>November 13, 1900</u>

Estimated Time of Arrival
Chapter 22, Upon Oceans for Limited Master/Mate

00601. At 1210 zone time on 1 December 1981, you depart Seattle, LAT 47° 36.0' N, LONG 122° 22.0' W (ZD +8). You are bound for Guam, LAT 13° 27.0' N, LONG 144° 37.0' E, and you estimate your speed of advance at 20 knots. The distance is 4,948 miles. What is your estimated zone time of arrival at Guam?

A. 1734, 11 December
B. 1934, 11 December
C. 0334, 12 December
D. 1334, 12 December

00602. At 1845 zone time on 24 October 1981, you depart Bimini Island, LAT 25° 50.0' N, LONG 77° 00.0' W (ZD +5). You are bound for Bishop Rock, LAT 49° 40.0' N, LONG 6° 34.0' W, and you estimate your speed of advance at 13.6 knots. The distance is 3,491 miles. What is your estimated zone time of arrival at Bishop Rock?

A. 0627, 3 November
B. 1642, 3 November
C. 0939, 4 November
D. 1627, 4 November

00603. At 0915 zone time on 7 November 1981, you depart Seattle, LAT 47° 36.0' N, LONG 122° 22.0' W (ZD +8). You are bound for Kobe, LAT 34° 40.0' N, LONG 135° 12.0' E, and you estimate your speed of advance at 18.5 knots. The distance is 4,527 miles. What is your estimated zone time of arrival at Kobe?

A. 1257, 17 November
B. 0657, 18 November
C. 1857, 18 November
D. 0657, 19 November

00604. At 1820 zone time on 21 March 1981, you depart San Francisco, LAT 37° 48.5' N, LONG 122° 24.0' W (ZD +8). You are bound for Melbourne, LAT 37° 49.2' S, LONG 144° 56.0' E, and you estimate your speed of advance at 21 knots. The distance is 6,970 miles. What is your estimated zone time of arrival at Melbourne?

A. 1214, 4 April
B. 2214, 4 April
C. 0814, 5 April
D. 1314, 5 April

00605. At 0915 zone time on 26 July 1981, you depart Yokohoma, LAT 35° 27.0' N, LONG 139° 39.0' E (ZD -9). You are bound for Seattle, LAT 47° 36.0' N, LONG 122° 22.0' W, and you estimate your speed of advance at 14 knots. The distance is 4,245 miles. What is your estimated zone time of arrival at Seattle?

A. 0728, 7 August
B. 1528, 7 August
C. 0028, 8 August
D. 1528, 8 August

00606. At 0915 zone time on 11 May 1981, you depart Yokohama, LAT 35° 27.0' N, LONG 139° 39.0' E (ZD -9). You are bound for Seattle, LAT 47° 36.0' N, LONG 122° 22.0' W, and you estimate your speed of advance at 19.5 knots. The distance is 4,276 miles. What is your estimated zone time of arrival at Seattle?

A. 1932, 19 May
B. 0332, 20 May
C. 1032, 20 May
D. 1232, 20 May

00607. At 0915 zone time on 6 March 1981, you depart Sydney, LAT 33° 51.5' S, LONG 151° 13.0' E (ZD -10). You are bound for Kodiak, LAT 57° 47.0' N, LONG 152° 25.0' W, and you estimate your speed of advance at 21 knots. The distance is 6,222 miles. What is your estimated zone time of arrival at Kodiak?

A. 0732, 17 March
B. 2132, 17 March
C. 0732, 18 March
D. 2132, 18 March

00608. At 1200 zone time on 10 October 1981, you depart San Francisco, LAT 37° 48.5' N, LONG 122° 24.0' W (ZD +8). You are bound for Yokohama, LAT 35° 27.0' N, LONG 139° 39.0' E, and you estimate your speed of advance at 22 knots. The distance is 4,536 miles. What is your estimated zone time of arrival at Yokohama?

A. 0111, 19 October
B. 0211, 19 October
C. 1011, 19 October
D. 1911, 19 October

00609. At 0915 zone time on 7 April 1981, you depart San Francisco, LAT 37° 48.5' N, LONG 122° 24.0' W (ZD +8). You are bound for Kobe, LAT 34° 40.0' N, LONG 135° 12.0' E, and you estimate your speed of advance at 17 knots. The distance is 4,819 miles. What is your estimated zone time of arrival at Kobe?

A. 0343, 18 April
B. 1243, 19 April
C. 2143, 19 April
D. 0443, 20 April

00610. At 0820 zone time on 10 April 1981, you depart Yokohoma, LAT 35° 27.0' N, LONG 139° 39.0'E (ZD -9). You are bound for Honolulu, LAT 21° 18.5' N, LONG 157° 52.2' W (ZD +10) and you estimate your speed of advance at 17.5 knots. The distance is 3,397 miles. What is your estimated zone time of arrival at Honolulu?

A. 0127, 17 April
B. 1527, 17 April
C. 0127, 18 April
D. 0927, 18 April

00611. At 0600 zone time on 22 October 1981, you depart Manilla, LAT 14° 35.0' N, LONG 120° 58.0' E (ZD -8). You are bound for Los Angeles, LAT 33° 46.0' N, LONG 118° 11.0' W, and you estimate your speed of advance at 20.2 knots. The distance is 6,385.9 miles. What is your estimated zone time of arrival at Los Angeles?

A. 1808, 3 November
B. 0208, 4 November
C. 1008, 4 November
D. 0208, 5 November

00612. At 0530 zone time on 20 December 1981, you depart Capetown (ZD -1). You are bound for New York, (ZD +5) and you estimate your speed of advance at 25 knots. The distance is 6,762 miles. What is your estimated zone time of arrival at New York?

A. 1200, 31 December
B. 0700, 31 December
C. 1100, 31 December
D. 0600, 31 December

00613. On 21 November at 2100 zone time, you depart LAT 32° 12.0' N, LONG 69° 26.0' W enroute to LAT 12° 05.0' N, LONG 7° 32.0' W. The distance is 3,519 miles and the average speed will be 12.5 knots. What is the zone time of arrival?

A. 1330, 3 December
B. 1530, 3 December
C. 1830, 3 December
D. 1530, 4 December

00614. Your vessel departs Arkhangel'sk, USSR from position LAT 64° 32' N, LONG 40° 31' E at 0236 zone time on 19 August. It is bound for New York, New York at position LAT 40° 42' N, LONG 74° 01' W. The distance is determined to be 4,216 miles, and you estimate that you will average 13.0 knots. What is your estimated zone time of arrival?

A. 1155, 31 August
B. 1755, 31 August
C. 0655, 1 September
D. 1155, 1 September

00615. Your vessel departs Yokohama from position LAT 35° 27.0' N, LONG 139° 39.0' E (ZD -9) at 1330 zone time on 23 July bound for Seattle at position LAT 47° 36.0' N, LONG 122° 22.0' W (ZD +8). The distance by great circle is 4,245 miles, and you estimate that you will average 13.6 knots. What is your estimated zone time of arrival?

A. 0438, 4 August
B. 2038, 4 August
C. 0438, 5 August
D. 1238, 5 August

00616. At 0800 zone time on 15 April your vessel is heading west in position LAT 15° 10.0' N, LONG 165° 15.0' W at a speed of 22 knots. The distance to your destination at LAT 15° 10.0'N, LONG 135° 15.0' E is 3,600 miles. What is your ETA?

A. 1439, 21 April
B. 0539, 22 April
C. 2339, 22 April
D. 0539, 23 April

00617. Your vessel will sail from a position in LAT 8° 51.0' N, LONG 81° 31.0' W to a position at LAT 33° 51.5' S, LONG 151° 13.0' E. The distance by great circle is 7,635 miles and you estimate an average speed of 15.0 knots. What is your estimated zone time of arrival if you depart at 1510 ZT on 23 July?

A. 1110, 14 August
B. 0110, 15 August
C. 1110, 16 August
D. 1510, 17 August

00618. Your vessel departs Seattle at 1010 zone time (ZD +8) on 28 May bound for Apra, Guam (ZD -10). The distance by great circle is 4,948 miles, and you estimate that you will average 18.5 knots. What is your estimated zone time of arrival?

A. 0737, 9 June
B. 1737, 9 June
C. 1937, 9 June
D. 0737, 10 June

00619. Your vessel departs Montevideo, Uruguay, LAT 34° 40.3' S, LONG 54° 09.1' W (ZD +4), at 1800 zone time on 15 October 1981. It is bound for New York, LAT 40° 27.5' N, LONG 73° 49.9' W, (ZD +5). The distance is 5,749 miles, and you expect to average 20 knots. What is your estimated zone time of arrival?

A. 0427, 26 October
B. 1627, 26 October
C. 1627, 27 October
D. 0427, 27 October

00620. On 21 May 1981, at 0630 PDT (ZD +7), your vessel takes departure at the San Francisco Sea Buoy, LAT 37° 45' N, LONG 122° 41.5' W, enroute to Kobe, LAT 33° 52' N, LONG 135° E via great circle. The distance is 4,245 miles, and you estimate that you will average 14.0 knots. What will be your estimated zone time of arrival?

A. 0442, 2 June
B. 1342, 2 June
C. 0442, 3 June
D. 1342, 3 June

00621. You are on a voyage from New York, NY to San Francisco, C
A. The distance from pilot to pilot is 5132 miles. The speed of advance is 13.5 knots. You estimate 32 hours for bunkering at Colon and 14 hours for the Panama Canal transit. If you take departure at 0600 hours (ZD +4) 16 May, what is your ETA (ZD +7) at San Francisco?

A. 0609, 1 June
B. 2109, 2 June
C. 0009, 3 June
D. 0409, 3 June

00622. You are on a voyage from Limoy, Costa Rica to Los Angeles, CA. The distance from pilot to pilot is 3150 miles. The speed of advance is 14.0 knots. You estimate 24.0 hours for bunkering at Colon and 12.0 hours for the Panama Canal transit. If you take departure at 1836 hours (ZD +6) 28 January. What is your ETA (ZD +8) at Los Angeles?

A. 1736, 9 February
B. 1736, 8 February
C. 1336, 8 February
D. 0536, 8 February

00623. You are on a voyage from Baltimore, MD to Seattle, W
A. The distance from pilot to pilot is 5960 miles. The speed of advance is 16.0 knots. You estimate 16 hours for bunkering at Colon and 12.0 hours for the Panama Canal transit. If you take departure at 0824 hours (ZD +5) 18 November, what is your ETA (ZD +8) at Seattle?

A. 1654, 5 December
B. 1354, 5 December
C. 2154, 4 December
D. 1354, 4 December

00624. You are on a voyage from San Diego, CA to New York, NY. The distance from pilot to pilot is 4860 miles. The speed of advance is 15.0 knots. You estimate 18 hours for bunkering at Colon and 14 hours for the Panama Canal transit. If you take departure at 0836 hours (ZD +7), 4 July. What is your ETA (ZD +4) at New York?

A. 0336, 20 July
B. 0036, 19 July
C. 0336, 19 July
D. 0736, 19 July

00625. You are on a voyage from Boston, MA to South Pass, LA. The distance is 1870 miles, and the speed of advance is 13.6 knots. You estimate 16.5 hours for bunkering enroute at Port Everglades, FL. If you sail at 0836 hours (ZD +5) 26, February, 1987. What is your ETA (ZD +6) at South Pass?

A. 2336, 3 March
B. 1136, 4 March
C. 1236, 4 March
D. 1736, 4 March

00626. You are on a voyage from St. John, Canada to Galveston, TX. The distance is 2280 miles, and the speed of advance is 15.0 knots. You estimate 16.5 hours for bunkering enroute at Ft. Lauderdale, FL. If you sail at 1642 hours (ZD +4) 27 February 1987 what is your ETA (ZD +6) at Galveston?

A. 1512, 6 March
B. 0812, 6 March
C. 0712, 6 March
D. 2312, 5 March

00627. You are on a voyage form Halifax, Nova Scotia to Galveston, TX. The distance is 2138 miles and the speed of advance is 12.5 knots. You estimate 18.0 hours for bunkering enroute at Port Everglades, FL. If you sail at 0648 hours (ZD +4), 12 June, what is your ETA (ZD +5) at Galveston?

A. 0250, 20 June
B. 1350, 20 June
C. 0350, 20 June
D. 0550, 20 June

00628. You are on a voyage from Valdez, AK to Panama Canal Zone. The distance from pilot to pilot is 4950 miles. The speed of advance is 15.0 knots. You estimate a layover in San Francisco, CA of 36.0 hours. If you take departure at 0800 (ZD +10) 29, October, what is your ETA (ZD +5) at Panama Canal Zone.

A. 1900, 13 Novemb43er
B. 1400, 13 November
C. 1400, 14 November
D. 0900, 13 November

4-69

Answers to USGG ETA Problems

00601 D
00602 D
00603 B
00604 C
00605 A
00606 A
00607 B
00608 D
00609 C
00610 B
00611 A
00612 D
00613 C
00614 C
00615 B
00616 C
00617 A
00618 A
00619 C
00620 D
00621 B
00622 C
00623 C
00624 D
00625 D
00626 A
00627 A
00628 A

ETA PROBLEMS WORKSHEET

0601 (1)	Month	day	Hour	Minutes
Departure ZT	12	01	12	10
ZD			+8	
Departure GMT	12	01	20	10
Dist. Run + Lay		10	07	24
Arrival GMT	12	12	03	34
Rev. ZD			+10	
Arrival ZT	12	12	13	34

0602 (2)	Month	day	Hour	Minutes
Departure ZT	10	24	18	45
ZD			+5	
Departure GMT	10	24	23	45
Dist. Run + Lay		10	16	41
Arrival GMT	11	04	16	26
Rev. ZD			0	
Arrival ZT	11	04	16	26

Distance Run plus lay time Calculations

$$\frac{4948}{20} = \frac{247.4}{24} = 10 \; Days$$

$$.30833333 \times 24 = 07 \; Hours$$

$$.4 \times 60 = 24 \; Minutes$$

Distance Run plus lay time Calculations

$$\frac{3491}{13.6} = \frac{256.6911765}{24} = 10 \; Days$$

$$.69546569 \times 24 = 16 \; Hours$$

$$.69117647 \times 60 = 41 \; Minutes$$

0603 (3)	Month	day	Hour	Minutes
Departure ZT	11	07	09	15
ZD			+8	
Departure GMT	11	07	17	15
Dist. Run + Lay		10	04	42
Arrival GMT	11	17	21	57
Rev. ZD			+9	
Arrival ZT	11	18	06	57

0604 (4)	Month	day	Hour	Minutes
Departure ZT	03	21	18	20
ZD			+8	
Departure GMT	03	22	02	20
Dist. Run + Lay		13	19	54
Arrival GMT	04	04	22	14
Rev. ZD			+10	
Arrival ZT	040	05	08	14

Distance Run plus lay time Calculations

$$\frac{4527}{18.5} = \frac{244.7527027}{24} = 10 \; Days$$

$$.1959459459 \times 24 = 04 \; Hours$$

$$.7027027027 \times 60 = 42 \; Minutes$$

Distance Run plus lay time Calculations

$$\frac{6970}{21} = \frac{331.9047619}{24} = 13 \; Days$$

$$.82936508 \times 24 = 19 \; Hours$$

$$.9047619 \times 60 = 54 \; Minutes$$

0605 (5)	Month	day	Hour	Minutes
Departure ZT	07	26	09	15
ZD			-9	
Departure GMT	07	26	00	15
Dist. Run + Lay		12	15	13
Arrival GMT	08	07	15	28
Rev. ZD			-8	
Arrival ZT	08	07	07	28

Distance Run plus lay time Calculations

$$\frac{4245}{14} = \frac{303.2142857}{24} = 12 \; Days$$

$$.63392857 \times 24 = 15 \; Hours$$

$$.2142857143 \times 60 = 13 \; Minutes$$

0606 (6)	Month	day	Hour	Minutes
Departure ZT	05	11	09	15
ZD			-9	
Departure GMT	05	09	00	15
Dist. Run + Lay		09	03	17
Arrival GMT	05	20	03	32
Rev. ZD			-8	
Arrival ZT	05	19	19	32

Distance Run plus lay time Calculations

$$\frac{4276}{19.5} = \frac{219.2820513}{24} = 9 \; Days$$

$$.136752137 \times 24 = 3 \; Hours$$

$$.2020512821 \times 60 = 17 \; Minutes$$

0607 (7)	Month	day	Hour	Minutes
Departure ZT	03	06	09	15
ZD			-10	
Departure GMT	03	05	23	15
Dist. Run + Lay		12	08	17
Arrival GMT	03	18	07	32
Rev. ZD			-10	
Arrival ZT	03	17	21	32

Distance Run plus lay time Calculations

$$\frac{6222}{21} = \frac{296.2857143}{24} = 12 \; Days$$

$$.3452380952 \times 24 = 8 \; Hours$$

$$.2857142857 \times 60 = 17 \; Minutes$$

0608 (8)	Month	day	Hour	Minutes
Departure ZT	10	10	10	00
ZD			+8	
Departure GMT	10	10	20	00
Dist. Run + Lay		08	14	11
Arrival GMT	10	19	10	11
Rev. ZD			+9	
Arrival ZT	10	19	19	11

Distance Run plus lay time Calculations

$$\frac{4526}{22} = \frac{206.1818182}{24} = 8 \; Days$$

$$.590909090909 \times 24 \times 24 = 14 \; Hours$$

$$.1818181818 \times 60 = 11 \; Minutes$$

0609 (9)	Month	day	Hour	Minutes
Departure ZT	04	07	9	15
ZD			-8	
Departure GMT	04	07	17	15
Dist. Run + Lay		11	19	28
Arrival GMT	04	19	12	43
Rev. ZD			+9	
Arrival ZT	04	19	21	43

Distance Run plus lay time Calculations

$$\frac{4819}{17} = \frac{283.4705882}{24} = 11 \; Days$$

$$.81127451 \times 24 = 19 \; Hours$$

$$.4705882353 \times 60 = 28 \; Minutes$$

0610 (10)	Month	day	Hour	Minutes
Departure ZT	04	10	08	20
ZD			-9	
Departure GMT	04	09	23	20
Dist. Run + Lay		08	02	07
Arrival GMT	04	18	01	27
Rev. ZD			-10	
Arrival ZT	04	17	15	27

Distance Run plus lay time Calculations

$$\frac{3397}{17.5} = \frac{194.1142857}{24} = 8 \; Days$$

$$.0880952381 \times 24 = 2 \; Hours$$

$$.1142857143 \times 60 = 6.85 \; Minutes$$

0611 (11)	Month	day	Hour	Minutes
Departure ZT	10	22	06	00
ZD			-8	
Departure GMT	10	21	22	00
Dist. Run + Lay		13	04	08
Arrival GMT	11	04	02	08
Rev. ZD			-8	
Arrival ZT	11	03	18	08

Distance Run plus lay time Calculations

$$\frac{6385.9}{20.2} = \frac{316.1336634}{24} = 13 \; Days$$

$$.1722359736 \times 24 = 4 \; Hours$$

$$.1336633663 \times 60 = 8.01 \; Minutes$$

0612 (12)	Month	day	Hour	Minutes
Departure ZT	12	20	05	30
ZD			-1	
Departure GMT	12	20	04	30
Dist. Run + Lay		11	06	29
Arrival GMT	12	31	10	59
Rev. ZD			-5	
Arrival ZT	12	31	05	59

Distance Run plus lay time Calculations

$$\frac{6762}{20} = \frac{270.48}{24} = 11 \; Days$$

$$.27 \times 24 = 6 \; Hours$$

$$.48 \times 60 = 28.8 \; Minutes$$

0613 (13)	Month	day	Hour	Minutes
Departure ZT	11	21	21	00
ZD			+5	
Departure GMT	11	22	02	00
Dist. Run + Lay		11	17	31
Arrival GMT	12	03	19	31
Rev. ZD			-1	
Arrival ZT	12	03	18	31

Distance Run plus lay time Calculations

$$\frac{3519}{12.5} = \frac{281.52}{24} = 11 \, Days$$

$$.73 \times 24 = 17 \, Hours$$

$$..52 \times 60 = 31 \, Minutes$$

0614 (14)	Month	day	Hour	Minutes
Departure ZT	08	18	23	36
ZD			-3	
Departure GMT	08	18	23	36
Dist. Run + Lay		13	12	19
Arrival GMT	09	01	11	55
Rev. ZD			-5	
Arrival ZT	09	01	06	55

Distance Run plus lay time Calculations

$$\frac{4216}{13} = \frac{324.3076923}{24} = 13 \, Days$$

$$.5128205128 \times 24 = 12 \, Hours$$

$$.3076923077 \times 60 = 18.46 \, Minutes$$

0615 (15)	Month	day	Hour	Minutes
Departure ZT	07	23	13	30
ZD			-9	
Departure GMT	07	23	04	30
Dist. Run + Lay		13	00	08
Arrival GMT	08	05	04	38
Rev. ZD			-5	
Arrival ZT	08	04	20	38

Distance Run plus lay time Calculations

$$\frac{4245}{13.6} = \frac{312.1323529}{24} = 13 \, Days$$

$$.00551471 \times 24 = 0 \, Hours$$

$$.1323529 \times 60 = 7.941174 \, Minutes$$

0616 (16)	Month	day	Hour	Minutes
Departure ZT	04	15	08	00
ZD			+11	
Departure GMT	04	15	19	00
Dist. Run + Lay		06	19	00
Arrival GMT	05	22	14	38
Rev. ZD			+9	
Arrival ZT	05	22	23	38

Distance Run plus lay time Calculations

$$\frac{3600}{22} = \frac{136.6363636}{24} = 6 \, Days$$

$$.8181818182 \times 24 = 19 \, Hours$$

$$.636363636364 \times 60 = 38.2 \, Minutes$$

0617 (17)	Month	day	Hour	Minutes
Departure ZT	07	23	15	10
ZD			+5	
Departure GMT	07	23	20	10
Dist. Run + Lay		21	5	00
Arrival GMT	08	14	01	10
Rev. ZD			+10	
Arrival ZT	08	14	11	10

Distance Run plus lay time Calculations

$$\frac{7635}{15} = \frac{509}{24} = 21\ Days$$

$$.2083333333 \times 24 = 5\ Hours$$

$$0\ Minutes$$

0618 (18)	Month	day	Hour	Minutes
Departure ZT	05	28	10	10
ZD			+8	
Departure GMT	05	28	18	10
Dist. Run + Lay		11	03	28
Arrival GMT	06	08	21	38
Rev. ZD			+10	
Arrival ZT	06	09	07	38

Distance Run plus lay time Calculations

$$\frac{4948}{18.5} = \frac{267.4594595}{24} = 11\ Days$$

$$.1441441441441 \times 24 = 3\ Hours$$

$$.4594594595 \times 60 = 27.56\ Minutes$$

0619 (19)	Month	day	Hour	Minutes
Departure ZT	11	15	18	00
ZD			+4	
Departure GMT	11	15	22	00
Dist. Run + Lay		11	23	27
Arrival GMT	11	27	21	27
Rev. ZD			-5	
Arrival ZT	11	27	16	27

Distance Run plus lay time Calculations

$$\frac{5749}{20} = \frac{287.45}{24} = 11\ Days$$

$$.9770833 \times 24 = 23\ Hours$$

$$..45 \times 60 = 27\ Minutes$$

0620 (20)	Month	day	Hour	Minutes
Departure ZT	05	21	06	30
ZD			+7	
Departure GMT	05	03	13	30
Dist. Run + Lay		12	15	13
Arrival GMT	06	03	04	43
Rev. ZD			+9	
Arrival ZT	06	03	13	43

Distance Run plus lay time Calculations

$$\frac{4245}{14} = \frac{3032142857}{24} = 12\ Days$$

$$.6339285714 \times 24 = 15\ Hours$$

$$2142857143 \times 60 = 12.85\ Minutes$$

0621 (21)	Month	day	Hour	Minutes
Departure ZT	05	16	06	00
ZD			+4	
Departure GMT	05	16	10	00
Dist. Run + Lay		17	18	09
Arrival GMT	06	03	04	09
Rev. ZD			-7	
Arrival ZT	06	02	21	09

Distance Run plus lay time Calculations

$$\frac{5132}{13.5} = \frac{372.5}{24} = 15 \; Days$$

$$.8395061728 \times 24 = 20 \; Hours$$

$$.1481481481 \times 60 = 8.9 \; Minutes$$

Plus and Lay Bunkering 1 Day 22 Hours

0622 (22)	Month	day	Hour	Minutes
Departure ZT	01	28	18	36
ZD			+6	
Departure GMT	01	29	00	36
Dist. Run + Lay		10	21	00
Arrival GMT	02	08	21	36
Rev. ZD			-8	
Arrival ZT	02	08	13	36

Distance Run plus lay time Calculations

$$\frac{3150}{14} = \frac{225}{24} = 9 \; Days$$

$$.375 \times 24 = 9 \; Hours$$

Plus Lay and Bunkering 1 Day 12 Hours

0623 (23)	Month	day	Hour	Minutes
Departure ZT	11	18	08	24
ZD			+5	
Departure GMT	11	18	13	24
Dist. Run + Lay		16	16	30
Arrival GMT	12	05	05	54
Rev. ZD			-8	
Arrival ZT	12	04	21	54

Distance Run plus lay time Calculations

$$\frac{5960}{16} = \frac{372.5}{24} = 15 \; Days$$

$$.52083333 \times 24 = 12 \; Hours$$

$$.5 \times 60 = 30 \; Minutes$$

Plus Lay and Bunkering 1 Day 04 Hours

0624 (24)	Month	day	Hour	Minutes
Departure ZT	07	04	08	36
ZD			+7	
Departure GMT	07	04	15	36
Dist. Run + Lay		14	20	00
Arrival GMT	07	19	11	36
Rev. ZD			-4	
Arrival ZT	07	19	07	36

Distance Run plus lay time Calculations

$$\frac{4860}{15} = \frac{324}{24} = 13 \; Days$$

$$.5 \times 24 = 12 \; Hours$$

Plus Lay and Bunkering 1 Day 08 Hours

0625 (25)	Month	day	Hour	Minutes
Departure ZT	02	26	08	36
ZD			+5	
Departure GMT	02	26	13	36
Dist. Run + Lay		06	10	00
Arrival GMT	03	04	23	36
Rev. ZD			-6	
Arrival ZT	03	04	17	36

0626 (26)	Month	day	Hour	Minutes
Departure ZT	02	27	16	42
ZD			+4	
Departure GMT	02	27	20	42
Dist. Run + Lay		07	00	30
Arrival GMT	03	06	21	12
Rev. ZD			-6	
Arrival ZT	03	06	15	12

Distance Run plus lay time Calculations

$$\frac{1870}{13.6} = \frac{137.5}{24} = 5\ Days$$

$$.729166667 \times 24 = 17\ Hours$$

$$.5 \times 60 = 30\ Minutes$$

Plus Bunkering 16 Hours 30 Minutes

Distance Run plus lay time Calculations

$$\frac{2280}{15} = \frac{152}{24} = 6\ Days$$

$$.333333 \times 24 = 8\ Hours$$

Bunkering 16 Hours 30 Minutes

0627 (27)	Month	day	Hour	Minutes
Departure ZT	06	12	06	48
ZD			+4	
Departure GMT	06	12	10	48
Dist. Run + Lay		07	21	02
Arrival GMT	06	20	07	50
Rev. ZD			-5	
Arrival ZT	06	20	02	50

0628 (28)	Month	day	Hour	Minutes
Departure ZT	10	29	08	00
ZD			+10	
Departure GMT	10	29	18	00
Dist. Run + Lay		15	06	00
Arrival GMT	11	14	00	00
Rev. ZD			-5	
Arrival ZT	11	13	19	00

Distance Run plus lay time Calculations

$$\frac{2138}{12.5} = \frac{171.04}{24} = 7\ Days$$

$$.12666667 \times 24 = 3 Hours$$

$$.040000008 \times 60 = 2.4\ Minutes$$

Plus 18 Hours

Distance Run plus lay time Calculations

$$\frac{5950}{15} = \frac{330}{24} = 13\ Days$$

$$.75 \times 24 = 18\ Hours$$

Plus lay time of 1 Day 12 Hours

USCG Local Apparent Noon Questions Worked-out

Chapter 12, Celestial Navigation (Upon Oceans Endorsement)

Danti's meridiana

This meridiana constructed by Egnatio Danti in the 16th century at the Torre dei Venti (Tower of Winds) in the Vatican shows a beam of sunlight (enhanced) shining through a hole in the south wall at local apparent noon and projected onto the floor. The position of the Sun's image on the calendar dates chiseled into the marble floor indicates the time of the year.

by
Alexander F. Hickethier MBA
and
DR. Hu Jia-Shen

Local Apparent Noon
Chapter 17, Celestial for Master/Mate limited Upon Oceans

00806. On 15 November 1981, your 0913 zone time fix gives you a position of LAT 22° 30.0' N, LONG 68° 28.0' W. Your vessel is on course 164° T, and your speed is 13.5 knots. Local apparent noon (LAN) occurs at 1218 zone time at which time a meridian altitude of the Sun's lower limb is observed. The observed altitude (Ho) for this sight is 49° 46.0'. What is the calculated latitude at local apparent noon (LAN)?

A. LAT 21° 36.0' N
B. LAT 21° 38.6' N
C. LAT 21° 40.0' N
D. LAT 21° 42.5' N

00807. On 12 February 1981, your 0542 zone time fix gives you a position of LAT 26° 42.0' N, LONG 60° 18.0' W. Your vessel is on course 300° T, and your speed is 9.8 knots. Local apparent noon (LAN) occurs at 1220 zone time at which time a meridian altitude of the Sun's lower limb is observed. The observed altitude (Ho) for this sight is 49° 10.0'. What is the calculated latitude at local apparent noon (LAN)?

A. LAT 27° 13.5' N
B. LAT 27° 16.3' N
C. LAT 27° 17.6' N
D. LAT 27° 19.2' N

00808. On 28 July 1981, your 0800 zone time fix gives you a position of LAT 25° 16.0' N, LONG 71° 19.0' W. Your vessel is on course 026° T, and your speed is 17.5 knots. Local apparent noon (LAN) occurs at 1149 zone time, at which time a meridian altitude of the Sun's lower limb is observed. The observed altitude (Ho) for this sight is 82° 28.7'. What is the calculated latitude at local apparent noon (LAN)?

A. LAT 26° 21.9' N
B. LAT 26° 23.4' N
C. LAT 26° 25.0' N
D. LAT 26° 27.7' N

00809. On 7 November 1981, your 0830 zone time fix gives you a position of LAT 27° 36.0' N, LONG 163° 19.0' W. Your vessel is on course 289° T, and your speed is 19.0 knots. Local apparent noon (LAN) occurs at 1138 zone time, at which time a meridian altitude of the Sun's lower limb is observed. The observed altitude (Ho) for this sight is 45° 35.0'. What is the calculated latitude at local apparent noon (LAN)?

A. LAT 27° 52.3' N
B. LAT 27° 53.4' N
C. LAT 27° 55.1' N
D. LAT 27° 57.2' N

00810. On 13 October 1981, your 0515 zone time fix gives you a position of LAT 26° 53.0' N, LONG 90° 05.0' W. Your vessel is on course 068° T, and your speed is 7.8 knots. Local apparent noon (LAN) occurs at 1145 zone time, at which time a meridian altitude of the Sun's lower limb is observed. The observed altitude (Ho) for this sight is 54° 51.5'. What is the calculated latitude at local apparent noon (LAN)?

A. LAT 27° 12.6' N
B. LAT 27° 14.1' N
C. LAT 27° 15.7' N
D. LAT 27° 16.2' N

00811. On 1 July 1981, your 0515 zone time fix gives you a position of LAT 24° 36.0' S, LONG 151° 42.0' W. Your vessel is on course 240° T, and your speed is 10.0 knots. Local apparent noon (LAN) occurs at 1215 zone time, at which time a meridian altitude of the Sun's lower limb is observed. The observed altitude (Ho) for this sight is 42° 55.0'. What is the calculated latitude at local apparent noon (LAN)?

A. LAT 24° 03.6' S
B. LAT 24° 02.5' S
C. LAT 24° 01.0' S
D. LAT 24° 00.0' S

00812. On 28 July 1981, your 0800 zone time fix gives you a position of LAT 25° 16.0' N, LONG 71° 19.0' W. Your vessel is on course 026° T, and your speed is 17.5 knots. Local apparent noon (LAN) occurs at 1150 zone time, at which time a meridian altitude of the Sun's lower limb is observed. The observed altitude (Ho) for this sight is 82° 28.7'. What is the latitude at 1200?

A. LAT 26° 25.0' N
B. LAT 26° 27.6' N
C. LAT 26° 29.8' N
D. LAT 26° 32.0' N

00813. On 7 November 1981, your 0830 zone time fix gives you a position of LAT 27° 36.0' N, LONG 162° 19.0' W. Your vessel is on course 289° T, and your speed is 19.0 knots. Local apparent noon (LAN) occurs at 1138 zone time, at which time a meridian altitude of the Sun's lower limb is observed. The observed altitude (Ho) for this sight is 45° 35.0'. What is the latitude at 1200?

A. LAT 27° 55.1' N
B. LAT 27° 57.2' N
C. LAT 27° 59.5' N
D. LAT 28° 01.9' N

00814. On 1 July 1981, your 0515 zone time fix gives you a position of LAT 23° 24.0' S, LONG 151° 42.0' W. Your vessel is on course 240° T, and your speed is 10.0 knots. Local apparent noon (LAN) occurs at 1215 zone time, at which time a meridian altitude of the Sun's lower limb is observed. The observed altitude (Ho) for this sight is 42° 55.0'. What is the latitude at 1200?

A. LAT 24° 02.5' S
B. LAT 24° 01.0' S
C. LAT 23° 59.7' S
D. LAT 23° 58.6' S

00815. On 13 October 1981, your 0515 zone time fix gives you a position of LAT 26° 53.0' N, LONG 90° 05.0' W. Your vessel is on course 068° T, and your speed is 7.8 knots. Local apparent noon (LAN) occurs at 1145 zone time, at which time a meridian altitude of the Sun's lower limb is observed. The observed altitude (Ho) for this sight is 54° 51.5'. What is the latitude at 1200?

A. LAT 27° 13.3' N
B. LAT 27° 14.6' N
C. LAT 27° 15.7' N
D. LAT 27° 16.8' N

00816. On 15 November 1981, your 0913 zone time fix gives you a position of LAT 22° 30.0' N, LONG 67° 28.0' W. Your vessel is on course 164° T, and your speed is 13.5 knots. Local apparent noon (LAN) occurs at 1215 zone time, at which time a meridian altitude of the Sun's lower limb is observed. The observed altitude (Ho) for this sight is 49° 46.0'. What is the latitude at 1200?

A. LAT 21° 39.9' N
B. LAT 21° 36.0' N
C. LAT 21° 33.3' N
D. LAT 21° 30.4' N

00844. On 12 September 1981, your 0600 zone time fix gives you a position of LAT 22° 51.9' N, LONG 133° 40.1' W. Your vessel is on course 062° T, and your speed is 12.3 knots. Local apparent noon (LAN) occurs at 1142 zone time, at which time a meridian altitude of the Sun's upper limb is observed. The observed altitude (Ho) for this sight is 70° 33.2'. What is the calculated latitude at local apparent noon (LAN)?

A. LAT 23° 23.0' N
B. LAT 23° 24.8' N
C. LAT 23° 26.5' N
D. LAT 23° 27.9' N

00845. On 16 September 1981, your 0600 zone time fix gives you a position of LAT 29° 47.2' N, LONG 65° 28.4' W. Your vessel is on course 242° T, and your speed is 13.5 knots. Local apparent noon (LAN) occurs at 1227 zone time, at which time a meridian altitude of the Sun's lower limb is observed. The observed altitude (Ho) for this sight is 63° 25.3'. What is the calculated latitude at local apparent noon (LAN)?

A. LAT 29° 07.9' N
B. LAT 29° 06.1' N
C. LAT 29° 04.7' N
D. LAT 29° 01.6' N

00846. On 22 February 1981, your 0612 zone time fix gives you a position of LAT 27° 16.2' S, LONG 37° 41.6' W. Your vessel is on course 298° T, and your speed is 14.2 knots. Local apparent noon (LAN) occurs at 1147 zone time, at which time a meridian altitude of the Sun's lower limb is observed. The observed altitude (Ho) for this sight is 73° 33.3'. What is the calculated latitude at local apparent noon (LAN)?

A. LAT 26° 31.4' S
B. LAT 26° 29.5' S
C. LAT 26° 27.1' S
D. LAT 26° 24.8' S

00847. On 17 December 1981, your 0600 zone time fix gives you a position of LAT 27° 16.7' N, LONG 138° 39.2' W. Your vessel is on course 137° T, and your speed is 14.8 knots. Local apparent noon (LAN) occurs at 1207 zone time, at which time a meridian altitude of the Sun's lower limb is observed. The observed altitude (Ho) for this sight is 40° 22.1'. What is the calculated latitude at local apparent noon (LAN)?

A. LAT 26° 09.9' N
B. LAT 26° 11.6' N
C. LAT 26° 13.0' N
D. LAT 26° 15.4' N

Answers Local Apparent Noon

1. 00806 B
2. 00807 B
3. 00808 C
4. 00809 D
5. 00810 A
6. 00811 C
7. 00812 B
8. 00813 C

9. 00814 C
10. 00815 A
11. 00816 B
12. 00844 B
13. 00845 C
14. 00846 A
15. 00847 D

Celestial Problems
Latitude by Meridian Passage of the Sun

LAN	
USCG #	806
Date	15 Nov
Lat:	22° 30' N
Long:	068° 28' W
ZT	1218
ZD	+5
GMT	1718
DEC	S 18° 35.2'
D (+.6)	+.2'
DEC	S 18° 35.4'
	89° 60.0'
- Ho	49° 46.0'
Z Dist	40° 14.0'
± Dec	18° 35.4'
LAT	21° 38.6'

LAN	
USCG#	807
Date	12 Feb
Lat:	26° 42' N
Long:	60° 18' W
ZT	1220
ZD	+4
GMT	1620
DEC	S 13° 34.0'
D (-.8)	-.3'
DEC	S 13° 33.7'
	89° 60.0'
- Ho	49° 10.0'
Z Dist	40° 50.0'
± Dec	13° 33.7'
LAT	27° 16.3'

LAN	
USCG#	808
Date	28 Jul
Lat:	25° 16' N
Long:	071° 19' W
ZT	1149
ZD	+5
GMT	1649
DEC	N 18° 54.2'
D (-.6)	-.5'
DEC	N 18° 53.7'
	89° 60.0'
- Ho	82° 28.7'
Z Dist	7° 31.3'
± Dec	18° 53.7'
LAT	26° 25.0'

LAN	
USCG#	809
Date	7 Nov
Lat:	27° 36' N
Long:	163° 19' W
ZT	1138
ZD	+11
GMT	2238
DEC	S 16° 27.4'
D (+.7)	+.4'
DEC	S 16° 27.8'
	89° 60.0'
- Ho	45° 35.0'
Z Dist	44° 25.0'
± Dec	16° 27.8'
LAT	27° 57.2'

LAN	
USCG#	810
Date	13 Oct
Lat:	26° 53' N
Long:	090° 05' W
ZT	1145
ZD	+6
GMT	1745
DEC	S 7° 55.2'
D (+.9)	+.7'
DEC	S 7° 55.9'
	89° 60.0'
- Ho	54° 51.5'
Z Dist	35° 08.5'
± Dec	7° 55.9'
LAT	27° 12.6'

LAN	
USCG#	811
Date	1 Jul
Lat:	24° 36' S
Long:	151° 42' W
ZT	1215
ZD	+10
GMT	2215
DEC	S 23° 22.2'
D (-.1)	0.0'
DEC	S 23° 04.0'
	89° 60.0'
- Ho	42° 55.0'
Z Dist	47° 05.0'
± Dec	23° 04.0'
LAT	24° 01.0'

LAN	
USCG #	812
Date	13 Oct
Lat:	25° 16' N
Long:	071° 19' W
ZT	1150
ZD	+5
GMT	1650
DEC	N 20° 54.2'
D (-.6)	-.5'
DEC	N 20° 53.7'
	89° 60.0'
- Ho	82° 28.7'
Z Dist	7° 31.3'
± Dec	18° 53.7'
LAT	26° 25.0'
LAT at 1200	26° 27.6'

$$\frac{10 \times 17.5}{60} = 2.916667$$
$$2.9 \times \cos 026 = 2.6$$

LAN	
USCG#	813
Date	7 Nov
Lat:	27° 36' N
Long:	162° 19' W
ZT	1138
ZD	+11
GMT	2238
DEC	S 16° 27.4'
D (+.7)	-.6'
DEC	S 16° 28.0'
	89°-60.0'
- Ho	45°-35.0'
Z Dist	44° 25.0'
± Dec	16° 28.0'
LAT	27°-57.0'
LAT at 1200	27° 59.3'

$$\frac{22 \times 19}{60} = 6.916667$$
$$7.0 \times \cos 289 = 2.27898$$

LAN	
USCG#	814
Date	1 Jul
Lat:	23° 40' S
Long:	151° 42' W
ZT	1215
ZD	+10
GMT	2215
DEC	N 23° 04.0'
D (-.2)	0'
DEC	N 23° 04.0'
	89° 60.0'
- Ho	42° 55.0'
Z Dist	47° 05.0'
± Dec	23° 04.0'
LAT	24° 01.0'
LAT at 1200	23° 59.7'

$$\frac{15 \times 10}{60} = 1.25$$
$$2.5 \times \cos 240 = 2.27898$$

LAN	
USCG#	815
Date	13 Oct
Lat:	26° 53' N
Long:	090° 05' W
ZT	1145
ZD	+6
GMT	1745
DEC	S 7° 55.2'
D (+.9)	+.3'
DEC	S 7° 55.5'
	89° 60.0'
- Ho	54° 51.5'
Z Dist	35° 08.5'
± Dec	7° 55.5'
LAT	27° 13.0'
Lat at 1200	27° 13.7'

$$\frac{15 \times 7.8}{60} = 1.95$$
$$2.0 \times \cos 068 = .749213$$

LAN	
USCG#	816
Date	15 Nov.
Lat:	22° 30' N
Long:	067° 28' W
ZT	1215
ZD	+4
GMT	1615
DEC	S 18° 34.5
D (+.6)	+.2
DEC	S 18° 34.7
	89° 60.0'
- Ho	49° 46.0'
Z Dist	40° 14.0'
± Dec	18° 34.7'
LAT	21° 39.3'
Lat at 1200	21° 36.0'

$$\frac{15 \times 13.5}{60} = 3.375$$
$$3.4 \times \cos 164 = 3.268289$$

LAN	
USCG#	844
Date	12 Sep
Lat:	22° 51.9' N
Long:	133° 40.1' W
ZT	1142
ZD	+9
GMT	2042
DEC	N 3°-58.8
D (-1.0)	-.7
DEC	N 3-58.1
	89° 60.0'
- Ho	70° 33.2'
Z Dist	19° 26.8'
± Dec	3° 58.1'
LAT	23° 24.9'

LAN	
USCG #	845
Date	16 Sep
Lat:	29° 47.2' N
Long:	065° 28.4' W
ZT	1227
ZD	+4
GMT	1627
DEC	N 2° 30.4'
D (+.1)	-.5'
DEC	N 2° 29.9'
	89° 60.0'
- Ho	63° 25.3'
Z Dist	26° 34.7'
± Dec	2° 29.9'
LAT	29° 04.6'

LAN	
USCG#	846
Date	22 Feb
Lat:	27° 16.2' S
Long:	037° 41.6' W
ZT	1147
ZD	+3
GMT	1447
DEC	S 10° 05.4'
D (-.9)	-.7'
DEC	S 10° 04.7'
	89° 60.0'
- Ho	73° 33.3'
Z Dist	16° 26.7'
± Dec	10° 04.7'
LAT	26° 31.4'

LAN	
USCG#	847
Date	17 Dec
Lat:	27° 16.7' N
Long:	138° 39.2' W
ZT	1207
ZD	+9
GMT	2107
DEC	S 23° 0.3'
D (+.1)	0.0'
DEC	S 23° 22.2'
	89° 60.0'
- Ho	40° 22.1'
Z Dist	49° 37.9'
± Dec	23° 22.2'
LAT	26° 15.7'

LATITUDE BY POLARIS
Chapter 16, Celestial Navigation (Upon Oceans Endorsement)

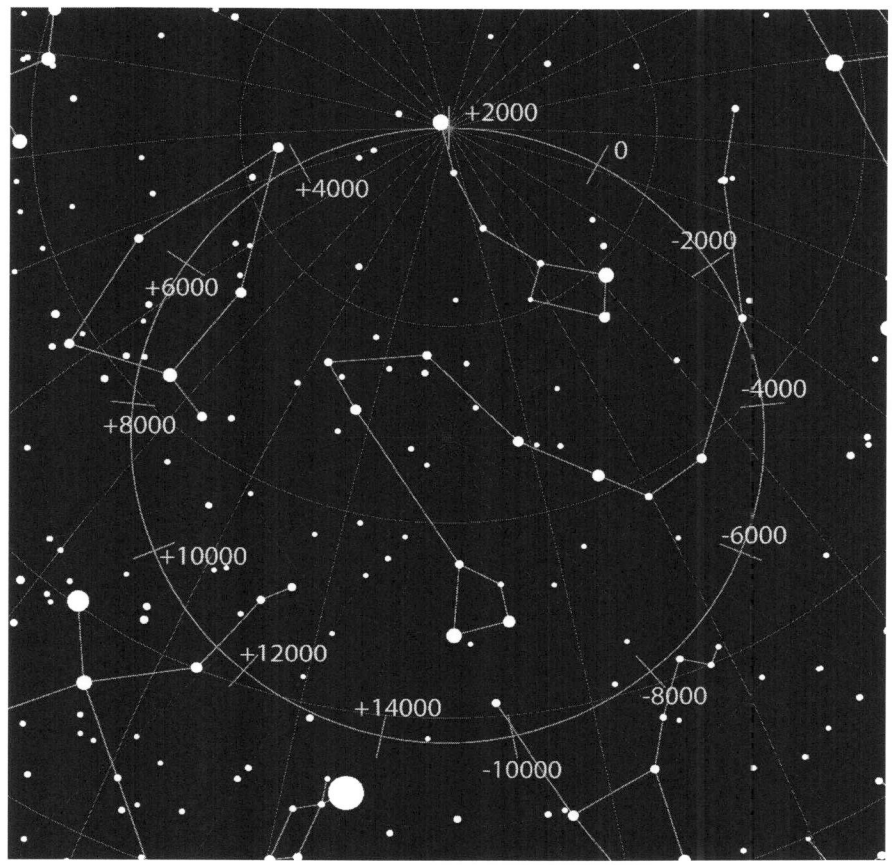

Latitude By Polaris

The Polaris tables in the *Nautical Almanac* list the corrections to Apparent Altitude to determine Latitude. The entering arguments for the table are LHA of Aries observer, latitude and Date.

by
Alexander F. Hickethier MBA
and
Dr. Hu Jia Shen

Latitude by Polaris
Chapter 16, Upon Oceans for Limited Master/Mate

00726. On 16 December 1981, your 1810 zone time DR position is LONG 129° 45.5' W. At that time you observe Polaris with a sextant altitude (hs) of 23° 56.8'. The chronometer time of the sight is 03h 12m 31s, and the chronometer error is 02m 16s fast. The index error is 2.5' off the arc, and the height of eye is 52.6 feet. What is your latitude by Polaris?

A. 23° 07.8' N
B. 23° 12.3' N
C. 24° 11.9' N
D. 24° 18.6' N

00727. On 11 February 1981, your 1832 zone time DR position is LONG 110° 52.6' W. At that time you observe Polaris with a sextant altitude (hs) of 26° 19.8'. The chronometer time of the sight is 01h 34m 56s, and the chronometer error is 02m 16s fast. The index error is 2.7' off the arc, and the height of eye is 60.2 feet. What is your latitude by Polaris?

A. 25° 27.2' N
B. 25° 34.2' N
C. 26° 27.2' N
D. 26° 34.2' N

00728. On 2 January 1981, your 1759 zone time DR position is LONG 45° 17.6' W. At that time you observe Polaris with a sextant altitude (hs) of 24° 16.5'. The chronometer time of the sight is 08h 57m 10s, and the chronometer error is 02m 16s slow. The index error is 3.5 on the arc, and the height of eye is 42.5 feet. What is your latitude by Polaris?

A. 22° 50.2' N
B. 23° 18.8' N
C. 23° 30.2' N
D. 24° 07.3' N

00729. On 24 September 1981, your 1841 zone time DR position is LONG 129° 34.5' E. At that time you observe Polaris with a sextant altitude (hs) of 25° 20.8'. The chronometer time of the sight is 09h 38m 12s, and the chronometer error is 03m 12s slow. The index error is 4.3' off the arc, and the height of eye is 52 feet. What is your latitude by Polaris?

A. 24° 28.1' N
B. 25° 16.0' N
C. 25° 37.6' N
D. 25° 42.3' N

00730. On 18 November 1981, your 1750 zone time DR position is LONG 110° 16.0' W. At that time you observe Polaris with a sextant altitude (hs) of 21° 29.8'. The chronometer time of the sight is 00h 52m 43s, and the chronometer error is 02m 18s fast. The index error is 3.2' on the arc, and the height of eye is 49.5 feet. What is your latitude by Polaris?

A. 21° 03.4' N
B. 21° 13.4' N
C. 21° 28.1' N
D. 21° 35.1' N

00731. On 2 January 1981, your 1759 zone time DR position is LONG 45° 17.6' W. At that time you observe Polaris with a sextant altitude (hs) of 24° 16.5'. The chronometer time of the sight is 08h 57m 10s, and the chronometer error is 02m 16s slow. The index error is 3.5' on the arc, and the height of eye is 42.5 feet. What is your latitude by Polaris?

A. 22° 50.2' N
B. 23° 18.8' N
C. 23° 30.8' N
D. 23° 48.8' N

00732. On 3 January 1981, your 1759 zone time DR position is LONG 60° 53.2' W. At that time you observe Polaris with a sextant altitude (hs) of 22° 55.8'. The chronometer time of the sight is 09h 57m 10s, and the chronometer error is 02m 26s slow. The index error is 2.9 off the arc, and the height of eye is 52.5 feet. What is your latitude by Polaris?

A. 21° 35.2' N
B. 21° 52.5' N
C. 22° 03.6' N
D. 22° 22.6' N

00733. On 12 March 1981, your 1846 zone time DR position is LONG 129° 16.5' W. At that time you observe Polaris with a sextant altitude (hs) of 28° 01.5'. The chronometer time of the sight is 03h 44m 10s, and the chronometer error is 01m 55s slow. The index error is 2.2' off the arc, and the height of eye is 59.8 feet. What is your latitude by Polaris?

A. 27° 33.7' N
B. 27° 40.9' N
C. 27° 54.4' N
D. 28° 06.9' N

00734. On 11 March 1981, your 1846 zone time DR position is LAT 25° 05.7' N, LONG 124° 29.0' W. At that time you observe Polaris with a sextant altitude (hs) of 25° 59.1'. The chronometer time of the sight is 02h 44m 01s, and the chronometer error is 02m 15s slow. The index error is 3.9' on the arc, and the height of eye is 42.7 feet. What is your latitude by Polaris?

A. 25° 14.2' N
B. 25° 17.9' N
C. 25° 28.1' N
D. 26° 15.2' N

00735. On 22 August 1981, your 1852 zone time DR position is LONG 155° 54.0' E. At that time you observe Polaris with a sextant altitude (hs) of 27° 36.9'. The chronometer time of the sight is 08h 54m 06s, and the chronometer error is 02m 20s fast. The index error is 3.6' off the arc, and the height of eye is 61.5 feet. What is your latitude by Polaris?

A. 27° 05.5' N
B. 27° 31.0' N
C. 28° 05.9' N
D. 28° 09.5' N

00736. On 6 March 1981, your 1854 zone time DR position is LAT 23° 51.5' N, LONG 73° 14.0' W. At that time you observe Polaris with a sextant altitude (hs) of 24° 16.5'. The chronometer time of the sight is 11h 52m 40s, and the chronometer error is 01m 56s slow. The index error is 5.0' on the arc, and the height of eye is 43.5 feet. What is your latitude by Polaris?

A. 23° 29.5' N
B. 23° 36.3' N
C. 23° 49.9' N
D. 24° 02.9' N

00737. On 29 July 1981, your 1930 zone time DR position is LONG 164° 26.0' E. At that time you observe Polaris with a sextant altitude (hs) of 23° 46.8'. The chronometer time of the sight is 08h 32m 18s, and the chronometer error is 02m 26s fast. The index error is 2.7' on the arc, and the height of eye is 56.0 feet. What is your latitude by Polaris?

A. 24° 01.9' N
B. 24° 19.5' N
C. 24° 31.7' N
D. 25° 19.6' N

00738. On 24 September 1981, your 1841 zone time DR position is LAT 25° 15.0' N, LONG 129° 34.5' E. At that time you observe Polaris with a sextant altitude (hs) of 25° 20.8'. The chronometer time of the sight is 09h 38m 12s, and the chronometer error is 03m 12s slow. The index error is 4.3' off the arc, and the height of eye is 52.0 feet. What is your latitude by Polaris?

A. 24° 28.4' N
B. 25° 16.0' N
C. 25° 37.6' N
D. 25° 42.3' N

00739. On 29 April 1981, your 1913 zone time DR position is LAT 22° 09.0' N, LONG 56° 16.0' W. At that time you observe Polaris with a sextant altitude (hs) of 22° 25.8'. The chronometer time of the sight is 11h 11m 14s, and the chronometer error is 02m 18s slow. The index error is 1.5' off the arc, and the height of eye is 61.5 feet. What is your latitude by Polaris?

A. 21° 39.9' N
B. 21° 55.7' N
C. 22° 39.9' N
D. 22° 48.8' N

5- 15

00740. On 14 March 1981, your 1846 zone time DR position is LAT 21° 57.6' N, LONG 132° 16.2' W. At that time you observe Polaris with a sextant altitude (hs) of 22° 16.8'. The chronometer time of the sight is 03h 45m 10s, and the chronometer error is 01m 32s slow. The index error is 3.2' off the arc, and the height of eye is 44.9 feet. What is your latitude by Polaris?

A. 21° 32.4' N
B. 21° 49.8' N
C. 21° 51.0' N
D. 21° 53.1' N

00741. On 16 February 1981, your 1845 zone time DR position is LAT 25° 50.5' N, LONG 46° 24.0' W. At that time you observe Polaris with a sextant altitude (hs) of 26° 25.5'. The chronometer time of the sight is 09h 47m 30s, and the chronometer error is 02m 16s fast. The index error is 2.5' off the arc, and the height of eye is 55.0 feet. What is your latitude by Polaris?

A. 25° 38.0' N
B. 25° 44.2' N
C. 26° 00.1' N
D. 26° 37.5' N

742. At 0447 zone time on 15 July 1981, your vessel's DR position is LAT 22° 42' N, LONG 126° 36' E. At approximately this time, you obtain a sextant altitude of Polaris. Given the following information, what is your latitude by Polaris?

Chronometer time:	08h 48m 28s
Chronometer error:	fast 1m 16s
Height of eye:	33 feet
Index error:	1.6' off the arc
Sextant altitude:	23° 46.2'

A. 22° 44.1' N
B. 22° 46.2' N
C. 22° 50.2' N
D. 22° 54.1' N

00743. On 7 March 1981 at ZT 1838 in DR position LAT 34° 26.9' N, LONG 58° 16.2' W, you observe Polaris for latitude. The sextant altitude (hs) is 35° 08.4'. The index error is 2.5' off the arc. The height of eye is 54'. What is the latitude at the time of the sight?

A. 34° 29.8' N
B. 34° 33.4' N
C. 34° 34.8' N
D. 34° 36.8' N

5- 16

744.   At 0440 zone time on 22 May 1981, your vessel's DR position is LAT 23° 24' N, LONG 110° 24' W. At approximately this time, you obtain a sextant altitude (hs) of Polaris. Given the following information, what is your latitude by Polaris?

Chronometer time:	11h 42m 14s
Chronometer error:	fast 2m 36s
Height of eye:	24 feet
Index error:	1.6' on the arc
Sextant altitude:	23° 40.9'

A. 23° 28.6' N
B. 23° 30.0' N
C. 23° 31.2' N
D. 23° 32.8' N

745.   At 1847 zone time on 13 October 1981, your vessel's DR position is LAT 42° 17.4' N, LONG 138° 46.2' W. At approximately this time, you obtain a sextant altitude of Polaris. Given the following information, what is your latitude by Polaris?

Chronometer time:	03h 45m 20s
Chronometer error:	slow 1m 32s
Height of eye:	44 feet
Index error:	3.2' on the arc
Sextant altitude:	42° 16.8'

A. 42° 09.1' N
B. 42° 12.5' N
C. 42° 16.0' N
D. 42° 19.5' N

00746. On 16 January 1981, at 1804 zone time, you take a sextant observation of Polaris. Your vessel's DR position is LAT 36° 12' N, LONG 124° 36' W, and your sextant reads (hs) 37° 16.4'. Your chronometer reads 02h 02m 12s, and is 01m 36s slow. Your height of eye is 60 feet, and the index error is 1.5' on the arc. From your observation of Polaris, what is the latitude of your vessel?

A. 36° 12.6' N
B. 36° 14.4' N
C. 36° 17.9' N
D. 36° 20.2' N

00747. On 14 March 1981, at 1845 zone time, you take a sextant observation of Polaris. Your DR position is LAT 29° 10' N, LONG 154° 30' W, and your sextant reads 29° 53.5'. Your chronometer reads 04h 42m 36s, and the chronometer error is 02m 24s slow. Your height of eye is 24 feet, and the index error is 1.3' off the arc. Determine the latitude by Polaris.

A. 29° 11.7' N
B. 20'15.5' N
C. 29'18.0' N
D. 29'21.3' N

5- 17

00748. On 7 May 1981, you observe Polaris for latitude at 0303 ZT. Your DR position is LAT 56° 35.4' N, LONG 05° 38.9' W. The sextant altitude is 56° 11.1'. The height of eye is 36' and the index error is 3.3' off the arc. What is the latitude at the time of sight?

A. 56° 24.6' N
B. 56° 32.6' N
C. 56° 35.0' N
D. 56° 38.7' N

00749. On 15 February 1981 at 0610 ZT in DR position LAT 56° 53.0' N, LONG 157° 02.9' E, you observe Polaris at a sextant altitude (hs) of 56° 10.4'. The index error is 2.5' on the arc, and the height of eye is 18 meters. What is the latitude?

A. LAT 56° 41.8' N
B. LAT 56° 47.9' N
C. LAT 56° 48.1' N
D. LAT 57° 10.6' N

750.   At 1754 zone time on 28 October 1981, your vessel's DR position is LAT 28° 30' N, LONG 63° 24' W. At this time, you obtain a sextant altitude of Polaris. Given the following information, what is your latitude by Polaris?

Chronometer time:	09h 50m 00s
Chronometer error:	slow 4m 14s
Height of eye:	28 feet
Index error:	2.4' on the arc
Sextant altitude:	28° 42.6'

A. 28° 25.2' N
B. 28° 30.6' N
C. 28° 34.1' N
D. 28° 41.3' N

00751. On 16 July 1981, at 2000 zone time, you take a sextant observation of Polaris. Your vessel's DR position is LAT 27° 22.0' N, LONG 148° 35.0' W, and your sextant reads 26° 57.5'. Your chronometer reads 05h 59m 16s, and your chronometer error is 01m 28s slow. Your height of eye is 48 feet, and the index error for your sextant is 1.3° off the arc. What is the latitude of your vessel from your observation of Polaris?

A. 26° 52.1' N
B. 26° 58.8' N
C. 27° 36.1' N
D. 27° 43.4' N

5- 18

00752. On 5 May 1981, at 1953 zone time, you take a sextant observation of Polaris. Your vessel's DR position is LAT 29° 30.0' N, LONG 66° 25.7' W, and your sextant reads 29° 07.2'. Your chronometer reads 11h 51m 45s, and your chronometer error is 01m 36s slow. Your height of eye is 56 feet, and the index error for your sextant is 1.5° on the arc. What is the latitude of your vessel from your observation of Polaris?

A. 29° 14.3' N
B. 29° 23.6' N
C. 29° 32.3' N
D. 29° 38.8' N

00753. On 10 June 1981, your 2010 zone time DR position is LAT 41° 10.0' N, LONG 61° 15.0' W. At that time you observe Polaris with a sextant altitude (hs) of 40° 35.8'. The chronometer time of the sight is 00h 08m 18s, and the chronometer error is 01m 54s slow. The index error is 2.0' on the arc, and the height of eye is 40 feet. What is your latitude by Polaris?

A. 41° 10.6' N
B. 41° 15.0' N
C. 41° 18.3' N
D. 41° 21.2' N

Answers to Latitude by Polaris

726.	A		740.	B
727.	A		741.	A
728.	B		742.	D
729.	C		743.	B
730.	A		744.	C
731.	B		745.	A
732.	C		746.	C
733.	A		747.	D
734.	B		748.	D
735.	C		749.	A
736.	B		750.	C
737.	B		751.	C
738.	C		752.	B
739.	C		753.	B

5- 19

Celestial Problems
Latitude By Polaris

Problem # (USCG) (0726)		Chapter 16	

Date:	16 Dec.	Time			LAT:	
			CT	03-12-31	LONG	129° 46.5′ W
	ZT	1810	CE	-2-16	S-	
	ZD	+9	CCT	03-10-15	C-	
17 Dec	GMT	0310	GMT	03-10-15		

Almanac

GHA	130° 39.4′	LHA a0	0° 16.2	Hs	23°56.8′
M/S	2° 34.2′	LAT a1	.5	Ic	+2.5′
GHA	133° 13.6′	DATE a2	1.0	Dip (52.6)	- 7.0′
±SHA/v		Total a	0° 17.7	Sum	-4.5′
Sum	133° 13.6′			Ha	23° 52.3′
a λ	- 129° 46.5′			Alt	- 2.2′
LHA	3° 27.1′			Ho	23°50.1′
Notes:				+ a	0° 17.7′
				Sum	24° 07.8′
				- 1°	- 1°
				Lat	23° 07.8′

Celestial Problems
Latitude By Polaris

Problem # (USCG) (0727)		Chapter 16	

Date:	11 Feb	Time			LAT:	
			CT	01-34-56	LONG	110° 52.6′
	ZT	18:32	CE	02-16	S-	
	ZD	+7	CCT	01-32-40	C-	
12 Feb	GMT	01:32	GMT	01-32-40		

Almanac

GHA	156° 59.7′	LHA a0	0-12.8	Hs	26° 19.8′
M/S	8° 11.3′	LAT a1	.6	Ic	+ 2.7′
GHA	165° 11.0′	DATE a2	.7	Dip (60.2)	- 7.5′
±SHA/v		Total a	0-14.1	Sum	- 4.8′
Sum	165° 11.0′			Ha	26° 15.0′
a λ	110° 52.6′			Alt	- 2.0′
LHA	54° 18.4′			Ho	26° 13.0′
Notes:				+ a	0-14.1′
				Sum	26° 27.1′
				- 1°	-1°
				Lat	25° 27.1′

Celestial Problems
Latitude By Polaris

Problem #   (USCG)   (0728)   Chapter   16

Date:	02 Jan	Time			LAT:	
			CT	08-57-10	LONG	45° 17.6' W
	ZT	1759	CE	02-16	S-	
	ZD	+9	CCT	20-59-26	C-	
	GMT	2059	GMT	20-59-26		

Almanac

GHA	42° 21.9'	LHA a0	0° 13.0'	Hs	24° 16.5'
M/S	14° 53.9'	LAT a1	.6'	Ic	- 3.5'
GHA	57° 15.8'	DATE a2	.7'	Dip (42.5)	- 6.3'
±SHA/v		Total a	0° 14.3'	Sum	- 9.8'
Sum	57° 15.8'			Ha	24° 06.7'
a λ	-45° 17.6'			Alt	- 2.2'
LHA	11° 58.2'			Ho	24° 04.5'
Notes:				+ a	0° 14.3'
				Sum	24° 08.8'
				- 1°	- 1°
				Lat	23° 08.8'

Celestial Problems
Latitude By Polaris

Problem #   (USCG)   (0729)   Chapter   16

Date:	24 Sep	Time			LAT:	
			CT	09-38-12	LONG	129° 34.0' e
	ZT	1841	CE	03-12	S-	
	ZD	- 9	CCT	09-41-24	C-	
	GMT	0941	GMT	09-41-24		

Almanac

GHA	138° 06.5'	LHA a0	1° 20.2'	Hs	25°20.8'
M/S	10° 22.7'	LAT a1	.4'	Ic	+ 4.3'
GHA	148° 29.2'	DATE a2	.9'	Dip (52)	- 7.0'
±SHA/v		Total a	1° 21.5'	Sum	- 2.7
Sum	148° 29.2'			Ha	25° 18.1'
a λ	129° 34.5'			Alt	- 2.0'
LHA	278° 03.7'			Ho	25° 16.1'
Notes:				+ a	1° 21.5'
				Sum	26° 37.6'
				- 1°	- 1°
				Lat	25° 37.6'

5- 13

Celestial Problems Latitude By Polaris				
Problem # (USCG) (0730)			Chapter 16	

Date:	18 Nov	Time			**LAT:**	
			CT	00-52-43	**LONG**	110° 16.0' W
	ZT	1750	**CE**	02-08	**S-**	
	ZD	+ 7	**CCT**	00-50-25	**C-**	
19 Nov	**GMT**	0050	**GMT**	00-50-25		

Almanac						
GHA	57° 56.1'	**LHA a0**	0° 44.8'	**Hs**	21°29.8'
M/S	12° 38.3'	**LAT a1**	.3'	**Ic**	- 3.2'
GHA	70° 34.4'	**DATE a2**	1.0'	**Dip (49.5)**	- 6.8'
±SHA/v		**Total a**	0° 46.1'	**Sum**	- 10.0'
Sum	70° 34.4'			**Ha**	21° 19.8'
a λ	- 110° 34.4'			**Alt**	- 2.5'
LHA	320° 18.4'			**Ho**	21° 17.3'
Notes:				**+ a**	0° 46.1'
				Sum	22° 03.4'
				- 1°	- 1°
				Lat	21° 03.4'

Celestial Problems Latitude By Polaris				
Problem # (USCG) (0731)			Chapter 16	

Date:	2 JAN	Time			**LAT:**	
			CT	08-57-10	**LONG**	45° 17.6' W
	ZT	1759	**CE**	+ 02-16	**S-**	
	ZD	+ 3	**CCT**	08-59-26	**C-**	
	GMT	2059	**GMT**	20-59-26		

Almanac						
GHA	42° 21.9'	**LHA a0**	0° 13.0'	**Hs**	24° 16.5'
M/S	14° 53.9'	**LAT a1**	.6'	**Ic**	- 3.5'
GHA	57° 15.8'	**DATE a2**	.7'	**Dip (42.5)**	- 6.3'
±SHA/v		**Total a**	0° 14.3'	**Sum**	- 9.8'
Sum	57° 15.8'			**Ha**	24° 06.7'
a λ	- 45° 17.6'			**Alt**	- 2.2'
LHA	11° 58.2'			**Ho**	24° 04.5'
Notes:				**+ a**	0° 14.3'
				Sum	24° 18.8'
				- 1°	- 1°
				Lat	23° 18.8'

Celestial Problems				
Latitude By Polaris				
Problem # (USCG) (0732)				Chapter 16

Date:	3 Jan		Time		**LAT:**	
			CT	09-57-10	**LONG**	60° 53.2′ W
	ZT	1759	**CE**	+ 02-26	**S-**	
	ZD	+ 4	**CCT**	09-59-36	**C-**	
2 Jan	**GMT**	2159	**GMT**	21-59-36		

Almanac						
GHA	58° 23.5′	**LHA a0**	0° 12.9′	**Hs**	22° 55.8′	
M/S	14° 56.4′	**LAT a1**	.6′	**Ic**	+ 2.9′	
GHA	73° 19.9′	**DATE a2**	.7′	**Dip (52.5)**	- 7.0′	
±SHA/v		**Total a**	0° 14.2′	**Sum**	- 4.1	
Sum	73° 19.9′			**Ha**	22° 51.7′	
a λ	- 60° 53.2′			**Alt**	- 2.3′	
LHA	12° 26.7′			**Ho**	22° 49.4′	
Notes:				**+ a**	0° 14.2′	
				Sum	23° 03.6′	
				- 1°	- 1°	
				Lat	22° 03.6′	

Celestial Problems				
Latitude By Polaris				
Problem # (USCG) (0733)				Chapter 16

Date:	12 March		Time		**LAT:**	
			CT	03-44-10	**LONG**	129° 16.5′ W
	ZT	1846	**CE**	+ 01-55	**S-**	
	ZD	+ 9	**CCT**	03-46-05	**C-**	
	GMT	0346	**GMT**	03-46-05		

Almanac						
GHA	215° 39.7′	**LHA a0**	0° 38.1′	**Hs**	28° 01.5′	
M/S	11°31.3′	**LAT a1**	.4′	**Ic**	+ 2.2′	
GHA	227° 11.0′	**DATE a2**	.9′	**Dip (59.8)**	- 7.5′	
±SHA/v		**Total a**	0° 39.4′	**Sum**	- 5.3	
Sum	227° 11.0′			**Ha**	27° 56.2′	
a λ	- 129° 16.5′			**Alt**	- 1.8′	
LHA	97° 54.5′			**Ho**	27° 54.4′	
Notes:				**+ a**	0° 39.4′	
				Sum	28° 33.8′	
				- 1°	- 1°	
				Lat	27° 33.8′	

Celestial Problems
Latitude By Polaris

Problem # (USCG) (0734)   Chapter   16

Date:	11 Mar	Time			LAT:	25° 05.7' N
			CT	02-44-01	LONG	124° 29.0' W
	ZT	1846	CE	+ 02-15	S-	
	ZD	+ 8	CCT	02-46-16	C-	
12 Mar	GMT	0246	GMT	02-46-16		

Almanac

GHA	119° 38.1'	LHA a0	0° 29.8'	Hs	25° 59.1'	
M/S	11° 58.6'	LAT a1	.4'	Ic	- 3.9'	
GHA	211° 14.0'	DATE a2	.8'	Dip (42.7)	- 6.4'	
±SHA/v		Total a	0° 31.0'	Sum	- 10.3'	
Sum	211° 14.0'			Ha	25° 48.8'	
a λ	- 124°29.0'			Alt	- 2.0'	
LHA	86° 45.0'			Ho	25° 46.8'	
Notes:				+ a	0° 31.0'	
				Sum	26° 18.0'	
				- 1°	- 1°	
				Lat	25° 18.0'	

Celestial Problems
Latitude By Polaris

Problem # (USCG) (0735)   Chapter   16

Date:	22 Aug.	Time			LAT:	
			CT	08-54-06	LONG	155° 54.0 E
	ZT	1852	CE	- 02-20	S-	
	ZD	- 10	CCT	08-51-46	C-	
	GMT	0852	GMT	08-51-46		

Almanac

GHA	90° 32.5'	LHA a0	1° 33.1'	Hs	27° 36.9'	
M/S	12° 58.6'	LAT a1	.5'	Ic	+ 3.6'	
GHA	103° 31.1'	DATE a2	.9'	Dip (61.5)	- 7.6'	
±SHA/v		Total a	1° 34.5'	Sum	- 4.0'	
Sum	103° 31.1'			Ha	27° 32.9'	
a λ	+ 155° 54.0'			Alt	- 1.9'	
LHA	259° 23.1'			Ho	27° 31.0'	
Notes:				+ a	1° 34.5'	
				Sum	29° 05.5'	
				- 1°	- 1°	
				Lat	28° 05.5'	

Celestial Problems
Latitude By Polaris

Problem # (USCG) (0736)				Chapter 16	
Date: 6 Mar.	Time			**LAT:**	23° 51.5′ N
	CT	11-52-40	**LONG**		73° 14.0′ W
ZT	1854	**CE**	+ 01-56	**S-**	
ZD	+5	**CCT**	11-54-36	**C-**	
GMT	2354	**GMT**	23-54-36		

Almanac

GHA	149° 35.0′	**LHA a0**	0° 32.1′	**Hs**	24° 16.5′
M/S	13° 41.2′	**LAT a1**	.4′	**Ic**	- 5.0′
GHA	163° 16.2′	**DATE a2**	.9′	**Dip (43.5)**	- 6.4′
±SHA/v		**Total a**	0° 33.4′	**Sum**	- 11.4′
Sum	163° 16.2′			**Ha**	24° 05.1′
a λ	- 73° 14.0′			**Alt**	- 2.2′
LHA	90° 02.2′			**Ho**	24° 02.9′
Notes:				**+ a**	0° 33.4′
				Sum	24° 36.3′
				- 1°	- 1°
				Lat	23° 36.3′

Celestial Problems
Latitude By Polaris

Problem # (USCG) (0737)				Chapter 16	
Date: 29 July	Time			**LAT:**	
	CT	08-32-18	**LONG**		164° 26.0′ E
ZT	1930	**CE**	- 02-26	**S-**	
ZD	- 11	**CCT**	08-29-52	**C-**	
GMT	0830	**GMT**	08-29-52		

Almanac

GHA	66° 53.1′	**LHA a0**	1° 43.3′	**Hs**	23° 46.8′
M/S	7° 14.2	**LAT a1**	.6′	**Ic**	- 2.7′
GHA	74° 07.3′	**DATE a2**	1.0′	**Dip (56.0)**	- 7.3′
±SHA/v		**Total a**	1° 44.9′	**Sum**	-10.0′
Sum	74° 07.3′			**Ha**	23° 36.8′
a λ	+ 164° 26.0′			**Alt**	- 2.2′
LHA	238° 33.3′			**Ho**	23° 34.6′
Notes:				**+ a**	1° 44.9′
				Sum	25° 19.5′
				- 1°	- 1
				Lat	24° 19.5′

5- 17

Celestial Problems Latitude By Polaris					
Problem # (USCG) (0738)				Chapter 16	
Date: 24 Sep	Time			**LAT:** 25° 15.0' N	
		CT	09-38-12	**LONG** 129° 34.5' E	
ZT	1841	**CE**	+ 03-12	**S-**	
ZD	- 9	**CCT**	09-41-24	**C-**	
GMT	0941	**GMT**	09-41-24		
Almanac					
GHA	138° 06.5'	**LHA a0**	1° 20.2'	**Hs**	25°20.8'
M/S	10° 22.7'	**LAT a1**	.4'	**Ic**	+ 4.3,
GHA	148° 29.2'	**DATE a2**	.9'	**Dip (52.0)**	- 7.0'
±SHA/v		**Total a**	1° 21.5'	**Sum**	- 2.7'
Sum	148° 29.2'			**Ha**	25° 18.1'
a λ	+ 129° 34.5'			**Alt**	- 2.0'
LHA	278° 03.7'			**Ho**	25° 16.1'
Notes:				**+ a**	1° 21.5'
				Sum	26° 37.6'
				- 1°	- 1
				Lat	25° 37.6'

Celestial Problems Latitude By Polaris					
Problem # (USCG) (0739)				Chapter 16	
Date: 29 Apr.	Time			**LAT:** 22° 09.0' N	
		CT	11-11-14	**LONG** 056° 16.0' W	
ZT	1913	**CE**	+ 02-18	**S-**	
ZD	+ 4	**CCT**	11-13-32	**C-**	
GMT	2313	**GMT**	23-13-32		
Almanac					
GHA	202° 48.5'	**LHA a0**	1° 21.2'	**Hs**	22° 25.8'
M/S	3° 23.6'	**LAT a1**	.3'	**Ic**	+ 1.5'
GHA	206° 12.2'	**DATE a2**	1.0'	**Dip (61.5)**	- 7.6'
±SHA/v		**Total a**	1° 22.5'	**Sum**	- 6.1'
Sum	206° 12.2'			**Ha**	22° 19.7'
a λ	- 56° 16.0'			**Alt**	- 2.4'
LHA	149° 56.2'			**Ho**	22° 17.3'
Notes:				**+ a**	1° 22.5'
				Sum	23° 39.9'
				- 1°	- 1°
				Lat	22° 39.9'

5- 18

Celestial Problems
Latitude By Polaris

Problem #   (USCG)   (0740)   Chapter   16

Date:	14 Mar.		Time		LAT:	21° 57.6' N
		CT	03-45-10	LONG		132° 16.2' W
	ZT	1846	CE	+ 01-32	S-	
	ZD	+ 9	CCT	03-46-42	C-	
15 Mar	GMT	0346	GMT	03-46-42		

Almanac

GHA	217° 38.0'	LHA a0	0° 37.3'	Hs	22° 16.8'
M/S	11° 42.4'	LAT a1	.4'	Ic	+ 3.2'
GHA	229° 20.4'	DATE a2	.9'	Dip (44.9)	- 6.5'
±SHA/v		Total a	0° 38.6'	Sum	- 3.3'
Sum	229° 20.4'			Ha	22° 13.5'
a λ	- 132° 16.2'			Alt	- 2.4'
LHA	97° 04.2'			Ho	22° 11.1'
Notes:				+ a	0° 38.6'
				Sum	22° 49.7'
				- 1°	-1°
				Lat	21° 49.7'

Celestial Problems
Latitude By Polaris

Problem #   (USCG)   (0741)   Chapter   16

Date:	16 Feb		Time		LAT:	25° 50.5 N
		CT	09-47-30	LONG		046° 24.0' W
	ZT	1845	CE	- 02-16	S-	
	ZD	+ 3	CCT	09-45-14	C-	
	GMT	2145	GMT	21-45-14		

Almanac

GHA	101° 45.6'	LHA a0	0° 17.8'	Hs	26° 25.5'
M/S	11° 20.4'	LAT a1	.5'	Ic	+ 2.5'
GHA	113° 06.0'	DATE a2	.8'	Dip (55.0)	- 7.2'
±SHA/v		Total a	0° 19.1'	Sum	- 4.7'
Sum	113° 06.0'			Ha	26° 20.8'
a λ	- 46° 24.0'			Alt	- 2.0'
LHA	66° 42.0			Ho	26° 18.8'
Notes:				+ a	0° 19.1'
				Sum	26° 37.9'
				- 1°	- 1°
				Lat	25° 37.9'

5- 19

Celestial Problems				
Latitude By Polaris				
Problem # (USCG) (0742)			Chapter 16	

Date:	15 Jul	Time		**LAT:**	22° 42.0 N
			CT	08-48-28	**LONG**	126° 36.0' E
	ZT	0447	CE	- 01-16		**S-**
	ZD	- 8	CCT	08-47-12		**C-**
14 Jul	**GMT**	2047	GMT	20-47-12		

Almanac						
GHA	232° 35.6'	**LHA a0**	0° 13.3'	**Hs**	23° 46.2'
M/S	11° 49.9'	**LAT a1**	.6'	**Ic**	+ 1.6'
GHA	244° 25.5'	**DATE a2**	.2'	**Dip (33.0)**	- 5.6'
±SHA/v		**Total a**	0° 14.1'	**Sum**	- 4.0'
Sum	244° 25.5'			**Ha**	23° 46.52'
a λ	126° 36.0'			**Alt**	- 2.2'
LHA	11° 01.5'			**Ho**	23° 40.0'
Notes:				**+ a**	0° 14.1'
				Sum	23° 54.1'
				- 1°	- 1°
				Lat	22° 54.1'

Celestial Problems				
Latitude By Polaris				
Problem # (USCG) (0743)			Chapter 16	

Date:	7 Mar.	Time		**LAT:**	34° 26.9' N
			CT		**LONG**	058° 16.2' W
	ZT	1838	CE			**S-**
	ZD	+ 4	CCT			**C-**
	GMT	2238	GMT			

Almanac						
GHA	135° 31.7'	**LHA a0**	0° 29.8'	**Hs**	35° 08.4'
M/S	9° 31.6'	**LAT a1**	.5'	**Ic**	+ 2.5'
GHA	145° 03.3'	**DATE a2**	.8'	**Dip (54.0)**	- 7.1'
±SHA/v		**Total a**	0° 31.1'	**Sum**	- 4.6'
Sum	145° 03.3'			**Ha**	35° 03.8'
a λ	- 58° 16.2'			**Alt**	- 1.4'
LHA	86° 47.1'			**Ho**	35° 02.4'
Notes:				**+ a**	0° 31.1'
				Sum	35° 33.5'
				- 1°	- 1°
				Lat	34° 33.5'

Celestial Problems
Latitude By Polaris

Problem # (USCG) (0744)   Chapter 16

Date:	22 May	Time			**LAT:**	23° 24.0' N
			CT	11-42-14	**LONG**	110° 24.0 W
	ZT	0440	**CE**	- 2-36	**S-**	
	ZD	+ 7	**CCT**	11-39-28	**C-**	
	GMT	1140	**GMT**	11-39-28		

Almanac

GHA	44° 59.1'	**LHA a0**	0° 58.4'	**Hs**	23° 40.9'
M/S	9° 53.6'	**LAT a1**	.3'	**Ic**	- 1.6'
GHA	54° 52.7'	**DATE a2**	.3'	**Dip (24.0)**	- 4.8'
±SHA/v		**Total a**	0° 59.0'	**Sum**	- 6.4'
Sum	54° 52.7'			**Ha**	23° 34.5'
a λ	- 110° 24.0'			**Alt**	-2.2'
LHA	304° 28.7'			**Ho**	23° 32.3'
Notes:				**+ a**	0° 59.0'
				Sum	24° 31.3'
				- 1°	- 1°
				Lat	23° 31.3'

Celestial Problems
Latitude By Polaris

Problem # (USCG) (0745)   Chapter 16

Date:	13 Oct.	Time			**LAT:**	42° 17.4' N
			CT	03-45-20	**LONG**	138° 46.2' W
	ZT	1847	**CE**	+ 1-32	**S-**	
	ZD	+ 9	**CCT**	03-52-46	**C-**	
14 Oct.	**GMT**	0347	**GMT**	03-52-46		

Almanac

GHA	67° 34.5'	**LHA a0**	1° 01.7'	**Hs**	42° 16.8'
M/S	11° 44.9'	**LAT a1**	.5'	**Ic**	- 3.2'
GHA	79° 19.4'	**DATE a2**	.9'	**Dip (44)**	- 6.4
±SHA/v		**Total a**	1° 03.1'	**Sum**	- 9.6
Sum	79° 19.4'			**Ha**	42° 07.2
a λ	- 138° 46.2'			**Alt**	- 1.1'
LHA	300° 33.2'			**Ho**	42° 06.1'
Notes:				**+ a**	1° 03.1'
				Sum	43° 09.2'
				- 1°	- 1°
				Lat	42° 09.2'

Alexander F. Hickethier MBA © 2011-2013

Celestial Problems
Latitude By Polaris

Problem # (USCG) (0746)				Chapter 16	

Date:	16 Jan	Time		LAT:	36° 12.0' N
		CT	02-02-12	LONG	124° 36.0' W
	ZT	1804	CE	+ 01-36	S-
	ZD	+ 8	CCT	02-03-48	C-
17 Jan	GMT	0204	GMT	02-03-48	

Almanac

GHA	146° 24.6'	LHA a0	0° 10.4'	Hs		37° 16.4
M/S	0° 57.2'	LAT a1	.6'	Ic		- 1.5'
GHA	147° 21.8'	DATE a2	.7'	Dip (60.0)		- 7.5'
±SHA/v		Total a	0° 11.7'	Sum		- 9.0
Sum	147° 21.8'			Ha		37° 07.4'
a λ	- 124° 36.0'			Alt		- 1.3'
LHA	22° 45.8'			Ho		37° 06.1'
Notes:				+ a		0° 11.7'
				Sum		37° 17.8'
				- 1°		- 1°
				Lat		36° 17.8'

Celestial Problems
Latitude By Polaris

Problem # (USCG) (0747)				Chapter 16	

Date:	14 Mar	Time		LAT:	29° 10.0' N
		CT	04-42-36	LONG	154° 30.0' W
	ZT	1845	CE	+ 02-24	S-
	ZD	+ 10	CCT	04-45-00	C-
15 Mar	GMT	0445	GMT	04-45-00	

Almanac

GHA	232° 40.4'	LHA a0	0° 31.1'	Hs		29° 53.5'
M/S	11° 16.8'	LAT a1	.6'	Ic		+ 1.3'
GHA	243° 57.2'	DATE a2	.8'	Dip (24)		- 4.8'
±SHA/v		Total a	0° 32.7'	Sum		- 3.5'
Sum	243° 57.2'			Ha		29°50.0'
a λ	- 154° 30.0'			Alt		-1.7'
LHA	89° 27.2'			Ho		29° 48.3'
Notes:				+ a		0° 32.7'
				Sum		30° 21.0'
				- 1°		- 1°
				Lat		29° 21.0'

Celestial Problems
Latitude By Polaris

Problem # (USCG) (0748)			Chapter 16	
Date: 7 May		Time	**LAT:** 56° 35.4' N	
		CT	**LONG** 005° 38.9' W	
ZT	0303	**CE**	S-	
ZD	0	**CCT**	C-	
GMT	0303	**GMT**		

Almanac

GHA	269° 52.3'	**LHA a0**	1° 29.6'	**Hs**	56° 11.1'
M/S	0° 45.1'	**LAT a1**	.7'	**Ic**	+ 3.3'
GHA	270° 37.4'	**DATE a2**	.5'	**Dip (36)**	- 5.8'
±SHA/v		**Total a**	1° 30.8'	**Sum**	- 2.5'
Sum	270° 37.4'			**Ha**	56° 08.6'
a λ	- 5° 38.9'			**Alt**	-.7'
LHA	264° 58.5'			**Ho**	56° 07.9'
Notes:				**+ a**	1° 30.8'
				Sum	57° 38.7'
				- 1°	- 1°
				Lat	56° 38.7'

Celestial Problems				
Latitude By Polaris				
Problem # (USCG) (0749)			Chapter 16	
Date: 15 Feb		Time	**LAT:** 56° 53.0'N	
		CT	**LONG** 157° 02.9' E	
ZT	0610	**CE**	S-	
ZD	- 10	**CCT**	C-	
GMT	2010	**GMT**		

Almanac

GHA	85° 44.0'	**LHA a0**	1° 40.7'	**Hs**	56° 10.4'
M/S	2° 30.4'	**LAT a1**	.6'	**Ic**	- 2.5'
GHA	88° 14.4'	**DATE a2**	.4'	**Dip (18)**	- 7.5'
±SHA/v		**Total a**	1° 41.7'	**Sum**	- 10.0'
Sum	88° 14.4'			**Ha**	56° 00.4'
a λ	+ 157° 02.9'			**Alt**	- .7
LHA	245° 17.3'			**Ho**	55° 59.7'
Notes:				**+ a**	1° 41.7'
				Sum	57° 41.1'
				- 1°	- 1°
				Lat	56° 41.1'

Alexander F. Hickethier MBA © 2011-2013

Celestial Problems
Latitude By Polaris

Problem # (USCG) (0750)   Chapter 16

Date:	28 Oct	Time			LAT:	28° 30.0' N
			CT	09-50-00	LONG	062° 24.0' W
	ZT	1754	CE	+ 04-14	S-	
	ZD	+ 4	CCT	09-54-14	C-	
	GMT	2154	GMT	21-54-14		

Almanac

GHA	352° 06.8'	LHA a0	0° 59.5'	Hs		28° 42.6'
M/S	13° 35.7'	LAT a1	.4'	Ic		- 2.4'
GHA	365° 42.5'	DATE a2	.9'	Dip (28)		- 4.9'
±SHA/v		Total a	1° 00.8'	Sum		- 7.3'
Sum	365° 42.5'			Ha		28° 35.3'
a λ	- 62° 24.0'			Alt		- 1.9'
LHA	303° 18.5'			Ho		28° 33.4'
Notes:				+ a		1° 00.8'
				Sum		29° 34.2'
				- 1°		- 1°
				Lat		28° 34.2'

Celestial Problems
Latitude By Polaris

Problem # (USCG) (0751)   Chapter 16

Date:	16 Jul	Time			LAT:	27° 22.0' N
			CT	05-59-16	LONG	148° 35.0' W
	ZT	2000	CE	+ 01-28	S-	
	ZD	+ 10	CCT	06-00-44	C-	
17 Jul	GMT	0600	GMT	06-00-44		

Almanac

GHA	24° 58.5'	LHA a0	1° 44.1'	Hs		26° 57.5'
M/S	0° 11.0'	LAT a1	.6'	Ic		+ 1.3'
GHA	25° 09.5'	DATE a2	1.0'	Dip (48)		-.67'
±SHA/v		Total a	1° 45.7'	Sum		-5.4'
Sum	25° 09.5'			Ha		26° 52.1'
a λ	- 148° 35.0'			Alt		- 2.0'
LHA	236° 34.5'			Ho		26° 50.1'
Notes:				+ a		1° 45.7'
				Sum		28° 35.8'
				- 1°		- 1°
				Lat		27° 35.8'

Celestial Problems
Latitude By Polaris

Problem # (USCG) (0752)				Chapter 16	
Date: 5 May	Time			LAT:	29° 30.0' N
		CT	11-51-45	LONG	066° 25.7' W
ZT	1953	CE	+ 01-36	S-	
ZD	+ 4	CCT	11-53-21	C-	
GMT	2353	GMT	23-53-21		

Almanac

GHA	208° 43.3'	LHA a0	1° 25.5'	Hs	29° 07.2'
M/S	13° 22.4'	LAT a1	.4'	Ic	- 1.5°
GHA	222° 05.7'	DATE a2	1.0'	Dip (56)	- 7.3'
±SHA/v		Total a	1° 26.9'	Sum	-8.8'
Sum	222° 05.7'			Ha	28° 58.4'
a λ	- 66° 25.7'			Alt	- 1.7'
LHA	155° 40.0'			Ho	28° 56.7'
Notes:				+ a	1° 26.9'1
				Sum	29° 23.6'
				- 1°	- 1°
				Lat	28° 23.6'

Celestial Problems
Latitude By Polaris

Problem # (USCG) (0753)				Chapter 16	
Date: 10 Jun	Time			LAT:	41° 10.0' N
		CT	00-08-18	LONG	061° 15.0' W
ZT	2010	CE	+ 01-54	S-	
ZD	+ 4	CCT	00-10-12	C-	
11 Jun GMT	0010	GMT	00-10-12		

Almanac

GHA	259° 14.8'	LHA a0	1° 46.8'	Hs	40° 35.8'
M/S	2° 33.4'	LAT a1	.6'	Ic	- 2.0'
GHA	261° 48.2'	DATE a2	1.0'	Dip (40)	- 6.1'
±SHA/v		Total a	1° 48.4'	Sum	- 8.1'
Sum	261° 48.2'			Ha	40° 27.7'
a λ	- 61° 15.0'			Alt	- 1.1'
LHA	200° 33.2'			Ho	40° 26.6'
Notes:				+ a	1° 48.4'
				Sum	42° 15.0'
				- 1°	- 1°
				Lat	41° 15.0'

5- 25

Rev. 20 December 2012

USCG CELESTIAL PROBLEMS WORKED-OUT
Chapter 7, Celestial Navigation (Upon Oceans Endorsement)
CALCULATING Ho

by

Alexander F. Hickethier MBA
and
DR. Hu Jia-Shen

Calculating Ho

Body: Enter the name of the body whose altitude you have measured. If using the Sun or the Moon, indicate which limb was measured.

Sextant Altitude (Hs): Enter the altitude of the body measured by the sextant.

Index Correction(IC): This is determined by the characteristics of the individual sextant used.

Sum: Enter the algebraic sum of the Sextant Altitude and the index correction.

Dip: The dip correction is a function of the height of eye of the observer. It is **always negative**; its magnitude is determined from the Dip Table on the inside front cover of the *Nautical Almanac*.

Apparent Altitude (Ha): Apply the correction determined above to the measured altitude and enter the result as the apparent altitude.

> **Altitude Correction:** Every observation requires an altitude correction. This correction is a function of the apparent altitude of the body and is the algebraic sum of Parallax, Refraction and simi-diameter. The *Almanac* contains tables for determining these corrections. For the Sun, planets, and stars, these tables are located on the inside front cover and facing page. For the Moon, these tables are located on the back inside cover and preceding page.

> **Mars or Venus Additional Correction:** As the name implies, this correction is applied to sights of Mars and Venus. The correction is a function of the planet measured, the time of year, and the apparent altitude. The inside front cover of the *Almanac* lists these corrections.

> **Additional Correction:** Enter this additional correction from Table A-4 located at the front of the *Nautical Almanac* when obtaining a sight under non-standard atmospheric temperature and pressure conditions. This correction is a function of atmospheric pressure, temperature, and apparent altitude.

> **Horizontal Parallax Correction:** This correction is unique to reducing Moon sights. Obtain the H.P. correction value from the daily pages of the *Almanac*. Enter the H.P correction table at the back of the *Almanac* with this value. The H.P correction is a function of the limb of the Moon used (upper or lower), the apparent altitude, and the H.P. correction factor. The H.P. correction is always added to the apparent altitude.

> **Moon Upper Limb Correction:** Enter -30' for this correction if the sight was of the upper limb of the Moon.

> **Correction to Apparent Altitude:** Sum the altitude correction, the Mars or Venus

6-3

additional correction, the additional correction, the horizontal parallax correction, and the Moon's upper limb correction. Be careful to determine and carry the algebraic sign of the corrections and their sum correctly. Enter this sum as the correction to the apparent altitude.

Observed Altitude: Apply the Correction to Apparent Altitude algebraically to the apparent altitude. The result is the observed altitude (**Ho**).

Ho SUN
USCG #
Date
Obj
Hs
I.C.
Dip(   ). _____
Sum
Ha
Alt (Sun) _____
Ho

Ho Planet
USCG #
Date
Obj
Hs
I.C.
Dip(   )
Sum _____
Ha
Alt (Star)
Add't Corr _____
Ho

Ho Star
USCG #
Date
Obj
Hs
I.C.
Dip(   )
Sum _____
Ha
Alt (Star) _____
Ho

Ho Moon
USCG #
Date
Obj
Hs
I.C.
Dip(   )
Sum _____
Ha
Alt Moon
HP U/L
Upper Limb   -30
Ho

CALCULATING HO
Chapter 8, Upon Oceans for Master Limited

02275. You observe the lower limb of the Sun at a sextant altitude (hs) of 24° 00.7' on 10 January 1981. The index error is 2.6' off the arc. The height of eye is 55 feet. What is the observed altitude (Ho)?

A. 24° 07.4'
B. 24° 08.9'
C. 24° 10.2'
D. 24° 11.8'

02276. You observe the lower limb of the Sun at a sextant altitude (hs) of 46° 20.3' on 1 April 1981. The index error is 4.5' off the arc. The height of eye is 57 feet. What is the observed altitude (Ho)?

A. 46° 24.2'
B. 46° 27.9'
C. 46° 30.1'
D. 46° 32.6'

02277. You observe the lower limb of the Sun at a sextant altitude (hs) of 41° 29.8' on 11 January 1981. The index error is 2.4' off the arc. The height of eye is 68 feet. What is the observed altitude (Ho)?

A. 41° 36.4'
B. 41° 39.4'
C. 41° 42.0'
D. 41° 44.5'

02278. You observe the lower limb of the Sun at a sextant altitude (hs) of 31° 31.5' on 6 March 1981. The index error is 2.5' on the arc. The height of eye is 76 feet. What is the observed altitude (Ho)?

A. 31° 35.3'
B. 31° 36.7'
C. 31° 38.2'
D. 31° 39.5'

02279. You observe the lower limb of the Sun at a sextant altitude (hs) of 58° 06.6' on 5 April 1981. The index error is 1.0' off the arc. The height of eye is 55 feet. What is the observed altitude (Ho)?

A. 58° 14.2'
B. 58° 15.8'
C. 58° 16.9'
D. 58° 18.1'

02280. You observe the lower limb of the Sun at a sextant altitude (hs) of 28° 24.7' on 17 May 1981. The index error is 1.5' off the arc. The height of eye is 86 feet. What is the observed altitude (Ho)?

A. 28° 29.7'
B. 28° 30.6'
C. 28° 31.5'
D. 28° 32.9'

02281. You observe the lower limb of the Sun at a sextant altitude (hs) of 62° 22.2' on 6 June 1981. The index error is 1.2 on the arc. The height of eye is 28 feet. What is the observed altitude (Ho)?

A. 62° 24.8'
B. 62° 26.9'
C. 62° 31.4'
D. 62° 36.7'

02282. You observe the lower limb of the Sun at a sextant altitude (hs) of 42° 44.0' on 22 June 1981. The index error is 0.8' off the arc. The height of eye is 70 feet. What is the observed altitude (Ho)?

A. 42° 19.8'
B. 42° 21.7'
C. 42° 51.7'
D. 42° 54.2'

02283. You observe the lower limb of the Sun at a sextant altitude (hs) of 22° 58.6' on 16 June 1981. The index error is 2.0' off the arc. The height of eye is 61 feet. What is the observed altitude (Ho)?

A. 23° 06.7'
B. 23° 09.9'
C. 23° 15.4'
D. 23° 22.2'

02284. You observe the lower limb of the Sun at a sextant altitude (hs) of 35° 26.3' on 25 June 1981. The index error is 1.5' on the arc. The height of eye is 58 feet. What is the observed altitude (Ho)?

A. 35° 28.2'
B. 35° 29.9'
C. 35° 32.1'
D. 35° 36.7'

02285. You observe the lower limb of the Sun at a sextant altitude (hs) of 45° 49.7' on 13 November 1981. The index error is 1.0' on the arc. The height of eye is 61 feet. What is the observed altitude (Ho)?

A. 45° 59.3'
B. 45° 56.4'
C. 45° 52.9'
D. 45° 49.8'

02286. You observe the lower limb of the Sun at a sextant altitude (hs) of 50° 26.9' on 9 November 1981. The index error is 1.5' on the arc. The height of eye is 56 feet. What is the observed altitude (Ho)?

A. 50° 04.2'
B. 50° 18.1'
C. 50° 33.5'
D. 50° 41.4'

02287. You observe the lower limb of the Sun at a sextant altitude (hs) of 34° 51.4' on 18 October 1981. The index error is 2.0' off the arc. The height of eye is 54 feet. What is the observed altitude (Ho)?

A. 35° 01.2'
B. 35° 03.6'
C. 35° 05.2'
D. 35° 07.4'

02288. You observe the lower limb of the Sun at a sextant altitude (hs) of 39° 48.7' on 11 October 1981. The index error is 2.0' on the arc. The height of eye is 63 feet. What is the observed altitude (Ho)?

A. 39° 39.9'
B. 39° 46.2'
C. 39° 50.7'
D. 39° 54.1'

02289. You observe the lower limb of the Sun at a sextant altitude (hs) of 38° 07.5' on 8 August 1981. The index error is 5.2' off the arc. The height of eye is 72 feet. What is the observed altitude (Ho)?

A. 38° 08.4'
B. 38° 13.3'
C. 38° 19.2'
D. 38° 23.4'

02290. You observe the lower limb of the Sun at a sextant altitude (hs) of 75° 12.3' on 6 August 1981. The index error is 1.5' off the arc. The height of eye is 32 feet. What is the observed altitude (Ho)?

A. 75° 18.6'
B. 75° 24.0'
C. 75° 30.7'
D. 75° 04.6'

Answers tom Ho Problems

1. 02275 C
2. 02276 D
3. 02277 B
4. 02278 A
5. 02279 B
6. 02280 C
7. 02281 C
8. 02282 C

9. 02283 A
10. 02284 C
11. 02285 B
12. 02286 C
13. 02287 A
14. 02288 D
15. 02289 C
16. 02290 B

Celestial Problems
Calculating Ho worked-out

Ho	
USCG #	2275
Date	10 Jan
Obj	Sun L/L
Hs	24° 00.7'
I.C.	+2.6'
Sum	24° 03.3'
Dip (55)	-7.2'
Ha	23° 56.1'
alt	+14.1'
Ho	24° 10.2'

Ho	
USCG #	2276
Date	1 Apr
Obj	Sun L/L
Hs	46° 20.3'
I.C.	+4.5'
Sum	46° 24.8'
Dip (57)	-7.3'
Ha	46° 17.5'
alt	+15.1'
Ho	46° 32.6'

Ho	
USCG #	2277
Date	11 Jan
Obj	Sun L/L
Hs	41° 29.8'
I.C.	+2.4'
Sum	41° 32.2'
Dip (68)	-8.0'
Ha	41° 24.2'
alt	+15.2'
Ho	41° 39.4'

Ho	
USCG #	2278
Date	6 Mar
Obj	Sun L/L
Hs	31° 31.5'
I.C.	-2.5'
Sum	31° 54.0'
Dip (76)	-8.4'
Ha	31° 20.6'
alt	+14.7'
Ho	31° 35.3'

Ho	
USCG #	2279
Date	5 Mar
Obj	Sun L/L
Hs	58° 06.6'
I.C.	+1.0'
Sum	58° 07.6'
Dip (55)	-7.2'
Ha	58° 00.4'
alt	+15.4'
Ho	58° 15.8'

Ho	
USCG #	2280
Date	17 May
Obj	Sun L/L
Hs	28° 24.7'
I.C.	+1.5'
Sum	28° 26.2'
Dip (86)	-8.9'
Ha	28° 17.3'
alt	+14.2'
Ho	28° 31.5'

Ho	
USCG #	2281
Date	6 Jun
Obj	Sun L/L
Hs	62° 22.2'
I.C.	-1.2'
Sum	62° 21.0'
Dip (28)	-5.1'
Ha	62° 15.9'
alt	+15.5'
Ho	62° 31.4'

Ho	
USCG #	2282
Date	22 Jun
Obj	Son L/L
Hs	42° 44.0'
I.C.	+.8'
Sum	42° 44.8'
Dip(70)	-8.1'
Ha	42° 36.7'
alt	+15.0'
Ho	42° 51.7'

Ho	
USCG #	2283
Date	16 Jun
Obj	Sun L/L
Hs	22° 56.6'
I.C.	+2.0'
Sum	22° 58.6'
Dip(61)	-7.6'
Ha	22° 51.0'
alt	+13.7'
Ho	23° 07.7'

Ho	
USCG #	2284
Date	25 Jun
Obj	Sun L/L
Hs	35° 26.3'
I.C.	-1.5'
Sum	35° 24.8'
Dip(58)	-7.4'
Ha	35° 17.4'
alt	+14.7'
Ho	35° 32.1'

Ho	
USCG #	2285
Date	13 Nov
Obj	Sun L/L
Hs	45° 49.7'
I.C.	-1.0'
Sum	45° 48.7'
Dip (61)	-7.6'
Ha	45° 41.1'
alt	+15.3'
Ho	45° 56.4'

Ho	
USCG #	2286
Date	9 Nov
Obj	Sun L/L
Hs	50° 26.9'
I.C.	-1.5'
Sum	50° 25.3'
Dip (56)	-7.3'
Ha	50° 18.1'
alt	+13.4'
Ho	50° 33.5'

Ho	
USCG #	2287
Date	18 Oct
Obj	Sun L/L
Hs	34°51.4'
I.C.	+2.0'
Sum	34° 53.4'
Dip (54)	-7.1'
Ha	34° 46.3'
alt	+14.9'
Ho	35° 01.2'

Ho	
USCG #	2288
Date	11 Oct
Obj	Sun L/L
Hs	39° 48.7'
I.C.	-2.0'
Sum	39° 46.7'
Dip (63)	-7.7'
Ha	39° 39.0'
alt	+15.1'
Ho	39° 54.1'

Ho	
USCG #	2289
Date	8 Aug
Obj	Sun L/L
Hs	38° 07.5'
I.C.	+5.2'
Sum	38° 12.7'
Dip (72)	-8.3'
Ha	38° 04.4'
alt	+14.8'
Ho	38° 19.2'

Ho	
USCG #	2290
Date	6 Aug
Obj	Sun L/L
Hs	75° 12.3'
I.C.	+1.5'
Sum	75° 13.8'
Dip (32)	-5.5'
Ha	75° 08.3'
alt	+15.7'
Ho	75° 24.0'

Ho	
USCG #	
Date	
Obj	
Hs	
I.C.	
Sum	
Dip( )	
Ha	
alt	
Ho	

SIGHT REDUCTION

Intercept (a), Course Angle (z) and Height Computed (Hc)
(Chapter 11, Navigation Celestial for Master/Mate limited Upon Oceans)

by

Alexander F. Hickethier MBA

and

DR. HU JIA-SHEN

CALCULATING Hc, ZN and INTERCEPT
Upon Oceans for Master Limited
Chapter 11

1. 02151. On 16 June 1981, at 0612 zone time morning stars were observed, and the vessel's position was determined to be LAT 27° 23.0' S, LONG 56° 22.0' W. Your vessel is steaming at 16.0 knots on a course of 212° T. A sextant observation of the Sun's lower limb is made at 0850 zone time. The chronometer reads 00h 53m 19s, and the sextant altitude is 22° 58.6'. The index error is 2.0' off the arc, and the chronometer error is 02m 43s fast. Your height of eye on the bridge is 61.0 feet. What is the azimuth (Zn) of this the bridge is 61.0 feet. What is the azimuth (Zn) of this sight using the assumed position?

A. 044.3°
B. 052.6°
C. 136.1°
D. 148.4°

2. 02152. On 25 June 1981, at 0612 zone time, morning stars were observed, and the vessel's position was determined to be LAT 28° 13.0' S, LONG 49° 34.0' E. Your vessel is steaming at 17.0 knots on a course of 066° T. A sextant observation of the Sun's lower limb is made at 1022 zone time. The chronometer reads 07h 19m 17s, and the sextant altitude is 35° 26.3'. The index error is 1.5' on the arc, and the chronometer error is 02m 51s slow. Your height of eye on the bridge is 58.0 feet. What is the azimuth (Zn) of this the bridge is 58.0 feet. What is the azimuth (Zn) of this sight using the assumed position?

A. 021.5°
B. 157.5°
C. 201.5°
D. 338.5°

3. 2153. At 0800 zone time, on 29 June 1981, your DR position is LAT 26° 00.0' N, LONG 75° 29.5' W. Given the following information, determine the computed altitude (Hc) of the Sun for the assumed position nearest to the above given latitude and longitude.

Chronometer Time: 01h 00m 00s

A. Hc 34° 38.6'
B. Hc 34° 48.6'
C. Hc 34° 58.6'
D. Hc 35° 18.6'

4. 02154. On 30 June 1981, at 0630 zone time morning stars were observed, and the vessel's position was determined to be LAT 25° 15.0' S, LONG 175° 36.0' E. Your vessel is steaming at 16.0 knots on a course of 302° T. A sextant observation of the Sun's lower limb is made at 1015 zone time. The chronometer reads 10h 14m 38s, and the sextant altitude is 32° 07.9'. The index error is 4.5' on the arc, and the chronometer error is 01m 25s slow. Your height of eye on the bridge is 58.0 feet. What is the azimuth (Zn) of this the bridge is 58.0 feet. What is the azimuth (Zn) of this sight using the assumed position?

A. 035.3° T
B. 144.7° T
C. 186.5° T
D. 248.5° T

5. 02155. On 17 May 1981, at 0501 zone time morning stars were observed, and the vessel's position was determined to be LAT 22° 16.0' S, LONG 103° 46.0' W. Your vessel is steaming at 24.0 knots on a course of 301° T. A sextant observation of the Sun's lower limb is made at 0845 zone time. The chronometer reads 03h 43m 32s, and the sextant altitude is 28° 24.7'. The index error is 1.5' off the arc, and the chronometer error is 02m 02s slow. Your height of eye on the bridge is 85.5 feetWhat is the azimuth (Zn) of this sight using the assumed position?

A. 051.0°
B. 052.5°
C. 054.2°
D. 055.7°

6. 2156. At 1300 zone time 9 May 1981, your DR position is LAT 24° 00' N, LONG 83° 26' W. Given the following information, determine the computed altitude (Hc) of the Sun for the assumed position (AP) nearest to the above given latitude and longitude.

Chronometer: 07h 00m 00s

A. Hc 68° 22.8'
B. Hc 68° 24.1'
C. Hc 68° 25.2'
D. Hc 68° 26.9'

7. 2157. On 25 May 1981, your vessel's 1917 zone time position is LAT 24° 16.0' N, LONG 017° 26.0' W. At that time a sextant observation of the planet Saturn was made. The sextant altitude is 63° 05.1', and the chronometer reads 08h 18m 24s. The index error is 4.5' off the arc, and the chronometer error is 01m 05s fast. Your height of eye is determined to be 62.0 feet. What is the azimuth (Zn) of this sight using the assumed position?

A. 143.8°
B. 147.3°
C. 148.7°
D. 149.9°

8. 02158. On 26 May 1981, your vessel's 1906 zone time position is LAT 27° 16.0' N, LONG 24° 37.0' W. At that time, a sextant observation of the planet Jupiter was made. The sextant altitude is 66° 27.6', and the chronometer reads 09h 05m 16s. The index error is 5.2' on the arc, and the chronometer error is 01m 25s slow. Your height of eye is determined to be 52.6 feet. What is the (Zn) of this sight using the assumed position?

A. 011.3°
B. 168.7°
C. 191.3°
D. 348.7°

9. 02159. On 25 May 1981, your vessel's 1858 zone time position is LAT 21° 05.0' N, LONG 143° 27.0' E. At that time a sextant observation of the planet Venus was made. The sextant altitude is 12° 53.4' and the chronometer reads 08h 59m 15s. The index error is 4.5' off the arc, and the chronometer error is 01m 25s fast. Your height of eye is determined to be 55.0 feet. What is the azimuth (Zn) of the sight using the assumed position?

A. 069.6°
B. 110.4°
C. 249.6°
D. 290.4°

10. 02160. On 17 April 1981, your vessel's 1856 zone time DR position is LAT 22° 35.0' N, LONG 63° 15.0' W. At that time, a sextant observation of the star Sirius is made. The sextant altitude is 42° 45.0' and the chronometer reads 10h 59m 27s. The index error is 2.6' off the arc, and the chronometer error is 03m 01s fast. Your height of eye is determined to be 45.0 feet. What is the computed altitude (hc) and azimuth (Zn) for this sight using the assumed position?

A. 42° 40.0', 214.9° T
B. 42° 40.0', 325.1° T
C. 42° 51.6', 214.9° T
D. 42° 51.6', 325.1° T

11. 02161. On 28 April 1981, your vessel's 0515 zone time position is LAT 23° 26' S, LONG 95° 30' E. At this time, the observed altitude (Ho) of the star Rigil Kentaurus is 24° 51.4'. Your chronometer reads 11h 16m 36s and is 01m 18s fast. What is the intercept (a) based on the assumed position method?

A. 30.9 miles
B. 32.3 miles
C. 33.1 miles
D. 34.4 miles

12. 02162. On 5 April 1981, at 0509 zone time morning stars were observed and the vessel's position was determined to be LAT 28° 32.0' N, LONG 177° 13.0' W. Your vessel is steaming at 19.0 knots on a course of 258° T. A sextant observation of the Sun's lower limb is made at 1021 zone time. The chronometer reads 10h 20m 09s, and the sextant altitude (hs) is 58° 06.6'. The index error is 1.0' off the arc, and the chronometer error is 00m 54s slow. Your height of eye on the bridge is 55.0 feet. What is the azimuth (Zn) of this sight using the assumed position?

A. 125.8°
B. 127.2°
C. 129.2°
D. 130.8°

13. 02163. On 1 April 1981, at 0515 zone time morning stars were observed, and the vessel's position was determined to be LAT 27° 05.0' N, LONG 16° 30.0' W. Your vessel is steaming at 19.0 knots on a course of 022° T. A sextant observation of the Sun's lower limb is made at 0930 zone time. The chronometer reads 10h 28m 25s, and the sextant altitude is 46° 20.3'. The index error is 4.5' off the arc, and the chronometer error is 02m 15s slow. Your height of eye on the bridge is 57.0 feet. What is the azimuth (Zn) of this sight using the assumed position?

A. 121.6°
B. 117.9°
C. 115.0°
D. 112.2°

14. 02164. On 6 March 1981, at 0550 zone time morning stars were observed, and the vessel's position was determined to be LAT 23° 56.0' N, LONG 27° 19.0' W. Your vessel is steaming at 25.0 knots on a course of 149.0° T. A sextant observation of the Sun's lower limb is made at 0830 zone time. The chronometer reads 10h 32m 05s, and the sextant altitude is 31° 31.5'. The index error is 2.5' on the arc, and the chronometer error is 01m 45s fast. Your height of eye on the bridge is 76.0 feet. What is the azimuth (Zn) of this sight using the assumed position?

A. 109.8°
B. 111.2°
C. 112.8°
D. 114.3°

15. 02165. On 25 February 1981, at 0622 ZT, you observe the upper limb of the Moon with a sextant altitude of 59° 58.6'. Your DR position is LAT 30° 28.3' S, LONG 102° 39.3 E. The chronometer reading at the time of the sight is 11h 21m 18s and the chronometer is 48s slow. The height of eye is 59 feet and the index error is 2.5' on the arc. What are the azimuth (Zn) and intercept (a) of this sight using the assumed position?

A. Zn 305.4° , a 4.2 T
B. Zn 234.6° , a 4.2 A
C. Zn 305.4° , a 1.5 T
D. Zn 305.4° , a 9.2 T

16. 02166. On 10 January 1981, at 0550 ZT, morning stars were observed, and the vessel's position was determined to be LAT 25° 16.0' N, LONG 123° 18.0' W. Your vessel is steaming at 22.0 knots on a course of 295° T. A sextant observation of the Sun's lower limb is made at 0915 ZT. The chronometer reads 05h 14m 02s, and the sextant altitude is 24° 00.7'. The index error is 2.6' off the arc, and the chronometer error is 01m 34s slow. Your height of eye on the bridge is 55.0 feet. What is the azimuth (Zn) of this sight using the assumed position?

A. 127.8°
B. 129.8°
C. 131.9°
D. 133.6°

17. 02167. On 4 July 1981, at 0630 ZT morning stars were observed, and the vessel's position was determined to be LAT 21° 15.0' S, LONG 21° 20.0' W. Your vessel is steaming at 13.0 knots on a course of 146° T. A sextant observation of the Sun's lower limb is made at 0915 ZT. The chronometer reads 10h 14m 27s, and the sextant altitude is 25° 29.8'. The index error is 3.1' off the arc, and the chronometer error is 0m 53s slow. Your height of eye on the bridge is 48.0 feet. What is the azimuth (Zn) of this sight using the assumed position?

A. 049.5°
B. 052.6°
C. 054.3°
D. 058.9°

18. 02168. On 22 July 1981, at 0448 ZT, morning stars were observed, and the vessel's position was determined to be LAT 21° 43.0' N, LONG 158° 39.0' E. Your vessel is steaming at 21.0 knots on a course of 028° T. A sextant observation of the Sun's lower limb is made at 0956 ZT. The chronometer reads 10h 54m 27s, and the sextant altitude is 54° 28.2'. The index error is 1.5' off the arc, and the chronometer error is 01m 38s slow. Your height of eye on the bridge is 56 feet. What is the azimuth (Zn) of this sight using the assumed position?

A. 080.9°
B. 082.2°
C. 084.2°
D. 086.9°

19. 2169. At 0600 ZT on 24 July 1981, your DR position is LAT 22° 37' N, LONG 32° 45' W. You are steering 185° T at a speed of 20.0 knots. Given the following information, determine the computed altitude (Hc) and azimuth (Zn) for an observation of the Sun's lower limb taken later that morning.

Zone time: 1030
Chronometer time: 00h 30m 16s
Chronometer error: slow 0m 31s

A. Hc 64° 37.1' Zn 089 3°
B. Hc 64° 38.8' Zn 090.1°
C. Hc 64° 41.9' Zn 087.8°
D. Hc 64° 43 2' Zn 091.7°

20. 02170. On 22 July 1981, at 0720 ZT in DR position LAT 20° 38.2' N, LONG 87° 16.0' W, you observe the Moon's lower limb. The sextant altitude (hs) is 38° 32.6, and the chronometer reads 01h 18m 14s. The chronometer is 01m 28s slow. The index error is 3.1' off the arc, and the height of eye is 68 feet. What is the azimuth (Zn) and intercept (a) of this sight from the assumed position?

A. Zn 291.4°, a 5.2A
B. Zn 111.4°, a 8.7A
C. Zn 248.6°, a 5.2T
D. Zn 068.6°, a 6.5T

21. 02171. On 8 August 1981, at 0545 ZT, morning stars were observed, and the vessel's position was determined to be LAT 26° 16.0' S, LONG 94° 16.0' E. Your vessel is steaming at 20.0 knots on a course of 346° T. A sextant observation of the Sun's lower limb is made at 0905 ZT. The chronometer reads 03h 02m 52s, and the sextant altitude (hs) is 38° 07.5'. The index error is 5.2' off the arc, and the chronometer error is 2m 17s slow. Your height of eye on the bridge is 72.0 feet. What is the observed altitude (Ho) and azimuth (Zn) of this sight using the assumed position?

A. 38° 19.4', 048.4° T
B. 38° 19.4', 131.6° T
C. 38° 54.9', 048.4° T
D. 38° 54.9', 131.6° T

22. 02172. On 11 October 1981, at 0516 ZT, morning stars were observed, and the vessel's position was determined to be LAT 23° 21.0' N, LONG 139° 27.0' W. Your vessel is steaming at 14.0 knots on a course of 293° T. A sextant observation of the Sun's lower limb is made at 0927 ZT. The chronometer reads 06h 30m 21s, and the sextant altitude (hs) is 39° 48.7'. The index error is 2.0' on the arc, and the chronometer error is 02m 56s fast. Your height of eye on the bridge is 63.0 feet What is the azimuth (Zn) of this sight using the assumed position?

A. 116.2°
B. 123.4°
C. 126.2°
D. 128.4°

23. 2173. At 1000 ZT, on 21 October 1981, your DR position is LAT 29° 00' N, LONG 134° 40' E. Given the following information, determine the computed altitude (Hc) of the Sun for the assumed position (AP) nearest to the above given latitude and longitude.

Chronometer: 01h 00m 00s

A. 42° 30.6'
B. 42° 32.1'
C. 42° 34.2'
D. 42° 35.3'

24. 02174. On 18 October 1981, at 0518 ZT, morning stars were observed and the vessel's position was determined to be LAT 25° 31.0' N, LONG 146° 29.2' E. Your vessel is steaming at 19.0 knots on a course of 308° T. A sextant observation of the Sun's lower limb is made at 0915 ZT. The chronometer reads 11h 17m 11s, and the sextant altitude (hs) is 34° 51.4'. The index error is 2.0' off the arc, and the chronometer error is 01m 57s fast. Your height of eye on the bridge is 54.0 feet. What is the azimuth (Zn) of this sight using the assumed position?

A. 120.6°
B. 121.9°
C. 125.5°
D. 127.3°

25. 02175. On 13 November 1981, at 0438 ZT, morning stars were observed and the vessel's position was determined to be LAT 22° 14.0' S, LONG 79° 23.0' E. Your vessel is steaming at 13.0 knots on a course of 242° T. A sextant observation of the Sun's lower limb is made at 0822 ZT. The chronometer reads 03h 20m 16s, and the sextant altitude (hs) is 45° 49.7'. The index error is 1.0' on the arc, and the chronometer error is 01m 47s slow. Your height of eye on the bridge is 61.0 feet. What is the azimuth (Zn) of this sight using the assumed position?

A. 092.6°
B. 096.2°
C. 098.7°
D. 099.7°

26. 02176. On 9 November 1981, at 0426 ZT, morning stars were observed and your position was determined to be LAT 25° 17.0' S, LONG 154° 16.0' E. Your vessel is steaming at 14.0 knots on course 066° T. A sextant observation of the Sun's lower limb is made at 0837 ZT. The chronometer reads 10h 35m 21s, and the sextant altitude (hs) is 50° 26.9'. The index error is 1.5' on the arc, and the chronometer error is 01m 48s slow. Your height of eye on the bridge is 56.0 feet. What is the observed altitude (Ho) and azimuth (Zn) of this sight using the assumed position?

A. 50° 18.1', 086.3° T
B. 50° 18.1', 093.7° T
C. 50° 33.5', 085.9° T
D. 50° 33.5', 093.7° T

27. 02177. On 21 November 1981, at 0430 ZT, morning stars were observed, and the vessel's position was LAT 22° 14.0 S, LONG 79° 23.0' E. Your vessel is steaming at 14.5 knots on a course of 246° T. A sextant observation of the Sun's lower limb is made at 0816 ZT. The chronometer reads 03h 14m 16s, and the sextant altitude (hs) is 44° 29.2'. The index error is 1.0' on the arc, and the chronometer error is 01m 47s slow. Your height of eye is 61.0 feet. What is the azimuth (Zn) and intercept (a) of this sight using the assumed position?

A. Zn 084.2°, a 6.6A
B. Zn 084.2°, a 6.6T
C. Zn 095.6°, a 6.6A
D. Zn 095.6°, a 6.6T

28. 02178. On 26 July 1981, your 1901 ZT position is LAT 28° 28' N, LONG 157° 16 E when you take an observation of Jupiter. The chronometer at the time of the sight reads 08h 54m 34s and is 06m 24s slow. The sextant altitude (hs) is 33° 51.5'. The index error is 2.8 off the arc, and the height of eye is 48 feet. What are the azimuth (Zn) and intercept (a) for this sight using the assumed position?

A. Zn 110.8°, a 32.0 T
B. Zn 249.2°, a 32.0 A
C. Zn 249.2°, a 34.2 T
D. Zn 290.8°, a 44.2 A

29. 02180. On 12 April 1981, at 0515 ZT, orning stars were observed, and the vessel's position was determined to be LAT 21° 05' S, LONG 16° 30' W. Your vessel is steaming at 19 knots on a course of 278° T. A sextant observation of the Sun's lower limb is made at 0930 ZT. The chronometer reads 10h 28m 25s, and the sextant altitude (hs) is 40° 15.9'. The index error is 2.5' off the arc, and the chronometer error is 2m 15s slow. What are the intercept (a) and azimuth (Zn) from the assumed position of this sight?

A. Zn 057.0°, a 15.4T
B. Zn 057.7°, a 17.7A
C. Zn 122.3°, a 17.7A
D. Zn 123.0°, a 22.7A

30. 02181. On 4 June 1981, at 0630 ZT, morning stars were observed, and the vessel's position was determined to be LAT 26° 15' S, LONG 121° 20' W. Your vessel is steaming at 13.0 knots on a course of 246° T. A sextant observation of the Sun's lower limb is made at 0915 ZT. The chronometer reads 05h 14m 27s, and the sextant altitude is 25° 57.8'. The index error is 2.1' off the arc, and the chronometer error is 0m 53s slow. Your height of eye is 39.0 feet. What is the intercept (a) and azimuth (Zn) of this sight using the assumed position method?

A. Zn 044.9°, a 1.7A
B. Zn 044.9°, a 2.5T
C. Zn 135.1°, a 1.7A
D. Zn 135.1°, a 2.5T

31. 02182. On 18 August 1981, at 0600 ZT, morning stars were observed, and the vessel's position was determined to be LAT 19° 48' N, LONG 108° 34' W. Your vessel is steaming on course 166° T at a speed of 16 knots. An observation of the Sun's lower limb is made at 1036 ZT. The chronometer reads 05h 34m 48s and is slow 01m 24s. What is the computed altitude (Hc) and azimuth (Zn) for this 1036 ZT observation using the assumed position method?

A. Hc 65° 18.5', Zn 102.1°
B. Hc 65° 14.8', Zn 100.4°
C. Hc 65° 11.3', Zn 099.4°
D. Hc 65° 07.2', Zn 101.2°

32. 2183. At 0800 ZT, on 29 June 1981, your DR position is LAT 26° 00.0' N, LONG 75° 29.5' W. Given the following information, determine the computed altitude (Hc) of the Sun for the assumed position nearest to the above given latitude and longitude.
Chronometer Time: 01h 00m 00s

A. Hc 34° 38.6'
B. Hc 34° 48.6'
C. Hc 34° 58.6'
D. Hc 35° 18.6'

33. 2184. At 1300 ZT, on 9 May 1981, your DR position is LAT 24° 00' N, LONG 83° 26' W. Given the following information, determine the computed altitude (Hc) of the Sun for the assumed position (AP) nearest to the above given latitude and longitude.

Chronometer: 07h 00m 00s

A. Hc 68° 22.8'
B. Hc 68° 24.1'
C. Hc 68° 25.2'
D. Hc 68° 26.9'

34. 2185. At 1000 ZT, on 21 October 1981, your DR position is LAT 29° 00' N, LONG 134° 40' E. Given the following information, determine the computed altitude (Hc) of the Sun for the assumed position (AP) nearest to the above given latitude and longitude.

Chronometer: 01h 00m 00s

A. Hc 42° 30.6'
B. Hc 42° 32.1'
C. Hc 42° 34.2'
D. Hc 42° 35.7'

1. 02151 A
2. 02152 A
3. 02153 C
4. 02154 A
5. 02155 B
6. 02156 D
7. 02157 B
8. 02158 B
9. 02159 D
10. 02160 C
11. 02161 D
12. 02162 C
13. 02163 C
14. 02164 C
15. 02165 A
16. 02166 C
17. 02167 A

18. 02168 D
19. 02169 C
20. 02170 C
21. 02171 A
22. 02172 B
23. 02173 D
24. 02174 C
25. 02175 A
26. 02176 C
27. 02177 D
28. 02178 C
29. 02180 B
30. 02181 B
31. 02182 B
32. 02183 C
33. 02184 D
34. 02185 D

Celestial Problems
Sight Reduction

Problem # 1 (USCG) (2151)			**Sun's Lower Limb**		Chapter 11	

Date:	**16 June**	Time		06:12	**LAT:**	27° 23.0 S
					LONG	56° 22.0 W
	ZT	08:50	**CT**	00 53 19	**C** - 212°	
	ZD	+ 4:00	**CE**	- 02 43	**S** -16.0 Kts	
	GMT	12:50	**CCT**	00 50 36		
			GMT	12 50 36	**DR**	
					Time	
					LAT	
					LONG	

Almanac

GHA	359° 51.2'	**DEC**	N 23° 21.3'	**Hs**	22° 58.6'
M/S	+ 12° 39.0'	**d (+.1)**	+ .1	**Ic**	+ 2.0'
GHA	372° 30.2'	**DEC**	N 23° 21.4'	**Dip (61)**	- 7.6'
±SHA/v				**Sum**	- 5.6'
Sum	372° 30.2'			**Ha**	22° 53.0'
a λ	- 56° 29.8'			**Alt**	+ 13.7'
LHA	316° 00.0'			**Ho**	23° 06.7'

LHA	**316°**	**DEC**	**N 23° 21.4**	**LAT**	**27 S**

Publication 229

		Z (23)	135.4	**Z to ZN**
Hc	24° 22.1'	**Z (24)**	136.2	
d	- 44.1	**d**	+ .8	ZN=180-Z
Inc Dec (X)	21.4	**Inc Dec (X)**	21.4	180 – 135.7 = 44.3°
Inv (÷)	60	**Inv (÷)**	60	**44.3**
Correction	-15.8	**Correction**	+ .3	
Hc	24° 06.3'	**Z**	**135.7**	
Ho	23° 06.7'			
a	**59.6 A**			

Notes:

Celestial Problems
Sight Reduction

Problem # 2 (USCG) (2152)		Sun's Lower Limb		Chapter 11	

Date:	25 June		Time	06:12	**LAT:**	28° 13.0' S
					LONG	049° 34.0' E
	ZT	10:22	**CT**	07:19:17	**C** - 066°	
	ZD	- 3:00	**CE**	+ 02:51	**S** -17 Kts	
	GMT	07:22	**CCT**	07:22:08		
			GMT	07:22:08	**DR**	1022-0612
					Time	
					LAT	27° 45.0' S
					LONG	50° 40.0' E

Almanac

GHA	284° 22.8'	**DEC**	N 23° 23.4'	**Hs**	35° 26.3'
M/S	+ 5° 32.0'	**d (+ .1)**	+ .1'	**Ic**	- 1.5'
GHA	289° 54.8'	**DEC**	N 23° 23.5'	**Dip (58)**	- 7.4'
±SHA/v				**Sum**	-8.9'
Sum	289° 54.8'			**Ha**	35° 17.4'
a λ	+ 51° 05.2			**Alt**	+ 14.0'
LHA	341° 00.0			**Ho**	35° 31.4'

LHA	340°	**DEC**	N 23° 23.5	**LAT**	28 S	CONTRARY

Publication 229

			Z (23)	158.3	**Z to ZN**
Hc	35° 48.3'	Z (24)	158.7	
d	- 56.1	d	+ .4	ZN=180-Z
Inc Dec (X)	23.5	**Inc Dec (X)**	23.5	180 – 158.5 = 22.5
Inv (÷)	60	**Inv (÷)**	60	**021.5**
Correction	- 22.0	**Correction**	+ .2	
Hc	36° 10.3'	**Z**	158.5	
Ho	35° 31.4'			
a	**39.9 A**			

Notes:

Alexander F. Hickethier MBA © 1999-2013

Celestial Problems
Sight Reduction

Problem #3 (USCG) (2153)	Sun's Lower Limb	Chapter 11

Date:	29 June	Time		08:00	LAT:	26° 00.0 N
					LONG	075° 29.5.0 W
	ZT	08:00	CT	01:00:00	C -	
	ZD	+ 5:00	CE		S -Kts	
	GMT	13:00	CCT	01:00:00		
			GMT	13:00:00	DR	
					Time	
					LAT	
					LONG	

Almanac

GHA	14° 09.5'	DEC	N 23°13.0'	Hs		
M/S	0	D (+.1)	0'	Ic		
GHA	14° 09.5'	DEC	N 23°13.0'	Dip ( )		
±SHA/v				Sum		
Sum	14° 09.5'			Ha		
a λ	- 75° 09.5'			Alt		
LHA	299° 00.0'			Ho		

LHA	299°	DEC	N 23° 13.0	LAT	26 N

Publication 229

						Z (34)	079.1	Z to ZN
	Hc	34° 55.'0		Z (24)	077.9		
	d	+ 16.8		d	- 1.2	ZN=Z
	Inc Dec (X)	13.0		Inc Dec (X)	13.0	**078.8**
	Inv (÷)	60		Inv (÷)	60	
	Correction	+ 3.6		Correction	- .3	
	Hc	**34° 58.6'**		Z	**078.8**	
	Ho					
	a					

Notes:

Alexander F. Hickethier MBA © 1999-2013

Celestial Problems
Sight Reduction

Problem # 4 (USCG) (2154)	Sun's Lower Limb		Chapter 11

Date:	30 June	Time	06:30	**LAT:**		25° 15.0 S
				LONG		175° 36.0 E
	ZT	10:15	**CT** 10:14:38	**C** - 302°		
	ZD	-12:00	**CE** + 01:25	**S** -16 Kts		
	GMT	22:15	**CCT** 10:16:03			
29 JUNE			**GMT** 22:16:03	**DR**		
				Time	10:15	
				LAT		24° 43.2' S
				LONG		174° 40.0' E

Almanac

GHA	149° 08.4'	**DEC**	N 23° 11.8'	**Hs**		32° 07.9'
M/S	+ 4° 00.8'	**d (- .1)**	0	**Ic**		- 4.5'
GHA	153° 09.2'	**DEC**	N 23° 11.8'	**Dip [58]**		- 7.4'
±SHA/v				**Sum**		- 11.9'
Sum	153° 09.2'			**Ha**		31° 56.0'
a λ	+ 174° 50.8'			**Alt**		+ 14.5'
LHA	328° 00.0'			**Ho**		32° 10.5'

LHA	**328°**	**DEC**	**N 21° 11.8**	**LAT**	**25 S**	**CONTRARY**

Publication 229

			Z (21)	144.5	**Z to ZN**
Hc	32° 50.7'	**Z (22)**	145.2	
d	-49.4	**d**	+ .7	ZN=180-Z
Inc Dec (X)	11.8	**Inc Dec (X)**	11.8	180 – 144.6 = **035.4**
Inv (÷)	60	**Inv (÷)**	60	**035.4**
Correction	- 9.7	**Correction**	+ .1	
Hc	32° 50.7'	**Z**	**144.6**	
Ho	32° 10.5'			
a	**40.2 T**			

Notes:

Celestial Problems
Sight Reduction

Problem # 5 (USCG) (2155)		Sun's Lower Limb		Chapter 11	

Date:	17 May	Time		05:01	LAT:	22° 16.0 S
					LONG	103° 46.0 W
	ZT	08:45	CT	03 43 32	C - 301°	
	ZD	+ 7:00	CE	+ 02 02	S -24 Kts	
	GMT	15:45	CCT	03 45 34		
			GMT	15 45 34	DR	3.733 X 24 = 89.6
					Time	08:45
					LAT	21° 29.0 S
					LONG	105° 11.0 W

Almanac

GHA	45° 55.1'	DEC	N 19° 23.9'	Hs	28° 47.7'		
M/S	+ 11° 23.5'	D (+ .6)	+ .5'	Ic	+ 1.5'		
GHA	57° 18.6'	DEC	N 19° 24.4'	Dip (85.5)	- 9.0'		
±SHA/v				Sum	- 7.5'		
Sum	57° 18.6'			Ha	28° 40.2'		
a λ	- 105° 18.6'			Alt	+ 14.3'		
LHA	312° 00.0'			Ho	28° 54.5'		

LHA	313°	DEC	N 19° 24.4'	LAT	21 S	+

Publication 229

		Z (19)	127.1	Z to ZN	
Hc	28° 17.6	Z (20)	128.0		
d	- 37.1	d	+ .9	ZN=180-Z	
Inc Dec (X)	24.4	Inc Dec (X)	24.4	180 − 127.5 = 052.5	
Inv (÷)	60	Inv (÷)	60	**052.5**	
Correction	- 15.1	Correction	+ .4		
Hc	28° 02.5	Z	127.5		
Ho	28° 54.5				
a	**21.8 T**				

Notes:

Celestial Problems
Sight Reduction

Problem # 6 (USCG) (2156)		Sun's Lower Limb		Chapter 11	

Date:	9 May		Time	13:00	LAT:	24° 00.0 N
					LONG	83° 26.0 W
	ZT	13:00	CT	07:00:00	C -	
	ZD	+ 6:00	CE		S -Kts	
	GMT	19:00	CCT	19:00:00		
			GMT		DR	
					Time	
					LAT	
					LONG	

Almanac

GHA	105°-54.4'	DEC	N 17°-29.0'	Hs	
M/S	0	D (+ .7)	0.0'	Ic	
GHA	105°-54.4'	DEC	N 17°-29.0'	Dip ( )	
±SHA/v				Sum	
Sum	105°-54.4'			Ha	
a λ	- 83°-54.4'			Alt	
LHA	22° 00.0'			Ho	

LHA	22°	DEC	N 17° 29.0'	LAT	24 N	SAME

Publication 229

			Z (17)	104.6	Z to ZN
Hc	68° 16.1'	Z (18)	102.1	
d	+ 21.8*	d	- 2.5	ZN=360-Z
Inc Dec (X)	29.0	Inc Dec (X)	29.0	360 − 103.4 = 256.6
Inv (÷)	60	Inv (÷)	60	**256.6**
Correction	+ 10.7	Correction	-1.2	
Hc	68° 26.8'	Z	103.4	
Ho				
a				

Notes:

+.2

Celestial Problems
Sight Reduction

Problem #7 (USCG) (2157)			**Saturn**		Chapter 11	

Date:	**25 MAY**		Time	19:17	**LAT:**	24° 16.0 N
					LONG	17° 26.0 W
	ZT	19:17	**CT**	08:18:24	**C** -	
	ZD	+ 1	**CE**	- 1:05	**S** -Kts	
	GMT	20:17	**CCT**	08:17:19		
			GMT	20:17:19	**DR**	
					Time	
					LAT	
					LONG	

Almanac

GHA	359° 28.3'	**DEC**	N 1°-06.3'	**Hs**	63° 05.1'
M/S	+ 4° 19.8'	**D (0.0)**	0.0'	**Ic**	+ 4.5'
GHA	003° 48.1'	**DEC**	N 1°-06.3'	**Dip (62)**	- 7.6'
±SHA/v (+ 2.5)	+ .7			**Sum**	- 3.1'
Sum	003° 48.8'			**Ha**	63° 02.0'
a λ	- 17° 48.8'			**Alt ***	- 0.5'
LHA	342° 00.0			**Ho**	63° 01.5'

LHA	346°	**DEC**	N 1° 06.3'	**LAT**	24 N	SAME

Publication 229

		Z (1)	147.4	**Z to ZN**
Hc	63° 18.0'	**Z (2)**	146.3	
d	+ 52.0	**d**	- 1.1	**ZN = Z**
Inc Dec (X)	06.3	**Inc Dec (X)**	06.3	
Inv (÷)	60	**Inv (÷)**	60	**147.3**
Correction	+ 5.5	**Correction**	-.1	
Hc	63° 12.5'	**Z**	**147.3**	
Ho	63° 01.5'			
a	**11.0 A**			

Notes:

Celestial Problems
Sight Reduction

Problem # 8 (USCG) (2158)		Jupiter		Chapter 11	

Date:	26 May	Time	19:06	**LAT:**	27° 16.0 N
				LONG	24° 37.0 W
	ZT	19:06	**CT** 09:05:16	**C -**	
	ZD	+ 2:00	**CE** + 01:25	**S -Kts**	
	GMT	21:06	**CCT** 09:06:41		
			GMT 21:06:41	**DR**	
				Time	
				LAT	
				LONG	

Almanac

GHA	18° 21.4′	**DEC**	N 1° 08.6′	**Hs**	63° 27.6′
M/S	+ 1° 40.3′	**D (0.0)**	0.0′	**Ic**	- 5.2′
GHA	20° 01.7′	**DEC**	N 1° 08.6′	**Dip (52.6)**	- 7.0′
±SHA/v(+ 2.5)	+0.3′			**Sum**	- 12.2′
Sum	20° 02.0′			**Ha**	63° 15.4′
a λ	- 25° 02.0′			**Alt ***	- 0.4′
LHA	355° 00.0′			**Ho**	63° 15.0′

LHA	357°	**DEC**	N 1°-08.6′	**LAT**	27 N	SAME

Publication 229

		Z (1)	168.7	**Z to ZN**
Hc	63° 33.6′	**Z (2)**	168.3	
d	+ 59.1	**d**	+ .4	**ZN = Z**
Inc Dec (X)	08.6′	**Inc Dec (X)**	08.6′	
Inv (÷)	60	**Inv (÷)**	60	**168.7**
Correction	+ 8.5	**Correction**	+ .0	
Hc	63° 42.1′	**Z**	168.7	
Ho	63° 15.0′			
a	**27.1 A**			

Notes:

Celestial Problems
Sight Reduction

Problem # 9 (USCG) (2159)		Venus		Chapter 11	

Date:	**25 May**	Time		18:58	**LAT:**	21° 05.0 N
					LONG	143° 27.0 E
	ZT	18:58	**CT**	08:59:15	**C -**	
	ZD	- 10:00	**CE**	- 01:25	**S -** Kts	
	GMT	08:58	**CCT**	08:57:50		
			GMT	08:57:50	**DR**	
					Time	
					LAT	
					LONG	

Almanac

GHA	287° 25.7'	**DEC**	N 23° 12.8'	**Hs**		12° 53.4'
M/S	+ 14°-27.5'	**D(+ .4)**	+ .4'	**Ic**		+ 4.5'
GHA	301° 53.2'	**DEC**	N 23° 13.2'	**Dip (55)**		- 7.2'
±SHA/v(-.9)	- .9'			**Sum**		- 2. 7'
Sum	301° 52.3'			**Ha**		12° 50.7'
a λ	+ 143° 17.7'			**Alt * + PL**	(- 4.5 + .1) = - 4.4'	
LHA	85° 00.0'			**Ho**		12° 46.3'

LHA	85°	**DEC**	N 23°-13.2'	**LAT**	21° N	SAME

Publication 229

		Z (23)	069.9	**Z to ZN**
Hc	12° 24.7'	**Z (24)**	068.9	
d	+ 16.2	**d**	- 1.0	ZN=1360-Z
Inc Dec (X)	13.2'	**Inc Dec (X)**	13.2'	360 − 069.7 = 290.3
Inv (÷)	60	**Inv (÷)**	60	**290.3**
Correction	+ 3.6	**Correction**	- .2	
Hc	12° 28.3'	**Z**	069.7	
Ho	12° 46.3'			
a	**18.0 T**			

Notes:

Celestial Problems
Sight Reduction

Problem # 10 (USCG) (2160)		Sirius		Chapter 11	

Date:	**17 April**		Time	18:56	**LAT:**	22' 35.0 N
					LONG	63' 15.0 W
	ZT	18:56	**CT**	10:59:27	**C -**	
	ZD	+ 4:00	**CE**	- 03:01	**S - ‹ts**	
	GMT	22:56	**CCT**	10:56:26		
			GMT	22:56:26	**DR**	
					Time	
					LAT	
					LONG	

Almanac

GHA	175° 56.3'	**DEC**	S 16° 41.7'	**Hs**	42° 45.0'
M/S	+ 14° 06.5'	**d**	0.0'	**Ic**	+ 2.6'
GHA	190°-02.8'	**DEC**	S 16° 41.7'	**Dip (45)**	- 6. 5'
±SHA/v	+ 258° 55.5'			**Sum**	- 3. 9'
Sum	448° 58.3'			**Ha**	42° 41.1'
a λ	- 62° 58.3'			**Alt ***	- 1. 1'
LHA	26° 00.0'			**Ho**	42° 40.0'

LHA	26°	**DEC**	S 16° 41.7'	**LAT**	23° N	CONTRARY

Publication 229

		Z (16)	144.5	**Z to ZN**
Hc	43° 26.4'	**Z (17)**	145.3	
d	- 50.0	**d**	+ .8	ZN=360-Z
Inc Dec (X)	41.7	**Inc Dec (X)**	41.7	360 − 145.1 = 214.9
Inv (÷)	60	**Inv (÷)**	60	214.9
Correction	- 34.8	**Correction**	+ .6	
Hc	42° 51.6'	**Z**	**145.1**	
Ho	42° 40.0'			
a	**11.6 A**			

Notes:

Celestial Problems
Sight Reduction

Problem # 11 (USCG) (2161)		**Rigil Kentaurus**		Chapter 11	
Date: **28 APRIL**	Time	05:15	**LAT:**	23° 26.0 S	
			LONG	095° 30.0 E	
ZT	05:15	**CT** 11:16:36	**C** -		
ZD	- 6:00	**CE** - 01:18	**S** -Kts		
GMT	23:15	**CCT** 11:15:18			
23:15 27 April		**GMT** 23:15:18	**DR**		
			Time		
			LAT		
			LONG		

Almanac

GHA	200° 50.2'	**DEC**	S 60° 45.4'	**Hs**		
M/S	+ 3° 49.5'	**d**	0.0	**Ic**		
GHA	204°-39.7'	**DEC**	S 60° 45.4'	**Dip ()**		_____
±SHA/v	+ 140° 24.6'			**Sum**		_____
Sum	345°-04.3'			**Ha**		
a λ	+ 95° 55.7'			**Alt ***		_____
LHA	81° 00.0'			**Ho**		24° 51.4'

LHA	81°	**DEC**	S 60° 45.4'	**LAT**	23° S	SAME

Publication 229

					Z to ZN
		Z (60)	032.8		
Hc	24° 13.7'	**Z (61)**	031.7		
d	+ 4.4	**d**	- 1.1		ZN=180+Z
Inc Dec (X)	45.4	**Inc Dec (X)**	45.4		180 + 031.9 = 211.9
Inv (÷)	60	**Inv (÷)**	60		**211.9**
Correction	+ 3.3	**Correction**	- .9		
Hc	24° 17.0'	**Z**	031.9		
Ho	24° 51.4'				
a	**34.4**				

Notes:

Celestial Problems
Sight Reduction

Problem # 12 (USCG) (2162)	Sun's Lower Limb		Chapter 11

Date:	5 April	Time	05:09	LAT:	28° 23.0 N
				LONG	177° 13.0 W
	ZT	10:21	CT	10:20:09	C - 258°
	ZD	+ 12:00	CE	+ 00:54	S -19.0 Kts
	GMT	22:21	CCT	10:21:03	
			GMT	22:21:03	DR	1021-0509
					Time	1021
					LAT	28° 53.5' S
					LONG	179° 02.0' W

Almanac

GHA	149° 16.8'	DEC	N 5° 55.4'	Hs	58° 06.6'
M/S	+ 5° 15.8'	D (+ .9)	+ .3'	Ic	+ 1.0'
GHA	154° 32.6'	DEC	N 5° 55.7'	Dip (55)	- 7.2'
±SHA/v	0.0'			Sum	- 6.2'
Sum	154°-32.6'			Ha	58° 00.4'
a λ	- 179° 32.6'			Alt *	+ 15.4'
LHA	335° 00.0'			Ho	58° 15.8'

LHA	335°	DEC	N 5° 55.7'	LAT	29 N	SAME

Publication 229

		Z (5)	130.6	Z to ZN
Hc	56° 17.7'	Z (6)	129.4	
d	+ 44.4	d	- 1.2	ZN=Z
Inc Dec (X)	55.7	Inc Dec (X)	55.7	
Inv (÷)	60	Inv (÷)	60	129.5
Correction	+ 42.2	Correction	- 1.1	
Hc	56° 59.9'	Z	129.5	
Ho	58° 15.8'			
a	75.9 T			

Notes:

Celestial Problems
Sight Reduction

Problem # 13 (USCG) (2163		Sun's Lower Limb		Chapter 11	

Date:	1 April	Time		05:15	LAT:	27° 05.0' N
					LONG	016° 30.0' W
	ZT	09:30	CT	10:28:25	C - 022°	
	ZD	+ 1:00	CE	+ 02:15	S -19.0 Kts	
	GMT	10:30	CCT	10:30:40		
			GMT	10:30:40	DR	0515-0930
					Time	0930
					LAT	28° 26.0' N
					LONG	015° 55.0' W

Almanac

GHA	329° 01.4'	DEC	N 4° 35.0'	Hs	46° 20.3'
M/S	+ 7° 40.0'	D(+ 1.0)	+ .5'	Ic	+ 4.5'
GHA	336° 41.4'	DEC	N 4° 35.5'	Dip (57)	- 6.0'
±SHA/v				Sum	- 2.5'
Sum	336° 41.4'			Ha	46° 17.8'
a λ	- 15° 41.4'			Alt	+ 15.1'
LHA	321° 00.0'			Ho	46° 22.9'

LHA	321°	DEC	N 4° 35.5'	LAT	28° N	SAME

Publication 229

			Z (4)	115.7	Z to ZN
Hc	45° 49.7'	Z (5)	114.6	
d	+ 35.9	d	- 1.1	ZN = Z
Inc Dec (X)	35.5	Inc Dec (X)	35.5	
Inv (÷)	60	Inv (÷)	60	115.0
Correction	+ 21.2	Correction	- .7	
Hc	46° 10.9'	Z	115.0	
Ho	46° 22.9'			
a	12.0 T			

Notes:

Celestial Problems
Sight Reduction

Problem # 14 (USCG) (2164)	Sun's Lower Limb	Chapter 11

Date:	6 March	Time	05:50	LAT:	23° 56.0' N
				LONG	027° 19.0' W
	ZT	08:30	CT	10:32:05	C-149° s
	ZD	+ 2:00	CE	- 01:45	S- 25.0 Kt
	GMT	10:21	CCT	10:30:20	
			GMT	10:30:20	DR
					Time
				LAT	22° 58.0' N
				LONG	026° 42.0' W

Almanac

GHA	327° 10.2'	DEC	S 5° 37.2'	Hs	31° 31.5'
M/S	+ 7° 35.0'	D(- 1.0)	- .5'	Ic	- 2.5'
GHA	334° 45.2'	DEC	S 5° 36.7'	Dip (76)	- 8.4'
±SHA/v				Sum	- 10.9'
Sum	334° 45.2'			Ha	31° 20.6'
a λ	- 26° 45.2'			Alt	+ 14.7'
LHA	308° 00.0'			Ho	31° 35.3'

LHA	308°	DEC	S 5° 36.7'	LAT	23 N	CONTRARY

Publication 229

		Z (5)	112.2	Z to ZN
Hc	32 02.4'	Z (6)	113.2	
d	-31.3	d	+ 1.0	ZN=Z
Inc Dec (X)	36.7	Inc Dec (X)	36.7	
Inv (÷)	60	Inv (÷)	60	112.8
Correction	- 19.1	Correction	+ .6	
Hc	31° 43.3'	Z	112.8	
Ho	31° 35.3'			
a	8.0 A			

Notes:

Celestial Problems

Sight Reduction

Problem #15 (USCG) (2165)	Moon Upper Limb	Chapter 11

Date:	25 Feb	Time	0622	LAT:	30° 28.3 S
				LONG	102° 39.3 E
	ZT	06:22	CT	11:21:18	
	ZD	- 7:00	CE	+ 00:48	
	GMT	23:22	CCT	11:22:06	
24 FEBRUARY			GMT	23:22:06	DR
					Time
					LAT
					LONG

Almanac

GHA	277° 10.3'	DEC	S 10° 52.8'	Hs	59° 58.6'
M/S	+ 5° 16.4'	D (+8.8)	+ 3.3'	Ic	- 2.5'
GHA	282° 26.7'	DEC	S 10° 56.1'	Dip (58)	- 7.5'
±SHA/v (+14.8)	+ 5.6'			Sum	- 10.0'
Sum	282° 32.3'			Ha	59° 48.6'
a λ	+ 102° 27.7'			Alt	+ 11.8'
LHA	25° 00.0'			Ho	60° 00.4'

LHA	25°	DEC	S 10° 56.1'	LAT	30 S	same

Publication 229

		Z (10)	125.4	Z to ZN
Hc	59° 17.6'	Z (11)	124.0	
d	41.3	d	-1.4	ZN=180+Z
Inc Dec (X)	56.1	Inc Dec (X)	56.1	180 + 124.1 = 304.1
Inv (÷)	60	Inv (÷)	60	**304.1**
Correction	38.6	Correction	-1.3	
Hc	59° 56.2'	Z	**124.1**	
Ho	60° 00.4'			
a	**4.2 T**			

Notes:

1. USCG used whole # of Declination 10 for Z and did not interpolate. 180 + = 205.4 = 305.4

HP 54.2
Alt (59° 50)   39.1
HP (54.3) UL   + 2.7
SUM   41.8
UL   - 30
Alt total   11.8

Celestial Problems
Sight Reduction

Problem # 16 (USCG) (2166)		Sun's Lower Limb		Chapter 11

Date:	**10 Jan**	Time	05:50	**LAT:**	25° 16.0' N
				LONG	123° 18.0' W
	ZT	09:15	**CT**	05:14:02	**C** - 295°
	ZD	+ 08:00	**CE**	+ 01:34	**S** -22.0 Kts
	GMT	17:15	**CCT**	05:15:36	
			GMT	17:15:36	**DR** 0550-0915
					Time 09:15
					LAT 25° 48.0' N
					LONG 124° 35.0' W

Almanac

GHA	73° 04.5'	**DEC**	S 21° 53.6'	**Hs**	24° 00.7'
M/S	+ 3° 54.0'	**D (- .4)**	- .1'	**Ic**	+ 2.6'
GHA	76° 58.5'	**DEC**	S 21° 53.5'	**Dip (55)**	- 7.2'
±SHA/v				**Sum**	- 4.6'
Sum	76° 58.5'			**Ha**	23° 56.1'
a λ	- 124° 58.5'			**Alt**	+ 14.3'
LHA	312° 00.0'			**Ho**	24° 10.3'

LHA	312°	**DEC**	S 21° 53.5'	**LAT**	26 N	CONTRARY

Publication 229

			Z (21)	130.7		**Z to ZN**
Hc	23° 51.1'		**Z (22)**	131.5		
d	- 41.1		**d**	+ .8		**ZN = Z**
Inc Dec (X)	53.5		**Inc Dec (X)**	53.5		
Inv (÷)	60		**Inv (÷)**	60		**131.4**
Correction	- 36.4		**Correction**	+ .7		
Hc	23° 15.2'		**Z**			
Ho	24° 10.3'					
a	**45.1 T**					

Notes:

Celestial Problems
Sight Reduction

Problem # 17 (USCG) (2167)		Sun's Lower Limb		Chapter 11	

Date:	4 July	Time	06:30	LAT:	21° 15.0 S
				LONG	21° 20.0 W
	ZT	09:15	CT	10:14 27	S- 146°
	ZD	+01:00	CE	+ 00:53	C-13.0 Kts
	GMT	10:15	CCT	10:15:20	
			GMT	10:15:20	DR
					Time	09:15
				LAT	20° 45.2 S
				LONG	20° 56.0 W

Almanac

GHA	328° 55.5'	DEC	N 22° 52.1'	Hs	25° 29.8'
M/S	+ 3° 50.0'	D (- .2)	- 0.1'	Ic	+ 3.1'
GHA	332° 45.5'	DEC	N 22° 52.0	Dip (48)	- 6.7'
±SHA/v				Sum	- 3.6'
Sum	332° 45.5'			Ha	25° 26.2'
a λ	- 20° 45.5'			Alt	+ 14.0'
LHA	312° 00.0'			Ho	25° 40.2'

LHA	312°	DEC	N 22° 52.0'	LAT	21° S	CONTRARY

Publication 229

			Z (22)	129.7	Z to ZN
Hc	26° 25.2'	Z (23)	130.6	
d	-38.1	d	+ .9	ZN=180-Z
Inc Dec (X)	52.0	Inc Dec (X)	52.0	180 – 130.5 = 049.5
Inv (÷)	60	Inv (÷)	60	**049.5**
Correction	- 33.0	Correction	+ .8	
Hc	25° 52.2'	Z	130.5	
Ho	25° 40.2'			
a	**12.0 T**			

Notes:

Celestial Problems
Sight Reduction

Problem # 18 (USCG) (2168)	Sun's Lower Limb	Chapter 11

Date:	22 July	Time	04:48	LAT:	21° 43.0' N
				LONG	158° 39.0' E
	ZT	09:56	CT	10:54:27	C - 028°
	ZD	- 11:00	CE	+ 01:38	S -21.0 Kts
	GMT	22:56	CCT	10:56:05	
21 July			GMT	22:56:05	DR
					Time	09:56
					LAT	23° 17.0' N
					LONG	159° 22.0' E

Almanac

	GHA	148° 25.0'	DEC	N 20° 21.4	Hs	54° 28.2'
	M/S	14° 01.3'	D (-.5)	- .5'	Ic	+ 1.5'
	GHA	162° 26.3'	DEC	N 20° 20.9'	Dip (56)	- 7.3'
	±SHA/v				Sum	- 5.8'
	Sum	162° 26.3'			Ha	54° 22.4'
	a λ	159° 33.7'			Alt	+ 153'
	LHA	322° 00.0'			Ho	54° 37.7'

LHA	322°	DEC	N 20° 20.9'	LAT	23° N	SAME

Publication 229

			Z (20)	087.5	Z to ZN
	Hc	54° 36.8'	Z (21)	085.8	
	d	+ 11.5	d	- 1.7	ZN = Z
	Inc Dec (X)	20.9	Inc Dec (X)	20.9	
	Inv (÷)	60	Inv (÷)	60	086.9
	Correction	+ 4.0	Correction	- .6	
	Hc	54° 40.8'	Z	086.9	
	Ho	54° 37.7'			
	a	3.1 A			

Notes:

Celestial Problems
Sight Reduction

Problem # 19 (USCG) (2169)		Sun's Lower Limb		Chapter 11	

Date:	**24 July**		Time		06:00	**LAT:**	22° 37.0' N
						LONG	032° 45.0' W
	ZT	10:30	**CT**	00:30:16		**S**- 185°	
	ZD	+02:00	**CE**	+ 00:31		**C**-20.0 Kts	
	GMT	12:30	**CCT**	12:30:47			
			GMT			**DR**	
						Time	06:00
						LAT	21° 07.3' N
						LONG	032° 54.0' W

Almanac

GHA	358° 23.8'		**DEC**	N 19° 49.8'	**Hs**	
M/S	+ 7° 41.8'		**D (-.5)**	- .3'	**Ic**	
GHA	006° 05.6'		**DEC**	N 19° 49.5'	**Dip (56)**	
±SHA/v					**Sum**	
Sum	006° 05.6'				**Ha**	
a λ	- 33° 05.6'				**Alt**	
LHA	333° 00.0'				**Ho**	

LHA	333°	**DEC**	N 19° 49.5'	**LAT**	21° N	SAME

Publication 229

			Z (19)	089.7		**Z to ZN**	
Hc	64° 34.8'		**Z (20)**	087.4			
d	+ 8.4*		**d**	- 2.3		**ZN = Z**	
Inc Dec (X)	49.5		**Inc Dec (X)**	49.5			
Inv (÷)	60		**Inv (÷)**	60		**087.8**	
Correction	+ 7.0		**Correction**	- 1.9			
Hc	64° 41. 8'		**Z**	087.8			
Ho							
a							

Notes:

* .1

Celestial Problems
Sight Reduction

Problem # 20 (USCG) (2170)		MOON L/L			Chapter 11

Date:	22 July		Time	07:20	LAT:	20° 38.2 N
					LONG	87° 16.0 W
	ZT	07:20	CT	01:18:14	S- 185°	
	ZD	+06:00	CE	+ 01:28	C-20.0 Kts	
	GMT	13:20	CCT	01:19:42		
			GMT	13:19:42	DR	
					Time	
					LAT	
					LONG	

Almanac

GHA	128° 25.4'	DEC	S 2° 13.9'	Hs	38°-32.6'
M/S	+ 4° 42.0'	D (- 11.4)	- 4.0'	Ic	+ 3.1'
GHA	133° 07.4'	DEC	S 2° 09.9'	Dip (68)	- 8.0'
±SHA/v (+11.2)	+ 3.6'			Sum	- 4.9'
Sum	133° 11.0'			Ha	38°-27.7'
a λ	- 87° 11.0'			Alt (54.6 + 5.9)	+ 1° 00.5'
LHA	46° 00.0'			Ho	38°-28.2'

LHA	46°	DEC	S 2° 09.9'	LAT	21° N	CONTRARY

Publication 229

			Z (2)	111.4	**Z to ZN**
Hc	39° 27.9'	Z (3)	112.5	
d	- 29.9	d	+ 1.1	ZN=360-Z
Inc Dec (X)	09.9'	Inc Dec (X)	09.9'	360 – 111.6 = 248.4
Inv (÷)	60	Inv (÷)	60	**248.4**
Correction	- 4.9	Correction	+ .2	
Hc	39° 23.0'	Z	111.6	
Ho	38° 28.2'			
a	5.2 T			

Notes:

HP 58.5
Alt (38° 30)   54.6
HP (58.5) UL   + 5.9
SUM   60.5
UL   -00
Alt total   + 60.5 or + 1° 00.5'

Celestial Problems
Sight Reduction

Problem # 21 (USCG) (2171)	Sun's Lower Limb		Chapter 11

Date:	8 Aug	Time	05:45	LAT:	26° 16.0' S
				LONG	094° 16.0' E
	ZT	09:05	CT	03 :02:52	S - 346°
	ZD	- 06:00	CE	+ 02:17	C-20.0 Kts
	GMT	03:05	CCT	03:05:09	
			GMT	03:05:09	DR
					Time
					LAT	25° 11.3' S
					LONG	093° 45.0' E

Almanac

GHA	223° 35.6'	DEC	N 16° 11.7'	Hs	38° 07.5'
M/S	+ 1° 17.3'	D(- .7)	- .1'	Ic	+ 5.2'
GHA	224° 52.9'	DEC	N 16° 11.7'	Dip (72)	- 8.1'
±SHA/v				Sum	- 2.9'
Sum	224° 52.9'			Ha	38° 04.6'
a λ	+ 094° 07.1'			Alt	+ 14.8'
LHA	319° 00.0'			Ho	38° 19.4'

LHA	319°	DEC	N 16° 11.7'	LAT	25 S	CONTRARY

Publication 229

			Z (16)	131.4	Z to ZN
Hc	32° 45.2'	Z (17)	132.3	
d	-42.6	d	+ .9	ZN=180-Z
Inc Dec (X)	11.7'	Inc Dec (X)	11.7'	180 – 131.8 =
Inv (÷)	60	Inv (÷)	60	**048.2**
Correction	- 8.3	Correction	+ .2	
Hc		Z	**131.6**	
Ho	38° 19.4'			
a				

Notes:

Celestial Problems
Sight Reduction

Problem # 22 (USCG) (2172)		Sun's Lower Limb		Chapter 11	

Date:	**11 Oct**	Time	05:16	**LAT:**	23° 21.0' N
				LONG	139° 27.0' W
	ZT	09:27	**CT** 06:30:21	**S** - 293°	
	ZD	+09:00	**CE** - 02:56	**C**-14.0 Kts	
	GMT	18:27	**CCT** 06:27:25		
			GMT 18:27:25	**DR**	0927-0516
				Time	0927
				LAT	23° 33.0' N
				LONG	140° 00.0' W

Almanac

GHA	93° 19.8'	**DEC**	S 7° 11.2'	**Hs**	39°-48.7'
M/S	+ 6° 51.8'	**D(+ .9)**	+ .4'	**Ic**	- 2.0'
GHA	100° 11.6'	**DEC**	S 7° 11.6'	**Dip (63)**	- 7.7'
±SHA/v				**Sum**	- 9.7'
Sum	100° 11.6'			**Ha**	39°-39.0'
a λ	140° 11.6'			**Alt**	+ 15.1'
LHA	320° 00.0'			**Ho**	39°-54.1'

LHA	320°	**DEC**	S 7° 11.6'	**LAT**	24 N	CONTRARY

Publication 229

			Z (7)	123.4	**Z to ZN**
Hc	40°10.1'	**Z (8)**	124.4	
d	- 38.7	**d**	+ 1.0	**ZN=Z**
Inc Dec (X)	11.6'	**Inc Dec (X)**	11.6'	
Inv (÷)	60	**Inv (÷)**	60	**123.6**
Correction	- 7.4	**Correction**	+ .2	
Hc	40° 02.7'	**Z**	123.6	
Ho	39°-54.1'			
a	**8.6 A**			

Notes:

Celestial Problems
Sight Reduction

Problem # 23 (USCG) (2173)	Sun's Lower Limb	Chapter 11

Date:	**21 Oct**	Time		10:00	**LAT:**	29° 00.0 N
					LONG	134° 40.0 E
	ZT	10:00	**CT**	01:00:00	**S** - 293°	
	ZD	- 09:00	**CE**	+ 00:00	**C**-14.0 Kts	
	GMT	01:00	**CCT**	01:00:00		
			GMT	01:00:00	**DR**	
					Time	
					LAT	
					LONG	

Almanac

GHA	198° 49.3'	**DEC**	S 10° 36.0'	**Hs**		
M/S	0	**D (+ .9)**	0	**Ic**		
GHA	198° 49.3'	**DEC**	S 10° 36.0'	**Dip (63)**		
±SHA/v				**Sum**		
Sum	198° 49.3'			**Ha**		
a λ	+ 134° 10.7'			**Alt**		
LHA	333° 00.0'			**Ho**		

LHA	333°	**DEC**	S 10° 36.0'	**LAT**	29 N	CONTRARY

Publication 229

		Z (10)	142.2	**Z to ZN**	
Hc	43° 06.0'	**Z (11)**	143.0		
d	-50.5	**d**	5 .8	**ZN = Z**	
Inc Dec (X)	36.0'	**Inc Dec (X)**	36.0'		
Inv (÷)	60	**Inv (÷)**	60	**142.7**	
Correction	-30.3	**Correction**	+ .5		
Hc	43° 35.7'	**Z**	142.7		
Ho					
a					

Notes:

Celestial Problems
Sight Reduction

Problem # 24 (USCG) (2174)			Sun's Lower Limb		Chapter 11	

Date:	**18 Oct**	Time		05:18	**LAT:**	25° 31.0 N
					LONG	146° 29.2 E
	ZT	09:15	**CT**	11:17:11	**S** - 308°	
	ZD	- 10:00	**CE**	- 01:57	**C**-19.0 Kts	
	GMT	23:15	**CCT**	11:15:04		
17 Oct			**GMT**	23:15:04	**DR**	0915-0518
					Time	0915
					LAT	26° 17.2' N
					LONG	145° 24.0' E

Almanac

GHA	168° 41.0'	**DEC**	S 9° 29.3	**Hs**		34°-51.4'	
M/S	+ 3° 46.0'	**D (+ .9)**	+ .2'	**Ic**		- 2.0'	
GHA	172° 27.0'	**DEC**	S 9° 29.5'	**Dip (54)**		- 7.0'	
±SHA/v				**Sum**		- 9.0'	
Sum	172° 27.0'			**Ha**		34°-42.4'	
a λ	+ 145° 33.0'			**Alt**		+ 14.9'	
LHA	318° 00.0'			**Ho**		34°-57.3'	

LHA	318°	**DEC**	S 9° 29.5'	**LAT**	26 N	CONTRARY

Publication 229

			Z (9)	125.0	**Z to ZN**
Hc	36 14.3'	**Z (10)**	125.9	
d	- 40.2	**d**	+ .9	**ZN = -Z**
Inc Dec (X)	29.5	**Inc Dec (X)**	29.5	
Inv (÷)	60	**Inv (÷)**	60	**125.4**
Correction	-19.8	**Correction**	+ .4	
Hc	36° 54.5'	**Z**	125.4	
Ho	34° 57.3'			
a	**57.2 A**			

Notes:

Celestial Problems
Sight Reduction

Problem #25 (USCG) (2175)	Sun's Lower Limb		Chapter 11

Date:	13 Nov		Time	04:38	LAT:	22° 14.0' S
					LONG	079° 23.0' E
	ZT	08:22	CT	03:20:16	S - 242°	
	ZD	- 5:00	CE	+ 01:47	C-13.0 Kts	
	GMT	03:22	CCT	03:22:03		
			GMT	03:22:03	DR	0822-0438
					Time	0822
					LAT	22° 36.7' S
					LONG	078° 36.0' E

Almanac

GHA	228° 56.1'	DEC	S 17° 54.9'	Hs	45°-49.7'
M/S	+ 5° 30.8'	D (+ .7)	+ .3'	Ic	- 1.0'
GHA	234° 26.9'	DEC	S 17° 55.2'	Dip (61)	- 7.6'
±SHA/v				Sum	- 8.6'
Sum	234° 26.9'			Ha	45°-41.1'
a λ	78° 33.1			Alt	+ 15.3'
LHA	313° 00.0'			Ho	45°-41.1'

LHA	313°	DEC	N 17° 55.2'	LAT	23 S	SAME

Publication 229

		Z (17)	088.8	Z to ZN
Hc	45° 36.6'	Z (18)	087.4	
d	+ 15.8	d	- 1.4	ZN=180-Z
Inc Dec (X)	55.2	Inc Dec (X)	55.2	180 – 087.5 = 092.5
Inv (÷)	60	Inv (÷)	60	**092.5**
Correction	+ 14.5	Correction	- 1.3	
Hc	45° 51.1'	Z	087.5	
Ho	45° 41.1'			
a	**10.0 A**			

Notes:

Celestial Problems
Sight Reduction

Problem # 26 (USCG) (2176)		Sun's Lower Limb		Chapter 11	

Date:	9 Nov		Time	04:26	**LAT:**	25° 17.0' S
					LONG	154° 16.0' E
	ZT	08:37	**CT**	10:35:21	**S - 066°**	
	ZD	- 10:00	**CE**	+ 01:48	**C-14.0 Kts**	
	GMT	22:37	**CCT**	10:37:09		
8 Nov			**GMT**	22:37:09	**DR**	0837-0426
					Time	0837
					LAT	24° 52.0' S
					LONG	155° 18.0' E

Almanac

GHA	154° 02.8'	**DEC**	S 16° 44.8'	**Hs**	50° 26.9'
M/S	+ 9° 17.3'	**D(+ .7)**	+ .4'	**Ic**	- 1.5'
GHA	163° 20.1'	**DEC**	S 16° 45.2'	**Dip (56)**	- 7.3'
±SHA/v				**Sum**	- 8.8'
Sum	163° 20.1'			**Ha**	50° 18.1'
a λ	155° 39.9'			**Alt**	+ 15.4'
LHA	319° 00.0'			**Ho**	50° 33.5'

LHA	319°	**DEC**	S 16° 45.2'	**LAT**	25° S	SAME

Publication 229

		Z (16)	095.1	**Z to ZN**
Hc	50° 42.8'	**Z (17)**	093.7	
d	+ 20.1	**d**	- 1.4	ZN=180-Z
Inc Dec (X)	45.2'	**Inc Dec (X)**	45.2'	180 - 094.0 = 086.0
Inv (÷)	60	**Inv (÷)**	60	**086.0**
Correction	+ 15.1	**Correction**	- 1.1	
Hc	50° 57.9'	**Z**	**094.0**	
Ho	50° 33.5'			
a	**24.4 A**			

Notes:

Celestial Problems
Sight Reduction

Problem # 27 (USCG) (2177)		Sun's Lower Limb		Chapter 11-1

Date:	**21 Nov 1981**		Time	0430	**LAT:**	22°-14.0' S
					LONG	79°-23.0' E
	ZT	08:16	**CT**	03:14:16	**C**-246°	
	ZD	-5:00	**CE**	+0:01:47	**S**-14.5 Kts	
	GMT	03:16	**CCT**	03:16:03		
			GMT	03:16:03	**DR**	08:16 – 04:30
					Time	08:16
					LAT	22° 36.3' S
					LONG	078° 30.0' E

	GHA	228° 32.9'	**DEC**	S 19°-52.4'	**Hs**	44°-29.2'
	M/S	+ 4° 00.8'	**D (+.5)**	+0.1'	**Ic**	-1.0'
	GHA	232° 33.7'	**DEC**	S 19°-52.5	**Dip (61)**	-7.6'
	±SHA/v				**Sum**	-8.6'
	Sum	232° 33.7'			**Ha**	44°-20.6'
	a λ	+78° 26.3'			**Alt**	+15.3'
	LHA	311° 00.0'			**Ho**	44°-35.9'

LHA	311°	**DEC**	S 19° 52.5'	**LAT**	23 S	CONTRARY

			Z (19)	085.4	**Z to ZN**
Hc	44° 17.0'	**Z (20)**	084.0	
d	+14.0	**d**	-1.4	ZN=180-Z
Inc Dec (X)	52.5	**Inc Dec (X)**	52.5	
Inv (÷)	60	**Inv (÷)**	60	180-84.2=
Correction	+12.3	**Correction**	-1.2	**095.8**
Hc	44° 29.3'	**Z**	**084.2**	
Ho	44° 35.9'			
a	**6.6 T**			

Notes:

Celestial Problems
Sight Reduction

Problem # 28 (USCG) (2178)			Jupiter		Chapter 11-2	

Date:	26 July		Time	1901	**LAT:**	28°-28.0' N
					LONG	157°-16.0' E
	ZT	19:01	**CT**	08:54:34	**C-**	
	ZD	-10:00	**CE**	+0:06:24	**S-**	
	GMT	09:01	**CCT**	09:00:58		
			GMT	09:00:58	**DR**	
					Time	
					LAT	
					LONG	

Almanac

GHA	253° 39.9'	**DEC**	S 0° 58.5'	**Hs**	33°-51.5'
M/S	+ 0° 14.5'	**d (+0.2)**		**Ic**	+2.8'
GHA	253° 54.4'	**DEC**	S 0° 58.5'	**Dip (48)**	-6.7'
±SHA/v				**Sum**	-3.9'
Sum	253° 54.4'			**Ha**	33° 47.6'
a λ	157° 05.6'			**Alt**	-1.4'
LHA	51° 00.0'			**Ho**	33° 46.2'

LHA	51°	**DEC**	S 0° 58.5'	**LAT**	28 S	SAME

Publication 229

		Z (0)	110.8	**Z to ZN**	
Hc	33° 45.4'	**Z (1)**	111.8		
d	-34.2	**d**	+ 1.0	ZN=180-Z	
Inc Dec (X)	58.5	**Inc Dec (X)**	58.5	360 - 111.8 =	
Inv (÷)	60	**Inv (÷)**	60	**248.2**	
Correction	-33.3	**Correction**	+ 1.0		
Hc	33° 12.1'	**Z**	**111.8**		
Ho	33° 46.2'				
a	**34.1**				

Notes:

Celestial Problems
Sight Reduction

Problem # 29 (USCG) (2180)		Sun's Lower Limb		Chapter 11 - 3

Date:	12 Apr	Time	05:15	**LAT:**	21°-05.0' S
				LONG	16°-30.0' W
	ZT	09:30	**CT** 10:28:25	**C-278°**	
	ZD	+1:00	**CE** + 2:15	**S-19 KTS**	
	GMT	10:30	**CCT** 10:30:40		
			GMT 10:30:40	**DR**	09:30 – 05:15
				Time	09:30
				LAT	20° 53.0' s
				LONG	017° 56.0' W

Almanac

GHA	329° 47.9'	**DEC**	N 8° 43.3'	**Hs**	40° 15.9'
M/S	+ 7° 40.0'	**d(+0.9)**	+ 0.5'	**Ic**	+2.5'
GHA	337° 27.9'	**DEC**	N 8° -43.8'	**Dip (57)**	-7.3'
±SHA/v				**Sum**	-4.8'
Sum	337° 27.9'			**Ha**	40° 11.1'
a λ	+17° 27.9'			**Alt**	+14.9'
LHA	320° 00.0'			**Ho**	40° 26.0'

LHA	320°	**DEC**	N 8° 43.8'	**LAT**	21 S	CONTRARY

Publication 229

			Z (8)	122.3	**Z to ZN**
Hc	41° 10.4'	**Z (9)**	123.3	
d	-36.6	**d**	+1.0	ZN = 180 - Z
Inc Dec (X)	43.8	**Inc Dec (X)**	43.8	180 – 123.0 = 057.0
Inv (÷)	60	**Inv (÷)**	60	**057.0**
Correction	-26.7	**Correction**	+0.7	
Hc	40° 43.7'	**Z**	**123.0**	
Ho	40° 26.0'			
a	**17.7A**			

Notes:

In USCG used closest Z

Celestial Problems

Sight Reduction

Problem # 30 (USCG) (2181)		Sun's Lower Limb		Chapter 11 4	

Date:	4 June	Time	06:30	**LAT:**	26° 15.0' S
				LONG	121° 20.0' W
ZT	09:15	**CT**	05:14:27	**C-**246°	
ZD	+8:00	**CE**	+0:53:	**S-**13 KTS	
GMT	17:15	**CCT**	05:15:20		
		GMT	17:15:20	**DR**	09:15 – 06:30
				Time	09:15
				LAT	26° 29.5' S
				LONG	121° 55.0' W

Almanac

GHA	75° 26.1'	**DEC**	N 22° 28.6'	**Hs**	25° 57.8'
M/S	+ 3° 50.0'	**d(+0.3)**	+0.1'	**Ic**	+2.1'
GHA	79° 16.1'	**DEC**	N 22° 28.7'	**Dip (39)**	-6.1'
±SHA/v				**Sum**	-4.0'
Sum	79° 16.1'			**Ha**	25°-53.8'
a λ	- 122° 16.1'			**Alt**	+14.0'
LHA	317° 00.0'			**Ho**	26°-07.8'

LHA	317°	**DEC**	N 22° 28.7'	**LAT**	26 S	CONTRARY

Publication 229

		Z (22)	135.1	**Z to ZN**
Hc	26° 26.4'	**Z (23)**	135.8	
d	-43.9	**d**	+0.7	ZN = 180 - Z
Inc Dec (X)	28.7	**Inc Dec (X)**	28.7	180 – 135.4 = 044.6
Inv (÷)	60	**Inv (÷)**	60	**044.6**
Correction	-21.0	**Correction**	+0.3	
Hc	26° 05.4'	**Z**	135.4	
Ho	26° 07.8'			
a	2.4 T			

Notes:

In USCG used closest Z Also you must have a very accurate DR.

Celestial Problems
Sight Reduction

Problem # 31 (USCG) (2182)			**Sun's Lower Limb**			Chapter 11

Date:	**18 Aug**	Time		06:00	**LAT:**	19° 48.0' N
					LONG	108° 34.0' W
	ZT	10:36	**CT**	05:34:48	**S**- 166	
	ZD	+ 7:00	**CE**	+ 01:24	**C**-16.0 Kts	
	GMT	17:36	**CCT**	05:35:12		
			GMT	17:35:12	**DR**	0600-1036
					Time	1036
					LAT	18° 36.0' N
					LONG	108° 16.0' W

Almanac

GHA	74° 04.0'	**DEC**	N 12° 58.4'	**Hs**	
M/S	+ 8° 48.0'	**D (-.8)**	- .5'	**Ic**	
GHA	82° 52.0'	**DEC**	N 12° 57.9'	**Dip (61)**	_____
±SHA/v	_____			**Sum**	_____
Sum	82° 52.0'			**Ha**	
a λ	- 107° 52.0'			**Alt**	_____
LHA	335° 00.0'			**Ho**	

LHA	335°	**DEC**	N 12° 57.9'	**LAT**	19 N	CONTRARY

Publication 229

	64° 56.6'	**Z (12)**	102.6	**Z to ZN**	
Hc		**Z (13)**	100.3		
d	+ 18.8*	**d**	- 2.3	**ZN=Z**	
Inc Dec (X)	57.9'	**Inc Dec (X)**	57.9'	**100.4**	
Inv (÷)	60	**Inv (÷)**	60		
Correction	+ 18.2	**Correction**	- 2.2		
Hc	65° 14.8'	**Z**	**100.4**		
Ho	_____				
a					

Notes:

Celestial Problems
Sight Reduction

Problem #32 (USCG) (2183)	Sun's Lower Limb	Chapter 11

Date:	29 June	Time	08:00	LAT:	26° 00.0 N
				LONG	75° 29.5 W
	ZT	08:00	CT	01:00:00	C -
	ZD	+ 5:00	CE	- 00:00	S -
	GMT	13:00	CCT	01:00:00	
			GMT	13:00:00	DR
					Time
					LAT
					LONG

Almanac

GHA	14° 09.5'	DEC	N 23° 13.0'	Hs	
M/S	0	d		Ic	
GHA	14° 09.5'	DEC	N 23° 13.0'	Dip (61)	
±SHA/v				Sum	
Sum	14° 09.5'			Ha	
a λ	- 75° 09.5'			Alt	
LHA	299° 00.0'			Ho	

LHA	299°	DEC	N 23° 13.0'	LAT	26° N	SAME

Publication 229

			Z (23)	079.1	Z to ZN
Hc	34° 55.0'	Z (24)	077.9	
d	+ 16.8	d	- 1.2	ZN=Z
Inc Dec (X)	13.0'	Inc Dec (X)	13.0'	
Inv (÷)	60	Inv (÷)	60	078.9
Correction	+ 3.6	Correction	- .3	
Hc	34° 58.6'	Z	078.9	
Ho				
a				

Notes:

Celestial Problems
Sight Reduction

Problem # 33 (USCG) (2184)	Sun's Lower Limb	Chapter 11

Date:	9 May		Time	13:00	**LAT:**	24° 00.0 N
					LONG	83° 26.0 W
	ZT	13:00	**CT**	07:00:00	**C -**	
	ZD	+ 6	**CE**	- 00:00	**S -**	
	GMT	19:00	**CCT**	07:00:00		
			GMT	19:00:00	**DR**	
					Time	
					LAT	
					LONG	

Almanac

GHA	105° 54.4'	**DEC**	N 17°29.0'	**Hs**	
M/S	0	**d**		**Ic**	
GHA	105° 54.4'	**DEC**	N 17°29.0'	**Dip (61)**	
±SHA/v				**Sum**	
Sum	105° 54.4'			**Ha**	
a λ	- 83° 54.4'			**Alt**	
LHA	22° 00.0'			**Ho**	

LHA	22°	**DEC**	N 17° 29.0'	**LAT**	24 N	SAME

Publication 229

			Z (17)	104.6	**Z to ZN**
Hc	68° 16.1'	**Z (18)**	102.1	
d	+ 21.8*	**d**	- 2.5	ZN=360-Z
Inc Dec (X)	29.0'	**Inc Dec (X)**	29.0'	360 – 103.4 = 256.6
Inv (÷)	60	**Inv (÷)**	60	**256.6**
Correction	+ 10.7*	**Correction**	-1.2	
Hc	68° 26.8'	**Z**	103.4	
Ho				
a				

Notes:

Celestial Problems
Sight Reduction

Problem #34 (USCG) (2185)	Sun's Lower Limb	Chapter 11

Date:	**21 Oct**	Time	10:00	**LAT:**	29° 00.0 N
				LONG	134° 40.0 E
	ZT	10:00	**CT**	01:00:00	**C-**
	ZD	- 9:00	**CE**	- 00:00	**S-**
	GMT	01:00	**CCT**	01:00:00	
			GMT	01:00:00	**DR**
					Time
					LAT
					LONG

Almanac

GHA	198° 49.3'	**DEC**	S 10° 36.0'	**Hs**	
M/S	0	**d**		**Ic**	
GHA	198° 49.3'	**DEC**	S 10° 36.0'	**Dip (61)**	
±SHA/v				**Sum**	
Sum	198° 49.3'			**Ha**	
a λ	+ 134° 10.7'			**Alt**	
LHA	333° 00.0 '			**Ho**	

LHA	64°	**DEC**	S 10° 36.0'	**LAT**	29 N	CONTRARY

Publication 229

		Z (10)	142.2	**Z to ZN**	
Hc	43° 06.0'	**Z (11)**	143.0		
d	- 50.5	**d**	+ .8	ZN =360 - Z	
Inc Dec (X)	36.0'	**Inc Dec (X)**	36.0'	360 - 142.7 = 217.3	
Inv (÷)	60	**Inv (÷)**	60	**217.3**	
Correction	- 30.3	**Correction**	+ .5		
Hc	42° 35.7'	**Z**	142.7		
Ho					
a					

Notes:

SIGHT REDUCTION
RUNNING FIX SUN AND LAN

Chapter 13, Celestial Navigation (Upon Oceans Endorsement)

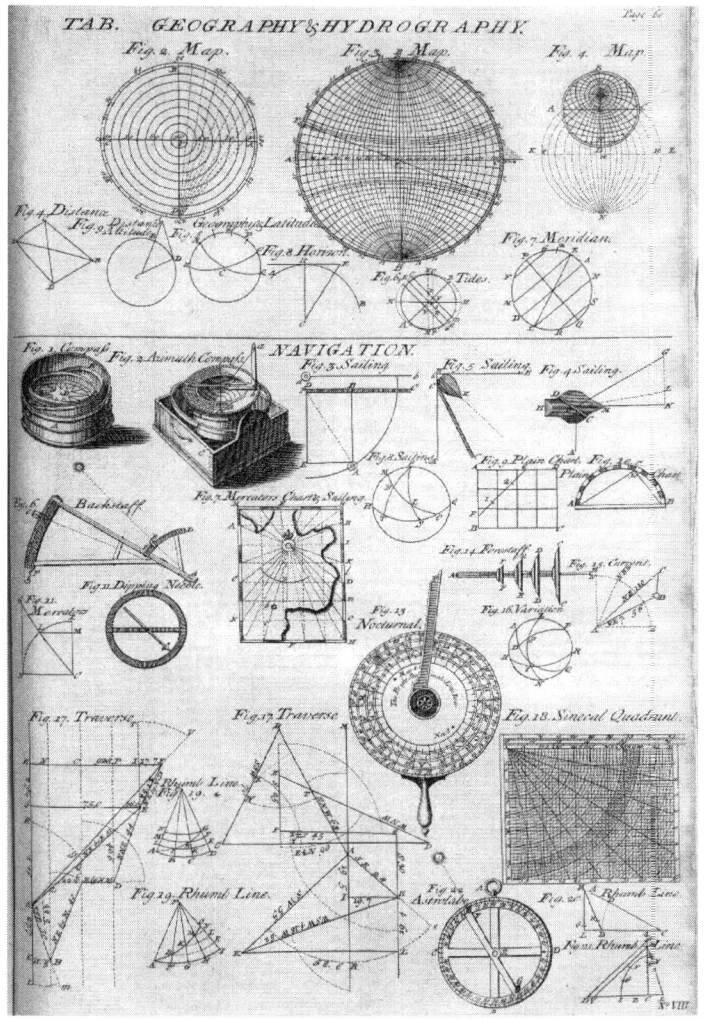

BY

Alexander F. Hickethier MBA

And

Dr. Hu, Jia Shen

Sight Reduction

In This module we will discussed the basic theory of sight reduction and presented a method to be followed when reducing sights. This section puts that method into practice in reducing sights of the Sun and LAN.

00998. On **23 May 1981**, your **0628** zone time position was **LAT 28° 18.0' S, LONG 102° 42.0' E**. Your vessel was steaming on course **040° T** at a speed of **20.0 knots**. An observation of the Sun's lower limb was made at **0758 ZT**. The chronometer read **01h 02m 06s** and was fast **04m 04s**. The observed altitude (Hc) was **13° 16.7'**. LAN occurred at **1201** zone time. The observed altitude (Ho) was **42° 32.0'**.

What was the longitude of your 1201 zone time running fix?

A. LONG 103° 57.9' E
B. LONG 104° 00.4' E
C. LONG 104° 03.5' E
D. LONG 104° 06.3' E

SECTION 1 Time, (Zone Time, Chronometer Time and GMT) DR Calculations

<table>
<tr><td colspan="8" align="center">Celestial Problems
Sight Reduction – LAN Running Fix</td></tr>
<tr><td colspan="4">Problem #   (USCG)   (00998)</td><td colspan="4" align="center">Chapter 13 - 9</td></tr>
<tr><td>Date:</td><td>23 May</td><td colspan="3" align="center">Time 06:28</td><td colspan="2">LAT:</td><td>28°-18.0 S</td></tr>
<tr><td></td><td></td><td></td><td></td><td></td><td colspan="2">LONG</td><td>102°-42.0 E</td></tr>
<tr><td></td><td>ZT</td><td>07:58</td><td>CT</td><td>01:02:06</td><td colspan="3">S-20.0°</td></tr>
<tr><td></td><td>ZD</td><td>-7:00</td><td>CE</td><td>-04:04</td><td colspan="3">C-040kts</td></tr>
<tr><td></td><td>GMT</td><td>00:58</td><td>CCT</td><td>00:58:02</td><td colspan="3"></td></tr>
<tr><td></td><td></td><td></td><td>GMT</td><td>00:58:02</td><td colspan="2">DR</td><td>1.8h x 20kts = 36 mi</td></tr>
<tr><td></td><td></td><td></td><td></td><td></td><td colspan="2">Time</td><td>06:28 to 08:16</td></tr>
<tr><td></td><td></td><td></td><td></td><td></td><td colspan="2">LAT</td><td>27° 40.4.0' S</td></tr>
<tr><td></td><td></td><td></td><td></td><td></td><td colspan="2">LONG</td><td>103° 0.05' E</td></tr>
</table>

Zone Time: (ZT) Correct the observation time with watch error to determine zone time.

Zone Description: (ZD) We determine **(ZD)** by dividing our Sight Time DR Longitude by 15 and rounding to the nearest whole number. Enter the zone description of the time zone indicated by the DR longitude. If the longitude is west of the Greenwich Meridian, the zone description is positive. Conversely, if the longitude is east of the Greenwich Meridian, the zone description is negative. The zone description represents the correction necessary to convert local time to Greenwich Mean Time.

Greenwich Mean Time: (GMT) Add to the zone description the zone time to determine Greenwich Mean Time.

Date: Carefully evaluate the time correction applied above and determine if the correction has changed the date.

Enter the GMT date.	23 May
Chronometer Time: (CT)	01:02:06
Chronometer Error: (ZT)	07:58
Corrected Chronometer Time (CTT)	00:58:02
Greenwich Mean Time: (GMT)	00:58:02 23 May

SECTION 2 Nautical Almanac Calculations

Almanac

GHA	180°-50.8'	DEC	N20°-31.1'		LAN	
M/S	14°-30.5'	d (+0.5)	+ 0.5'	ZT		12:01
GHA	195°-21.3'	DEC	N20°-31.6'	ZD		-7:00
a λ	102°-38.7'			GMT		05:01
LHA	298°-00.0'			DEC		N20°-33.5'
				d (+0.5)		0
				DEC		N 20°-33.5'
						89°-60.0'
				- Ho		42°-32.0'
				Z Dist		47°-28.0'
				± Dec		- 20°-33.5'
				LAT		26°-54.5'

In this section we determine two of the three arguments required to enter *Pub. 229*: Local Hour Angle (LHA) and Declination, using the Nautical Almanac. This section employs the principle that a celestial body's LHA is the algebraic sum of its Greenwich Hour Angle (GHA) and the observer's longitude. Therefore, the basic method employed in this section is:

(1) Determine the body's GHA;
(2) Determine an assumed longitude;
(3) Algebraically combine the two quantities, remembering to subtract a western assumed longitude from GHA and to add an eastern longitude to GHA; and
(4) Extract the declination of the body from the appropriate *Almanac* table, correcting the tabular value if required.

Tabulated GHA and (2) *v* Correction Factor:
For the Sun, the Moon, or a planet, extract the value for the whole hour of GHA corresponding to the sight. For example, if the sight was obtained at 00:58:02 GMT, extract the GHA value for 0000. For a star sight reduction, extract the value of the GHA of Aries (GHA), again using the value corresponding to the whole hour of the time of the sight.

For a planet or Moon sight reduction, enter the *v* correction value. This quantity is not applicable to a Sun or star sight. The *v* correction for a planet sight is found at the bottom of the column for each particular planet. The *v* correction factor for the Moon is located directly beside the tabulated hourly GHA values. The *v* correction factor for the Moon is always positive. If a planet's *v* correction factor is listed without sign, it is positive. If listed with a negative sign, the planet's *v* correction factor is negative. This *v* correction factor is not the magnitude of the *v* correction; it is used later to enter the Increments and Correction table to determine the magnitude of the correction.

GHA Increment: The GHA increment serves as an interpolation factor, correcting for the time that the sight differed from the whole hour. For example, in the sight at 13-50-45 discussed above, this increment correction accounts for the 50 minutes and 45 seconds after the whole hour at which the sight was taken. Obtain this correction value from the Increments and Corrections tables in the *Almanac*. The entering arguments for these tables are the minutes and seconds after the hour at which the sight was taken and the body sighted. Extract the proper correction from the applicable table and enter the correction.

Sidereal Hour Angle or *v* Correction: If reducing a star sight, enter the star's Sidereal Hour Angle (SHA). The SHA is found in the star column of the daily pages of the *Almanac*. The SHA combined with the GHA of Aries results in the star's GHA. The SHA entry is applicable only to a star. If reducing a planet or Moon sight, obtain the *v* correction from the Increments and Corrections Table. The correction is a function of only the *v* correction factor; its magnitude is the same for both the Moon and the planets.

GHA: A star's GHA equals the sum of the Tabulated GHA of Aries, the GHA Increment, and the star's SHA. The Sun's GHA equals the sum of the Tabulated GHA and the GHA Increment. The GHA of the Moon or a planet equals the sum of the Tabulated GHA, the GHA Increment, and the *v* correction.

+ or – 360° (if needed): Since the LHA will be determined from subtracting or adding the assumed longitude to the GHA, adjust the GHA by 360° if needed to facilitate the addition or subtraction.

Assumed Longitude: If the vessel is west of the prime meridian, the assumed longitude will be subtracted from the GHA to determine LHA. If the vessel is east of the prime meridian, the assumed longitude will be added to the GHA to determine the LHA. Select the assumed longitude to meet the following two criteria: (1) When added or subtracted (as applicable) to the GHA determined above, a whole degree of LHA will result; and (2) It is the longitude closest to that DR longitude that meets criterion (1).

Local Hour Angle (LHA): Combine the body's GHA with the assumed longitude as discussed above to determine the body's LHA.

Tabulated Declination and *d* Correction factor:

(1) Obtain the tabulated declination for the Sun, the Moon, the stars, or the planets from the daily pages of the *Almanac*. The declination values for the stars are given for the entire three day period covered by the daily page of the *Almanac*. The values for the Sun, Moon, and planets are listed in hourly increments. For these bodies, enter the declination value for the whole hour of the sight. For example, if the sight is at 12-58-40, enter the tabulated declination for 1200.

(2) There is no *d* correction factor for a star sight. There are *d* correction factors for Sun, Moon, and planet sights. Similar to the v correction factor discussed above, the *d* correction factor does not equal the magnitude of the *d* correction; it provides the argument to enter the Increments and Corrections tables in the *Almanac*. The sign of the *d* correction factor, which determines the sign of the *d* correction, is determined by the trend of declination values, not the trend of *d* values. The *d* correction factor is simply an interpolation factor; therefore, to determine its sign, look at the declination values for the hours that frame the time of the sight. For example, suppose the sight was taken on a certain date at 12-30-00. Compare the declination value for 1200 and 1300 and determine if the declination has increased or decreased. If it has increased, the *d* correction factor is positive. If it has decreased, the *d* correction factor is negative.

d **correction:** Enter the Increments and Corrections table with the *d* correction factor discussed above. Extract the proper correction, being careful to retain the proper sign.

True Declination: Combine the tabulated declination and the *d* correction to obtain the true declination.

Assumed Latitude: Choose as the assumed latitude that whole value of latitude closest to the vessel's DR latitude. If the assumed latitude and declination are both north or both south, label the assumed latitude "Same." If one is north and the other is south, label the assumed latitude "Contrary."

SECTION FOUR uses the arguments of assumed latitude, LHA, and declination determined in Section Three to enter *Pub. 229* to determine azimuth and computed altitude. Then, Section Four compares computed and observed altitudes to calculate the altitude intercept. From this the LOP is plotted.

LHA	298°	DEC	N 20°-31.6	LAT	27°-40.4 S
		Publication 229			
		Z (20)	121.5	**Z to ZN**	
Hc	13°-45.4	Z (21)	122.2		
d	-35.5	d	+0.7	ZN=180-Z	
Inc Dec (X)	31.6	Inc Dec (X)	31.6	180 – 121.9 = **58.1**	
Inv (÷)	60	Inv (÷)	60		
Correction	-18.7	Correction	+0.4		
Hc	13°-26.7	Z	121.9		
Ho	13°-16.7				
A	10.0A				

Declination Increment and *d* Interpolation Factor: Note that two of the three arguments used to enter *Pub. 229*, LHA and latitude, are whole degree values. Section Three does not determine the third argument, declination, as a whole degree. Therefore, the navigator must interpolate in *Pub. 229*, for declination, given whole degrees of LHA and latitude. The first steps of Section Four involve this interpolation for declination. Since declination values are tabulated every whole degree in *Pub. 229*, the declination increment is the minutes and tenths of the true declination. For example, if the true declination is 20°-31.6', then the declination increment is 31.6'.

Pub. 229 also lists a *d* Interpolation Factor. This is the magnitude of the difference between the two successive tabulated values for declination that frame the true declination. Therefore, for the hypothetical declination listed above, the tabulated *d* interpolation factor listed in the table would be the difference between declination values given for 20° and 21°. If the declination increases between these two values, *d* is positive. If the declination decreases between these two values, *d* is negative.

Computed Altitude (Tabulated): Enter *Pub. 229* with the following arguments:
(1) LHA from Section Three;
(2) assumed latitude from Section Three;
(3) the whole degree value of the true declination. For example, if the true declination were 13° 15.6', then enter *Pub. 229* with 20° as the value for declination. Record the tabulated computed altitude.

Double Second Difference Correction: Use this correction when linear interpolation of declination for computed altitude is not sufficiently accurate due to the nonlinear change in the computed altitude as a function of declination. The need for double second difference interpolation is indicated by the *d* interpolation factor appearing in italic type followed by a small dot. When this procedure must be employed, refer to detailed instructions in the introduction to *Pub. 229*.

Total Correction: The total correction is the sum of the double second difference (if required) and the interpolation corrections. Calculate the interpolation correction by dividing the declination increment by 60' and multiply the resulting quotient by the *d* interpolation factor.

Computed Altitude (h$_c$): Apply the total correction, being careful to carry the correct sign, to the tabulated computed altitude. This yields the computed altitude. 13° 26.7'

Observed Altitude (h_o): Enter the observed altitude from the USCG Question

Altitude Intercept: Compare h_c and h_o. Subtract the smaller from the larger. The resulting difference is the magnitude of the altitude intercept. If h_o is greater than h_c, then label the altitude intercept "Toward." If h_c is greater than h_o, then label the altitude intercept "Away."

Azimuth Angle: Obtain the azimuth angle (Z) from *Pub. 229*, using the same arguments which determined tabulated computed altitude. Visual interpolation is sufficiently accurate.

True Azimuth: Calculate the true azimuth (Z_n) from the azimuth angle (Z) as follows:

a)   If in northern latitudes:

        LHA > 180°, then $Z_n = Z$
        LHA < 180°, then $Z_n = 360° - Z$

b)   If in southern latitudes:

        LHA > 180°, then $Z_n = 180° - Z$
        LHA < 180°, then $Z_n = 180° + Z$

Running Fix using the Sun AND LAN
Chapter 13, Celestial for Master/Mate limited Upon Oceans

1. 00976. On 7 November 1981, your 0830 zone time position was LAT 27° 36.0' N, LONG 162° 19.0' W. Your vessel was steaming on course 289° T at a speed of 19.0 knots. An observation of the Sun's lower limb was made at 0945 ZT. The chronometer read 08h 43m 11s and was slow 01m 51s. The observed altitude (Ho) was 38° 21.1'. LAN occured at 1138 zone time. The observed altitude (Ho) was 45° 35.0'. What was the longitude of your 1200 zone time running fix?

A. LONG 163° 38.8' W
B. LONG 163° 34.0' W
C. LONG 163° 30.2' W
D. LONG 163° 26.0' W

2. 00977. On 8 February 1981, your 0800 zone time position was LAT 28° 55.0' S, LONG 52° 27.0' W. Your vessel was steaming on course 036° T at a speed of 19.0 knots. An observation on the Sun's lower limb was made at 0938 ZT. The chronometer read 12h 37m 23s and was slow 01m 24s. The observed altitude (Ho) was 45° 29.2'. LAN occurred at 1240 zone time. The observed altitude (Ho) was 77° 10.5'. What was the longitude of your 1200 zone time running fix?

A. LONG 51° 29.6' W
B. LONG 51° 31.4' W
C. LONG 51° 33.1' W
D. LONG 51° 35.4' W

3. 00978. On 11 November 1981, your 0730 zone time position was LAT 19° 58.0' N, LONG 143° 54.0' W. Your vessel was steaming on course 084° T at a speed of 15.0 knots. An observation of the Sun's lower limb was made at 0931 ZT. The chronometer read 07h 29m 22s and was slow 02m 22s. The observed altitude (Ho) was 44° 17.6'. LAN occurred at 1125 zone time (ZD+10).The observed altitude (Ho) was 52° 17.4'. What was the longitude of your 1200 zone time running fix?

A. LONG 142° 34.7' W
B. LONG 142° 37.1' W
C. LONG 142° 40.2' W
D. LONG 142° 44.2' W

4. 00980. On 29 April 1981, your 0530 zone time position was LAT 23° 04.0' S, LONG 162° 12.0' E. Your vessel was steaming on course 120° T at a speed of 9.0 knots. An observation of the Sun's upper limb was made at 0830 ZT. The chronometer read 09h 27m 32s and was slow 02m 24s. The observed altitude (Ho) was 24° 58.0'. LAN occurred at 1205 zone time. The observed altitude (Ho) was 52° 04.0'. What was the longitude of your 1200 zone time running fix?

A. LONG 163° 02.1' E
B. LONG 163° 06.0' E
C. LONG 163° 09.5' E
D. LONG 163° 11.3' E

5. 00981. On 20 September 1981, your 0730 zone time position was LAT 28° 58.0' N, LONG 152° 26.0' W. Your vessel was steaming on course 225° T at a speed of 19.0 knots. An observation of the Sun's lower limb was made at 0931 ZT. The chronometer 07h 29m 20s and was slow 02m 22s. The observed altitude (Ho) was 44° 14.4'. LAN occurred at 1206 zone time. The observed altitude (Ho) was 62° 49.5'. What was the longitude of your 1200 zone time running fix?

A. LONG 153° 32.5' W
B. LONG 153° 27.2' W
C. LONG 153° 24.5' W
D. LONG 153° 20.0' W

6. 00982. On 15 August 1981, your 0512 zone time position was LAT 29° 18.0' N, LONG 57° 24.0' W. Your vessel was steaming on course 262° T at a speed of 20.0 knots. An observation of the Sun's lower limb was made at 0824 ZT. The chronometer read 00h 22m 24s and was slow 01m 34s. The observed altitude (Ho) was 38° 16.7'. LAN occurred at 1204 zone time. The observed altitude (Ho) was 74° 58.0'. What was the longitude of your 1204 zone time running fix?

A. LONG 59° 52.0' W
B. LONG 59° 54.0' W
C. LONG 59° 58.5' W
D. LONG 60° 02.0' W

7. 00983. On 17 January 1981, your 0730 zone time position was LAT 22° 26.0' N, LONG 152° 17.0' E. Your vessel was steaming on course 136° T at a speed of 17.0 knots. An observation of the Sun's lower limb was made at 1015 ZT. The chronometer read 00h 13m 23s and was slow 01m 49s. The observed altitude (Ho) was 40° 25.7'. LAN occurred at 1222 zone time. The observed altitude (Ho) was 47° 48.1'. What was the longitude of your 1200 zone time running fix?

A. LONG 153° 04.2' E
B. LONG 153° 08.3' E
C. LONG 153° 13.1' E
D. LONG 153° 18.6' E

8. 00984. On 28 July 1981, your 0800 zone time fix gives you a position of LAT 25° 16.0' N, LONG 71° 19.0' W. Your vessel is steaming a course of 026° T at a speed of 17.5 knots. An observation of the Sun's upper limb is made 0905 zone time, and the observed altitude (Ho) is 51° 06.8'. The chronometer reads 02h 07m 10s, and the chronometer error is 02m 24s fast. Local apparent noon occurs at 1149 zone time, and a meridian altitude of the Sun's lower limb is made. The observed altitude (Ho) for this sight is 82° 28.7'. Determine the vessel's 1200 zone time position.

A. LAT 26° 21.9' N, LONG 70° 46.1' W
B. LAT 26° 25.0' N, LONG 70° 46.0' W
C. LAT 26° 25.0' N, LONG 70° 48.1' W
D. LAT 26° 27.9' N, LONG 70° 45.5' W

17.0' E. Your vessel is steaming on a course of 116° T at a speed of 17 knots. An observation of the Sun's lower limb is made at 1015 zone time. The chronometer reads 00h 13m 23s, and the chronometer error is 01m 49s slow. The observed altitude (Ho) is 66° 02.1'. LAN occurs at 1152 zone time and a meridian altitude of the Sun's lower limb is made. Determine the vessel's observed altitude (Ho) is 87° 54.2'. Determine the vessel's 1200 zone time position.

A. LAT 22° 53.8' S, LONG 153° 25.6' E
B. LAT 22° 53.8' S, LONG 153° 28.8' E
C. LAT 22° 56.3' S, LONG 153° 25.6' E
D. LAT 22° 56.3' S, LONG 153° 28.8' E

10. 00988. On 29 June 1981, your 0800 zone time fix gives you a position of LAT 26° 16.0' S, LONG 61° 04.0' E. Your vessel is steaming a course of 079° T at a speed of 15.5 knots. An observation of the Sun's upper limb is made at 0905 zone time, and the observed altitude (Ho) is 25° 20.1. The chronometer reads 05h 08m 12s, and the chronometer error is 02m 27s fast. Local apparent noon occurs at 1154 zone time, and a meridian altitude of the Sun's lower limb is made. The observed altitude (Ho) for this sight is 40° 44.2'. Determine the vessel's 1200 zone time position.

A. LAT 26° 01.7' S, LONG 62° 03.1' E
B. LAT 26° 02.0' S, LONG 62° 23.2' E
C. LAT 26° 05.1' S, LONG 62° 06.3' E
D. LAT 25° 56.0' S, LONG 62° 03.0' E

9. 00987. On 17 January 1981, your 0730 zone time fix gives you a position of LAT 22° 26.0' S, LONG 152°

11. 00989. On 2 April 1981, your 0830 zone time fix gives you a position of LAT 20° 16.0' S, LONG 4° 12.0' E. Your vessel is steaming a course of 143° T at a speed of 18.0 knots. An observation of the Sun's upper limb is made at 0903 zone time, and the observed altitude (Ho) is 42° 39.6'. The chronometer reads 09h 05m 40s, and the chronometer error is 02m 15s fast. Local apparent noon occurs at 1145 zone time, and a meridian altitude of the Sun's lower limb is made. The observed altitude (Ho) for this sight is 63° 46.2'. Determine the vessel's 1200 zone time position.

A. LAT 21° 10.1' S, LONG 004° 53.9' E
B. LAT 21° 14.0' S, LONG 004° 55.0' E
C. LAT 21° 18.0' S, LONG 005° 00.5' E
D. LAT 22° 42.0' S, LONG 004° 57.0' E

12. 00990. On 24 March 1981, your 0800 zone time fix gives you a position of LAT 22° 16.0' N, LONG 31° 45.0' W. Your vessel is steaming a course of 285° T at a speed of 16.5 knots. An observation of the Sun's upper limb is made at 0938 zone time, and the observed altitude (Ho) is 46° 32.2'. The chronometer reads 11h 41m 01s, and the chronometer error is 02m 50s fast. Local apparent noon occurs at 1214 zone time, and a meridian altitude of the Sun's lower limb is made. The observed altitude (Ho) for this sight is 68° 55.8'. Determine the vessel's 1200 zone time position.

A. LAT 22° 35.0' N, LONG 30° 29.0' W
B. LAT 22° 35.0' N, LONG 32° 51.0' W
C. LAT 22° 36.0' N, LONG 32° 10.5' W
D. LAT 22° 36.0' N, LONG 32° 55.2' W

13. 00995. On 17 October 1981, your 0536 zone time position was LAT 24° 34.0' N, LONG 150° 46.0' W. Your vessel was steaming on course 075° T at a speed of 12.0 knots. An observation of the Sun's lower limb was made at 0830 ZT. The chronometer read 06h 32m 48s and was fast 02m 42s. The observed altitude (Ho) was 31° 20.7'. LAN occurred at 1143 zone time. The observed altitude (Ho) was 55° 37.6'. What was the longitude of your 1200 zone time running fix?

A. LONG 149° 19.3' W
B. LONG 149° 22.4' W
C. LONG 149° 26.8' W
D. LONG 149° 29.2' W

14. 00996. On 30 August 1981, your 0554 zone time position was LAT 25° 39.0' S, LONG 31° 51.0' E. Your vessel was steaming on course 325° T at a speed of 15.0 knots. An observation of the Sun's lower limb was made at 0836 ZT. The chronometer read 06h 38m 36s and was fast 02m 24s. The observed altitude (Ho) was 30° 49.2'. LAN occurred at 1157 zone time. The observed altitude (Ho) was 56° 40.0'. What was the longitude of you 1157 zone time running fix?

A. LONG 30° 59.8' E
B. LONG 30° 57.6' E
C. LONG 30° 55.9' E
D. LONG 30° 52.5' E

15. 00997. On 20 November 1981, your 0612 zone time position was LAT 25° 38.0' N, LONG 166° 54.0' W. Your vessel was steaming on course 126° T at a speed of 20.0 knots. An observation of the Sun's lower limb was made at 0854 ZT. The chronometer read 07h 51m 14s and was slow 02m 52s. The observed altitude (Ho) was 27° 58.3'. LAN occurred at 1147 zone time. The observed altitude (Ho) was 45° 35.0'. What was the longitude of you 1147 zone time running fix?

A. LONG 165° 20.2' W
B. LONG 165° 18.4' W
C. LONG 165° 15.8' W
D. LONG 165° 12.5' W

16. 00998. On 23 May 1981, your 0628 zone time position was LAT 28° 18.0' S, LONG 102° 42.0' E. Your vessel was steaming on course 040° T at a speed of 20.0 knots. An observation of the Sun's lower limb was made at 0758 ZT. The chronometer read 01h 02m 06s and was fast 04m 04s. The observed altitude (Ho) was 13° 16.7'. LAN occurred at 1201 zone time. The observed altitude (Ho) was 42° 32.0'. What was the longitude of your 1201 zone time running fix?

A. LONG 103° 57.9' E
B. LONG 104° 00.4' E
C. LONG 104° 03.5' E
D. LONG 104° 06.3' E

17. 00999. On 16 February 1981, your 0640 zone time position was LAT 23° 46.0' N, LONG 156° 24.0' W. Your vessel was steaming on course 222° T at a speed of 18.0 knots. An observation of the Sun's lower limb was made at 0910 ZT. The chronometer read 07h 08m 06s and was slow 01m 56s. The observed altitude (Ho) was 27° 15.8'. LAN occurred at 1245 zone time (ZD +10). The observed altitude (Ho) was 55° 25.3'. What was the longitude of your 1245 zone time running fix?

A. LONG 157° 37.2' W
B. LONG 157° 42.0' W
C. LONG 157° 45.7' W
D. LONG 157° 47.2' W

18. 01008. On 27 March 1981, your 0730 zone time position is LAT 28° 16' N, LONG 56° 37' W. Your vessel is on course 158° T at a speed of 15.0 knots. An observation of the Sun's lower limb is made at 0915 zone time. The chronometer reads 01h 14m 11s, and the chronometer error is 00m 53s slow. The observed altitude (Ho) is 45° 10.7'. LAN occurs at 1150 zone time, and a meridian altitude of the Sun's lower limb is made. The observed altitude (Ho) is 65° 32.8'. Determine the vessel's 1200 zone time position.

A. LAT 27° 08.8' N, LONG 56° 04.2' W
B. LAT 27° 08.8' N, LONG 56° 10.3' W
C. LAT 27° 11.6' N, LONG 56° 04.2' W
D. LAT 27° 11.6' N, LONG 56° 10.3' W

19. 01009. On 22 February 1981, your 0800 zone time position is LAT 24° 16' S, LONG 95° 37' E. Your vessel is on course 126° T at a speed of 14 knots. An observation of the Sun's lower limb is made at 0945 zone time. The chronometer reads 03h 47m 22s, and the chronometer error is 02m 37s fast. The observed altitude (Ho) is 57° 02.1'. LAN occurs at 1148 zone time, and a meridian altitude of the Sun's lower limb is made. The observed meridian altitude (Ho) is 75° 22.3'. Determine the vessel's 1200 zone time position. Determine the vessel's 1200 zone time position.

A. LAT 24° 49.3' S, LONG 96° 24.0' E
B. LAT 24° 49.3' S, LONG 96° 27.2' E
C. LAT 24° 52.2' S, LONG 96° 24.0' E
D. LAT 24° 52.2' S, LONG 96° 27.2' E

20. 01010. On 8 February 1981, your 0800 zone time position is LAT 21° 55' S, LONG 52° 27' W. Your vessel is on course 056° T at a speed of 17.5 knots. An observation of the Sun s lower limb is made at 0938 zone time, and the observed altitude (Ho) is 46° 06.5'. The chronometer reads 12h 37m 23s, and the chronometer error is 1m 24s slow. LAN occurs at 1243 zone time, and a meridian altitude of the Sun's lower limb is madeDetermine the vessel's 1200 zone time position. 83° 56.1' Determine the vessel's 1200 zone time position.

A. LAT 20° 57.0' S, LONG 51° 21.5' W
B. LAT 20° 58.0' S, LONG 51° 25.5' W
C. LAT 21° 04.0' S, LONG 51° 12.0' W
D. LAT 21° 04.0' S, LONG 51° 21.5' W

ANSWERS

1.	00976 A		12.	00990 B
2.	00977 D		13.	00995 B
3.	00978 C		14.	00996 D
4.	00980 B		15.	00997 D
5.	00981 C		16.	00998 C
6.	00982 C		17.	00999 B
7.	00983 C		18.	01008 A
8.	00984 D		19.	01009 C
9.	00987 A		20.	01010 D
10.	00988 A			
11.	00989 C			

Celestial Problems				
Sight Reduction – LAN Running Fix				
Problem # 1 (USCG) (00976)			Chapter 13	

Date:	7 Nov	Time	0830	**LAT:**	27° 36.0' N
				LONG	162° 19.0' E
	ZT	09:45	**CT**	08:43:11	**C**-289°
	ZD	+ 11:00	**CE**	+ 01:51	**S** -19.0 kts
	GMT	20:45	**CCT**	08:45:02	
			GMT	20:45:02	**DR**	0830 - 0945
					Time	0945
					LAT	27° 43.7' N
					LONG	162° 44.0' E

Almanac					
GHA	124° 03.9'	**DEC**	S 16° 26.0'		**LAN**
M/S	+ 11° 15.5'	**d (+0.7)**	+ .5'	**ZT**	11:38
GHA	135° 19.4'	**DEC**	S 16° 26.5'	**ZD**	+ 11:00
a λ	- 162° 19.4'			**GMT**	22:38
LHA	333° 00.0'			**DEC**	S 16° 27.4'
				d (+0.7)	+ .4'
				DEC	S 16° 27.8'
					89° 60.0'
				- Ho	45° 35.0'
				Z Dist	44° 25.0'
				± Dec	- 16° 27.8'
				LAT	27° 57.2'

LHA	333°	**DEC**	S 16° 26.5'	**LAT**	28 N	CONTRARY

Publication 229					
		Z (16)	145.9		**Z to ZN**
Hc	39° 49.0'	**Z (17)**	146.6		
d	- 51.2'	**d**	+ .7		ZN=Z
Inc Dec (X)	26.5'	**Inc Dec (X)**	26.5		146.0
Inv (÷)	60	**Inv (÷)**	60		
Correction	- 22.5'	**Correction**	+ .3		
Hc	38° 26.5'	**Z**	**146.0**		
Ho	38° 21.1'				
A	5.4 A				

Notes:
Required Fix at 12:00
DR   1200 - 0945 = 135 X 19/60= 42.8 NM
DR   1138 - 1200 = 22 X 19/60 = 7.0
Dlat =   7.0 x cos 289 = 2.3

Celestial Problems					
Sight Reduction – LAN Running Fix					
Problem # 2 (USCG) (00977)				Chapter 13	

Date:	8 Feb		Time	0800	**LAT:**	28° 55.0′ S
					LONG	052° 27.0′ E
	ZT	09:38	**CT**	12:37:23	**C**-036°	
	ZD	+ 3:00	**CE**	+ 01:24	**S** -19.0 kts	
	GMT	12:38	**CCT**	12:38:47		
			GMT	12:38:47	**DR**	0800 - 0938
					Time	0938
					LAT	29° 20.0′ S
					LONG	052° 49.0′ E

Almanac						
GHA	356° 26.4′	**DEC**	S 14° 55.5′		**LAN**	
M/S	+ 9° 41.8′	**d (-0.8)**	- .5	**ZT**		12:40
GHA	366° 08.2′	**DEC**	S 14° 55.0	**ZD**		+ 3:00
a λ	- 52° 08.2′			**GMT**		15:40
LHA	314° 00.0′			**DEC**		S 14° 53.1′
				d (+0.8)		- .5′
				DEC		S 14° 52.6′
						89° 60.0′
				- Ho		77° 10.5′
				Z Dist		12° 49.5′
				± Dec		+ 14° 52.6′
				LAT		27° 42.1′

LHA	314°	**DEC**	S 14° 55.0′	**LAT**	28 S	SAME

Publication 229					
		Z (14)	098.4	**Z to ZN**	
Hc	45° 07.8′	**Z (15)**	097.1		
d	+ 25.7′	**d**	+ 1.3	ZN=180-Z	
Inc Dec (X)	55.0′	**Inc Dec (X)**	55.0		
Inv (÷)	60′	**Inv (÷)**	60	**180 – 97.2 = 82.8**	
Correction	23.6′	**Correction**	- 1.2		
Hc	45° 31.4′	**Z**	97.2		
Ho	45° 29.2′				
A	**2.2 A**				

Notes:

Required Fix at 12:00

DR   0938 - 1200 = 142 X 19/60 = 44.96

DR   1200 - 1240 = 40 X 19 /60 = 12.66

Dlat =   12.7 X cos 036 = 10.3

Celestial Problems					
Sight Reduction – LAN Running Fix					
Problem # 3 (USCG) (00978)				Chapter 13	

Date:	11 Nov		Time	0800	**LAT:**	19° 58.0' N
					LONG	143° 54.0' W
	ZT	09:31	**CT**	07:29:22	**C**-084°	
	ZD	+ 10:00	**CE**	+ 02:22	**S** -15.0 kts	
	GMT	19:31	**CCT**	07:31:44		
			GMT	19:31:44	**DR**	0730 - 0931
					Time	0931
					LAT	20° 01.2' N
					LONG	143° 22.0' W

Almanac						
GHA	108° 58.6'	**DEC**	S 17° 33.3'		**LAN**	
M/S	+ 7° 56.0'	**d (+0.7)**	+ .4'	**ZT**		11:25
GHA	116° 54.6'	**DEC**	S 17° 33.7'	**ZD**		+ 10
a λ	- 142° 54.6'			**GMT**		21:25
LHA	334			**DEC**		S 17° 34.6'
				d (+0.7)		+ .3'
				DEC		S 17° 34.9'
						89° 60.0'
				- Ho		52° 17.4'
				Z Dist		37° 42.6'
				± Dec		- 17° 34.9'
				LAT		20° 07.7'

LHA	334°	**DEC**	S 17° 33.7'	**LAT**	20 N	CONTRARY

Publication 229						
			Z (17)	143.6	**Z to ZN**	
Hc	45° 02.8'	**Z (18)**	144.4		
d	- 48.9'	**d**	+ .8	ZN=Z	
Inc Dec (X)	33.7'	**Inc Dec (X)**	33.7	**144.0**	
Inv (÷)	60'	**Inv (÷)**	60		
Correction	- 27.5'	**Correction**	+ .4		
Hc	44° 35.3'	**Z**	**144.0**		
Ho	44° 17.6'				
A	**17.7 A**				

Notes:	
Required Fix at 12:00	
DR	0931-1200 = 149 X 15/60 = 37.25
DR	1125 -1200 =35 X 15/60 = + .8.75
Dlat =	8.75 X cos 84 = .9

Alexander F. Hickethier MBA © 2011-2013

Celestial Problems Sight Reduction – LAN Running Fix						
Problem # 4 (USCG) (00980)				Chapter 13		

Date:	29 Apr	Time	0800	**LAT:**	23° 04.0' S	
				LONG	162° 12.0' E	
	ZT	O8:30	**CT**	09:27:32	**C**-120°
	ZD	- 11:00	**CE**	+ 02:24	**S** -9.0 kts
	GMT	21:30	**CCT**	09:29:56	
28 Apr			**GMT**	21:29:56	**DR**	0530 - 0830
					Time	0830
					LAT	23° 17.5' S
					LONG	162° 37.5' E

Almanac					
GHA	135° 39.1'	**DEC**	N 14° 19.6'	**LAN (29 Apr)**	
M/S	+ 7° 29.0'	**d (+0.8)**	+ .4	**ZT**	12:05
GHA	143° 08.1'	**DEC**	N 14° 20.0'	**ZD**	- 11:00
a λ	+ 162° 51.9'			**GMT**	01:05
LHA	306° 00.0'			**DEC**	N 14° 22.7'
				d (+0.8)	+ .1'
				DEC	N 14° 22.8'
					89° 60.0'
				- Ho	52° 04.0'
				Z Dist	37° 56.0'
				± Dec	- 14° 22.8'
				LAT	23° 33.2'

LHA	306°	**DEC**	N 14° 20.0'	**LAT**	23 S	CONTRARY

Publication 229					
		Z (14)	119.6	**Z to ZN**	
Hc	25° 29.8'	**Z (15)**	120.5		
d	- 34.1'	**d**	+ .9	ZN=180-Z	
Inc Dec (X)	20.0'	**Inc Dec (X)**	20.0	180 – 119.9 =	
Inv (÷)	60'	**Inv (÷)**	60	**060.1**	
Correction	- 11.4'	**Correction**	+ .3		
Hc	25° 18.4'	**Z**	119.9		
Ho	24° 58.0'				
A	**20.4 A**				

Notes:

Required Fix at 1200

DR   0830-1200 = 210 X 9/60 = 31.5

DR   1205-1200 = 5 X 9/60 =.75 (Remember to retard the DR)

Dlat =   .75X COS 120 =.4

Celestial Problems					
Sight Reduction – LAN Running Fix					
Problem # 5 (USCG) (00981)				Chapter 13	

Date:	20 Sep.		Time		0730	**LAT:**	28° 58.0' N
						LONG	152° 26.0' W
	ZT	09:31	**CT**	07:29:20		**C-** 225°	
	ZD	+ 10:00	**CE**	+ 02:22		**S** -19.0 kts	
	GMT	19:12	**CCT**	07:31:42			
			GMT	19:31:42		**DR**	0730 - 0931
						Time	0931
						LAT	28° 29.0'N
						LONG	152° 45.0' W

Almanac						
GHA	106° 40.6'	**DEC**	N 0° 54.6'		**LAN**	
M/S	7° 55.5'	**d (-1.0)**	- .5	**ZT**		12:06
GHA	114° 36.1'	**DEC**	N 0° 54.1'	**ZD**		+ 10:00
a λ	- 152° 36.1'			**GMT**		22:06
LHA	322° 00.0'			**DEC**		N 0° 51.6'
				d (-1.0)		- .1'
				DEC		N 0° 51.5'
						89° 60.0'
				- Ho		62° 49.5'
				Z Dist		27° 10.5'
				± Dec		0° 51.0'
				LAT		28° 11.5'

LHA	322°	**DEC**	N 0° 54.1'	**LAT**	28 N	SAME

Publication 229					
		Z (0)	121.0	**Z to ZN**	
Hc	44° 05.3'	**Z (1)**	119.9		
d	+ 38.9'	**d**	- 1.1	**ZN=Z**	
Inc Dec (X)	54.1'	**Inc Dec (X)**	54.1		
Inv (÷)	60.0'	**Inv (÷)**	60.0	**120.0**	
Correction	35.1'	**Correction**	- 1.0		
Hc	44° 40.4'	**Z**	**120.0**		
Ho	44° 14.4'				
A	**26.0 A**				

Notes:
Required Fix at 1200
DR   1200 – 0931 = 229 x 19.0 / 60 = 72.5
DR   1206 – 1200 = 6 x 19.0 / 60 = 1.9
Dlat =   1.9 x cos 225° = 1.3

Celestial Problems				
Sight Reduction – LAN Running Fix				
Problem # 6 (USCG) (00982)			Chapter 13	

Date:	15 Aug.	Time	0512	**LAT:**	29° 18.0′ N
				LONG	57° 24.0′ W
	ZT	08:24	**CT** 00:22: 24	**C**-262°	
	ZD	+ 4:00	**CE** + 01:34	**S** -20.0 kts	
	GMT	12:12	**CCT** 00:23:58		
			GMT 12:23:58	**DR**	0515 - 0824
				Time	0824
				LAT	29° 09.0′ N
				LONG	058° 34.0′ W

Almanac						
GHA	358° 53.8′	**DEC**	N 13° 59.7′		**LAN**	
M/S	5° 59.5′	**d (-0.8)**	- .3′	**ZT**		12:04
GHA	364° 53.3′	**DEC**	N 13° 59.4′	**ZD**		+ 4:00
a λ	58° 53.3′			**GMT**		16:04
LHA	306° 00.0′			**DEC**		N 13° 56.6′
				d (-0.8)		0′
				DEC		N 13° 56.6′
						89° 60.0′
				- Ho		74° 58.8′
				Z Dist		15° 01.2′
				± Dec		13° 56.6′
				LAT		28° 57.8′

LHA	306°	**DEC**	N 13° 59.4′	**LAT**	29 N	SAME

Publication 229					
		Z (13)	095.9	**Z to ZN**	
Hc	37° 35.2′	**Z (14)**	094.7		
d	+ 26.7′	**d**	- .8	**ZN=Z**	
Inc Dec (X)	59.4′	**Inc Dec (X)**	59.4′		
Inv (÷)	60.0′	**Inv (÷)**	60.0′	**094.7**	
Correction	+ 26.4′	**Correction**	- .8		
Hc	38° 01.6′	**Z**	094.7		
Ho	38° 16.7′				
A	15.1 T				

Notes:

Required Fix at 1204

DR   1204 – 1024 = 220 x 20.0 / 60 = 73.3

DR   Fix time is time of LAN

Dlat =

Celestial Problems Sight Reduction – LAN Running Fix					
Problem # 7 (USCG) (00983)				Chapter 13	

Date:	17 Jan.		Time	0730	**LAT:**	22° 26.0' N
					LONG	152° 17.0' E
	ZT	10:15	**CT**	00:13:23	**C**-136°	
	ZD	- 10:00	**CE**	+ 01:49	**S** -17.0 kts	
	GMT	00:15	**CCT**	00:15:12		
			GMT	00:15:12	**DR**	0730 - 1015
					Time	1015
					LAT	21° 52.0' N
					LONG	152° 40.0' E

Almanac							
GHA	177° 29.8'	**DEC**	S 20° 47.9'			**LAN**	
M/S	3° 48.0'	**d (-0.5)**	- .1'	**ZT**			12:22
GHA	181° 17.8'	**DEC**	S 20° 47.8'	**ZD**			- 10:00
a λ	+ 152° 42.2'			**GMT**			02:22
LHA	334° 00.0'			**DEC**			S 20° 46.9'
				d (-0.5)			- .2'
				DEC			S 20° 46.7'
							89°-60.0'
				- Ho			47° 48.1'
				Z Dist			43° 11.9'
				± Dec			20° 46.7'
				LAT			22° 25.2'

LHA	334°	DEC	S 20° 47.8'	LAT	22 N	CONTRARY

Publication 229					
		Z (20)	147.0	**Z to ZN**	
Hc	40° 55.0'	**Z (21)**	147.7		
d	- 50.7'	**d**	+ .7	**ZN=Z**	
Inc Dec (X)	47.8'	**Inc Dec (X)**	47.8		
Inv (÷)	60.0'	**Inv (÷)**	60.0	**147.6**	
Correction	- 40.4'	**Correction**	+ .6		
Hc	40° 14.6'	**Z**	147.6		
Ho	40° 25.7'				
A	**11.1 T**				

Notes:
Required Fix at 1200
DR   1015 - 1200 = 105 x 17.0 / 60 =29.75
DR   1222 - 1200 = 22 x 17.0 / 60 = 6.2
Dlat =   6.2 x cos 136° = 4.5

Celestial Problems						
Sight Reduction – LAN Running Fix						
Problem # 8 (USCG) (00984)					Chapter 13 - 1	

Date:	28 July 1981		Time	0800	LAT:	25° 16.0 N
					LONG	071° 19.0 W
	ZT	09:05	**CT**	02:07:10	C- 026°	
	ZD	+5:00	**CE**	-0:02:24	S-17.5 kts	
	GMT	14:05	**CCT**	02:04:10		
			GMT	14:04:46	**DR**	08:16 - 0905
					Time	0905
					LAT	25° 33.0' N
					LONG	071° 10.0' E

						LAN	
GHA	28°-23.9'	**DEC**	N 18°-55.4'				
M/S	+ 1° 11.5'	**d (-.6)**	.0	**ZT**	11:49		
GHA	29° 35.4'	**DEC**	N 18° 53.7'	**ZD**	+5:00		
a λ	- 71° 35.4'			**GMT**	16:49		
LHA	319° 00.0'			**DEC**	N 18° 54.2'		
				D (-.6)	-.5'		
				DEC	N 18° 54.7'		
					89° 60.0'		
				- Ho	- 82° 28.7'		
				Z Dist	7° 31.3'		
				± Dec	+ 18° 53.7'		
				LAT	26° 25.0'		

LHA	319°	**DEC**	N 18° 55.4	**LAT**	26 N	SAME

		Z (18)	092.1		Z to ZN
Hc	50° 25.0'	**Z (19)**	090.6		
d	+19.3	**d**	-1.5		ZN=Z
Inc Dec (X)	55.4	**Inc Dec (X)**	55.4		
Inv (÷)	60	**Inv (÷)**	60		090.7
Correction	+17.8	**Correction**	-1.4		
Hc	50° 42.8'	**Z**	090.7		
Ho	51° 06.8'				
a	24.0 A				

Notes:

Required fix at 1200
DR   0905 – 1200 = 175 x 17.5 / 60 = 51.0 nm
DR   1149 - 1200 = 11 x 17.5 / 60 = 3.2 nm
Dlat =   3.2 x cos 026 = 2.79

Celestial Problems						
Sight Reduction – LAN Running Fix						
Problem # 9 (USCG) (00987)				Chapter 13 - 2		

Date:	17 Jan		Time	0730	**LAT:**	22° 26.0' S
					LONG	152° 17.0' E
	ZT	10:15	**CT**	00:13:23	**C-**116°	
	ZD	-10:00	**CE**	+1:49	**S-**17 kts	
	GMT	00:15	**CCT**	00:15:12		
			GMT	00:15:12	**DR**	0730 - 1015
					Time	1015
					LAT	22° 45.0' S
					LONG	153° 03.0' E

Almanac						
GHA	177° 29.8'	**DEC**	S 20°47.9'		**LAN**	
M/S	+ 3° 48.0'	**d (-0.5)**	- 0.1'	**ZT**	11:52	
GHA	181° 17.8'	**DEC**	S 20° 47.8'	**ZD**	-10:00	
a λ	+ 152° 42.2'			**GMT**	01:52	
LHA	334° 00.0'			**DEC**	S 20° 47.4'	
				D (-.5)	-0.4'	
				DEC	S 20° 47.0'	
					89° 60.0'	
				- Ho	- 87° 54.2'	
				Z Dist	2° 05.8'	
				± Dec	+ 20° 47.0'	
				LAT	22° 52.8'	

LHA	334°	**DEC**	S 20° 47.9	**LAT**	23° S	SAME

Publication 229						
			Z (20)	092.1	**Z to ZN**	
Hc	65°-39.4'	**Z (21)**	089.7		
d	+11.1'	**d**	- 2.4	ZN=180 - Z	
Inc Dec (X)	47.8'	**Inc Dec (X)**	47.8	180 – 090.2 = 089.8	
Inv (÷)	60'	**Inv (÷)**	60	**089.8**	
Correction	+8.0'	**Correction**	-1.9		
Hc	65°-48.2'	**Z**	090.2		
Ho	66° 02.1'				
a	**13.9 T**				

Notes:
Required Fix at 12:00
DR   1015 – 1200 = 105 x 17 / 60 = 29.75
DR   1152 – 1200 = 8 x 17 / 60 = 2.3
Dlat   2.3 x cos 116 = 1.0

Celestial Problems							
Sight Reduction – LAN Running Fix							
Problem # 10 (USCG) (0988)					Chapter 13 -3		

Date:	29 June		Time	0800	**LAT:**	26° 16.0' S	
					LONG	061° 04-0' E	
	ZT	09:05	**CT**	05:08:12	**C**-079°		
	ZD	-4:00	**CE**	- 0:02:27	**S**-15.5 Kts		
	GMT	05:05	**CCT**	05:05:45			
			GMT		**DR**	08:00 - 0905	
					Time	0905	
					LAT	26° 12.0' S	
					LONG	061° 22.0' E	

Almanac						
GHA	254° 10.5'	**DEC**	N 23° 14.1'		**LAN**	
M/S	+ 1° 26.3'	**d (-0.1)**	0'	**ZT**	11:54	
GHA	255° 36.8'	**DEC**	N 23° 14.1'	**ZD**	-4:00	
a λ	+ 61° 23.2'			**GMT**	07:54	
LHA	317° 00.0'			**DEC**	N 23° 13.9'	
				D(-0.1)	-0.1'	
				DEC	N 23° 13.8'	
					89° 60.0'	
				- Ho	- 40° 44.2'	
				Z Dist	49° 15.8'	
				± Dec	-23° 13.8'	
				LAT	26° 02.0'	

LHA	317°	**DEC**	N 23° 14.1'	**LAT**	26 S	CONTRARY

Publication 229				
		Z (23)	135.8	**Z to ZN**
Hc	25°-42.5'	**Z (24)**	136.6	
d	- 44.1'	**d**	+ 0.8	ZN=180-Z
Inc Dec (X)	14.1'	**Inc Dec (X)**	14.1	180-136.0 = 044.0
Inv (÷)	60'	**Inv (÷)**	60	**044.0**
Correction	-10.4'	**Correction**	+0.2	
Hc	25° 32.1'	**Z -**	136.0	
Ho	25° 20.1'			
a	**12.0 A**			

Notes:

Required Fix at 12:00

DR   0905 – 1200 = 175 x 15.5 / 60 = 45.2 nm

DR   1154 – 1200 = 6 X 15.5 /60 = 1.6 nm

Dlat = 1.6 x cos 079 = .73

Celestial Problems Sight Reduction – LAN Running Fix						
Problem # 11 (USCG) (00989)				Chapter 13-4		

Date:	2 April		Time	0830	**LAT:**	20° 16.0' S
					LONG	004° 12.0' E
	ZT	09:03	**CT**	09:05:40	**C**-143°	
	ZD	00:00	**CE**	-0:02:15	**S** -18.0 kts	
	GMT	09:03	**CCT**	09:03:25		
			GMT	09:03:25	**DR**	08:30 - 0903
					Time	0903
					LAT	20° 23.0' S
					LONG	004° 18.0' E

Almanac						
GHA	314° 05.7'	**DEC**	N 4° 57.1'		**LAN**	
M/S	+ 0° 51.3'	**D (+1.0)**	+ 0.1'	**ZT**		11:45
GHA	314° 57.0'	**DEC**	N 4° 57.2'	**ZD**		0
a λ	+ 4° 03.0'			**GMT**		11:45
LHA	319° 00.0'			**DEC**		N 4° 59.0'
				D (+1.0)		+ 0.7'
				DEC		N 4° 59.7'
						89° 60.0'
				- Ho		- 63° 46.2'
				Z Dist		26° 13.8'
				± Dec		- 4° 59.7'
				LAT		21° 14.1'

LHA	319°	**DEC**	N 4° 57.2'	**LAT**	20 S	CONTRARY

Publication 229						
		-	**Z (4)**	116.3	**Z to ZN**	
Hc	43°-07.6'		**Z (5)**	117.4		
d	- 32.5'		**d**	+1.1	ZN=180-Z	
Inc Dec (X)	57.2'		**Inc Dec (X)**	57.2	180-117.3 =	
Inv (÷)	60'		**Inv (÷)**	60	**062.7**	
Correction	-31.0'		**Correction**	117.3		
Hc	42° 36.6'		**Z**			
Ho	42° 39.6'					
a	**3.0 T**					

Notes:

Required Fix at 12:00

DR 0903 – 1200 = 177 X 18 / 60 = 53.1

DR 1145 – 1200 = 15 X 18 / 60 = 4.5

Dlat = 4.5 x cos 143 = 3.6

Celestial Problems					
Sight Reduction – LAN Running Fix					
Problem # 12 (USCG) (00990)				Chapter 13 - 5	

Date:	24 March		Time	0800	**LAT:**	22° 16.0' N
					LONG	031° 45.0' W
	ZT	09:38	**CT**	11:41:01	**C-**285°	
	ZD	+2:00	**CE**	-2:50	**S-**16.5 kts	
	GMT	11:38	**CCT**	11:38:11		
			GMT	11:38:11	**DR**	08:00 - 0938
					Time	0938
					LAT	22° 23.0' N
					LONG	32° 14.0' W

Almanac						
GHA	343° 25.3'	**DEC**	N 1° 28.7'		**LAN**	
M/S	+ 9° 32.8'	**D (+1.0)**	+ 0.6'	**ZT**	12:14	
GHA	352° 58.1'	**DEC**	N 1°-29.3'	**ZD**	+2:00	
a λ	- 31° 58.1'			**GMT**	14:14	
LHA	321° 00.0'			**DEC**	N1° 31.6'	
				D(+1.0)	+ 0.2'	
				DEC	N1° 31.8'	
					89° 60.0'	
				- Ho	- 68° 55.8'	
				Z Dist	21° 04.2'	
				± Dec	+ 1° 31.8'	
				LAT	22° 36.0'	

LHA	321°	**DEC**	N 1° 29.3'-	**LAT**	23 N	SAME

Publication 229					
		Z (1)	113.6	**Z to ZN**	
Hc	46° 38.1'	**Z (2)**	112.4		
d	+31.2'	**d**	-1.2	**ZN=Z**	
Inc Dec (X)	29.3'	**Inc Dec (X)**	29.3	**113.0**	
Inv (÷)	60'	**Inv (÷)**	60		
Correction	+15.2'	**Correction**	-0.6		
Hc	46° 53.3'	**Z**	113.0		
Ho	46° 32.2'				
a	**21.1A**				

Notes:
Required Fix at 12:00
DR   0938 – 1200 = 142 x 16.5 / 60 = 39.1
DR   1214 – 1200 = 14 x 16.5 / 60 = -3.9 (Remember to retard the DR 1.0 nm)
Dlat =   3.9 x cos 285 = 1.00

Celestial Problems				
Sight Reduction – LAN Running Fix				
Problem # 13 (USCG) (00995)			Chapter 13 - 6	

Date:	17 October		Time	0536	LAT:	24° 34.0′ N
					LONG	150° 46.0′ W
	ZT	08:30	**CT**	06:32:48	**C**-075°	
	ZD	+10:00	**CE**	- 02:42	**S**-12.0 kts	
	GMT	18:30	**CCT**	06:30:06		
			GMT	18:30:06	**DR**	0536 - 0830
					Time	0830
					LAT	24° 43.0′ N
					LONG	150° 08.0′ W

Almanac						
GHA	93° 40.4′	**DEC**	S 9° 24.7′		**LAN**	
M/S	+ 7° 31.5′	**D(+0.9)**	+ 0.5′	**ZT**	11:43	
GHA	101° 11.9′	**DEC**	S 9° 25.2′	**ZD**	+10	
a λ	+ 149° 11.9′			**GMT**	21:43	
LHA	312° 00.0′			**DEC**	S 9° 27.4′	
				D(+0.9)	+ 0.7′	
				DEC	S 9° 28.1′	
					89° 60.0′	
				- Ho	- 55° 37.6′	
				Z Dist	34° 22.4′	
				± Dec	- 9° 28.1′	
				LAT	24° 53.3′	

LHA	312°	**DEC**	S 9° 25.2′	**LAT**	25 N	CONTRARY

Publication 229					
		Z (9)	119.8	**Z to ZN**	
Hc	31° 11.9′	**Z (10)**	120.8		
D	- 36.5′	**d**	+1.0	ZN=Z	
Inc Dec (X)	25.2′	**Inc Dec (X)**	25.2		
Inv (÷)	60′	**Inv (÷)**	60	**120.2**	
Correction	-15.3′	**Correction**	0.4		
Hc	30° 56.6′	**Z**	120.2		
Ho	31° 20.7′				
a	**24.1 T**				

Notes:

Required Fix at 12:00
DR   0830 – 1200 = 210 x 12.0 / 60 = 42.0
DR   1143 – 1200 = 26 x 12.0 / 60 = 5.2
Dlat =   5.2 x cos 075 = 1.3

Celestial Problems				
Sight Reduction – LAN Running Fix				
Problem # 14 (USCG) (00996)				Chapter 13 - 7
Date: 30 August	Time		0554	**LAT:** 25° 39.0' S
				LONG 31° 51.0' E
ZT 08:36	**CT**	06:38:36		**C-325°**
ZD -02:00	**CE**	-02:24		**S-15.0 kts**
GMT 06:36	**CCT**	06:36:12		
	GMT	06:36:12	**DR**	0554 - 0836
			Time	0836
			LAT	25° 05.0' S
			LONG	031° 24.0' E

Almanac

					LAN	
GHA	269°.50.2'	**DEC**	N9°-01.5'			
M/S	+ 9° 03.0'	**D(-0.9)**	- 0.5'	**ZT**	11:57	
GHA	278°53.2'	**DEC**	N 9° 01.0'	**ZD**	-2:00	
a λ	+ 31° 06.8'			**GMT**	09:57	
LHA	310°-00.0'			**DEC**	N8° 58.8'	
				d (-0.9)	- 0.9'	
				DEC	N8° 57.9'	
					89° 60.0'	
				- Ho	56° 40.0'	
				Z Dist	33° 20.0'	
				± Dec	8° 57.9'	
				LAT	24° 22.1'	

LHA	310°	**DEC**	N 9° 01.0'	**LAT**	24 S	CONTRARY

Publication 229

		Z (9)	118.5	**Z to ZN**
Hc	30° 36.9'	**Z (10)**	119.4	
d	-35.6	**d**	0.9	ZN=180-Z
Inc Dec (X)	1.5'	**Inc Dec (X)**	1.5	180- 118.5 =
Inv (÷)	60'	**Inv (÷)**	60	**061.5**
Correction	-0.9'	**Correction**	0.02	
Hc	30° 36.0'	**Z**	118.5	
Ho	30° 49.2'			
a	**13.2 T**			

Notes:

Required Fix at 11:57

DR   0836 – 1157 = 201 x 15 / 60 = 50.3

DR   Fix time is time of LAN

Dlat =

Celestial Problems						
Sight Reduction – LAN Running Fix						

Problem # 15 (USCG) (00997)	Chapter 13 - 8

Date:	20 Nov.		Time	0612	**LAT:**	25° 38.0' N
					LONG	166° 54.0' W
	ZT	08:54	**CT**	07:51:14	**C**-126°	
	ZD	+11:00	**CE**	+2:52	**S**-20.0 kts	
	GMT	19:54	**CCT**	07:54:06		
			GMT	19:54:06	**DR**	0612 - 0854
					Time	0854
					LAT	25° 06.0' N
					LONG	166° 05.0' W

Almanac						
GHA	108° 34.1'	**DEC**	S 19° 48.0'		**LAN**	
M/S	+ 13° 31.5'	**D (+0.6)**	+ 0.5'	**ZT**	11:47	
GHA	122° 05.6'	**DEC**	S 19° 48.5'	**ZD**	+11	
a λ	+ 167° 05.6'			**GMT**	22:47	
LHA	315°-00.0'			**DEC**	S19° 49.6'	
				d (- 0.6)	- 0.5'	
				DEC	S 19° 50.1'	
					89° 60.0'	
				- Ho	- 45° 35.0'	
				Z Dist	44° 25.0'	
				± Dec	-19° 50.1'	
				LAT	24° 34.9'	

LHA	315°	**DEC**	S 19° 48.5'	**LAT**	25 N	CONTRARY

Publication 229					
		Z (19)	130.8	**Z to ZN**	
Hc	27° 55.6'	**Z (20)**	131.6		
d	-41.4'	**d**	+0.8	ZN=Z	
Inc Dec (X)	48.5'	**Inc Dec (X)**	48.5		
Inv (÷)	60'	**Inv (÷)**	60	**131.5**	
Correction	-33.5'	**Correction**	0.7		
Hc	27° 22.1'	**Z**	131.5		
Ho	27° 58.3'				
a	**36.2 T**				

Notes:
Required Fix at 11:47
DR   0854 – 1147 = 173 x 20 / 60 = 57.7
DR Fix time is time of LAN
Dlat =

Alexander F. Hickethier MBA © 2011-2013

Celestial Problems					
Sight Reduction – LAN Running Fix					
Problem # 16 (USCG) (00998)				Chapter 13 - 9	

Date:	23 May	Time	0628	**LAT:**	28° 18.0' S
				LONG	102° 42.0' E
	ZT	07:58	**CT**	01:02:06	**C**-040°
	ZD	-7:00	**CE**	- 04:04	**S** -20.0 kts
	GMT	00:58	**CCT**	00:58:02	
			GMT		**DR**	0628 - 0758
				Time	0758
				LAT	27° 54.0' S
				LONG	103° 04.0' E

Almanac

GHA	180° 50.8'	**DEC**	N 20° 31.1'		**LAN**	
M/S	+ 14° 30.5'	**d (+0.5)**	+ 0.5'	**ZT**	12:01	
GHA	195° 21.3'	**DEC**	N 20° 31.6'	**ZD**	-7:00	
a λ	+ 102° 38.7'			**GMT**	05:01	
LHA	298° 00.0'			**DEC**	N20° 33.5'	
				d (+0.5)	0'	
				DEC	N 20° 33.5'	
					89° 60.0'	
				- Ho	- 42° 32.0'	
				Z Dist	47° 28.0'	
				± Dec	- 20° 33.5'	
				LAT	26° 54.5'	

LHA	298°	**DEC**	N 20° 31.6'	**LAT**	27 S	CONTRARY

Publication 229

			Z (20)	121.5	**Z to ZN**	
Hc	13° 45.4'	**Z (21)**	122.2		
d	-35.5'	**d**	+0.9	ZN=180-Z	
Inc Dec (X)	31.6'	**Inc Dec (X)**	31.6	180-121.8 =	
Inv (÷)	60'	**Inv (÷)**	60	**058.2**	
Correction	-18.7'	**Correction**	+0.5		
Hc	13° 26.7'	**Z**	121.8		
Ho	13° 16.7'				
A	**10.0 A**				

Notes:

Required Fix at 12:01

DR   0758 – 1201 = 243 x 20 / 60 = 81

DR   Fix time is time of LAN

Dlat =

Celestial Problems						
Sight Reduction – LAN Running Fix						
Problem # 17 (USCG) (0999)				Chapter 13		

Date:	16 Feb	Time		0640	**LAT:**	23° 46.0' N
					LONG	156° 24.0' W
ZT		09:10	**CT**	07:08:06	**C**-222°	
ZD		-10:00	**CE**	+ 01:56	**S** -18.0 kts	
GMT		19:10	**CCT**	07:10:02		
			GMT	19:10:02	**DR**	0640-0910
					Time	0910
					LAT	23° 13.0' N
					LONG	156° 59.0' W

Almanac						
GHA	101° 28.4'	**DEC**	S 12° 09.5'		**LAN**	
M/S	2° 30.5'	**d (-0.9)**	- .2'	**ZT**		12:45
GHA	103° 58.9'	**DEC**	S 12° 09.3'	**ZD**		+ 10:00
a λ	- 156° 58.9'			**GMT**		22:45
LHA	307° 00.0'			**DEC**		S 12° 06.9'
				d (+0.9)		+ .7'
				DEC		S 12° 07.7'
						89° 60.0'
				- Ho		55° 25.3'
				Z Dist		34° 34.7'
				± Dec		12° 07.7'
				LAT		22° 27.0'

LHA	307°	**DEC**	S 12° 09.3'	**LAT**	23 N	CONTRARY

Publication 229					
		Z (12)	118.3	**Z to ZN**	
Hc	27° 25.7'	**Z (13)**	119.3		
d	33.8	**d**	+ 1.0	ZN=Z	
Inc Dec (X)	9.3'	**Inc Dec (X)**	9.3		
Inv (÷)	60'	**Inv (÷)**	60	**118.5**	
Correction	- 5.5'	**Correction**	+ .2		
Hc	27° 25.2'	**Z**	118.5		
Ho	27° 15.8'				
A	9.4 A				

Notes:
Required Fix at 12:45
DR   0910-1245 = 215 x 18/60 = 64.5
DR   Fix time is time of LAN
Dlat =

Celestial Problems
Sight Reduction – LAN Running Fix

Problem # 18 (USCG) (01008)				Chapter 13	

Date:	27 Mar		Time	0730	**LAT:**	28° 16.0' N
					LONG	056° 37.0' W
	ZT	09:15	**CT**	01:14:11	**C**-158°	
	ZD	+ 4:00	**CE**	+ 00:53	**S** -15.0 kts	
	GMT	13:15	**CCT**	01:15:04		
			GMT	13:15:04	**DR**	0730 - 0915
					Time	0915
					LAT	28° 51.2' N
					LONG	056° 26.0' W

Almanac

					LAN	
GHA	13° 39.4'	**DEC**	N 2° 41.3'			
M/S	+ 3° 46.0'	**d (+1.0)**	+ .3'	**ZT**	11:50
GHA	17° 25.4'	**DEC**	N 2° 41.6'	**ZD**	+ 4:00
a λ	- 56° 25.4'			**GMT**	15:50
LHA	321° 00.0'			**DEC**	N 2° 43.2'
				d (+1.0)	+ .8'
				DEC	N 2° 44.0'
					89° 60.0'
				- Ho	65° 32.8'
				Z Dist	24° 27.2'
				± Dec	2° 44.0'
				LAT	27° 11.2'

LHA	321°	**DEC**	N 2° 41.6	**LAT**	28 N	SAME

Publication 229

		Z (2)	118.0	**Z to ZN**	
Hc	44° 36.0'	**Z (3)**	116.8		
d	+ 37.2'	**d**	- 1.2	ZN=Z	
Inc Dec (X)	41.6'	**Inc Dec (X)**	41.6	**117.2**	
Inv (÷)	60'	**Inv (÷)**	60		
Correction	+ 25.8'	**Correction**	- .8		
Hc	45° 01.8'	**Z**	117.2		
Ho	45° 10.7'				
A	8.9 A				

Notes:

Required Fix at 12:00
DR   0915-1200 = 165 X 15/60 = 41.25
DR   1150-1200 = 10 X 15/60 = 2.5
Dlat =   2.5 X cos 158 = 2.3

Celestial Problems Sight Reduction – LAN Running Fix				
Problem # 19 (USCG) (01009)			Chapter 13	

Date:	22 Feb	Time	0800	**LAT:**	24° 16.0' S
				LONG	095° 37.0' W
	ZT	09:45	**CT**	03:47:22	**C** -126°
	ZD	- 6:00	**CE**	- 02:37	**S** -14.0 kts
	GMT	03:45	**CCT**	03:44:45	
			GMT	03:44:45	**DR**	0800-0945

				DR	0800-0945
				Time	0945
				LAT	24° 30.4' S
				LONG	095° 07.0' W

Almanac						
GHA	221° 36.3'	**DEC**	S 10° 15.5'		**LAN**	
M/S	+ 11° 11.0'	**d (10.9)**	- .6'	**ZT**		11:48
GHA	232° 47.3'	**DEC**	S 10° 14.9'	**ZD**		- 6:00
a λ	+ 96 12.7'			**GMT**		05:48
LHA	329° 00.0'			**DEC**		S 10° 13.6'
				d (-0.9		- .7'
				DEC		S 10° 12.9'
						89° 60.0'
				- Ho		75° 22.3'
				Z Dist		14° 37.7'
				± Dec		+ 10° 12.9'
				LAT		24° 50.6'

LHA	329°	**DEC**	S 10° 14.9'	**LAT**	25 S	SAME

Publication 229					
		Z (10)	111.5	**Z to ZN**	
Hc	56° 58.6'	**Z (11)**	109.9		
d	+ 30.3'	**d**	- .6	ZN=180-Z	
Inc Dec (X)	14.9'	**Inc Dec (X)**	14.9	180 – 111.4 =	
Inv (÷)	60'	**Inv (÷)**	60	**068.6**	
Correction	+ 7.5'	**Correction**	- .1		
Hc	57° 06.1'	**Z**	111.4		
Ho	57° 02.1'				
A	**4.0 A**				

Notes:
Required Fix at 12:00
DR   0945-1200 = 135 x 14/60 = 31.5
DR   1148-1200 = 12 x 14 / 60 = 2.8
Dlat =   2.8 X COS 126 = 1.6

Alexander F. Hickethier MBA © 2011-2013

Celestial Problems				
Sight Reduction – LAN Running Fix				
Problem # 20 (USCG) (01010)				Chapter 13

Date:	8 Feb		Time	0800	**LAT:**	21° 55.0' S
					LONG	052° 27.0' W
	ZT	09:38	**CT**	12:37:23	**C**-056°	
	ZD	+ 3:00	**CE**	+ 01:24	**S** -17.5 kts	
	GMT	12:38	**CCT**	12:38:47		
			GMT	12:38:47	**DR**	0800 - 0938
					Time	0938
					LAT	21° 39.0' S
					LONG	52° 03.0' W

Almanac

GHA	356° 26.4'	**DEC**	S 14° 55.5'		**LAN**	
M/S	9° 41.8'	**d (-0.9)**	- .6'	**ZT**		12:43
GHA	006° 08.2'	**DEC**	S 14° 54.9'	**ZD**		+ 3:00
a λ	-052° 08.2'			**GMT**		15:43
LHA	314° 00.0'			**DEC**		S 14° 55.5'
				d (-0.9)		- .7'
				DEC		S 14° 54.8'
						89°-60.0'
				- Ho		83° 56.1'
				Z Dist		6° 03.9'
				± Dec		+ 14° 54.8'
				LAT		20° 58.7'

LHA	314°	**DEC**	S 14° 54.9'	**LAT**	21 S	SAME

Publication 229

			Z (14)	091.3	**Z to ZN**
Hc	45° 43.3'		**Z (15)**	089.9	
d	+ 15.9'		**d**	- 1.4	ZN=180-Z
Inc Dec (X)	54.9'		**Inc Dec (X)**	54.9	180 – 090.0
Inv (÷)	60'		**Inv (÷)**	60	**090.0**
Correction	+ 15.8'		**Correction**	- 1.3	
Hc	45° 57.8'		**Z**	090.0	
Ho	46° 06.5'				
A	8.7 T				

Notes:

Required Fix at 12:00

DR   0938-1200 = 142' X 17.5 = 41.4

DR   1200-1243 = 43 X 17.5/60 = 12.54

Dlat =   12.54 X cos 56 = 7.0

Alexander F. Hickethier MBA © 2011-2013

3 LOP FIXES

Chapter 14, Celestial Navigation (Upon Oceans Endorsement)

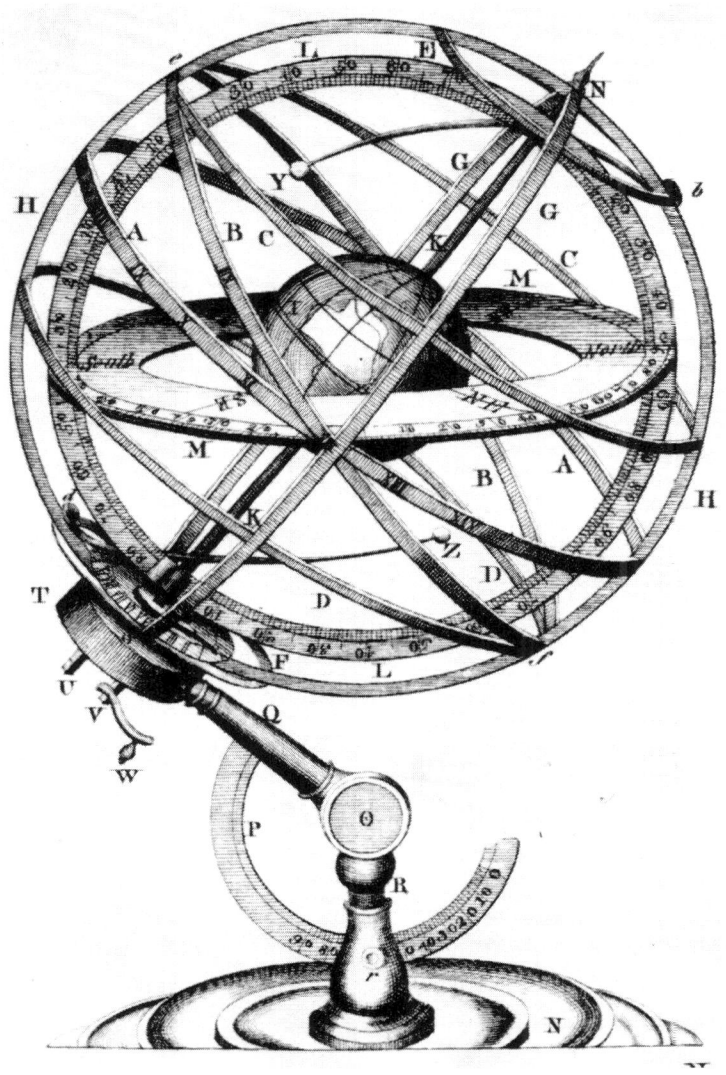

by
Alexander F. Hickethier MBA
and
Dr. HU Jia-Shan

3 LOP FIXES (SUN)
Chapter 18, Upon Ocean for Master Limited

1.

0986 At 0900 zone time, on 23 September, your DR position is LAT 28° 48.0' N, LONG 153° 11.5' W. You are steering course 257 °T at a speed of 18.0 knots. You observed 3 morning sun lines. Determine the latitude and longitude of your 1020 running fix?

ZONE TIME	GHA	OBSERVED ALTITUDE	DECLINATION
0915	110° 44.9'	40° 01.9'	S 0° 15.8'
0950	119° 27.4'	46° 22.9'	S 0° 16.3'
1020	127° 00.9'	51° 21.7'	S 0° 16.8'

A.   LAT 28°43.3' N,   LONG 153°32.1' W
B.   LAT 28°46.4' N,   LONG 153°34.6' W
C.   LAT 28°49.1' N,   LONG 153°37.0' W
D.   LAT 28°52.8' N,   LONG 153°30.6' W

2.

993 Your 0745 ZT, 15 July, position is LAT 29° 04.0' N, LONG 71° 17.5' W. You are on course 165° T, and your speed is 8.0 knots. You observed 3 morning sun lines. Determine the latitude and longitude of your 1130 running fix?

ZONE TIME	GHA	OBSERVED ALTITUDE	DECLINATION
0830	021°01.8'	44° 16.4'	N 21° 29.2'
0930	036°01.7'	57° 25.5'	N 21° 28.8'
1130	066°01.6'	81° 30.2'	N 21° 28.0'

A.   LAT 28° 35.0' N,   LONG 71° 08.5' W
B.   LAT 28° 39.8' N,   LONG 71° 04.0' W
C.   LAT 28° 40.5' N,   LONG 71° 13.0' W
D.   LAT 28° 43.3' N,   LONG 71° 02.5' W

3 LOP FIXES (STARS, SUN, MOON AND PLANES)

1.
1076.   On 25 March, your 0500 ZT DR position is LAT 28° 14.0' S, LONG 93° 17.0' E. You are on course 291° T at a speed of 16.0 knots. The following bodies are observed and information determined:

BODY	ZONE TIME	GHA	OBSERVED ALTITUDE (Ho)	DECLINATION
Peacock	0520	226° 18.5'	49° 42.9'	S 56° 47.6'
Altair	0535	238° 38.2'	43° 53.1'	N 8° 48.9'
Spica	0550	338° 48.5'	21° 11.7'	S 11° 03.8'

What are the latitude and longitude of your 0550 zone time running fix?

A. LAT 28° 15.9' S,   LONG 92° 56.9' E
B. LAT 28° 19.3' S,   LONG 92° 59.0' E
C. LAT 28° 06.4' S,   LONG 93° 02.5' E
D. LAT 27° 53.2' S,   LONG 93° 17.6' E

2.
1077.   On 15 July, your 1845 ZT DR position is LAT 27° 42.0' N, LONG 167° 02.0' E. You are on course 243° T at a speed of 16.0 knots. The following bodies are observed and information determined:

BODY	ZONE TIME	GHA	OBSERVED ALTITUDE (Ho)	DECLINATION
Deneb	1905	104° 08.0'	19° 52.4'	N 45° 12.8'
Antares	1924	172° 02.1'	32° 22.1'	S 26° 23.5'
Denebola	1945	247° 20.6'	38° 22.3'	N 14° 40.7'

What are the latitude and longitude of your 1945 zone time running fix?

A. LAT 27° 31.1' N,   LONG 166° 43.0' E
B. LAT 27° 38.5' N,   LONG 166° 45.1' E
C. LAT 27° 45.3' N,   LONG 166° 32.2' E
D. LAT 27° 46.9' N,   LONG 166° 39.8' E

Alexander F. Hickethier MBA © 2011-2013

3.

1078.   On 6 April, your 1830 ZT DR position is LAT 26° 33.0' N, LONG 64° 31.0' W. You are on course 082° T at a speed of 16 knots. The following bodies are observed and information determined:

BODY	ZONE TIME	GHA	OBSERVED ALTITUDE (Ho)	DECLINATION
Sirius	1836	073° 02.7'	46° 00.5'	S 16° 41.7'
Regulus	1842	023° 46.9'	49° 07.2'	N 12° 03.5'
Mirfak	1900	129° 24.3'	35° 51.6'	N 49° 47.7'

What are the latitude and longitude of your 1900 zone time running fix?

A. LAT 26° 49.5' N,   LONG 64° 06.5' W
B. LAT 26° 32.5' N,   LONG 64° 27.1' W
C. LAT 26° 28.7' N,   LONG 64° 32.1' W
D. LAT 26° 31.2' N,   LONG 64° 32.1' W

4.

1079.   On 12 December, your 1830 ZT DR position in LAT 24° 16.0' S, LONG 41° 18.0' W. You are on course 235° T at a speed of 16.0 knots. The following bodies are observed and information determined:

BODY	ZONE TIME	GHA	OBSERVED ALTITUDE (Ho)	DECLINATION
Rigel	1845	329° 19.7'	19° 54.7'	S 08° 13.4'
Peacock	1910	107° 58.4'	32° 43.9'	S 56° 47.8'
Markab	1930	073° 04.1'	39° 53.1'	N 15° 06.5'

What are the latitude and longitude of your 1930 zone time running fix?

A. LAT 24° 12.5' S,   LONG 41° 10.9' W
B. LAT 24° 16.9' S,   LONG 41° 18.2' W
C. LAT 24° 25.2' S,   LONG 41° 39.9' W
D. LAT 27° 46.9' S,   LONG 41° 31.2' W

6-93

5.

1080.　　On 20 February, your 0530 ZT DR position is LAT 24° 15.0' N, LONG 137° 33.0' W. You are on course 033° T at a speed of 18 knots. The following bodies are observed and information determined:

BODY	ZONE TIME	GHA	OBSERVED ALTITUDE (Ho)	DECLINATION
Regulus	0540	218° 35.9'	13° 02.2'	N 12° 03.5'
Antares	0552	26° 23.5'	38° 04.1'	S 26° 23.3'
Vega	0600	096° 23.2'	52° 33.5'	N 38° 45.8'

What are the latitude and longitude of your 0600 zone time running fix?

A. LAT 24° 23.3' N,　　LONG 137° 35.5' W
B. LAT 24° 26.0' N,　　LONG 137° 25.8' W
C. LAT 24° 27.5' N,　　LONG 137° 31.8' W
D. LAT 24° 30.1' N,　　LONG 137° 24.5' W

6.

1081.　　On 14 September, your 1810 ZT DR position is LAT 27° 12.0' S, LONG 71° 10.0' E. You are on course 060° T at a speed of 15.0 knots. The following bodies are observed and information determined:

BODY	ZONE TIME	GHA	OBSERVED ALTITUDE (Ho)	DECLINATION
Venus	1810	341° 30.4'	38° 48.9'	S 12° 48.1'
Altair	1816	255° 00.4'	41° 20.3'	N 8° 49.3'
Peacock	1822	247° 55.8'	48° 39.5	S 56° 47.8'

What are the latitude and longitude of your 1822 zone time running fix?

A. LAT 27° 11.0' S,　　LONG 71° 14.5' E
B. LAT 27° 07.5' S,　　LONG 71° 28.6' E
C. LAT 27° 09.2' S,　　LONG 71° 01.3' E
D. LAT 27° 04.5' S,　　LONG 71° 22.4' E

7.

1082.   On 20 November, your 1030 ZT DR position is LAT 27° 16.0' N, LONG 157° 13.6' E. You are on course 060° T at a speed of 20 knots. The following bodies are observed and information determined:

BODY	ZONE TIME	GHA	OBSERVED ALTITUDE (Ho)	DECLINATION
Moon	1030	259° 24.4'	34° 01.5'	N 9° 47.3'
Sun	1116	202° 30.5'	43° 00.0'	S 19° 38.0'
Venus	1200	162° 57.7'	24° 26.9'	S 26° 02.4'

What are the latitude and longitude of your 1200 zone time running fix?

A. LAT 27° 16.8' N,   LONG 157° 30.5' E
B. LAT 27° 22.6' N,   LONG 157° 37.8' E
C. LAT 27° 29.7' N,   LONG 157° 43.0' E
D. LAT 27° 33.4' N,   LONG 157° 48.2' E

8.

1083.   On 21 November, your 1146 ZT DR position is LAT 26° 05.0' N, LONG 90° 02.0' W. You are on course 300° T at a speed of 20.0 knots. The following bodies are observed and information determined:

BODY	ZONE TIME	GHA	OBSERVED ALTITUDE (Ho)	DECLINATION
Sun L/L	1146	090° 02.0'	43° 50.5'	S 20° 00.0'
Venus	1216	046° 53.6'	23° 16.3'	S 25° 49.1'
Moon L/L	1246	154° 30.6'	23° 56.1'	N 01° 57.3'

What are the latitude and longitude of your 1246 zone time running fix?

A. LAT 26° 09.0' N,   LONG 90° 10.5' W
B. LAT 26° 14.5' N,   LONG 90° 15.8' W
C. LAT 26° 19.0' N,   LONG 90° 21.0' W
D. LAT 26° 24.2' N,   LONG 90° 24.0' W

9.

1084.   On 4 December, your 1500 ZT DR position is LAT 18° 06.0' N, LONG 75° 42.0' W. You are on course 020° T at a speed of 15.0 knots. The following bodies are observed and information determined:

BODY	ZONE TIME	GHA	OBSERVED ALTITUDE (Ho)	DECLINATION
Venus	1500	073° 51.1'	48° 29.5'	S 23° 22.1'
Sun L/L	1524	128° 25.7'	24° 24.9'	S 22° 18.6'
Moon L/L	1548	037° 54.1'	43° 24.8'	S 9° 43.0'

What are the latitude and longitude of your 1548 zone time running fix?

A. LAT 18° 10.3' N,   LONG 75° 34.5' W
B. LAT 18° 12.6' N,   LONG 75° 42.0' W
C. LAT 18° 14.0' N,   LONG 75° 40.0' W
D. LAT 18° 17.3' N,   LONG 75° 37.7' W

10.

1085. On 20 February, your vessel is enroute from Honolulu, HI to San Francisco, CA, steering course 033° T and making a speed of 18 knots. Your 0530 zone time DR is LAT 24° 15.0' N, LONG 137° 33.0' W. Three stars are observed, and the following information is determined:

STAR	BODY'S ZT	BODY'S GHA	DECLINATION	OBSERVED ALTITUDE (Ho)
Regulus	0540	218° 35.9'	N 12° 03.5'	13° 02.2'
Antares	0552	126° 23.5'	S 26° 23.3'	38° 04.1'
Vega	0600	096° 23.2'	N 38° 45.8'	52° 33.5'

What is the position of your vessel at 0600?

A. LAT 24° 24.3' N,   LONG 137° 35.5' W
B. LAT 24° 26.0' N,   LONG 137° 25.8' W
C. LAT 24° 27.5' N,   LONG 137° 31.8' W
D. LAT 24° 30.1' N,   LONG 137° 24.5' W

11.

1086.   On 15 July, your vessel is enroute from Portland, OR to Singapore, Malaysia, steering course 243° T and making a speed of 16 knots. Your 1845 zone time DR is LAT 27° 42.0' N, LONG 167° 02.0' E. Three stars are observed, and the following information is determined:

STAR	BODY'S ZT	BODY'S GHA	DECLINATION	OBSERVED ALTITUDE (Ho)
Deneb	1905	104° 08.0'	N 45° 12.8'	19° 52.4'
Antares	1924	172° 02.1'	S 26° 23.5'	32° 22.1'
Denebola	1945	247° 20.6'	N 14° 40.7'	38° 22.3'

What is the position of your vessel at 1945?

A. LAT 27° 31.1' N,   LONG 166° 43.0' E
B. LAT 27° 38.5' N,   LONG 166° 45.1' E
C. LAT 27° 45.3' N,   LONG 166° 32.2' E
D. LAT 28° 18.1' N,   LONG 166° 39.8' E

12.

1087. On 15 August, your vessel is enroute from Bombay, India to San Francisco, CA, steering course 020° T and making a speed of 20.0 knots. Your 1830 zone time DR is LAT 26° 13.0' N, LONG 135° 18.0' W. Three stars are observed, and the following information is determined:

STAR	BODY'S ZT	BODY'S GHA	DECLINATION	OBSERVED ALTITUDE (Ho)
Spica	1848	180° 24.3'	S 11° 03.8'	32° 21.4'
Altair	1910	089° 29.8'	N 8° 49.3'	43° 06.3'
Kochab	1935	170° 33.4'	N 74° 14.3'	39° 12.0'

What is the position of your vessel at 1935?

A. LAT 26° 15.9' N,   LONG 135° 03.6' W
B. LAT 26° 35.3' N,   LONG 135° 24.8' W
C. LAT 26° 40.5' N,   LONG 135° 21.6' W
D. LAT 26° 48.1' N,   LONG 135° 20.7' W

13.

1089.   At 1830 zone time on 6 April, your DR position is LAT 26° 33.0' N, LONG 64° 31.0' W. You are steering course 082° T at a speed of 16.0 knots. Three stars are observed, and the following information is determined:

STAR	ZONE TIME	STAR'S GHA	OBSERVED ALTITUDE (Ho)	STAR'S DECLINATION
Sirius	1836	073° 02.7'	46° 00.5'	S 16° 41.7'
Regulus	1842	023° 46.9'	49° 07.2'	N 12° 03.5'
Mirfak	1900	129° 24.3'	35° 50.5'	N 49° 47.7'

What are the latitude and longitude of your 1900 zone time running fix?

A. LAT 26° 20.1' N,   LONG 64° 19.4' W
B. LAT 26° 23.7' N,   LONG 64° 29.3' W
C. LAT 26° 28.4' N,   LONG 64° 32.1' W
D. LAT 26° 32.5' N,   LONG 64° 27.1' W

14.

1090.   At 0450 zone time on 25 June, your DR position is LAT 21° 26.0' N, LONG 160° 24.5' W. You are steering course 100° T at a speed of 10 knots. Three stars are observed at intervals of 12 minutes. Given the following information, determine your position at 0514 zone time.

STAR	ZONE TIME	STAR'S GHA	OBSERVED ALTITUDE (Ho)	STAR'S DECLINATION
Mirfak	0450	100° 25.9'	35° 27.4'	N 49° 47.5'
Fomalhaut	0502	169° 59.9'	38° 01.3'	S 29° 43.1'
Altair	0514	219° 39.9'	31° 39.5'	N 8° 49.1'

A. LAT 21° 27.0' N,   LONG 160° 17.0' W
B. LAT 21° 25.0' N,   LONG 160° 18.0' W
C. LAT 21° 22.0' N,   LONG 160° 17.0' W
D. LAT 21° 20.0' N,   LONG 160° 15.5' W

15.

1091.   On 10 August, your 0430 ZT position is LAT 29° 56.7' S, LONG 139° 11.0' E. Your course is 321° T, speed 18.2 knots. Three stars are observed and the following information determined:

STAR	ZT	GHA	DECLINATION	OBSERVED ALT. (Ho)
Fomalhaut	0452	272° 03.3'	S 29° 43.1'	46° 05.3'
Canopus	0459	162° 05.5'	S 52° 41.0'	41° 48.9'
Achernar	0510	236° 28.2'	S 57° 19.6'	60° 26.5'

What is the 0500 position of your vessel?

A. LAT 29° 46.0' S,   LONG 138° 54.0' E
B. LAT 29° 49.2' S,   LONG 138° 57.0' E
C. LAT 29° 56.0' S,   LONG 139° 03.8' E
D. LAT 30° 07.5' S,   LONG 138° 55.2' E

16.

1093.   On 22 November, your vessel is enroute from Accra, Ghana, to Montevideo, Uruguay, on course 240° T and making a speed of 15.0 knots. Your 1129 DR position is LAT 28° 25.0' S, LONG 42° 40.0' W. Three bodies are observed, and the following information determined:

BODY	ZONE TIME	BODY'S GHA	DECLINATION	OBSERVED ALTITUDE (Ho)
Venus	1129	350° 00.1'	S 25° 41.8'	43° 26.8'
Moon	1134	082° 54.7'	S 01° 46.5'	43° 15.0'
Sun	1137	042° 38.0'	S 20° 11.7'	81° 44.7'

What is the position of your vessel at 1137 zone time?

A. LAT 28° 27.0' S,   LONG 42° 38.0' W
B. LAT 28° 25.0' S,   LONG 42° 36.0' W
C. LAT 28° 23.4' S,   LONG 42° 42.0' W
D. LAT 28° 25.2' S,   LONG 42° 40.0' W

6-99

17.

1094.   On 12 October, your vessel is on course 081° T, speed 20 knots. Your 1800 zone time DR position is LAT 26° 11.0' S, LONG 77° 18.0' E. Three stars are observed, and the following information is determined:

STAR	ZONE TIME	GHA	BODY'S DECLINATION	OBSERVED ALTITUDE (Ho)
Vega	1810	299° 26.6'	N 38° 46.3'	23° 08.7'
Fomalhaut	1823	237° 37.0'	S 29° 43.2'	50° 23.9'
Antares	1835	337° 43.4'	S 26° 23.4'	40° 53.1'

What is the position of your vessel at 1835?

A. LAT 26° 05.5' S,   LONG 77° 14.5' E
B. LAT 26° 07.5' S,   LONG 77° 34.0' E
C. LAT 26° 09.0' S,   LONG 77° 27.5' E
D. LAT 26° 12.0' S,   LONG 77° 31.0' E

18.

1095.   On 25 October, your 0430 zone time DR position is LAT 24° 48.0' N, LONG 65° 21.1' W. Your vessel is on course 030° T at a speed of 18 knots. Three stars are observed and the following information is determined:

STAR	ZONE TIME	BODY'S GHA	BODY'S DECLINATION	OBSERVED ALTITUDE (Ho)
Mirfak	0430	110° 23.1'	N 49° 47.7'	47° 20.8'
Regulus	0440	011° 48.3'	N 12° 03.5'	37° 49.9'
Sirius	0455	066° 19.5'	S 16° 41.3'	48° 25.3'

What is the position of your vessel at 0455?

A. LAT 24° 53.0' N,   LONG 65° 28.3' W
B. LAT 24° 54.0' N,   LONG 65° 17.3' W
C. LAT 24° 53.0' N,   LONG 65° 12.5' W
D. LAT 25° 03.0' N,   LONG 65° 18.5' W

Answers to 3 LOP Fixes

3 LOP FIXES (SUN)

1. 00986 C
2. 00993 A

3 LOP FIXES
(STARS, SUN, MOON AND PLANETS)

1. 01076 A
2. 01077 A
3. 01078 B
4. 01079 B
5. 01080 C
6. 01081 A
7. 01082 C
8. 01083 C
9. 01084 D
10. 01085 C
11. 01086 A
12. 01087 D
13. 01089 D
14. 01090 B
15. 01091 B
16. 01093 A
17. 01094 D
18. 01095 A

3 LOP FIXES (SUN)

1.		23 September	
USCG # 0986	Latitude		28°48.0'N
0900	Longitude		153°11.5' W
		C- 257°	S- 18.0
Sun at	0915	0950	1020
ZT Sight	0915	0950	1020
Fix Time	1020	1020	1020
D	65	30	0
Speed x Time	18 x 65	18 x 30	18 x 0
Divided by 60	60	60	60
= Advance	19.5	9.0	0
	Convert GHA to LHA		
GHA	110° 44.9'	119° 27.4'	127° 00.9
±Longitude	-153° 44.9'	-153°- 27.4'	-153° 00.9'
LHA	317° 00.0'	326° 00.0'	334° 00.0'
	Declination		
Declinatio n	S 0° 15.8'	S 0° 16.3'	S 0° 16.8'
	CONTRARY	CONTRARY	CONTRARY
	Pub 229 Work		
	Intercept Computed		
Hc	39° 46.0'	46° 28.6'	51° 49.4'
d	- 38.1	-42.5	- 47.3
Dec inc (x)	15.8'	16.1	16.8'
60 (\)	60	60	60
Correction	- 10.0	- 11.5'	- 13.2
HC Corrected	39° 36.0'	46° 17.7'	51° 36.2'
Ho	40° 01.9'	46° 22.9'	51° 21.7'
a: (intercept)	**25.9 T**	**5.8 T**	**14.5 A**
	Direction Computer		
Z	117.5	125.7	134.8
Z	118.5	126.7	135.8
d	+ 1.0'	1.0''	+ 1.0'
Dec inc (x)	15.8'	16.3'	16.8'
60 (\)	60'	60'	60'
Correction	+ .3'	+ .3'	+ .3'
Corrected Z	117.8	126.0	135.1
± 180, 360			
Convert Z to Zn	**117.8**	**126.0**	**135.1**

2.		15 July	
USCG # 993	Latitude		29°04.0' N
0745	Longitude		071°17.5' W
		C- 165°	S- 8.0
Sun at	0830	0930	1130
ZT Sight	0830	0930	1130
Fix Time	1130	1130	1130
D	180	120	0
Speed x Time	8 x 180	8 x 120	8 x 0
Divided by 60	60	60	60
= Advance	24.0	16.0	0
	Convert GHA to LHA		
GHA	21° 01.8'	036° 01.7'	066° 01.6'
± Longitude	- 71° 01.8'	- 071° 01.7'	- 071° 01.6'
LHA	310° 00.0'	325° 00.0'	355° 00.0'
	Declination		
Declination	N 21° 29.2'	N 21° 28.8'	N 21° 28.0'
	SAME	SAME	SAME
	Pub 229 Work		
	Intercept Computed		
Hc	44° 18.9'	57° 24.9'	81° 40.4'
d	+ 20.6	+ 21.1	+50.0
Dec inc (x)	29.2'	28.8'	28.0'
60 (\)	60	60	60
Correction	+ 10.0	+ 10.1	+ 23.3
HC Corrected	44° 28.9'	57°35.0'	82° 03.7'
Ho	44° 16.4'	57° 25.5'	81° 30.2'
a: (intercept)	**12.5 A**	**9.5 A**	**33.5 A**
	Direction Computer		
Z	088.2	096.1	46.1
Z	086.9	094.4	142.0
d	- 1.3'	- 1.7'	- 4.1'
Dec inc (x)	29.2'	28.8'	28.0'
60 (\)	60'	60'	60'
Correction	- .6'	- .8'	- 1.9'
Corrected Z	86.3	095.3	144.2
± 180, 360	0	0	0
Convert Z to Zn	**086.3**	**095.3**	**144.2**

3 LOP FIXES
(STARS, SUN, MOON AND PLANETS)

1.		25 March	
USCG # 1076	Latitude		28° 14.0' S
0500	Longitude		093° 17.0' E
		C- 291	S- 16.0
Object Name	**Peacock**	**Antares**	**Spica**
ZT Sight	0520	0535	0550
Fix Time	0550	0550	0550
D	30	15	0
Speed x Time	16 x 30	16 x 15	16 x 15
Divided by 60	60	60	60
= Advance	8.0	4.0	0

Convert GHA to LHA			
GHA	226° 18.5'	238° 38.2'	338° 48.5'
± Longitude	+ 093° 41.5'	+ 093° 21.8'	+ 093° 11.5
LHA	320° 00.0'	332° 00.0'	072° 00.0'

Declination			
Declination	S 56° 47.6'	N 8° 48.9'	S 11° 03.8'
	SAME	CONTRARY	SAME

Pub 229 Work			
Intercept Computed			
Hc	50° 07.4	44° 57.9'	20° 56.5
d	- 28.3	- 48.8	+ 26.1
Dec inc (x)	47.6'	48.9'	03.8'
60 (\)	60'	60'	60'
Correction	- 22.5'	- 39.7'	+ 1.7'
HC Corrected	49° 44.9'	44° 18.2	20° 58.2'
Ho	49° 42.9'	43° 53.1'	21° 11.7'
a: (intercept)	**2.0 A**	**25.1 A**	**13.5 T**

Direction Computer			
Z	034.1	138.9	088.4
Z	032.7	139.7	087.4
d	- 1.4'	+ .8'	- 1.0'
Dec inc (x)	47.6'	48.9'	03.8'
60 (\)	60'	60'	60
Correction	- 1.1'	+ .8'	- .1
Corrected Z	033.0	138.5	088.3
± 180, 360	180 -	180 -	180 -
Convert Z to Zn	**147.0**	**041.5**	**268.3**

2.		15 July	
USCG # 1077	Latitude		27° 42.0' N
1845	Longitude		167° 02.0' E
		C -243	S - 16
Object Name	**Deneb**	**Antares**	**Denebola**
ZT Sight	1905	1924	1945
Fix Time	1945	1945	1945
D	40	21	
Speed x Time	16 x 40	16 x 40	16 x 0
Divided by 60	60	60	60
= Advance	10.7	5.5	0

Convert GHA to LHA			
GHA	104° 08.0'	172° 02.1'	247° 20.6'
± Longitude	+ 166° 52.0'	+ 166° 57.9'	+ 166° 39.4'
LHA	271° 00.0'	339° 00.0'	054° 00.0'

Declination			
Declination	N 45° 12.8'	S 26° 23.5'	N 14° 40.7'
	SAME	CONTRARY	SAME

Pub 229 Work			
Intercept Computed			
Hc	20° 03.1'	32° 20.9'	38° 06.5'
d	+ 20.3	- 55.6	+ 24.8
Dec inc (x)	12.8'	23.5'	40.7'
60 (\)	60'	60'	60'
Correction	+ 4.3'	- 21.7'	+ 16.8'
HC Corrected	20° 07.4'	31° 29.2'	38° 23.3'
Ho	19° 52.4'	32° 22.1'	38° 22.3'
a: (intercept)	**15.0 A**	**22.9 T**	**1.0 A**

Direction Computer			
Z	048.8	157.6	093.9
Z	047.8	158.0	092.8
d	- 1.0'	+ .4'	- 1.1'
Dec inc (x)	12.8'	23.5'	40.7'
60 (\)	60	60'	60
Correction	- .2	+ .2'	- .7
Corrected Z	048.6	157.8	093.2
± 180, 360			180 -
Convert Z to Zn	**048.6**	**157.8**	**266.8**

3.		**6 April**			4.		**12 December**		
USCG # 1078	Latitude			26° 33.0' N	USCG # 1079	Latitude			24° 16.0' S
1830	Longitude			064° 31.0' W	1830	Longitude			041° 18.0' W
		C- 082	S- 16.0				C - 235°	S – 16.0	
Object Name	**Sirius**	**Regulus**	**Mirfak**		Object Name	**Rigel**	**Peacock**	**Markab**	
ZT Sight	1836	1842	1900		ZT Sight	1845	1910	1930	
Fix Time	1900	1900	1900		Fix Time	1930	1930	1930	
D	24	18	0		D	45	20	0	
Speed x Time	16 x 24	16 x 18	16 x 15		Speed x Time	16 x 30	16 x 20	16 x 0	
Divided by 60	60	60	60		Divided by 60	60	60	60	
= Advance	6.4	4.8	0		= Advance	12.0	5.3	0	

Convert GHA to LHA					Convert GHA to LHA				
GHA	73° 02.7'	23° 46.9'	129° 24.3'		GHA	329° 19.7'	107° 58.4'	073° 04.1'	
± Longitude	64° 02.7'	64° 46.9'	064°24.3'		± Longitude	- 41° 19.7'	-40° 58.5'	- 41° 04.1'	
LHA	009° 00.0'	319° 00.0'	065° 00.0'		LHA	288° 00.0'	067° 00.0'	032° 00.0'	

Declination					Declination				
Declination	S 16° 41.7'	N 12° 03.5'	N 49° 47.7'		Declination	S 8° 13.4'	S 56° 47.8'	N 15° 06.5'	
	CONTRARY	SAME	SAME			SAME	SAME	CONTRARY	

Pub 229 Work
Intercept Computed

Pub 229 Work — Intercept Computed					Pub 229 Work — Intercept Computed				
Hc	46° 07.3'	48° 46.6'	36° 08.0'		Hc	19° 38.6	33° 01.4	40° 01.2'	
d	- 58.8	+ 27.2	+ .7		d	+ 23.0	- 6.1	- 46.6'	
Dec inc (x)	41.8'	03.5'	47.7'		Dec inc (x)	13.4'	47.8'	06.5'	
60 (\)	60'	60'	60'		60 (\)	60'	60	60'	
Correction	- 40.9'	+ 1.6'	+ .6'		Correction	+ 5.1'	- 4.9	- 5.0'	
HC Corrected	45° 26.4'	48° 48.2'	36° 08.6'		HC Corrected	19° 43.7'	32° 56.5'	39° 56.2'	
Ho	46° 00.5'	49° 07.2'	35° 51.6'		Ho	19° 54.7'	32° 43.9'	39° 53.1'	
a: (intercept)	**34.1 T**	**19.0 T**	**17.0 A**		a: (intercept)	**11.0 T**	**12.6 A**	**3.1 A**	

Direction Computer					Direction Computer				
Z (16)	167.5	103.1	047.4		Z	089.8	037.6	138.1	
Z (17)	167.7	101.8	046.2		Z	088.9	036.4	138.9	
d	+ .3'	- 1.3'	- 1.2'		d	- .9'	- 1.2'	+ .8'	
Dec inc (x)	41.8'	03.5'	47.7'		Dec inc (x)	13.4'	47.8'	06.5'	
60 (\)	60'	60'	60'		60 (\)	60'	60'	60'	
Correction	+ .2'	- .1'	1.0		Correction	- .2'	- 1.0'	+ .1'	
Corrected Z	167.7	103.0	46.2		Corrected Z	089.6	036.6	138.2	
± 180, 360	360 -		360		± 180, 360	180 -	180 +	180 +	
Convert Z to Zn	**192.3**	**103.0**	**313.8**		Convert Z to Zn	**090.4**	**216.6**	**318.2**	

Alexander F. Hickethier MBA © 2011-2013

5.		**20 February**	
USCG # 1080	Latitude		24° 15.0' N
0530	Longitude		137° 33.0' W
		C- 033	S- 18.0
Object Name	**Regulus**	**Antares**	**Vega**
ZT Sight	0540	0552	0600
Fix Time	0600	0600	0600
D	20		0
Speed x Time	18 x 20	18 x 8	18 x 0
Divided by 60	60	60	60
= Advance	6.0	2.4	0

Convert GHA to LHA			
GHA	218° 35.9'	126° 23.5'	96° 23.2'
± Longitude	- 137° 35.6'	- 137° 23.5'	- 137° 23.2'
LHA	81° 00.0'	349° 00.0'	319° 00.0'

Declination			
Declination	N 12° 03.5'	S 26° 23.3'	N 38° 45.8'
	SAME	CONTRARY	SAME

Pub 229 Work
Intercept Computed

Hc	12° 57.9'	38° 52.8'	52° 32.0'
d	+ 22.5	- 58.5	- 10.9
Dec inc (x)	03.5'	23.3'	45.8'
60 (\)	60'	60'	60'
Correction	+ 1.3'	- 22.7'	- 8.3'
HC Corrected	12° 59.2'	38° 30.1'	52° 24.7
Ho	13° 02.2'	38° 04.1'	52° 33.5'
a: (intercept)	**3.0 T**	**26.0 A**	**8.8 T**

Direction Computer			
Z		082.5	167.3	058.2
Z		081.5	167.6	056.6
d		- 1.0'	+ .3'	- 1.6'
Dec inc (x)		03.5'	23.3'	45.8'
60 (\)		60'	60'	60'
Correction		- .1'	+ 1'	- 1.2'
Corrected Z		082.4	167.4	057.0
± 180, 360		360 -		
Convert Z to Zn		**277.6**	**167.4**	**057.0**

6.		**14 September**	
USCG # 1081	Latitude		27° 12.0' S
1810	Longitude		71° 10.0' E
		C - 060°	S – 15.0
Object Name	**Venus**	**Altair**	**Peacock**
ZT Sight	1810	1816	1822
Fix Time	1822	1822	1822
D	12		
Speed x Time	15 x 12	15 x 6	15 x 0
Divided by 60	60	60	60
= Advance	3.0	1.5	0

Convert GHA to LHA			
GHA	341° 30.4'	255° 00.4'	247° 55.8'
± Longitude	+ 71° 29.6'	+ 71° 59.6	+ 71° 04.2'
LHA	053° 00.0'	327° 00.0'	319° 00.0'

Declination			
Declination	S 12° 48.1'	N 8° 49.3'	S 56° 47.8'
	SAME	CONTRARY	SAME

Pub 229 Work
Intercept Computed

Hc	38° 14.1	42° 35.7'	48°47.9'
d	+ 25 1	- 45.4	- 28.1
Dec inc (x)	48.1'	49.3'	47.8'
60 (\)	60'	60'	60'
Correction	+ 20.1'	- 37.3'	- 22.4'
HC Corrected	38° 34.2'	41° 58.4'	48° 25.5'
Ho	38° 48.9'	41° 20.3'	48° 39.5'
a: (intercept)	**14.7 T**	**38.1 A**	**14.0 T**

Direction Computed			
Z		096.0	132.9	033.8
Z		094.8	133.8	32.5
d		- 1.2'	+ .9'	- 1.3'
Dec inc (x)		48.1'	49.3'	47.8'
60 (\)		60'	60'	60'
Correction		- 1.0'	+ .7'	- 1.0'
Corrected Z		095.0	133.6	032.8
± 180, 360		180 +	180 -	180 -
Convert Z to Zn		**275.0**	**46.4**	**147.2**

7.		**20 November**	
USCG # 1082	Latitude		27° 16.0' N
1030	Longitude		157° 18.6' E
		C- 060	S- 20.0
Object Name	**Moon L/L**	**Sun L/L**	**Venus**
ZT Sight	1030	1116	1200
Fix Time	1200	1200	1200
D	90	44	0
Speed x Time	20 x 90	20 x 44	20 x 0
Divided by 60	60	60	60
= Advance	30	14.7	0
Convert GHA to LHA			
GHA	259° 24.4'	202° 30.5'	162° 57.7'
±Longitude	+157° 35.6'	+157° 29.5'	+157° 02.3'
LHA	057° 00.0'	360° 00.0'	320° 00.0'
Declination			
Declination	N 9° 47.3'	S 19° 38.0'	S 26° 02.4'
	SAME	CONTRARY	CONTRARY
Pub 229 Work			
Intercept Computed			
Hc	33° 23.3'	44° 00.0'	24° 29.1'
d	+26.5	- 60.0	- 46.7
Dec inc (x)	47.3'	38.0'	02.4'
60 (\)	60'	60'	60'
Correction	+ 20.9'	- 38.0'	- 1.9'
HC Corrected	33° 44.2'	43° 22.0'	24° 27.2'
Ho	34° 01.5'	43° 00.0'	24° 26.9'
a: (intercept)	**17.3 T**	**22.0 A**	**.3 A**
Direction Computer			
Z	097.2	180.0	140.6
Z	096.1	180.0	141.3
d	- 1.1'	0'	+ .7'
Dec inc (x)	47.3'	38.0'	02.4'
60 (\)	60'	60'	60'
Correction	- .9'	0'	0'
Corrected Z	096.3	180.0	140.6
± 180, 360	360 -		
Convert Z to Zn	**263.7**	**180.0**	**140.6**

8.		**21 November**	
USCG # 1083	Latitude		26° 05.0' N
1146	Longitude		90° 02.0' W
		C - 300	S- 20.0
Object Name	**Sun L/L**	**Venus**	**Sun L/L**
ZT Sight	1146	1216	1246
Fix Time	1246	1246	1246
D	60	30	0
Speed x Time	20 x 60	20 x 30	20 x 0
Divided by 60	60	60	60
= Advance	20.0	10	0
Convert GHA to LHA			
GHA	90° 02.0'	46° 53.6	154° 30.6'
± Longitude	90° 02.0'	- 89° 53.6	- 90° 30.6'
LHA	- 000° 00.0'	317° 00.0'	064° 00.0'
Declination			
Declination	S 20° 00.0'	S 25° 49.1'	N 01° 57.3'
	CONTRARY	CONTRARY	SAME
Pub 229 Work			
Intercept Computed			
Hc	44° 00.0'	24° 14.1'	23° 40.7'
d	- 60.0	- 44.5	+ 28.1
Dec inc (x)	0	49.1'	57.3'
60 (\)	60'	60'	60'
Correction	0'	- 36.4'	+ 26.8'
HC Corrected	44° 00.0'	23° 37.7'	24° 07.5'
Ho	43° 50.5'	23° 16.3'	23° 56.1'
a: (intercept)	**9.5 A**	**21.4 A**	**11.4 A**
Direction Computer			
Z	180.0	137.3	101.1
Z	180.0	138.1	100.1
d	0'	+ .4'	- 1.0'
Dec inc (x)	0'	49.1'	57.3'
60 (\)	60'	60'	60'
Correction	0	+ .3'	- 1.0'
Corrected Z		138.0	100.1
± 180, 360			
Convert Z to Zn	**180**	**138.0**	**100.1**

9.		4 December	
USCG # 1084	Latitude	18° 06.0' N	
1500	Longitude	075° 42.0' W	
		C- 020	S- 15.0
Object Name	**Venus**	**Sun L/L**	**Moon L/L**
ZT Sight	1500	1524	1548
Fix Time	1548	1548	1548
D	48	24	0
Speed x Time	15 x 48	15 x24	15 x 0
Divided by 60	60	60	60
= Advance	12.0	6.0	0
Convert GHA to LHA			
GHA	73° 51.1'	128° 25.7'	37° 54.1'
± Longitude	- 75° 51.1'	- 75° 25.7'	- 75° 54.1'
LHA	358° 00.0'	053° 00.0'	322° 00.0'
Declination			
Declination	S 23° 22.1'	S 22° 18.6'	S 9° 43.0'
	CONTRARY	CONTRARY	CONTRARY
Pub 229 Work			
Intercept Computed			
Hc	48° 57.2'	24° 30.9'	43° 46.7'
d	- 59.9	- 33.2	- 35.4
Dec inc (x)	22.1'	18.6'	43.0'
60 (\)	60'	60'	60'
Correction	- 22.1'	- 10.3'	- 25.4'
HC Corrected	48° 35.1'	24° 20.6'	43° 21.3'
Ho	48° 29.5'	24° 24.9'	43° 24.8'
a: (intercept)	**5.6 A**	**4.3 T**	**3.5 T**
Direction Computer			
Z	177.2	125.5	122.6
Z	177.3	126.4	123.7
d	+ .1'	+ .9'	+ 1.1'
Dec inc (x)	22.1'	18.6'	43.0'
60 (\)	60'	60'	60'
Correction	0'	+ .3'	+ .8'
Corrected Z	177.3	125.9	123.4
± 180, 360	O	360-	0
Convert Z to Zn	**177.3**	**234.1**	**123.4**

10.		20 February	
USCG # 1085	Latitude	24° 15.0' N	
0530	Longitude	137° 33.0' W	
		C -033	S – 18.0
Object Name	**Regulus**	**Antares**	**Vega**
ZT Sight	0540	0552	0600
Fix Time	0600	0600	0600
D	20	8	0
Speed x Time	18 x 40	18 x 8	18 x 0
Divided by 60	60	60	60
= Advance	6.0	2.4	0
Convert GHA to LHA			
GHA	218° 35.9'	126° 23.5	96° 23.2'
± Longitude	- 137° 35.9'	- 137° 23.5'	- 137° 23.2'
LHA	081° 0.0'	349° 00.0'	319° 00.0'
Declination			
Declination	N 12° 03.5'	S 26° 23.3'	N 38° 45.8'
	SAME	CONTRARY	SAME
Pub 229 Work			
Intercept Computed			
Hc	12° 57.9'	38° 52.8'	52° 33.0
d	+ 22.5	-58.5	- 10.9
Dec inc (x)	03.5'	23.3'	45.8'
60 (\)	60'	60'	60'
Correction	+ 1.3'	- 22.7'	- 8.3'
HC Corrected	12° 59.2	38° 30.1'	52° 24.7'
Ho	13° 02.2'	38° 04.1'	52° 33.5'
a: (intercept)	**3.0 T**	**26.0 A**	**8.8 T**
Direction Computer			
Z	082.5	167.3	058.2
Z	081.5	167.6	056.6
d	- 1.0'	+ .3'	-1.6'
Dec inc (x)	03.5'	23.3'	45.8'
60 (\)	60'	60'	60'
Correction	- .1'	+ .1'	- 1.2'
Corrected Z	082.4	167.4	057.0
± 180, 360	360-	0	0
Convert Z to Zn	**277.6**	**167.4**	**057.0**

6-107

11.		**15 July**	
USCG # 1086	Latitude		27° 42.0' N
1845	Longitude		167° 02.0' E
		C- 243	S- 16.0
Object Name	**Deneb**	**Antares**	**Denebola**
ZT Sight	1905	1924	1945
Fix Time	1945	1945	1945
D	40	24	0
Speed x Time	16 x 40	16 x24	16 x 0
Divided by 60	60	60	60
= Advance	10.7	6.4	0
Convert GHA to LHA			
GHA	104° 08.0'	172° 02.1'	247° 20.6'
±Longitude	+167° 52.0'	+167°57.9'	+ 167° 39.4'
LHA	272° 00.0'	340° 00.0'	55° 00.0'
Declination			
Declination	N 45° 12.8'	S 26° 23.5'	N 14° 40.7'
	SAME	CONTRARY	SAME

Pub 229 Work
Intercept Computed

Hc	20° 03.6'	33° 36.5'	37°16.8'
d	+ 18.9	- 55.9	+ 23.6
Dec inc (x)	12.8'	23.5'	40.7'
60 (\)	60'	60'	60'
Correction	+ 4.0'	- 21.9'	+ 16.0'
HC Corrected	20° 07.6'	33° 14.2'	37° 32.8
Ho	19° 52.4'	32° 22.1'	38° 22.3'
a: (intercept)	**25.2 A**	**52.1 A**	**49.5 T**
Direction Computer			
Z	048.8	158.3	092.7
Z	047.8	158.8	091.5
d	- 1.0'	+ .5'	- 1.2'
Dec inc (x)	12.8'	23.5'	40.7'
60 (\)	60'	60'	60'
Correction	- .2'	+ .2'	- .6'
Corrected Z	048.6	158.5	092.1
± 180, 360	0	0	360 -
Convert Z to Zn	**048.6**	**158.5**	**267.9**

12.		**15 August**	
USCG # 1087	Latitude		26° 13.0' N
1830	Longitude		135° 18.0' W
		C -020	S – 20.0
Object Name	**Spica**	**Altair**	**Kochab**
ZT Sight	1848	1910	1935
Fix Time	1935	1935	1935
D	47	25	0
Speed x Time	20 x 47	20 x 25	18 x 0
Divided by 60	60	60	60
= Advance	15.7	8.3	0
Convert GHA to LHA			
GHA	180° 24.3'	89° 29.8'	170° 33.4'
±Longitude	-135° 24.3'	-135°29.8'	-135° 33.4'
LHA	45° 00.0'	314° 00.0'	35° 00.0'
Declination			
Declination	S 11° 03.8'	N 8° 49.3'	N 74° 14.3
	CONTRARY	SAME	SAME

Pub 229 Work
Intercept Computed

Hc	32° 41.9'	42° 47.3	38° 38.0'
d	- 39.2	+ 28.0	- 45.3
Dec inc (x)	03.8'	49.3'	14.3'
60 (\)	60'	60'	60'
Correction	- 2.5'	+ 23.0'	- 10.8'
HC Corrected	32° 39.4'	42° 24.3	38° 27.2'
Ho	32° 21.4'	43° 06.3'	39° 12.0'
a: (intercept)	**18.0 A**	**42.0 T**	**44.0 T**
Direction Computer			
Z	124.4	103.9	011.7
Z	125.3	102.7	010.8
d	+ .9'	- 1.2'	- .9'
Dec inc (x)	03.8'	49.3'	14.3'
60 (\)	60'	60'	60'
Correction	+ .1'	+ 1.0'	- .2'
Corrected Z	124.5	102.9	011.5
± 180, 360	360 -	0	0
Convert Z to Zn	**235.5**	**102.9**	**011.5**

6-108

13.		**6 April**		
USCG # 1089	Latitude		26° 33.0' N	
1830	Longitude		64° 31.0' W	
		C- 082°	S- 16.0	
Object Name	**Sirius**	**Regulus**	**Mirfak**	
ZT Sight	1836	1842	1900	
Fix Time	1900	1900	1900	
D	24	18	0	
Speed x Time	16 x 24	16 x18	16 x 0	
Divided by 60	60	60	60	
= Advance	6.4	4.8	0	
Convert GHA to LHA				
GHA	73° 02.7'	23° 46.9'	129° 24.3'	
±Longitude	-64° 57.3'	-64° 13.1	-64° 35.7'	
LHA	009° 00.0'	319° 00.0'	64° 00.0'	
Declination				
Declination	S 16° 41.7'	N 12° 03.5'	N 49° 47.7'	
	CONTRARY	SAME	SAME	
Pub 229 Work				
Intercept Computed				
Hc	46° 07.3'	48° 46.6'	36° 08.0	
d	- 58.8	- 27.2	+ .7	
Dec inc (x)	41.7'	03.5'	47.7'	
60 (\)	60'	60'	60'	
Correction	- 40.6'	- 1.6'	+.6'	
HC Corrected	45° 26.4'	48° 45.0'	36° 08.6'	
Ho	46° 00.5'	49° 07.2'	35° 50.5'	
a: (intercept)	**34.0 T**	**22.2 T**	**18.1 A**	
Direction Computer				
Z		167.5	10.31	047.4
Z		167.8	101.8	046.2
d		+ .3'	- 1.3'	- 1.2'
Dec inc (x)		41.7'	03.5'	47.7'
60 (\)		60'	60'	60'
Correction		+ .2'	- .1'	- 1.0'
Corrected Z		167.3	103.0	046.4
± 180, 360		360 -	0	360 -
Convert Z to Zn		**192.7**	**103.0**	**313.6**

14.		**25 June**		
USCG # 1090	Latitude		21° 26.0' N	
0450	Longitude		160° 24.5' W	
		C -100°	S – 10.0	
Object Name	**Mirfak**	**Fomalhaut**	**Altair**	
ZT Sight	0450	0502	0514	
Fix Time	0514	0514	0514	
	24	12	0	
Speed x Time	10 x 24	10 x 12	18 x 0	
Divided by 60	60	60	60	
= Advance	4.0	2.0	0	
Convert GHA to LHA				
GHA	100° 25.9'	169° 59.9'	219° 39.9'	
± Longitude	- 160°25.9'	- 160° 59.9'	- 160° 39.9'	
LHA	300° 00.0'	010° 00.0'	059° 00.0'	
Declination				
Declination	N 49° 47.5'	S 29° 43.1'	N 8° 49.1'	
	SAME	CONTRARY	SAME	
Pub 229 Work				
Intercept Computed				
Hc	35° 13.2'	39° 04.7'	31° 44.2'	
d	- 9.0	- 58.7	+ 20.1	
Dec inc (x)	47.5'	43.1'	49.1'	
60 (\)	60'	60'	60'	
Correction	- 7.1'	- 42.2'	+ 16.4'	
HC Corrected	35° 06.1'	38° 22.5'	32° 00.6'	
Ho	35° 27.4'	38° 01.3'	31° 39.5	
a: (intercept)	**21.3 T**	**21.2 A**	**27.1 A**	
Direction Computer				
Z		044.1	168.7	093.6
Z		042.9	169.0	092.5
d		- 1.2'	+ .3'	- 1.1'
Dec inc (x)		47.5'	43.1'	49.1'
60 (\)		60'	60'	60'
Correction		- 1.0'	+ .2'	- .9'
Corrected Z		043.1	168.9	092.7
± 180, 360		180 -	180 +	180 +
Convert Z to Zn		**136.9**	**348.9**	**272.7**

6-109

15.		**10 August**			16.		**22 November**		
USCG # 1091	Latitude		29° 56.7' S		USCG # 1093	Latitude		28° 25.0' S	
0430	Longitude		139° 11.0' E		1400	Longitude		42° 40.0' W	
		C- 321°	S- 18.2				C- 240°	S- 15.0	
Object Name	**Fomalhaut**	**Canopus**	**Achernar**		Object Name	**Venus**	**Moon**	**Sun**	
ZT Sight	0452	0459	0510		ZT Sight	1129	1134	1137	
Fix Time	0500	0500	0500		Fix Time	1137	1137	1137	
D	8	1	10		D	6	3	0	
Speed x Time	18.2 x 8	18.2 x1	18.2 x 10		Speed x Time	15 x 48	15 x24	15 x 0	
Divided by 60	60	60	60		Divided by 60	60	60	60	
= Advance	2.4	.3	3.0		= Advance	1.5	.75	0	

	Convert GHA to LHA					Convert GHA to LHA			
GHA	272° 03.3'	162° 05.5	236° 28.2'		GHA	350° 00.1'	082° 54.7'	042° 38.0'	
± Longitude	+139° 56.7'	+139° 54.5'	+139° 31.8'		± Longitude	- 42° 00.1'	- 42° 54.7'	- 42° 38.0'	
LHA	52° 00.0'	302° 00.0'	16° 00.0'		LHA	308° 00.0'	40° 00.0'	000° 00.0'	

	Declination					Declination			
Declination	S 29° 43.1'	S 52° 41.0'	S 57° 19.6'		Declination	S 25° 41.8'	S 01° 46.5'	S 20° 11.7'	
	SAME	SAME	SAME			SAME	SAME	SAME	

Pub 229 Work
Intercept Computed

Hc	45° 07.9'	42° 34.5'	60° 46.7		Hc	42° 50.6'	43° 49.0'	82° 00.0'	
d	+ 14.7'	- 4.9'	- 52.6'		d	+ 16.0	+ 38.6	+ 60	
Dec inc (x)	43.1'	41.0'	19.6'		Dec inc (x)	41.8'	46.5'	11.7'	
60 (\)	60'	60'	60'		60 (\)	60'	60'	60'	
Correction	+ 10.6'	- 3.3'	- 17.2'		Correction	+ 11.1'	+ 29.9'	+ 11.7'	
HC Corrected	45° 18.5'	42° 31.2'	60° 29.5		HC Corrected	43° 01.7'	44° 18.9'	82° 11.7'	
Ho	46° 05.3'	41° 48.9'	60° 26.5'		Ho	43° 26.8'	43° 15.0'	81° 44.7'	
a: (intercept)	**46.8 T**	**42.3 A**	**3.0 A**		a: (intercept)	**25.1 T**	**63.9 A**	**27.0 A**	

	Direction Computer					Direction Computer			
Z	077.7	045.2	017.9		Z	080.8	117.1	180.0	
Z	076.3	043.8	016.9		Z	079.5	116.0	180.0	
d	- 1.4'	- 1.4'	- 1.0'		d	- 1.3'	- 1.1'	0'	
Dec inc (x)	43.1'	41.0'	19.6'		Dec inc (x)	41.8'	46.5'	11.7'	
60 (\)	60'	60'	60'		60 (\)	60'	60'	60'	
Correction	- 1.0'	- 1.0'	- .3'		Correction	- .9'	- .9'	0'	
Corrected Z	076.7	044.2	017.6		Corrected Z	079.9	116.2	180	
± 180, 360	180 +	180 -	180 +		± 180, 360	180 -	180 +	180 +	
Convert Z to Zn	**256.7**	**135.8**	**197.6**		Convert Z to Zn	**100.1**	**296.2**	**360**	

6-110

17.	**12 October**		
USCG # 1094	Latitude		26° 11.0' S
	Longitude		077° 18.0' E
		C -081°	S – 20.0
Object Name	**Vega**	**Fomalhaut**	**Antares**
ZT Sight	1810	1823	1835
Fix Time	1835	1835	1835
D	25	12	0
Speed x Time	20x 25	20 x 12	20 x 0
Divided by 60	60	60	60
= Advance	8.3	4.0	0
Convert GHA to LHA			
GHA	299° 26.6'	237° 37.0'	337° 43.4'
± Longitude	+ 77° 33.4'	+ 77° 23.0'	+ 77° 16.7
LHA	17° 00.0'	161° 00.0'	261° 00.0'
Declination			
Declination	N 38° 46.3'	S 29° 43.2'	S 26° 23.4'
	CONTRARY	SAME	SAME
Pub 229 Work			
Intercept Computed			
Hc	24° 02.6'	50° 12.5'	40° 57.6'
d	- 57.5	+ 6.5	+ 12.9
Dec inc (x)	46.3'	43.2'	23.4'
60 (\)	60'	60'	60'
Correction	- 44.4'	+ 4.7'	+ 5.0'
HC Corrected	23° 18.2'	50° 17.2'	41° 02.6'
Ho	23° 08.7'	50° 23.9'	40° 53.1'
a: (intercept)	**905 A**	**6.7 T**	**9.5 A**
Direction Computer			
Z	165.4	075.1	077.1
Z	165.7	073.5	175.8
d	+ .3'	- 1.6'	- 1.3'
Dec inc (x)	46.3'	43.2'	23.4'
60 (\)	60'	60'	60'
Correction	+ .2'	- .7'	- .7'
Corrected Z	165.6	074.4	076.4
± 180, 360	180 +	180 +	180 -
Convert Z to Zn	**345.0**	**254.4**	**103.6**

18.	**25 October**		
USCG # 1095	Latitude		24° 48.0' N
	Longitude		65° 21.1' W
		C- 030°	S- 18.0
Object Name	**Mirfak**	**Regulus**	**Sirius**
ZT Sight	0430	0440	0455
Fix Time	0455	0455	0455
D	25	15	0
Speed x Time	18 x 25	18 x15	18 x 0
Divided by 60	60	60	60
= Advance	7.5	4.5	0
Convert GHA to LHA			
GHA	110° 23.1'	011° 48.3'	066° 19.5'
± Longitude	- 65° 23.1'	- 65° 48.3'	- 65° 19.5'
LHA	45° 00.0'	306° 00.0'	001° 00.0'
Declination			
Declination	N 49° 47.7'	N 12° 03.5'	S 16° 41.3'
	SAME	SAME	CONTRARY
Pub 229 Work			
Intercept Computed			
Hc	46° 57.0'	37° 34.5'	49° 59.3'
d	- 19.9	+ 21.3	- 60.0
Dec inc (x)	47.7'	03.5'	41.3'
60 (\)	60'	60'	60'
Correction	- 15.8'	+ 1.2'	- 41.3'
HC Corrected	46° 41.2'	37° 35.7'	49°18.0'
Ho	47° 20.8'	37° 49.9'	48° 25.3'
a: (intercept)	**39.6 T**	**14.2 T**	**52.7 A**
Direction Computer			
Z	042.8	093.2	178.5
Z	041.4	092.0	178.5
d	- 1.4'	- 1.2'	0'
Dec inc (x)	47.7'	03.5'	41.3'
60 (\)	60'	60'	60'
Correction	- 1.1'	- .1'	0'
Corrected Z	041.7	093.1	178.5
± 180, 360	360 -	0	360 -
Convert Z to Zn	**318.3**	**093.1**	**181.5**

Star identification and Selection

Chapter 14, Celestial Navigation (Upon Oceans Endorsement)

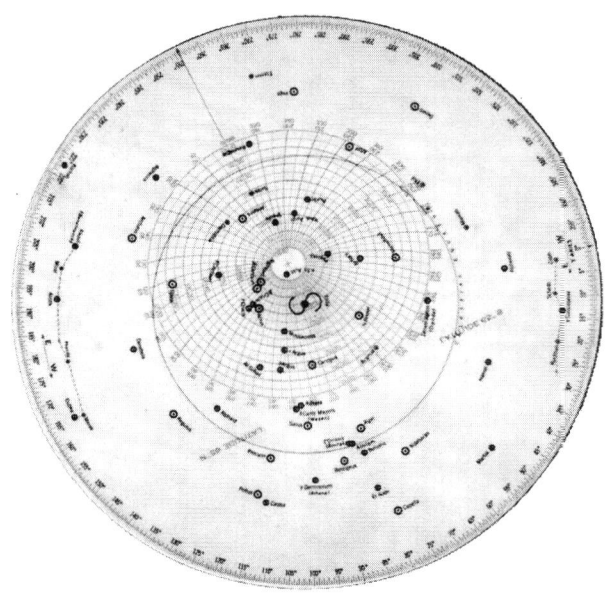

By

Alexander F. Hickethier, MBA

and

Dr. Hu, Jia-Shen

Star Identification and Selection
Chapter 14 Celestial for Master/Mate limited Upon Oceans

Various devices have been invented to help an observer find individual stars. The most widely used is the **Star Finder and Identifier**, formerly published by the U.S. Navy Hydrographic Office as *No. 2102D*, but it is still available commercially. Currently available navigation calculator or computer programs are much quicker, more accurate, and less tedious. They are NOT allowed in the Testing room thus we will discuss the use of the Star Finder and Identifier below.

The data required by the calculator or program consists of the DR position, the sextant altitude of the body, the time, and the azimuth of the body. The name of the body is not necessary because there will be only one possible body meeting those conditions, which the computer will identify. Computer sight reduction programs can also automatically predict twilight on a moving vessel and create a plot of the sky at the vessel's twilight location (or any location, at any time). This plot will be free of the distortion inherent in the mechanical star finders and will show all bodies, even planets, Sun, and Moon, in their correct relative orientation centered on the observer's zenith. It will also indicate which stars provide the best geometry for a fix.

Computer sight reduction programs or celestial navigation calculators are especially useful when the sky is only briefly visible thorough broken cloud cover. The navigator can quickly shoot any visible body without having to identify it by name, and let the computer do the rest.

Using the Rude Star Finder and Identifier

The unit consists of a base plate (northern hemisphere on one side, southern on the other) plus

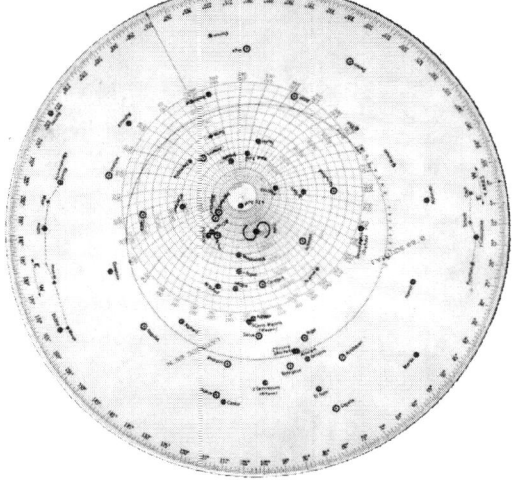

a set of latitude plates. Use the **nautical almanac** to look up the Greenwich Hour Angle of Aries for the time of interest (usually Civil Twilight - also obtained from the nautical almanac), then set the closest latitude disk on the base plate. Rotate the arrow on the latitude disk to the Local Hour Angle of Aries on the graduated edge of the base-plate, and you have in your hand a picture of the sky around you, showing the stars visible at twilight. From the disk you can read the azimuths (bearings), and altitudes (angular height above the horizon) of the stars. The planets, sun and moon can be marked in pencil onto the base-plate for a specific date and their approximate positions in the sky obtained at the same time as the starts.

STAR IDENTIFICATION - MAJOR
Chapter 14, Upon Oceans for Limited Master

01851. On 23 September 1981, while taking stars for an evening fix, an unidentified star is observed bearing 261° T at an observed altitude of 61° 35'. Your 1836 zone time DR position is LAT 25° 18' S, LONG 162° 36' E. The chronometer reads 07h 34m 12s, and the chronometer error is 01m 54s slow. Your vessel is steaming on a course of 230° T at a speed of 18 knots. Which star did you observe?

A. Antares
B. Canopus
C. Achernar
D. Sirius

01852. On 26 November 1981, at 0535 ZT while taking sights for a morning fix, you observe an unidentified planet bearing 074° T at an observed altitude (Ho) of 38° 29.8'. Your DR position is LAT 27° 18.9' S, LONG 30° 18.4' E. The chronometer time of the sight is 03h 33m 16s, and the chronometer is 01m 48s slow. Which planet did you observe?

A. Saturn
B. Jupiter
C. Mars
D. Venus

01853. On 8 April 1981, while taking observations for an evening fix, you observe an unidentified star bearing 250.7° T at an observed altitude of 51° 44.8'. Your DR position at the time of the sight was LAT 22° 16.0' N, LONG 157° 58.3' W. The chronometer reads 05h 09m 57s and is 01m 23s slow. Which star did you observe?

A. Betelgeuse
B. Aldebaran
C. Alnilam
D. Bellatrix

01854. On 22 July 1981, your 1759 ZT DR position is LAT 24° 50.2 S, LONG 005° 16.0' E. You observe an unidentified star bearing 231° T at an observed altitude (Ho) of 26° 10.0'. The chronometer reads 06h 01m 31s and is 02m 15s fast. What star did you observe?

A. Acamar
B. Capella
C. Miaplacidus
D. Suhail

01855. On 22 July 1981, your 0442 ZT DR position is LAT 26° 35.6' N, LONG 22° 16.7' W. You observe an unidentified star bearing 112° T at an observed altitude (Ho) of 44° 16.0'. The chronometer reads 05h 39m 03s and is 03m 14s slow. What star did you observe?

A. Hamal
B. Rigel
C. Menkar
D. Acamar

01856. On 22 June 1981, your 0424 ZT DR position is LAT 26° 18.5' N, LONG 124° 18.2' W. You observe an unidentified star bearing 031° T at an observed altitude (Ho) of 49° 26.0'. The chronometer reads 00h 23m 24s and is 01m 32s slow. What star did you observe?

A. Peacock
B. Schedar
C. Ankaa
D. Alioth

01857. On 22 May 1981, your 0437 ZT DR position is LAT 25° 18.5' N, LONG 51° 18.0' W. You observe an unidentified star bearing 097° T at an observed altitude (Ho) of 48° 20.0'. The chronometer reads 07h 40m 40s and is 03m 24s fast. What star did you observe?

A. Markab
B. Diphda
C. Sabik
D. Hamal

01858. On 22 April 1981, your 1852 ZT DR position is LAT 23° 54.5' N, LONG 117° 36.8' W. You observe an unidentified star bearing 129° T at an observed altitude (Ho) of 27° 10.0'. The chronometer reads 02h 54m 53s and is 02m 51s fast. What star did you observe?

A. Diphda
B. Betelgeuse
C. Gienah
D. Arcturus

01859. On 22 March 1981, your 0519 ZT DR position is LAT 27° 20.6' N, LONG 69° 25.6' W. You observe an unidentified star bearing 094° T at an observed altitude (Ho) of 30° 15.0. The chronometer reads 10h 16m 47s and is 02m 15s slow. What star did you observe?

A. Acamar
B. Enif
C. Menkar
D. Rigel

01860. On 22 March 1981, your 1834 ZT DR position is LAT 26° 13.5' S, LONG 108° 36.5' W. You observe an unidentified star bearing 077° T at an observed altitude (Ho) of 43° 10.5'. The chronometer reads 01h 32m 37s and is 01m 50s slow. What star did you observe?

A. Regulus
B. Menkar
C. Rigel
D. Alphard

7-5

01861. On 22 February 1981, your 1857 ZT DR position is LAT 23° 46.0' S, LONG 93° 16.5' E. You observe an unidentified star bearing 159° T at an observed altitude (Ho) of 34° 30.0'. The chronometer reads 01h 00m 35s and is 03m 25s fast. What star did you observe?

A. Adhara
B. Miaplacidus
C. Avior
D. Suhail

01862. On 14 January 1981, your 0550 ZT DR position is LAT 25° 26.0' N, LONG 38° 16.0' W. You observe an unidentified star bearing 004.5° T at an observed altitude (Ho) of 40° 10.0'. The chronometer reads 08h 48m 51s and is 01m 22s slow. What star did you observe?

A. Gienah
B. Kochab
C. Gacrux
D. Eltanin

01863. On 14 January 1981, your 1922 ZT DR position is LAT 27° 18.5' S, LONG 67° 18.0' E. You observe an unidentified star bearing 029° T at an observed altitude (Ho) of 29° 35.0'. The chronometer reads 03h 25m 43s and is 03m 15s fast. What star did you observe?

A. Elnath
B. Fomalhaut
C. Pollux
D. Markab

01864. At 0520 zone time on 17 March 1981, while taking stars for a morning fix, you observe an unidentified star bearing 050° T at an observed altitude (Ho) of 45° 00.0'. Your DR position at the time of the sight is LAT 27° 23.0' N, LONG 39° 42.0' W. The chronometer time of the sight is 08h 22m 15s, and the chronometer error is 01m 45s fast. Your vessel is steaming on a course of 300° T at a speed of 18 knots. Which star did you observe?

A. Altair
B. Alkaid
C. Arcturus
D. Deneb

01865. At 1845 zone time on 17 March 1981, while taking stars for an evening fix, you observe an unidentified star bearing 200° T at an observed altitude of 53° 45.0'. Your DR position at the time of the sight is LAT 25° 10.0' N, LONG 66° 48.0' W. The chronometer time of the sight is 10h 47m 49s, and the chronometer error is 1m 54s fast. Your vessel is steaming on a course of 290° T at a speed of 18.0 knots. Which star did you observe?

A. Capella
B. Mirfak
C. Pollux
D. Rigel

01851	A	01859	B
01852	A	01860	D
01853	D	01861	B
01854	D	01862	B
01855	C	01863	A
01856	B	01864	D
01857	A	01865	D
01858	C		

Celestial Problems
Unknown Star

Problem # (USCG) (1851)				Chapter 1	

Date:	23 Sept		Time		
				LAT:	25° 18′ S
				LONG	162° 36′ E
	ZT	1836	**CT**	07:34:12	**C-230°**
	ZD	- 11	**CE**	+ 01:54	**S- 18 kts**
	GMT	0736	**CCT**	07:36:06	
			GMT	07:36:06	**Unknown Star**
				Ho	61° 35′
				Bearing	261°

Almanac		Star Finder (Notes)
GHA Aries	107° 02.4′	
M/S	9° 03.0′	
GHA Aries	116° 05.4′	
±SHA/v		
Sum	116° 05.4′	
Long	+ 162° 36.0′	
LHA Aries	278° 41.4′	

Celestial Problems
Unknown Planet

Problem # (USCG) (1852)				Chapter 1	

Date:	26 Nov		Time		
				LAT:	27° 18.9′ S
				LONG	30° 18.4′ E
	ZT	0535	**CT**	03:33:16	**C-**
	ZD	- 2	**CE**	+ 01:48	**S-**
	GMT	0335	**CCT**	03:35:04	
			GMT	03"35:04	**Unknown Star**
				Ho	38° 29.8′
				Bearing	074°

Almanac		Star Finder (Notes)			
GHA Aries	109° 57.7′				
M/S	+ 8° 32.4′	Name	360 - SHA	= RA	Dec
GHA Aries	118° 30.1′				
±SHA/v		Saturn	360 - 162°	198°	S 05° 11.8′
Sum	118° 30.1′	Jupiter	360 - 152°	208°	S 11° 22.1′
Long	+ 30° 18.4′	Mars	360 - 189°	171°	N 05° 38.8′
LHA Aries	148° 48.5′	Venus	360 - 69°	291°	S 25° 07.9′

Celestial Problems					
Unknown Star					
Problem # (USCG) (1853)				Chapter 1	
Date: 8 April		Time		**LAT:**	22° 16.0' N
				LONG	157° 58.3' W
ZT	1800	**CT**	05:09:57	**C-**	
ZD	+ 11	**CE**	+ 01:23	**S-**	
GMT	2900	**CCT**	05:11:20		
9 April 05:00		**GMT**	05:11:20	**Unknown Star**	
				Ho	51° 44.8'
				Bearing	230.7°

Almanac		Star Finder (Notes)
GHA Aries	271° 22.2'	
M/S	+ 2° 50.5'	
GHA Aries	274° 12.7'	
±SHA/v		
Sum	274° 12.7'	
Long	- 157° 58.3'	
LHA Aries	117° 14.4'	

Celestial Problems					
Unknown Star					
Problem # (USCG) (1854)				Chapter 1	
Date: 22 July		Time1759		**LAT:**	24° 50.2' S
				LONG	005° 16.0' E
ZT	17:59	**CT**	06 :01:31	**C-**	
ZD	0	**CE**	- 02:15	**S-**	
GMT	1759	**CCT**	05:59:16		
		GMT	05:59:16	**Unknown Star**	
				Ho	26° 10.0'
				Bearing	231°

Almanac		Star Finder (Notes)
GHA Aries	14° 51.8'	
M/S	+ 14° 49.0'	
GHA Aries	29° 40.8'	
±SHA/v		
Sum	29° 40.8'	
Long	+ 5° 16.0'	
LHA Aries	34° 56.8'	

7-9

Celestial Problems Unknown Star					
Problem # (USCG) (1855)				Chapter 1	
Date: 22 July		Time	0442	**LAT:** 26° 35.6' N	
				LONG 022° 16.7'	
ZT	0442	**CT**	05:39:03	**C-**	
ZD	+ 1	**CE**	+ 03:32	**S-**	
GMT	0542	**CCT**	05:42:35		
		GMT	05:42:35	**Unknow44° 16.0n Star**	
				Ho 44° 16.0	
				Bearing 112°	

Almanac		Star Finder (Notes)
GHA Aries	014° 51.8'	
M/S	+ 0° 40.5'	
GHA Aries	025° 32.3'	
±SHA/v		
Sum	025° 32.3'	
Long	- 022° 16.7'	
LHA Aries	003° 15.6'	

Celestial Problems Unknown Star					
Problem # (USCG) (1856)				Chapter 1	
Date: 22 June		Time	0424	**LAT:** 26° 18.5' N	
				LONG 124° 18.2' W	
ZT	0424	**CT**	00:23:24	**C-**	
ZD	+ 8	**CE**	+ 01:32	**S-**	
GMT	1224	**CCT**	00:24:56		
		GMT	12:24:56	**Unknown Star**	
				Ho 49° 26.0'	
				Bearing 031°	

Almanac		Star Finder (Notes)
GHA Aries	090° 34.9'	
M/S	+ 6° 15.0'	
GHA Aries	096° 49.9'	
±SHA/v		
Sum	096° 49.9'	
Long	- 124° 18.2'	
LHA Aries	332° 31.7'	

Celestial Problems						
Unknown Star						
Problem # (USCG) (1857)				Chapter 1		

Date:	22 May		Time	0437	**LAT:**	25° 18.5' N
					LONG	51° 18.0' W
	ZT	0437	**CT**	07:40:40	**C-**	
	ZD	+ 3	**CE**	- 03:24	**S-**	
	GMT	0737	**CCT**	07:37:16		
			GMT	07:37:16	**Unknown Star**	
					Ho	48° 20.0'
					Bearing	097°

Almanac		Star Finder (Notes)
GHA Aries	334° 49.2'	
M/S	9° 20.2'	
GHA Aries	344° 09.4'	
±SHA/v		
Sum	344° 09.4'	
Long	- 51° 18.0'	
LHA Aries	342° 51.4'	

Celestial Problems						
Unknown Star						
Problem # (USCG) (1858)				Chapter 1		

Date:	22 April		Time	1852	**LAT:**	23° 54.5' N
					LONG	117° 36.8' W
	ZT	1852	**CT**	02:54:53	**C-**	
	ZD	+ 8	**CE**	- 02:51	**S-**	
	GMT	2652	**CCT**	02:52:02		
23 April 0252			**GMT**	02:52:02	**Unknown Star**	
					Ho	27° 10.0'
					Bearing	129°

Almanac		Star Finder (Notes)
GHA Aries	241° 01.9'	
M/S	+ 13° 02.4'	
GHA Aries	254° 04.3'	
±SHA/v		
Sum	254° 04.3'	
Long	- 117° 36.8'	
LHA Aries	136° 27.5'	

Celestial Problems						
Unknown Star						
Problem # (USCG) (1859)					Chapter 1	
Date:	22 March		Time	0519	**LAT:**	27° 20.6' N
					LONG	069° 25.6' W
	ZT	0519	**CT**	10:16:47	**C-**	
	ZD	+ 5	**CE**	+ 02:15	**S-**	
	GMT	1019	**CCT**	10:19:02		
			GMT	10:19:02	**Unknown Star**	
					Ho	30° 15.0'
					Bearing	094°

Almanac		Star Finder (Notes)
GHA Aries	329° 49.2'	
M/S	+ 4° 46.3'	
GHA Aries	334° 35.5'	
±SHA/v		
Sum	334° 35.5'	
Long	- 69° 25.6'	
LHA Aries	265° 09.9'	

Celestial Problems						
Unknown Star						
Problem # (USCG) (1860)					Chapter 1	
Date:	22 March		Time	1834	**LAT:**	26° 13.5' S
					LONG	108° 36.5' W
	ZT	1834	**CT**	01:32:37	**C-**	
	ZD	+ 7	**CE**	+ 01:50	**S-**	
	GMT	2534	**CCT**	01:34:27		
23 March 0124			**GMT**	01:34:27	**Unknown Star**	
					Ho	43° 10.5'
					Bearing	077°

Almanac		Star Finder (Notes)
GHA Aries	209° 29.5'	
M/S	+ 8° 38.2'	
GHA Aries	218° 51.3'	
±SHA/v		
Sum	218° 51.3'	
Long	- 108° 36.5'	
LHA Aries	110° 14.8'	

Celestial Problems Unknown Star					
Problem # (USCG) (1861)				Chapter 1	

Date:	22 February		Time	1857	**LAT:**	23° 46.0' S
					LONG	093° 16.5' E
	ZT	1857	**CT**	01:00:35	**C-**	
	ZD	- 6	**CE**	- 03:25	**S-**	
	GMT	1257	**CCT**	00 :57:10		
			GMT	12:57:10		
					Unknown Star	
					Ho	34° 30.0'
					Bearing	159°

Almanac		Star Finder (Notes)
GHA Aries	332° 18.2'	
M/S	+ 14° 19.8'	
GHA Aries	346° 38.0'	
±SHA/v		
Sum	346° 38.0'	
Long	+ 093° 16.5'	
LHA Aries	439° 54.5'	
	079° 54.85'	

Celestial Problems Unknown Star					
Problem # (USCG) (1862)				Chapter 1	

Date:	14 January		Time	0550	**LAT:**	25° 26.0' N
					LONG	038° 16.0' W
	ZT	0550	**CT**	08:48:51	**C-**	
	ZD	+ 3	**CE**	+ 01:22	**S-**	
	GMT	0850	**CCT**	08:50:13		
			GMT	08:50:13		
					Unknown Star	
					Ho	40° 10.0'
					Bearing	004.5°

Almanac		Star Finder (Notes)
GHA Aries	233° 42.0'	
M/S	+ 12° 35.3'	
GHA Aries	266° 17.3'	
±SHA/v		
Sum	266° 17.3'	
Long	- 38° 16.0'	
LHA Aries	228° 01.3'	

7-13

Celestial Problems		
Unknown Star		
Problem # (USCG) (1863)		Chapter 1

Date:	14 January		Time	1922	**LAT:**	27° 18.5' S
					LONG	067° 18.0' E
	ZT	1922	**CT**	03:25:43	**C-**	
	ZD	- 4	**CE**	- 03:15	**S-**	
	GMT	1522	**CCT**	03:22:28		
			GMT	15:22:28	**Unknown Star**	
					Ho	29° 35.0'
					Bearing	029°

Almanac		Star Finder (Notes)
GHA Aries	338° 59.2'	
M/S	+ 5° 37.9'	
GHA Aries	344° 37.1'	
±SHA/v		
Sum	344° 37.1'	
Long	+ 67° 18.0'	
LHA Aries	411° 55.1'	

Celestial Problems		
Unknown Star		
Problem # (USCG) (1864)		Chapter 1

Date:	17 March		Time	0520	**LAT:**	27° 23.0' N
					LONG	039° 42.0' W
	ZT	0520	**CT**	08:22:15	**C-**	
	ZD	+ 3	**CE**	- 01:45	**S-**	
	GMT	0820	**CCT**	08:20:30		
			GMT	08:20:30	**Unknown Star**	
					Ho	45° 00.0'
					Bearing	050°

Almanac		Star Finder (Notes)
GHA Aries	294° 48.6'	
M/S	+ 5° 08.3'	
GHA Aries	299° 56.9'	
±SHA/v		
Sum	299° 56.9'	
Long	- 39° 42.0'	
LHA Aries	260° 14.9'	

Celestial Problems				
Unknown Star				
Problem # (USCG) (1865)			Chapter 1	

Date:	17 March		Time			LAT:	25° 10.0' N
						LONG	056° 48.0' W
	ZT	1800	CT	10:47:49		C-	
	ZD	+ 4	CE	- 01:54		S-	
	GMT	2200	CCT	10:45:55			
			GMT	22:45:55		**Unknown Star**	
						Ho	53° 45.0
						Bearing	200°

Almanac		Star Finder (Notes)
GHA Aries	145° 23.1'	
M/S	+ 11° 30.6'	
GHA Aries	156° 53.7'	
±SHA/v		
Sum	156° 53.7'	
Long	- 66° 48.0'	
LHA Aries	90° 05.7'	

7-15

STARS SELECTION
(Chapter 14 Celestial for Master/2nd Mate limited Upon Oceans)

02001. On 3 February 1981, your 0451 zone time DR position is LAT 24° 15.0' S, LONG 124° 24.0' W. Considering their magnitude, azimuth, and altitude, which of the following groups includes the three bodies best suited for a fix at star time?

A. Alphard, Denebola, Acrux
B. Spica, Venus, Procyon
C. Jupiter, Dubhe, Antares
D. Mars, Arcturus, Spica

02002. On 16 July 1981, your 1810 zone time DR position is LAT 24° 16.5' S, LONG 162° 52.0' E. Considering their magnitude, azimuth, and altitude, which of the following groups includes the three bodies best suited for a fix at star time?

A. Arcturus, Spica, Antares
B. Jupiter, Acrux, Alphecca
C. Pollux, Mars, Deneb
D. Vega, Hadar, Venus

02003. On 20 June 1981, your 1742 zone time DR position is LAT 24° 55.0' S, LONG 8° 19.6' E. Considering their magnitude, azimuth, and altitude, which of the following groups includes the three stars best suited for a fix at star time?

A. Regulus, Canopus, Antares
B. Spica, Arcturus, Alioth
C. Arcturus, Achernar, Pollux
D. Avior, Sabik, Fomalhaut

02004. On 28 February 1981, your 1850 zone time DR position is LAT 27° 49.0' N, LONG 159° 24.0' W. Considering their magnitude, azimuth, and altitude, which of the following groups includes the three stars best suited for a fix at star time?

A. Rigel, Schedar, Regulus
B. Sirius, Mirfak, Elnath
C. Hamal, Alkaid, Canopus
D. Bellatrix, Vega, Regulus

02005. On 17 July 1981, your 1951 zone time DR position is LAT 24° 26.0' N, LONG 51° 16.0' W. Considering their magnitude, azimuth, and altitude, which of the following groups includes the three bodies best suited for a fix at star time?

A. Hadar, Deneb, Alphard
B. Regulus, Venus, Antares
C. Mars, Vega, Dubhe
D. Kochab, Jupiter, Rasalhague

02006. On 8 November 1981, your 1731 zone time DR position is LAT 27° 16.0'N, LONG 137° 25.0' W. Considering their magnitude, azimuth, and altitude, which of the following groups includes the three stars best suited for a fix at star time?

A. Alphecca, Fomalhaut, Schedar
B. Antares, Rasalhague, Altair
C. Sirius, Hamal, Dubhe
D. Peacock, Ankaa, Alnair

02007. On 4 September 1981, your 1813 zone time DR position is LAT 24° 18.0' S, LONG 95° 16.0' E. Considering their magnitude, azimuth, and altitude, which of the following groups includes the three stars best suited for a fix at star time?

A. Enif, Miaplacidus, Alkaid
B. Betelgeuse, Acrux, Hamal
C. Rasalhague, Fomalhaut, Spica
D. Deneb, Altair, Vega

02008. On 24 July 1981, your 1912 zone time DR position is LAT 24° 28.0' N, LONG 73° 46.5' W. Considering their magnitude, azimuth, and altitude, which of the following groups includes the three stars best suited for a fix at star time?

A. Fomalhaut, Rigel, Pollux
B. Arcturus, Acrux, Hadar
C. Spica, Altair, Alioth
D. Vega, Deneb, Regulus

7-17

02009. On 16 July 1981, your 1920 zone time DR position is LAT 25° 36.0' N, LONG 172° 18.9' W. Considering their magnitude, azimuth, and altitude, which of the following groups includes the three bodies best suited for a fix at star time?

A. Rasalhague, Spica, Arcturus
B. Venus, Antares, Vega
C. Vega, Mars, Antares
D. Saturn, Acrux, Spica

02010. On 3 February 1981, your 0550 zone time DR position is LAT 26° 16.0' N, LONG 112° 25.0' W. Considering their magnitude, azimuth, and altitude, which of the following groups includes the three bodies best suited for a fix at star time?

A. Spica, Antares, Saturn
B. Vega, Jupiter, Dubhe
C. Venus, Regulus, Vega
D. Spica, Kochab, Rasalhague

02011. On 3 February 1981, your 0547 zone time DR position is LAT 24° 18.5' N, LONG 167° 25.0' E. Considering their magnitude, azimuth, and altitude, which of the following groups includes the three bodies best suited for a fix at star time?

A. Regulus, Deneb, Antares
B. Altair, Saturn, Regulus
C. Arcturus, Kochab, Venus

02012. On 24 March 1981, your vessel is enroute from Cadiz to Norfolk. Evening twilight will occur at 1830 zone time, and your vessel's DR position will be LAT 35° 06' N, LONG 60° 48' W. Considering their azimuth, altitude, and magnitude, which of the following groups of stars is best suited for plotting a star fix at star time?

A. Adhara, Rigel, Suhail
B. Regulus, Denebola, Alkaid
C. Adhara, Procyon, Alphard
D. Sirius, Dubhe, Mirfak

02013. On 28 October 1981, morning twilight will occur around 0524 zone time in LAT 25° 25' N, LONG 32° 33.3' W. Considering their magnitude and location, which of the following will be the three stars best suited to observe for a star fix at star time?

A. Sirius, Hamal, Denebola
B. Sirius, Denebola, Dubhe
C. Sirius, Capella, Denebola
D. Sirius, Mirfak, Hamal

02014. On 16 October 1981, evening twilight will occur 1746 ZT, and your DR position will be LAT 28° 43.2' N, LONG 60° 29.8' W. Considering their magnitude and location, which of the following are the three best stars to select for a fix at star time?

A. Antares, Altair, Alphecca
B. Deneb, Polaris, Vega
C. Antares, Deneb, Vega
D. Vega, Polaris, Enif

02022. On August 24 1981, your vessel is enroute from Perth, Austrailia to Bombay, India. Evening twilight will occur at 1807 zone time, and your vessel's DR position for this time will be LAT 27° 17'.0 S, LONG 83° 17'.0 E. Considering their magnitude and location, which of the following are the three stars best suited to observe for a fix at star time?

A. Arcturus, Antares, Atria
B. Spica, Altair, Acrux
C. Pollux, Canopus, Hamal
D. Rasalhague, Spica, Kochab

02023. On 1 October 1981, you determine the zone time of evening twilight will be 1835. Your DR position at this time is LAT 27° 18.0' N, LONG 48° 52.0 W. Considering their magnitude and location, which of the following groups of three stars are best suited to be used in obtaining a fix at star time?

A. Altair, Rasalhague, Vega
B. Alphecca, Kochab, Deneb
C. Diphda, Hamal, Mirfak
D. Antares, Rigil Kentaurus, Peacock

7-18

02024. On 3 December 1981, evening twilight for your vessel will occur at 1901 zone time. Your vessel's DR position for this time will be LAT 24° 18.5' S, LONG 110° 30.6' W. Considering their magnitude and location, which of the following are the three stars best suited to observe for a fix at star time?

A. Canopus, Hamal, Deneb
B. Alpheratz, Achernar, Nunki
C. Antares, Fomalhaut, Mirfak
D. Rigel, Canopus, Regulus

Answers to Star Selection

1. 02001 A
2. 02002 B
3. 02003 A
4. 02004 A
5. 02005 D
6. 02006 A
7. 02007 C
8. 02008 C
9. 02009 B

10. 02010 B
11. 02011 A
12. 02012 D
13. 02013 C
14. 02014 A
15. 02022 B
16. 02023 B

Celestial Problems
Star Selection

Problem # 1 (USCG) (2001)			Chapter 14	

Date:	3 Feb	Time		LAT:	24° 15.0' S
				LONG	124° 24.0' W
	ZT	0451	CT	C-	
	ZD	+ 8	CE	S-	
	GMT	1251	CCT		
			GMT	Star Selection	
				Ho	
				Bearing	

Almanac

			Star Finder (Notes)			
			Plotting the Planets			
GHA	313° 34.6'		360 -	SHA	=	RA	DEC
M/S	+ 12° 47.1'					
GHA	326° 21.7'	Venus	360	058°	=	302°	S 21
±SHA/v		Mars	360	030°	=	330°	S 13
		Jupiter	360	170°	=	190°	S 3
Sum	326° 21.7'					
Long	- 124° 24.0'					
LHA	201° 57.7'					

Celestial Problems
Star Selection

Problem # 2 (USCG) (2002)			Chapter 14	

Date:	16 Jul	Time	1810	LAT:	24° 16.5' S
				LONG	162° 52.0' E
	ZT	1810	CT	C-	
	ZD	- 11	CE	S-	
	GMT	0710	CCT		
			GMT	Star Selection	
				Ho	
				Bearing	

Almanac

			Star Finder (Notes)			
			Plotting the Planets			
GHA	39° 01.9'		360 -	SHA	=	RA	DEC
M/S	+ 2° 30.4'					
GHA	41° 32.3'	Venus	360	217°	=	143°	N 16
±SHA/v		Mars	360	271°	=	089°	N 23
		Jupiter	360	176°	=	184°	S 0
Sum	41° 32.3'					
Long	+ 162° 52.0'					
LHA	204° 24.3'					

Celestial Problems
Star Selection

Problem # 3 (USCG) (2003) Chapter 14

Date:	20 June	Time		1742	**LAT:**	24° 55.0' S
					LONG	008° 19.6' E
	ZT	1742	**CT**		**C-**	
	ZD	- 1	**CE**		**S-**	
	GMT	1642	**CCT**			
			GMT		**Star Selection**	
					Ho	
					Bearing	

Almanac		Star Finder (Notes)
GHA	148° 46.4'	
M/S	+ 10° 31.7'	
GHA	159° 18.1'	
±SHA/v		
Sum	159° 18.1'	
Long	+ 008° 19.6'	
LHA	167° 37.7'	

Celestial Problems
Star Selection

Problem # 4 (USCG) (2004) Chapter 14

Date:	28 Feb	Time		1850	**LAT:**	27° 49.0' N
					LONG	159° 24.0' W
	ZT	1850	**CT**		**C-**	
	ZD	+ 11	**CE**		**S-**	
Mar 1	**GMT**	0550	**CCT**			
			GMT		**Star Selection**	
					Ho	
					Bearing	

Almanac		Star Finder (Notes)
GHA	233° 54.9'	
M/S	+ 12° 31.1'	
GHA	246° 24.0'	
±SHA/v		
Sum	246° 24.0'	
Long	- 159° 24.0'	
LHA	87° 02.0'	

7-22

Celestial Problems
Star Selection

Problem # 5 (USCG) (2005) Chapter 14

Date:	17 July	Time		1951	LAT:	24° 26.0' N
					LONG	051° 16.0' W
	ZT	1951	CT		C-	
	ZD	+ 3	CE		S-	
	GMT	2251	CCT			
			GMT		Star Selection	
					Ho	
					Bearing	

Almanac / Star Finder (Notes)

	Almanac			Star Finder (Notes)		
GHA	265° 38.0'		Plotting the Planets			
M/S	+ 12° 45.0'		360 -	SHA	=	RA	DEC
GHA	278° 23.0'	Venus	360	217°	=	143°	N 16
±SHA/v		Mars	360	271°	=	089°	N 23
		Jupiter	360	176°	=	184°	S 0
Sum	278° 23.0'					
Long	-51° 16.0'					
LHA	227° 07.0'					

Celestial Problems
Star Selection

Problem # 6 (USCG) (2006) Chapter 14

Date:	8 Nov	Time		1731	LAT:	
					LONG	
	ZT	1731	CT		C-	
	ZD	+ 9	CE		S-	
9 Nov	GMT	0231	CCT			
			GMT		Star Selection	
					Ho	
					Bearing	

Almanac / Star Finder (Notes)

	Almanac	Star Finder (Notes)
GHA	78° 09.6'	
M/S	+ 7° 46.3'	
GHA	86° 55.9'	
±SHA/v		
Sum	86° 55.9'	
Long	+ 137° 25.0'	
LHA	308° 30.9'	

Celestial Problems
Star Selection

Problem # 7 (USCG) (2007)   Chapter 14

Date:	4 Sep	Time		1813	**LAT:**	24° 18.0'
					LONG	95° 16.0 E
	ZT	1813	**CT**		**C-**	
	ZD	- 6	**CE**		**S-**	
	GMT	1213	**CCT**			
			GMT		**Star Selection**	
					Ho	
					Bearing	

Almanac		Star Finder (Notes)
GHA	163° 31.1'	
M/S	+ 3° 15.5'	
GHA	166° 46.6'	
±SHA/v		
Sum	166° 46.6'	
Long	+ 95° 25.0'	
LHA	262° 02.6	

Celestial Problems
Star Selection

Problem # 8 (USCG) (2008)   Chapter 14

Date:	24 Jul	Time		1912	**LAT:**	24° 28.0' N
					LONG	73° 46.5' W
	ZT	1912	**CT**		**C-**	
	ZD	+ 5	**CE**		**S-**	
25 Jul	**GMT**	0012	**CCT**			
			GMT		**Star Selection**	
					Ho	
					Bearing	

Almanac		Star Finder (Notes)
GHA	302° 26.9'	
M/S	+ 3° 00.5'	
GHA	305° 37.4	
±SHA/v		
Sum	305° 37.4	
Long	+ 73° 46.5'	
LHA	231°50.9'	

Celestial Problems
Star Selection

Problem # 9 (USCG) (2009)   Chapter 1

Date:	16 Jul	Time		1920	**LAT:**	25° 36.0'
					LONG	172° 18.9'
	ZT	1920	**CT**		**C-**	
	ZD	+ 11	**CE**		**S-**	
17 Jul	**GMT**	0620	**CCT**			
			GMT		**Star Selection**	
					Ho	
					Bearing	

Almanac			Star Finder (Notes)				
GHA	24° 58.5'		Plotting the Planets				
M/S	+ 5° 00.8'		360 -	SHA	=	RA	DEC
GHA	29° 59.3'	Venus	360	217°	=	143°	N 16
±SHA/v		Mars	360	271°	=	089°	N 23
Sum	29° 59.3'	Satern	360	175°	=	185°	N 0
Long	- 172° 18.9'						
LHA	217° 40.4'						

Celestial Problems
Star Selection

Problem # 10 (USCG) (2010)   Chapter 14

Date:	3 Feb	Time		0550	**LAT:**	26° 16.0' N
					LONG	112° 25.0' W
	ZT	0550	**CT**		**C-**	
	ZD	+ 7	**CE**		**S-**	
	GMT	1250	**CCT**			
			GMT		**Star Selection**	
					Ho	
					Bearing	

Almanac			Star Finder (Notes)				
GHA	313° 34.6'		Plotting the Planets				
M/S	+ 12° 31.1'		360 -	SHA	=	RA	DEC
GHA	326° 05.7'	Venus	360	058°	=	302°	S 21
±SHA/v		Saturn	360	170°	=	190°	S 1
Sum	326° 05.7'	Jupiter	360	170°	=	190°	S 3
Long	+ 112° 25.0'						
LHA	212° 02.1'						

7-25

Celestial Problems
Star Selection

Problem # 11 (USCG) (2011)			Chapter 14

Date:	3 Feb	Time		0547	**LAT:**	24° 18.0' N
					LONG	167° 25.0' E
	ZT	0547	**CT**		**C-**	
	ZD	- 11	**CE**		**S-**	
2 Feb	**GMT**	1847	**CCT**			
			GMT		**Star Selection**	
					Ho	
					Bearing	

Almanac		Star Finder (Notes)				
GHA	42° 50.2'		Plotting the Planets			
M/S	+ 11° 46.9'		360 -	SHA	=	RA	DEC
GHA	59° 37.1'	Venus	360	058°	=	302°	S 21
±SHA/v		Saturn	360	170°	=	190°	S 1
Sum	59° 37.1'					
Long	+ 167° 25.0'					
LHA	222°02.1'					

Celestial Problems
Star Selection

Problem # 12 (USCG) (2012)			Chapter 14

Date:		Time		1830	**LAT:**	36° 06.0' N
					LONG	60° 48.0' W
	ZT	1830	**CT**		**C-**	
	ZD	+ 4	**CE**		**S-**	
	GMT	2230	**CCT**			
			GMT		**Star Selection**	
					Ho	
					Bearing	

Almanac		Star Finder (Notes)
GHA	152° 17.0'	
M/S	+ 7° 31.2'	
GHA	159° 48.2'	
±SHA/v		
Sum	159° 48.2'	
Long	- 60° 48.0'	
LHA	99° 00.2'	

Celestial Problems
Star Selection

Problem # 2013 (USCG) (2013)   Chapter 14

Date:	28 Oct	Time		0524	**LAT:**	25° 25.0' N

					LONG	032° 33.3' W
	ZT	0524	**CT**		**C-**	
	ZD	+ 2	**CE**		**S-**	
	GMT	0724	**CCT**			
			GMT		**Star Selection**	
					Ho	
					Bearing	

Almanac — **Star Finder (Notes)**

GHA	141° 32.3'
M/S	+ 6° 01.0'
GHA	147° 33.3'
±SHA/v	
Sum	147° 33.3'
Long	- 32°33.3'
LHA	115° 00.0'

Celestial Problems
Star Selection

Problem # 14 (USCG) (2014)   Chapter 14

Date:	16 Oct	Time		1746	**LAT:**	28° 43.2' N

					LONG	60° 29.8' W
	ZT	1746	**CT**		**C-**	
	ZD	+ 4	**CE**		**S-**	
	GMT	2146	**CCT**			
			GMT		**Star Selection**	
					Ho	
					Bearing	

Almanac — **Star Finder (Notes)**

GHA	340° 17.1'
M/S	+ 11° 31.9'
GHA	351° 49.0'
±SHA/v	
Sum	351° 49.0'
Long	- 60° 29.8'
LHA	291° 19.2'

7-27

Alexander F. Hickethier MBA © 2008-2012

Celestial Problems
Star Selection

Problem # 22 (USCG) (2022)   Chapter 14

Date:	24 Aug	Time		1807	LAT:	27° 17.0' S
					LONG	83° 17.0' E
ZT		1807	CT			C-
ZD		- 6	CE			S-
GMT		1207	CCT			
			GMT			Unknown Star
					Ho	
					Bearing	

Almanac		Star Finder (Notes)
GHA	152° 40.6'	
M/S	+ 1° 45.3'	
GHA	154° 25.9'	
±SHA/v		
Sum	154° 25.9'	
Long	+ 83° 17.0'	
LHA	237° 42.9'	

Celestial Problems
Star Selection

Problem # 23 (USCG) (2023)   Chapter 14

Date:	1 Oct	Time		1835	LAT:	27° 18.0' N
					LONG	048° 52.0' W
ZT		1835	CT			C-
ZD		+ 3	CE			S-
GMT		2135	CCT			
			GMT			Star Selection
					Ho	
					Bearing	

Almanac		Star Finder (Notes)
GHA	92° 36.3'	
M/S	+ 8°46.4'	
GHA	101°22.7'	
±SHA/v		
Sum	101°22.7'	
Long	- 048° 52.0'	
LHA	52° 30.7'	

7-28

Celestial Problems
Star Selection

Problem # 24 (USCG) (2024)				Chapter 14	

Date:		3 Dec	Time		1901	**LAT:**	24° 18.5' S
						LONG	110° 30.6' W
	ZT		1901	**CT**		**C-**	
	ZD		+ 7	**CE**		**S-**	
4 Dec'	**GMT**		0201	**CCT**			
				GMT		**Star Selection**	
						Ho	
						Bearing	

Almanac		**Star Finder (Notes)**
GHA	102° 48.1'	
M/S	+ 0°15.0'	
GHA	103° 03.1'	
±SHA/v		
Sum	103° 03.1'	
Long	- 110° 30.6'	
LHA	352° 32.5'	

5929851R00250

Printed in Great Britain
by Amazon.co.uk, Ltd.,
Marston Gate.